COSMO-MODERNISM AND THEATER IN INDIA

MODERNIST LATITUDES

MODERNIST LATITUDES

Jessica Berman and Paul Saint-Amour, Editors

Modernist Latitudes aims to capture the energy and ferment of modernist studies by continuing to open up the range of forms, locations, temporalities, and theoretical approaches encompassed by the field. The series celebrates the growing latitude ("scope for freedom of action or thought") that this broadening affords scholars of modernism, whether they are investigating little-known works or revisiting canonical ones. Modernist Latitudes will pay particular attention to the texts and contexts of those latitudes (Africa, Latin America, Australia, Asia, Southern Europe, and even the rural United States) that have long been misrecognized as ancillary to the canonical modernisms of the global North.

Laura Winkiel, *Modernism and the Middle Passage*

Shir Alon, *Static Forms: Writing the Present in the Modern Middle East*

Mat Fournier, *Dysphoric Modernism: Undoing Gender in French Literature*

Nergis Ertürk, *Writing in Red: Literature and Revolution Across Turkey and the Soviet Union*

Cate I. Reilly, *Psychic Empire: Literary Modernism and the Clinical State*

Adam McKible, *Creating Jim Crow America: George Horace Lorimer, the Saturday Evening Post, and the War Against Black Modernity*

Hannah Freed-Thall, *Modernism at the Beach: Queer Ecologies and the Coastal Commons*

Daniel Ryan Morse, *Radio Empire: The BBC's Eastern Service and the Emergence of the Global Anglophone Novel*

Jill Richards, *The Fury Archives: Female Citizenship, Human Rights, and the International Avant-Gardes*

Claire Seiler, *Midcentury Suspension: Literature and Feeling in the Wake of World War II*

Elizabeth Outka, *Viral Modernism: The Influenza Pandemic and Interwar Literature*

Ben Conisbee Baer, *Indigenous Vanguards: Education, National Liberation, and the Limits of Modernism*

Aarthi Vadde, *Chimeras of Form: Modernist Internationalism Beyond Europe, 1914–2014*

For a complete list of books in this series, please see the Columbia University Press website.

Cosmo-Modernism and Theater in India

WRITING AND STAGING MULTILINGUAL MODERNISMS

Aparna Bhargava Dharwadker

Columbia University Press
New York

Columbia University Press
Publishers Since 1893
New York   Chichester, West Sussex

Copyright © 2025 Columbia University Press
All rights reserved

Library of Congress Cataloging-in-Publication Data
Names: Dharwadker, Aparna Bhargava, 1955–, author
Title: Cosmo-modernism and theater in India : writing and staging
multilingual modernisms / Aparna Bhargava Dharwadker.
Description: New York : Columbia University Press, 2025. | Series: Modernist Latitudes |
Includes bibliographical references and index.
Identifiers: LCCN 2025000690 | ISBN 9780231213844 hardback |
ISBN 9780231213851 trade paperback | ISBN 9780231560061 ebook
Subjects: LCSH: Indic drama—20th century—History and criticism |
Modernism (Literature)—India | Theater—India—History—20th century |
LCGFT: Literary criticism
Classification: LCC PK5421 .D47 2025 | DDC 891.4—dc23/eng/20250508

Cover design: Chang Jae Lee
Cover image: *Andha yug* at Purana Qila

GPSR Authorized Representative: Easy Access System Europe,
Mustamäe tee 50, 10621 Tallinn, Estonia, gpsr.requests@easproject.com

For Aneesha and Sachin
beloved children, simpatico friends

CONTENTS

ACKNOWLEDGMENTS ix

AUTHOR'S NOTE xiii

ABBREVIATIONS xv

PART I: APPROACHING INDIAN MODERNISMS

Introduction. Indian Modernisms in a Global Frame   3

Chapter One
Modernism, India, and the Axis of Language   31

Chapter Two
Modernity, Modernism, and Indian Theater   65

PART 2: WRITING AND STAGING MODERNISM

Chapter Three
Palimpsests of the Past   113

CONTENTS

Chapter Four
Modernism, Realism, and the Postcolonial Urban Present   160

Chapter Five
Modernism and Tradition   209

Conclusion: Cosmo-Modernism and Theater in Retrospect   259

NOTES   273

BIBLIOGRAPHY   309

INDEX   321

ACKNOWLEDGMENTS

My principal challenge during the formative stages of this book was to determine how the burgeoning map of global modernisms could accommodate the large but resistant body of non-Anglophone Indian modernist writing. I would first like to thank Katherine Kelly, Penny Farfan, Rebecca Walkowitz, Elin Diamond, Chelva Kanaganayakam, Martin Puchner, Siyuan Liu, Ameet Parameswaran, Will Broadway, and Julia Walker for including me in the symposia, conference panels, lecture series, encyclopedias, and special journal issues that enabled me to arrive at a qualitatively new understanding of modernism and to bring Indian cultural forms into the critical conversation. Working through primary sources in modern and contemporary Indian theater theory during a yearlong fellowship at the International Research Center in Berlin (2015–16) revealed with unusual clarity the sharp turn toward modernism in mid-twentieth-century theater; a Resident Fellowship at UW-Madison's Institute for Research in the Humanities (spring 2017) provided the time and space for conceptualizing a book around that rupture in theory and practice. Editorial work on *A Poetics of Modernity* (2019), my collection of primary texts in modern Indian theater theory, occupied me for the next two years, but I resumed my focus specifically on modernism in 2020. Martin Puchner, Elin Diamond, and Glenn Odom graciously agreed to referee grant proposals that secured me uninterrupted time for writing. At UW-Madison, the Graduate

School Research Committee offered substantial salary support in summer 2021; a multiyear Kellett award from the Graduate School and Wisconsin Alumni Research Foundation (2022-) facilitated travel to India and all other research-related costs; and sabbatical leave during the spring 2023 semester (granted by the Provost's Office) allowed me to complete the process of writing and revision. Florence Hsia, Associate Vice Chancellor for the Arts and Humanities in the Graduate School, offered valuable advice and guidance during these years that led to successful extramural as well as intramural awards. A publishing subvention from the Office of the Vice Chancellor for Research, with funding from the Wisconsin Alumni Research Foundation, offset production costs, especially those associated with the large number of illustrations. I gratefully acknowledge the generosity of all these institutions and colleagues.

In the English Department at Madison, I was singularly fortunate in having Susan Friedman and Teju Olaniyan as colleagues, interlocutors, well-wishers, and friends for two decades. Quite simply, I wrote this book because Susan believed in it—India's expressive culture had an important place in her planetary thinking, both scholarly and pedagogic, and it was because of her vocal enthusiasm that I made the subcontinent's historically ingrained multilingual literacy the core of my argument about Indian modernisms. Susan's insistence on the reperiodization of modernism, her use of cultural parataxis as a reading strategy, and the decentering of Western modernity in her definition of planetarity were also brilliantly compelling models as I reoriented myself to the new modernist studies in the new century. Losing her would have been hard at any time, but to know that she will not be a reader of this book is a lot harder: her last email of February 2023 offers me congratulations on the coming contract with Columbia. Teju, the thought provocateur par excellence, left us without warning in 2019, and took with him the power to cut through irrelevant distractions and get to the heart of postcolonial politics and aesthetics in ways that often felt epiphanic. Shaped by very different cultural geographies, Teju and I nonetheless shared methods that gave the same priority to authors, languages, and cultural forms within the complicated sociopolitical contexts of our respective regions, and we preferred theories that could explain rather than merely legislate what Teju liked to call "the reality on the ground." Addressing the relationship between culture and politics, especially in the unruly genre of theater, we also saw the excesses of the

ACKNOWLEDGMENTS

postcolonial nation-state as a more urgent problem in the present than the determinisms of colonial discourse in the past. What I learned from reading, hearing, and talking to Susan and Teju has shaped this book in fundamental ways, and it is my bittersweet way of thanking and remembering them.

Euro-American "high" modernists were a powerful presence in our daily lives at the time when Vinay Dharwadker and I were completing degrees in physics and English, respectively, at the University of Delhi. His diasporic transformation into a scholar of the South Asian humanities was more astonishing than mine, and his essays on Indian modernisms belong in a class of their own. Vinay's work on cosmopolitanism, print culture, modernity, translation, and the formation of the modern Indian literary and cultural spheres has been a vital part of my understanding of these topics for a long time now, and as always, it is a pleasure to acknowledge these debts. The anonymous external reviewers of my manuscript at various stages of its progress were generous in their comments and perceptive in their suggestions: their responses have enabled me to improve the book in numerous respects. I am especially grateful to Jessica Berman for feedback and conversation that led to an important course correction in the spring of 2023 and streamlined the writing that followed.

The always difficult task of securing photographs for a book about theater was made easier by a number of colleagues and friends: Alan Joseph of the Alkazi Theatre Archive, Kirti Jain, and Anjala Maharishi in Delhi; Mahesh Dattani, Raell Padamsee, Sunil Shanbag, Rajeev Puri, and Bhavikk Shah in Mumbai; Mahesh Elkunchwar in Nagpur; Madhuchhanda Ghosh of the Natya Shodh Sansthan, Rustom Bharucha, and Ananda Lal in Kolkata; Nageen Tanvir in Bhopal; and Neil Scharnick of Carthage College in Kenosha, Wisconsin. Frances Belsham of Sotheby's (London) and the photographer Filip Dujardin of Ghent (Belgium) had the kindness to respond to permission requests from a stranger. I am beholden to all of them for images that have immeasurably enhanced this book. Special thanks to Deepak Kumar for his extraordinary generosity and courtesy in guiding me through the permission process at the National School of Drama (New Delhi), and to Chittaranjan Tripathy, the school's Director, for making the iconic photograph on the cover of this book available to us. Most of the images were prepared for submission by my son Sachin, a filmmaker who moonlights graciously as my tech support for all such needs.

Chapters 1 and 2 incorporate portions of my essay "Mohan Rakesh, Modernism, and the Postcolonial Present," in "Staging Modernism," ed. Katherine Kelly and Penny Farfan, special issue, *South Central Review* 25, no. 1 (2008): 136–62. Chapter 3 incorporates my introductions to Girish Karnad's play *Yayati*, which appeared in volumes 1 and 3 of his *Collected Plays* (Oxford University Press, 2005 and 2017), and brief excerpts from my essay "Cultural Interweaving and Translation: Three Iconic Moments in Indian Theater, 1859-1979" (ed. Erika Fischer-Lichte et al., Routledge, 2020). Chapters 2 and 5 incorporate my essay "Modernism, 'Tradition,' and History in the Postcolony: Vijay Tendulkar's *Ghashiram kotwal* (1972)," in "Modernism," ed. Penny Farfan, special issue, *Theatre Journal* 65 (2013): 467–87. For permission to reprint this material I am grateful to Oxford University Press, Johns Hopkins University Press, and Routledge.

Watching Aneesha and Sachin grow up into creative, intelligent, emotionally grounded, and ethical adults has been the great pleasure and comfort of my life. That passage has been punctuated over the years by the books I have generated—this one is dedicated to them with love and admiration.

AUTHOR'S NOTE

I have translated all of the original primary and secondary materials from Hindi and Marathi that are discussed and cited in this book. In the case of plays that already existed in published English translations from these two languages, I have referred to and occasionally cited the editorial content (introductions, prefaces, forewords, and afterwords), but quotations from the plays have been translated afresh from the original version. Any exceptions to this practice are recorded in the text or in the notes.

English translations are provided for the titles of all Indian-language works—plays, poems, essays, and books of various kinds. For each play, I have translated the title when the work is mentioned for the first time and periodically thereafter to maintain clarity of reference. However, to preserve the integrity of the Indian-language materials, I have used the original rather than translated titles in extended discussions. The dating of plays is based on publication or first performance, whichever comes earlier.

Many major Indian cities have been renamed in the past three decades to "correct" anglicized spellings from the colonial period or to "recover" ostensibly more authentic precolonial or even ancient names. Among theatrically active cities, Bombay became Mumbai, Calcutta became Kolkata, Madras became Chennai, Trivandrum became Thiruvananthapuram, and

Bangalore became Bengaluru. Throughout the book, for historical accuracy I have used the names for these cities that were current during the time period in question. When my reference is to an event since the official name change, I have used the new spelling; when it is important to invoke the continuity of a city's identity over the modern period as a whole, I have mentioned both names.

ABBREVIATIONS

BK	Mohan Rakesh, *Bakalam khud* (By his own pen)
DBG	*Dharamvir bharati granthavali* (The works of Dharamvir Bharati)
Hirma	Habib Tanvir, *Hirma ki amar kahani* (The immortal tale of Hirma)
IPTA	Indian People's Theatre Association
LTH	Habib Tanvir, *The Living Tale of Hirma*, trans. Anjum Katyal and Prabha Katyal
MRR	*Mohan rakesh rachanavali* (The works of Mohan Rakesh)
NV	Mohan Rakesh, *Natya vimarsh* (Reflections on theater)
NSD	National School of Drama, New Delhi
Ninasam	Nilakanteshwara Natya Seva Sangh, Heggodu (Karnataka)
ODSR	Mohan Rakesh, *One Day in the Season of Rain*, trans. Aparna Dharwadker and Vinay Dharwadker
POM	*A Poetics of Modernity: Indian Theatre Theory, 1850 to the Present*, ed. Aparna Dharwadker
PTT	Vijay Tendulkar, *The Play Is the Thing*
SAS	Mohan Rakesh, *Sahitya aur sanskriti* (Literature and culture)
SN	*Mohan rakesh ke sampurna natak* (The complete plays of Mohan Rakesh)
SNA	Sangeet Natak Akademi (National Performing Arts Academy), New Delhi

PART I
Approaching Indian Modernisms

INTRODUCTION

Indian Modernisms in a Global Frame

AN INDIAN'S MODERNISMS: THEN AND NOW

In the curricula for the bachelor's and master's degrees in English that I received in India some decades ago, the Anglo-American high modernists—Yeats, Conrad, Joyce, Eliot, Lawrence, Stevens, Williams, et al.—marked a heady moment of liberation in a relentless and mandatory literary-historical sequence that began with Chaucer and Malory and ended with Auden. The first version of the "modernist canon" was firmly in place by the 1970s, and works such as *Heart of Darkness, The Wild Swans at Coole, Prufrock and Other Observations, A Portrait of the Artist as a Young Man, Harmonium, Women in Love,* and *Four Quartets* were among those that represented our first full-fledged encounter with the twentieth-century avant-garde, creating in us the feeling that we had finally arrived at a fearlessly experimental, sexually liberated, irreplaceable, and deeply satisfying modernity. Belonging mainly to the English-educated urban Indian middle class and with neither the motivation nor the intellectual equipment to begin questioning our unreflecting neocolonialism, we saw the modernists as kindred spirits—poets, novelists, theorists, and critics who were ideally positioned to serve as touchstones of "our" cultural experience. The Indian academy's fascination with close reading and its reverence for "the text" were also perfect instruments for immersion in what appeared to be an endless array of modernist verbal icons. As a young lecturer in English at Delhi University, I became especially passionate about Yeats, Joyce, and Eliot, reading systematically through their work (creative and critical) to understand fully the worlds that had made their singular achievements possible. When I left Delhi to enter a PhD program in the United States, I expected to write a dissertation on Eliot's interwar journal, *The Criterion* (1922–1939), all eighteen volumes of which I had gone through during an intense eight-week stint in the Reading Room of the Delhi University Library.

Between that unfulfilled goal and this book on modernist drama and theater in India lies the long arc of a fundamental cultural, political, and intellectual reeducation that has marked the professional lives of most Indian literary scholars of my generation in the Western academy. The New Critical habits I had inherited were quickly challenged in the American classroom by the methodological claims of structuralism, poststructuralism, feminism, neo-Aristotelianism, neo-Marxism, and new historicism (among other approaches). This evolving pedagogical environment was reinforced by more or less extended contact with some of its key proponents, including Jonathan Culler, Tzvetan Todorov, Geoffrey Hartman, J. Hillis Miller, Wayne Booth, Gerald Graff, Hayden White, Sandra Gilbert, Susan Gubar, and Stephen Greenblatt. Doctoral work in British drama of the late seventeenth and early eighteenth centuries—a relatively neglected and misrepresented field I had never expected to enter—taught me how to "read" texts in/for performance as contingent constructs entangled in volatile sociopolitical and institutional conditions. Perhaps more important, the experience shifted my scholarly interests from poetry and fiction to theater. Crucial disciplinary and curricular changes in the 1990s also enabled me to make a timely transition to Indian, postcolonial, diasporic, and world literature studies as new areas of research and teaching expertise, again with theater at the center. The methods I had developed for the study of mainstream and marginal British materials were repurposed during this time so that I, like many of my peers, could take up non-Western cultural forms without resorting to philologically oriented area studies approaches.[1] The publication of my monograph *Theatres of Independence* in 2005 formalized the shift from Euro-American topics to twentieth-century India and from Europhone colonial and postcolonial writing in various parts of the world to the novel challenges of non-Europhone, multilingual, Indian cultural forms that were responding to similar historical-political circumstances.[2]

In 2019, my anthology *A Poetics of Modernity* expanded the scholarly field further by bringing together selections from a multilingual archive of theoretically significant source texts, which were presented either in the original English or in English translation from ten other Indian languages.[3]

Cosmo-Modernism and Theater in India represents a second major critical shift—from cultural and political modernity/modernization in India to postcolonial modern*ism*—that redirected my long-standing interest in the topic toward the familiar yet surprisingly new territory of the subcontinent, now ready to be grasped through the changed critical outlooks of the present. The global or planetary turn within modernist studies has decisively decentered the idea of a Euro-American (primarily Anglophone) modernist canon and introduced non-Eurocentric critical perspectives that can potentially balance the global horizons of modernism with qualities intrinsic to particular cultural geographies. It has also fundamentally reconfigured the spatiotemporal boundaries, chronologies, and hierarchical relations of modernism, bringing non-Western and postcolonial regions meaningfully into the movement's ambit for the first time. Many of the generative concepts created by this revisionary energy—especially those of "geomodernism," a shared "geocultural consciousness," "polycentric modernities," "circulating modernisms," "planetary modernism," and "cultural parataxis"—have been instrumental in clearing the theoretical space that enables me, for instance, to formulate my central claim: that the midcentury revolution in urban cultural forms accompanying the end of British colonialism in India created the largest clustering of "modernist" as well as "postcolonial" writing outside the circuits of Europhone textuality and performance. The emphasis on locational particularity in current modernist scholarship also has the potential to accommodate the unique circumstance that Indian modernisms intersect fully with a millennium-long history of multilingual literacy in nearly twenty indigenous languages, which arrived at their developed modern forms over the course of the nineteenth century. However, in the ambitious recent remapping of modernism as a global movement, the theory, history, aesthetics, reception, and interpretation of Indian modernisms have not received commensurate attention for two main reasons. First, in an intranational frame, the study of Indian modernisms across the entire spectrum of literary and performative genres is hampered by the unbridged gap between modernism's pervasive presence as a late-colonial and postcolonial aesthetic-political movement in the country, and the tentative, more or less erratic formulation of Indian modernist studies as a critical field. Second, in a transnational frame, the problems of linguistic and cultural access posed by India's voluminous non-Europhone output and the lack of critical attention to the intrinsic qualities and intercultural politics of modernism's global languages have kept multilingual Indian modernisms on the margins of even the new modernist studies.

Considered synchronically in the early twenty-first century, these divergent elements underscore the singularity of India as a geomodernist location. The *plurality* of languages separates India from national spaces around the globe in which a single language dominates literary culture, even when other languages are present in spoken and written forms—an attribute shared by France and Germany in Europe, the United States and Argentina in the Americas, and Japan and China in Asia. The plurality of *non-Europhone languages* separates India not only from the West but also from former colonies in sub-Saharan Africa and the Caribbean, where languages such as English and French have emerged as the dominant media of expression for the "new national and postcolonial" literatures. English has been a vital literary/modernist medium in India as it is in other former British colonies, but as a colonial and postcolonial configuration it coexists uniquely *within a single national space* with the largest number of other fully developed literary languages. In "reading" these non-Anglophone Indian modernisms, it is not possible to circumvent scholarly expertise in the original language and its modern literary history, however much these are mediated now by relevant perspectives from postcolonial studies, cosmopolitics, and world literature or by the activity and frequency of translation. The issue of language is central, not only because non-European languages remain marginal in modernist studies but also because Indian-language writing—modernist or otherwise—is initially available only to those who have knowledge of the medium in question. With the exception (again) of English, the primarily regional compass of modern Indian languages also generates criticism that focuses on a single language and region, most often in the language *of* that region, and hence occludes the understanding of modernism as a transregional, national, and transnational movement. In sum, the need for "insider knowledge," the paucity of holistic perspectives, and the degrees of critical disinterest (in India and elsewhere) position Indian literary/theatrical modernisms as compelling objects of recovery that are paradoxically indecipherable.

INTRODUCTION

In *Cosmo-Modernism and Theater* I develop an approach to Indian modernisms that acknowledges the particulars of literary and cultural history in all their trans/national complexity, and within those frames of reference I consider the theory, practice, and reception of modernist drama, attending fully to its dual existence in writing/print and performance. The key terms in this book's title encapsulate its conceptual schema. "Cosmo-modernism," a neologism I first used in 2005, signals both the centrality of modernism as an aesthetic-political movement in postindependence India and the complex affiliations its major practitioners maintain with modernisms beyond the nation's borders. Indian modernists, I argue, combine an acute awareness of their historical positioning within the old-but-new nation of India with a "full consciousness of the world" that connects them as intellectuals and artists to modernities in a global frame. "Theater," my chosen form, poses unique challenges as a modernist category because it was almost invisible even in Euro-American modernist studies until the 1990s and always involves the complex interplay of multiple modalities—of "drama" as text, of "theater" as institutionalized performance, and of "reception" as the response of an actual audience to live enactment. In India, all of these factors are complicated by the continuous processes of cross-cultural exchange, the proliferation of languages, and, most important, the pressures of sustaining theater in a resolutely decommercialized postindependence performance economy. The activities of "writing" and "staging" modernism in India—invoked in my subtitle—take place in an environment created by the intermixture of these intrinsic and extrinsic factors. Finally, the presence of "multilingual modernisms" demands attention because it reflects intrinsic, historically determined conditions of modern Indian writing and performance, reshapes all of the Euro-Western cultural influences activated by colonialism and postcolonialism, and offers a significant variation on the current (and growing) Western interest in linguistic plurality as a measure of social, political, cultural, and racial diversity.

In the remainder of this introduction, I address three distinct issues that are germane to my argument and explain how they are amplified in subsequent chapters. The first issue relates to language—not how language is used *in* modernist works (a major focus of modernist studies since its inception) but how the languages *of* modernism have proliferated around the globe during the twentieth and twenty-first centuries and the extent to which modernist studies has addressed or failed to address the implications of this expansion for our relational understanding of global modernisms. The second involves a peculiar conflation of the concepts of "modernity" and "modernism" in Indian-language terminology, which obscures fundamental aesthetic differences between works produced at different times, the evolution of literary/theatrical history during the colonial and postcolonial periods, and the logic of periodization. The third stems from the historic marginality of the genres of live performance in modernist studies, which has been redressed to some extent by recent scholarly efforts to bring such works saliently into the modernist fold through new theoretical models, historicizing strategies, and methods of textual interpretation. The critical valences created by this earlier scholarship help clarify the particular features of modernist theater in India and provide comparative frames for the dramatic genres I have chosen for analysis.

The next three sections have a "metacritical" orientation because they demonstrate as well as explain the virtual exclusion of Indian-language modernisms (literary and theatrical) from the old and new modernist studies, the underdeveloped state of Indian modernist studies, and the undervaluation of theater (especially Indian theater) in modernist studies. To address these critical gaps, in part 1 of the book I occasionally point to specific trends in modernist scholarship, but my approach is comparative, evaluative, and contestatory, not descriptive: I focus on positions that obscure or clarify the Indian-language materials I am concerned with to clear the *conceptual* space for a commensurate inclusion of these materials in global perspectives on modernism. The chapters in part 2 then chart the formation of major modernist genres for print and performance around a variety of narratives rooted in the past and present. Taken together, these multiple lines of argument articulate the threefold objectives of *Cosmo-Modernism*: to position Indian modernisms clearly in relation to transnational modernist studies, to accentuate the performative in modernist studies, and to give Indian theater a new visibility in modernist theater studies.

GLOBAL MODERNISMS, GLOBAL LANGUAGES

The rapid expansion in the spatiotemporal boundaries of modernism around the globe, especially over the past decade, has also meant a corresponding proliferation of the global *languages* of modernism. As critical overviews of modernist studies noted in the 1990s, English had initially dominated the modernist canon because the emergence of the field in Anglo-American academic institutions during the 1960s, under the strong influence of New Criticism, positioned Anglophone high modernists such as Yeats, Joyce, Eliot, Pound, and Woolf firmly at the center of this "retrospectively constructed" movement. By the end of the century, however, many other European languages had joined the modernist fold, and their significance as theoretical and creative mediums could be examined in comparative frameworks. In an anthology published in 1998, for example, German, French, Russian, Spanish, Hungarian, Italian, Swedish, and Romanian appeared with varying degrees of prominence alongside English as national languages in which primary works from the 1840–1940 period could be assembled to create new perspectives on the pan-European emergence of the modern, the formation of avant-gardes, and self-reflexive commentaries on modernism by writers and critics.[4] Since 2005, the appearance of comprehensive collections and monographs organized around the concepts of "geomodernism," "cosmopolitanism," "national and transnational modernisms," "global modernisms," "the modernist world," "metageographies," and "planetary modernisms" have gradually added a large number of major languages from Europe, Asia, Oceania, the Americas, Africa, and the Caribbean to the modernist output, consolidating the claims of modernism's global reach.[5]

This new cartography of modernism has established compelling although widely varying connections between nation, region, and language but has paid surprisingly little specific attention to the relations of power *between* languages that determine the visibility and accessibility of modernist repertoires. Because of the complexities of moving from Western-centric to transnational, global, and planetary schemas, much of the recent energy in modernist studies has been focused on reconceptualizing and reperiodizing modernism (especially in relation to colonial/postcolonial histories) and on formulating coeval definitions of modernism that accommodate locational differences while preserving a qualitative sense of the "family resemblances that make multiple modernisms recognizable as members of a class."[6] The default position in these revisionary initiatives has been to treat language as a transparently available and neutral medium rather than as a volatile instrument that is enmeshed in historical, cultural, and political contests and is dependent for its status on an always shifting relation to other languages. In mapping the globality that is now a prominent feature of modernist studies, for instance, the emerging practice is to organize criticism around transnational *spatial* categories—such as "transatlantic," "Scandinavian," "Oceanic," "Pacific Rim," "sub-Saharan," "Afro-Caribbean," "Caribbean," "South Asian," and "the Global South"—which foreground geography but subsume or erase the pervasive geopolitics of language.[7]

My fundamental premise in this book is that the relationship between geography, language, and expressive culture is shaped by broader relations of power, and modernisms in various global locations cannot be understood without reference to the resulting hierarchies that have affected or even determined the aesthetic scope of various languages in transnational/global contexts. A synchronic twenty-first-century vantage point reveals at least four distinct configurations that are relevant to modern cultural forms, including those of global modernism.

1. European countries in which the development of the modern nation-state is intimately connected with the development of a dominant national language (Britain, France, Germany, Spain, Portugal, the Netherlands, Norway, Sweden, Finland, Italy, and so on). In relation to national culture this is the most prominent model of literary activity, whereas in transnational comparisons within Europe it offers a densely interdependent yet manifestly competitive field.

2. Settler colonies in which a European language becomes dominant and contributes to nation formation in ways similar to Europe, but by suppressing and often eradicating the indigenous/native languages of the region (Ireland, the United States, Canada, Latin America, settler colonies in the Greater Antilles, Australia, New Zealand). The "nationalization" of English, French, Spanish, and Portuguese in these locations is therefore based on the systematic destruction of other tongues.

3. Imperial/crown colonies in Africa, South Asia, and Southeast Asia, where European colonialism imposes a dominant new language on cultures with already highly developed oral or written languages. The cultural politics of language, the tension between acceptance and resistance, the issues of derivativeness and belatedness, and the conditions of epistemic violence are at their most complex and intense in this model, both during the period of colonialism and in the extended subsequent process of decolonization.

INTRODUCTION

4. Countries or regions (such as the "Arab world," Iran, China, and Japan) that did not undergo conventional colonization by Europe and in which a dominant language anchors literary activity in ways analogous to the national languages of Europe. Unlike the first three models, in which European languages are hegemonic or dominant, this one offers literary cultures that are outside the direct control of the West and in which indigenous linguistic systems thoroughly mediate Western influences.

Indian literary and theatrical modernisms are suspended uncertainly between these formations because in one direction the millennium-long tradition of multilingual literacy precludes the model of a single dominant "national" language that can be charted as a modernist medium (as it can be in Japan or China) and in another direction the dynamic of modernity and modernism in the indigenous languages becomes deeply entangled with the impact of the imperial language, English, after the mid-nineteenth century (as in the former British colonies of sub-Saharan Africa). Indian modernisms represent, in fact, the foremost contemporary example of the complicating effects of language because of the singular role English has played as an imperial-colonial import that evolved into a major creative medium on the subcontinent and now functions as both a Western and an Indian language, alongside the full range of modern Indian languages. When compared with the indigenous languages of the subcontinent, English became an active participant in the cultural conversation belatedly, only around the mid-nineteenth century, yet its role as a national link language is now more important than that of any other Indian language. This is especially true with reference to spoken and written communication and the spheres of nonliterary and literary translation. Furthermore, the qualities of English as a world language—its links to colonial and postcolonial history; its association with the political, social, and literary elite; and, most recently, its dominance as a literary medium in the global South Asian diaspora—have placed it in a position of distinct privilege in relation to the other Indian languages *but without critically displacing the latter*. One can indeed argue that the availability of English has predetermined the manner in which modernist studies, postcolonial studies, diaspora studies, and discussions of cosmopolitanism have approached Indian writing; however, the purpose of this argument is not to raise ahistorical objections against English but to draw attention to the resulting imbalances. The presence of

Anglophone writing has allowed scholars in the West, including scholars of Indian origin, to bring "India" into the critical matrix without having to consider Indian languages that are less readily accessible than English. If English were the dominant literary language in India, as it is in Anglophone postcolonial Africa and the Caribbean, its dominance within the critical discourses would not be so problematic or problematic in the same way. If, on the other hand, India did not have English, scholars would be compelled to pay attention to writing in the other Indian languages, as they do in the case of major non-Western languages such as Chinese, Japanese, and Arabic. It is the position of English as both inside and outside, Indian and not-Indian, and national and global that has created the peculiar problems of inclusion and exclusion.[8]

This paradox creates an unresolvable asymmetry: regardless of its actual creative status in relation to specific genres, the presence of English occludes work in the other Indian languages. In prose fiction, for example, English enabled the pioneering careers of authors such as Mulk Raj Anand, Raja Rao, and R. K. Narayan in the 1930s, and since the 1980s it has secured a global readership for the next generation of authors, including Anita Desai, Salman Rushdie, Amitav Ghosh, Rohinton Mistry, and Arundhati Roy, who figure prominently in arguments about the emergence of a late-twentieth-century postcolonial and cosmopolitan modernism.[9] But the mid-twentieth-century modernist revolution in *non-Anglophone* Indian poetry and fiction, announced as the arrival of the "new poetry," the "new novel," and the "new short story" in a succession of languages, remains almost entirely absent from the purview of the "new modernist studies." In modern/ist Indian drama and theater, the alchemy of English is even more complicated because as the medium of original composition it has remained secondary to languages such as Bengali, Marathi, Hindi, and Kannada since the mid-nineteenth century, but as the target language of translation it has emerged as a singularly important means of giving regional-language plays access to national and international communities of readers and viewers.

These complicated relationships lead to yet another paradox: the plurality of regional Indian languages and the relatively subsidiary role of English as the language of original composition create a unique profile for India in the postcolonial sphere, but they are also the factors that render the field of modern/ist Indian theater largely inaccessible to audiences outside India unless the works are translated into English and other world languages. The activity of translation then becomes another measure of stark disparity because since the nineteenth century an immense body of Western and world theater has been consumed in India through translation into multiple Indian languages (including English), but movement in the opposite direction—from India to the world—is hampered by the dominance of Anglophone Indian writing abroad and the consequent disinterest in other Indian source languages, which in any case are not "national" languages along Western lines.[10]

The preceding catalogue of cultural singularities indicates that India can have substantive theoretical/critical representation in transnational frames of reference only when there is a direct focus on particular non-European locations *and languages* as modernist media. The comprehensive recent collections charting modernism as a global movement, however, have continued to focus almost entirely on Anglophone Indian writing (especially prose fiction) or visual, plastic, popular, and mass-cultural forms (painting, photography, architecture, and cinema).[11] The few notable exceptions to this pattern have appeared so far in essays by Vinay Dharwadker that specifically address non-Anglophone Indian modernisms and the section on India in Alys Moody and Stephen J. Ross's anthology, *Global Modernists on Modernism*.[12] Invoking the "precolonial divergences of multilingualism, multi-literacy, and multiple literatures" in India, Dharwadker locates the foundation for modernist innovation in "the social dimension of the subcontinent's modernity—rather than its aesthetic dimension" and establishes the important disciplinary principle that twentieth-century Indian modernisms are not separable from the continuities of Indian literary culture before, during, and after the colonial phase that has shaped the most recent discourses on modernity and modernization.[13] Moody and Ross note that their collection represents nineteen languages and take the crucial step of acknowledging that language instrumentally creates the very conditions of writing: "The decision (forcible or voluntary) to write in one language over another, in one place or another, is constitutive to a given writer's modernist practice, rather than incidental to it."[14] Presenting materials written originally in English, Hindi, Urdu, Bengali, Marathi, and Malayalam in the section on South Asia, Rudrani Gangopadhyay invokes "the immense linguistic diversity of the region," which means that "any attempt to identify a modernist moment is necessarily pluralized as well."[15] The volume thus offers a pioneering glimpse into non-Western modernist positions shaped by region, language, period, class, caste, politics, genre, and occasion, outlining a model of autonomous enunciation and diversity that is necessary in any approach to South Asia/India; it also prefigures the potentially radical reconceptualization of modernism that would become possible through a full-scale engagement with Indian multilingualism and Indian languages as modernist vehicles.

The focus on language in this section has moved toward an overdetermined conclusion: when global practices are at issue, language has to become a fourth axis of criticism in modernist studies, regardless of genre, because the issues it raises as the medium of original composition and translation cannot be fully settled by reference to the spatial, temporal, and vertical expansions charted by the new modernist studies. We can provisionally call this the expressive or lexical dimension, and in the multilingual Indian context it involves a dense network of histories, forms, texts, and cultures, both indigenous and foreign, that together generate modern/ist Indian writing and performance. The full implications of this position—that the relational political-cultural status of modernism's languages is a vital aspect of the movement's global dynamic, especially from the standpoint of a multilingual non-Western former colony such as India—are explored in chapter 1.

MODERNITY, MODERNISM, AND THE PROBLEMS OF DEFINITION

In the theory and criticism that have debated competing ideas of cultural modernity since the 1980s, "modern," "modernity," "modernism," and "modernization" are routinely recognized as interconnected terms, although the precise relationship between them varies according to the frames of reference. For Tim Armstrong, "the demand to 'make it new' places modernism and modernity in proximity, and often involves a violent rejection of the petrified values of 'art' in favour of 'life' or reform."[16] In Susan Stanford Friedman's definition, modernism is "the domain of creative expressivity *within* modernity's dynamic of rapid change," although she delinks both terms from the norms of Western modernity and locates their disruptive energy in unexpected spatiotemporal configurations around the world.[17] In other frameworks the idea of interconnection gives way to the idea of identity or interchangeability, as in Michael Wood's contention that "all films are modernist, that the cinema itself is an accelerated image of modernity, like the railway and the telephone."[18] As Western genres, drama and theater seem to encourage this semantic conflation to an even greater extent because the rupture from convention represented by late-nineteenth-century pioneers in "modern" drama (such as Ibsen, Strindberg, Chekhov, and Shaw) can plausibly be seen as prefiguring the "modernist" practices of playwrights such as Eugene O' Neill, John Galsworthy, Arthur Miller, and Tennessee Williams. In general, the terminological switch from modern to modernist and back again in Western and other critical sources is simply too widespread to support arguments for more precise usage.

In the case of India, there has been a growing scholarly interest in *precolonial* forms of modernity, such as the Hindu and Muslim imperial state formations straddling more than two millennia (fifth century BCE to eighteenth century CE) and the nationwide movement of religious reform and protest known as *bhakti* (worship or devotion). The normative meanings of modernity, however, are still firmly yoked to the transformations brought about by Anglo-European influences and the colonial experience during the nineteenth and early twentieth centuries. As Dipesh Chakrabarty notes, "The very colonial crucible in which Bengali [read Indian] modernity originated ensured that it would not be possible to fashion a historical account of the birth of this modernity without reproducing some aspect of European narratives of the modern subject—for European modernity was present at this birth."[19] In the cultural sphere, however, the mediation of colonial modernity by "naïve" Indian aesthetic practices, the preoccupation with classical India encouraged by European Orientalism, and the late-colonial cult of romantic nationalism create relationships not of proximity or identity but of overt antagonism between the earlier permutations and mid-twentieth-century modernisms. Without being named explicitly, modern*ism* becomes by the 1950s the expression of a "true" or "real" modernity capable of confronting the chaos of independence, partition, inherently unjust social structures, and disenchantment with the new nation-state. This specific history has to be read into the Indian terminology, and its implications for aesthetic theory and practice across the colonial/postcolonial divide have to be drawn out carefully. As Ross and Lindgren have argued, "If we are going to take seriously the challenge to think plural modernisms globally, then we must accept a shifting terminological, as well as conceptual and aesthetic, terrain."[20] Because in India the idea of plurality operates so powerfully at the *intra*national level, it is also important to consider how modernizing processes intersect with the conditions of inherited multilingualism, how each language responds to cultural transmutations, and how the various languages interact with one another. Indian-language modernisms in literature and theater therefore have to be situated within the specific and distinctive history of Indian cultural modernity as defined in relation to colonialism and its aftermath. This entails a discussion of the conceptual relation between modernity and modernism in Indian theory and criticism, the relevance of that relation to the development of cultural forms after the mid-nineteenth century, and the convergence of aesthetic and political interests that mark the advent of a modernist turn in the mid-twentieth century.

The inquiry into terms and concepts, however, runs immediately into complications because Indian languages do not make a distinction that is commonplace in English: the universally used adjective *adhunik* means both modern and modernist, and the abstract noun *adhunikata* denotes both modernity and modernism. Both terms appear with the greatest frequency in two leading literary languages of the modern period, Hindi and Bengali, but have transregional currency across the full spectrum of modern languages.[21] However, the equivalent terms for "modern*ism*" and "postmodern*ism*"—*adhunikatavad* and *uttara-adhunikatavad*—are not visible in the discourse of either authors or critics in India, and although *uttara-adhunik* ("postmodern") brings up a small number of critical works focused mainly on poetry, in a broader terminological context these are completely dwarfed by the ubiquity of *adhunik* and *adhunikata*. The Indian-language aesthetic vocabulary therefore recognizes the existence of modern and postmodern works, but by evading the suffix "*vad*" it resolutely resists the instrumentalization of these qualities into "isms." Consequently, there is no substantial body of Indian criticism *specifically on literary modernism*, no existing history of "the modernist movement in Indian literature/theater," and no broadly shared understanding of what constitutes modernist practice—instead, the theory and practice of the movement are buried in the discourses on/of modernity. Furthermore, the modernist attributes of novels, poems, and plays are not usually articulated self-reflexively by the author but have to be inferred hermeneutically by the critic, who also has to bear in mind that modernism in Indian performative genres is entangled in a powerful rhetoric of tradition and traditionalism.

INTRODUCTION

The theoretical imprecision of the modernity/modernism conflation also spills over into actual usage, in which *adhunik* and *adhunikata* designate an extended chronology—circa 1850 to the present—as well as a complex of literary, cultural, and political qualities. In the cultural-political sphere, the terms define a period ("the modern age"); a phase in the history of society and the nation ("modern India"); and particular ways of thinking ("modern" attitudes to, say, society, the family, sexuality, and gender). In the literary sphere, they denote a body of writing ("modern" Bengali or Punjabi or Gujarati literature); a phase in the development of a language ("modern" Assamese); specific authors ranging widely in time and place (Bankimchandra Chatterjee [1838–1894], Rabindranath Tagore [1861–1941], Buddhadeva Bose [1908–1974], Gopal Krishna Adiga [1918–1992], and Girish Karnad [1938–2019], to name a few); and particular qualities in literary genres, forms, poetic and fictional techniques, and even fictional characters in novels or plays. *Adhunik* (modern/modernist) is also variously synonymous with *naya, navya,* or *naveen* ("new"); *samakaleen* ("contemporary"); *pragatisheel* ("progressive"); and even *svatantrayottara* ("postindependence"). Its established antonym across all these usages is *parampara* ("tradition").

The absence of a lexical/conceptual distinction between modernity and modernism in Indian usage presents a notable contrast to the West, which continues to regard modernism as a *specific* aesthetic-political expression of modernity, however permeable its spatiotemporal boundaries.[22] In relation to literary modernity, therefore, the Indian usage has to be understood as a complex response to the disruptive effects of colonialism in a subcontinental region with a continuous, two-millennium-long precolonial history of cultural production. *Conceptually,* Indian modernity (*adhunikata*) comes to be defined primarily by/as the rupture from "intrinsic" tradition brought about by the "extrinsic" forces of colonialism, with the further assumption that this process profoundly influences the subsequent course of culture and accommodates later disjunctions as extensions of the original breach.[23] For example, a recent anthology of "modern Indian literature" begins chronologically with Michael Madhusudan Dutt (born in 1824) and ends with Sunetra Gupta (born in 1965)—a strategy of periodization and grouping that has no parallel in Western representations of modernity.[24] It is possible for critics writing just a decade apart to describe Mohan Rakesh (born in 1925) as the "messiah of modern theatre" and the Hindi poet-playwright

Bharatendu Harishchandra (born in 1850) as a "fountainhead of Indian modernity."[25] As a chronological and qualitative category, Indian literary modernity encapsulates part of the nineteenth century and all of the twentieth, as well as the work of individual authors anywhere along the spectrum.[26] However, Tagore is the only author whose modernity (*adhunikata*) is rendered explicitly as "modernism" in the English translation of a Bengali critical study.[27] Admittedly, the use of the terms *adhunik* and *adhunikata* has accelerated tremendously since independence.[28] This suggests that the *formulation* of the idea of modernity has been mainly a postindependence preoccupation (some theorists even assert that "real" modernity belongs only to the postindependence writers, not their colonial precursors). But in periodizing terms, the most common usage posits "modernity" as a process that began in the nineteenth century as a corollary to colonialism and continues into the present without any overt acknowledgment of a *modernist* configuration in the course of the twentieth century.

Major Indian modernists have to negotiate this conceptual failure, but demarcating modernism as a particular phase within the continuum of modernity is important because of the intensity of the rupture between colonial and postcolonial forms of expression across the whole spectrum of genres and languages. The question of when and why modernism emerged as a distinctive twentieth-century aesthetic in Indian literature has been answered in varying ways. Sudipta Kaviraj suggests intriguingly that the colonial writers possessed a "travestic modernity" in which the accomplishments of one generation were canceled out and "made impossible" by the next. In Bengali, even major authors such as Dutt and Tagore could not create "a repertoire of acknowledged styles in which literary writing could be carried on for the indefinite future," leading to a demand for change "in the fundamental aesthetic itself."[29] The foundational colonial-era precursors were thus not modern enough for their twentieth-century modernist successors. Anantha Murthy refers to the 1920s reaction against the "Tagore syndrome" as a flash point, suggesting that romantic mysticism and ardent nationalism were the two major ideologies countered by modernist experimentalism as India moved through the stages of intensifying anticolonial nationalism, the Second World War, the Bengal famine, the holocaust of Partition, and independence (circa 1920–1947).[30] Vinay Dharwadker offers yet another template by demarcating four distinct phases in a longer chronology of modernism that moves from social reformist/realist and anticolonial/experimental phases (1882–1922 and 1922–1947) to radically "new" postindependence movements (1950–1980), and then to the displacements of a cosmopolitan postcolonial diaspora (1980-).[31]

The timelines for modernism suggested by Anantha Murthy and Dharwadker point to important differences between print genres such as fiction, nonfiction, poetry, theory, and criticism and the performative genres of drama and theater. With the city as the primary site of transformation, print culture allowed literary authors autonomy and privacy of a kind that made possible the emergence of "modern" proprietary authorship as early as the 1850s (within a half century of the arrival of print), and the medium of print fixed language and form within the material confines of the book as a consumable object. Correspondingly, the conjuncture of a colonial-style education, increasing professionalization, and relative economic stability—especially in colonial metropolises such as Calcutta, Bombay, and Madras and the older imperial capitals of Delhi, Agra, Lucknow, Hyderabad, and Mysore—created new "reading publics" in the modern Indian languages, enabling authors and readers to connect directly within a widening literary-cultural sphere.[32] Furthermore, as "new" nineteenth-century forms shaped by European influences, the novel, the short story, the autobiography, the verse epic, the confessional lyric, and the theoretical essay do not have close antecedents in the precolonial culture of writing; their novelty is moored more solidly in the historical present than in the past. These factors have enabled recent critical *re*appraisals in which major authors of the 1880–1920 period, especially Tagore and Premchand, are viewed not only as modern but modernist in a specifically Indian literary trajectory.

In contrast, drama and theater involve the economies of textuality and print as well as private and public performance, and although plays are published from the 1850s onward, with a few exceptions performance remains drama's primary mode of existence until the 1940s, pushing the modernist potential of individual authorship to the periphery. The institutional demands of theatrical production position the dramatic "text" as only one element in a collective commercial enterprise that is far more invested in entertainment and spectacle for a live paying audience than in literary or cultural capital. Finally, because of the prestige of Sanskrit and the unbroken history of indigenous forms of theater and performance on the subcontinent, late-nineteenth-century theater grapples with classical legacies and "traditional" precolonial forms (especially in music and dance) on a qualitatively different scale from the genres of print. The modernist turn in theater therefore takes longer to materialize and represents a decisive break with the proximate past through the post-1940 forms of theory, authorial self-fashioning, aesthetic practice, and reception discussed in chapter 2.

MODERNIST STUDIES AND (INDIAN) THEATER

My focus on Indian theater connects in challenging ways to modernist studies at large because even in the West "drama" was relegated to the margins of this field until almost the turn of the twenty-first century. Christopher Innes observed a decade ago that "at first sight it might seem contradictory to include drama in a discussion of Modernism" but also noted the incongruity inherent in this marginalization: "Standard books like Peter Faulkner's *Modernism* ignore drama almost altogether, dismissing the whole genre as intrinsically unsuited to 'the complexities of modernism'—yet the list of people at the forefront of the Modernist movement who wrote plays is long."[33] Many of these "people at the forefront" were in fact largely responsible for the contradiction noted by Innes: the iconic poetry, fiction, and nonfiction of such writers as Yeats, Joyce, Eliot, and Gertrude Stein ensured the long-lasting dominance of these textual print genres in modernist studies, obscuring even their own output in drama. The relative insignificance of performative forms in modernist studies could be explained in additional ways. The public and collaborative nature of theater appeared incompatible with the modernist valorization of authorial exclusivity and autonomy; some modernist "plays" were categorically not intended for performance; others remained outside the powerful circuits of commercial production, especially those represented by Broadway and the West End; and still others maintained an ambiguous status in relation to the radical twentieth-century traditions of avant-garde, epic, and absurdist theater.

Many overviews of modernism (those by Bradshaw and Dettmar, Matthews, and most recently by Latham and Rogers, and Mao, for example) continue to marginalize or entirely ignore the drama-theater-performance triad.[34] But many productive frameworks have also emerged to enable the progressive (although far from complete) recovery of these genres in modernist studies. One major initiative involves the recognition of modernist elements in the work of major modern playwrights, which recast the foundational figures of "modern drama" as key figures in modernism. For example, numerous field-defining essays treat "modern drama" or "the drama of modernity" as alternative labels for "modernist drama," bringing figures such as Ibsen, Strindberg, Zola, Pirandello, Brecht, and August Wilson into a domain that usually focuses on Yeats, Eliot, Stein, and Beckett.[35] Other recuperative strategies include a focus on modernist drama/theater in collections that "rethink" modernisms or serve as "companions" to modernism (Thormahlen, Levenson); discussions of modernism specifically in relation to theater theory, history, and practice (Innes and Marker); an intentional focus on the performative rather than the textual (Ackerman and Puchner, Diamond, and Farfan *Performing*); the use of topoi such as primitivism and disease as thematically significant structuring devices (Eisen, Knapp, and Kelly); and reference to categories such as gender, subalternity, popular culture, and visual culture in diverse discussions of "modernism from below" (Farfan "Editorial," and Kelly and Farfan).[36] Constructing carefully theorized genealogies of modernist theater within the longer history of modern drama, Puchner and Taxidou offer suggestively antithetical views of "literariness" and "performance" in their respective interpretations. Puchner characterizes the negation of theater-as-performance—not only by closet playwrights such as Joyce and Gertrude Stein but by conspicuously successful practitioners such as Brecht and Beckett—as a form of "stage fright," whereas Taxidou relates modernism to "moments of performance that are at once literary and theatrical, textual and discursive," stressing the interdependence of these categories.[37] Taxidou's position has been strengthened during the past two decades by the momentum that concepts such as "staging modernism" and "performing modernism" have acquired in what is now a clearly established Euro-American field of modernist theater studies.[38]

Such "studies" are almost completely absent in relation to India, but the scholarly positions outlined here clarify the modernist attributes of Indian-language drama and theater and also throw into relief some unusual perspectives that Indian theater brings to modernist theater studies. First, the modernity of urban Indian theater results from a unique mediation of precolonial materials and practices by Anglo-European colonial influences. In aesthetic and institutional terms, this synthesis separates the new (colonial, urban, secular, commercial) theater from the predominantly nonurban forms of postclassical and premodern performance in India as well as from contemporaneous Western practices. Hence the "modern" continuum that accommodates "modernist" divergences begins as a singular *tabula rasa* in the mid-nineteenth century, and its displacement by the modernist revisions of the mid-twentieth century establishes a more intensely polarized relationship between the two phases than is the case in Western theater.

Second, the non-Europhone, concurrent multilingualism of this theater does not have a parallel in either the Euro-American or the postcolonial cultural spheres because drama is written, published, and performed simultaneously in numerous languages that are largely unknown outside India. Since multilingualism also continuously generates the activity of translation, the national and transnational dissemination of modernist plays across languages, geographical regions, and temporal frames becomes a notable component of the afterlife of Indian modernist theater.

Third, modernist playwrights, directors, and other theater artists participate actively in the attack on colonial models of commercial theater in the 1940s and 1950s, even though they do not share the political positions or cultural goals of the other two coteries demanding an end to the theatrical marketplace—left-wing activists and bourgeois-nationalist policy makers. Consequently, Indian modernist theater provides powerful late-twentieth century lessons in how a large number of major works can be written and staged successfully in an effectively noncapitalized theater culture.

Fourth, modernist playwrights in India reject the immediate colonial past but connect with a much older past to retrieve narratives that can be shaped by the aesthetic-political principles, dramatic forms, and representational styles of the present. At first glance this choice seems to align with the cultural-nationalist project of retrieving precolonial "tradition" for the effective decolonization of artistic practices after independence—an especially intense preoccupation in India because of the long history and rich variety of the culture's performative repertoires. However, modernism subjects the past in all its instrumental forms—as narrative source, theoretical resource, and aesthetic model—to irony, and its practitioners use the devices of tradition mainly to deconstruct nationalist master narratives. Modernism therefore occupies its own distinctive niche in an atypical field of theater practice in which classical, early modern, and modern Indian performance traditions maintain a fraught coexistence in the postcolonial present.

INTRODUCTION

ANATOMY OF *COSMO-MODERNISM*

The issues of culture, language, historical positioning, theoretical signification, critical terminology, and aesthetic practice addressed in the preceding sections shape multilingual Indian modernisms and inform the two-part structure of this book. In chapter 1, "Modernism, India, and the Axis of Language," I take the relative obscurity of Indian-language modernisms as a point of departure and argue that as cultural forms fundamentally dependent on language modernist literature and theater in India offer a hermeneutic field qualitatively more complex than forms such as cinema, the visual arts, dance, and architecture. The singular effects of India's multilingual literacy on modernist expression can also be gauged only through a full consideration of the historically determined cultural identity and territorial circulation of India's active modern languages. As an important corollary to this discussion, I question the reductive description of these languages as "vernacular" mediums caught up in a deterministic Eurocentric hierarchy of "center-periphery" relations. The relevance of new initiatives in modernist studies to Indian modernist forms, including drama and theater, becomes easier to ascertain when Indian languages assume their rightful status as creative media.

Chapter 2, "Modernity, Modernism, and Indian Theater," situates Indian-language modernisms in literature and theater within the specific history of Indian cultural modernity, which concludes part 1 of the book. I trace the formation of modernism as an aesthetic-political project from the late-colonial antitheatricalism of major literary playwrights such as Bharatendu Harishchandra and Rabindranath Tagore to the full-scale midcentury rupture with colonial models of drama-as-text and theater-as-performance, and I describe the emergence of "new, really new" thematic and formal constructs, especially between 1950 and 1990. The terminological muddle between "modernity" and "modernism" in Indian languages, I argue, does not prevent or preclude the full articulation of authorial positions and artistic practices that we can label "modernist" against the backdrop of the colonial theatrical past as well as contemporary modernisms elsewhere. The *writing* of modernist drama is enabled by systematic theorizing and reflexive self-fashioning among authors, many of whom are also leading figures in a range of other literary and performative genres. The *staging* of this work involves unique processes of deferral and actualization linked to the idiosyncrasies of a noncommercial postindependence performance economy. Generative artistic relationships between playwrights and theater professionals, contingent material strategies, and productive support from readers, translators, and viewers come together in a "movement" that ensures the full realization of modernist plays in performance.

Following the discussion of the constitutive features of Indian theatrical modernism in chapter 2, in part 2 of the book (chapters 3 through 5) I connect the resulting body of drama to the planetary terrain of modernism as a movement and critical subject, and I use formal-thematic principles to differentiate and analyze some major modernist genres that appear after 1950. In *Theatres of Independence* I had used the idea of "genres in context" to discuss notable formations in postindependence theater around the narratives of myth and history, the conventions of realism, and the alternative stages made possible by the cumulative resources of "Indian tradition." These developments are central to the aesthetic, cultural, and ideological trajectories of later twentieth-century theater, and they partially undergird the content of *Cosmo-Modernism*—but with important differences. My purpose now is to approach categories such as myth, history, realism, and tradition through the lens of comparative modernist theory and practice and to focus on qualities that constitute not just "postindependence" but *modernist* form and affect in particular works. I also extend the critical field chronologically and qualitatively by acknowledging that modernist models in theater begin to dissipate in the 1990s as India moves toward economic globalization and full-blown neoliberalism and the public sphere becomes an increasingly fraught arena for contests over gender, sexuality, class, caste, religion, language, and region. In describing the following chapters, I outline some "family resemblances" within the field of modernist theater and indicate the range of works I draw on for my analysis of particular theatrical kinds.

Chapter 3, "Palimpsests of the Past," deals with the first notable modernist formation of the 1950s and 1960s, which brings an intensely critical vision to bear on the received narratives of Indian myth and history and demystifies the imagined ideal past invoked in orientalist and cultural-nationalist discourses after the early nineteenth century. The centrifugal energies of myth originate in the Sanskrit epic *Mahabharata*, which had served during the colonial period as a heroic source for culturally self-validating plays about the golden past or thinly disguised attacks on the colonial state but which moves to a satiric-ironic register after independence and becomes the "epic of ambivalence." The narratives of history are even more conspicuous in postindependence modernist drama, their revisionary fictions fashioned around iconic but more or less deromanticized figures of the classical, postclassical, and early colonial periods. I approach post-1950 plays based on myth and history as examples of a radical cultural reckoning that Indian playwrights undertake on a much larger scale than their postcolonial counterparts elsewhere because of the magnitude of racial/cultural memory: at any given moment in time the past stretches back into remote antiquity but is also symbolically and existentially continuous with the present. The verisimilitude and dialogism of drama, I argue, make it an inherently palimpsestic form, exceptionally open to the superimposition of one text over another. In a notable variant of this quality that I define as "palimpsestic modernism," the source narratives provide a structure that playwrights want to rework for their time but also need to revisit *over* time because the new meanings remain tenuous and elusive. My principal examples of this process of compulsive return are Girish Karnad's first play, *Yayati* (1961), which is based on the well-known episode about the eponymous king in book 1 of the *Mahabharata*, and Mohan Rakesh's second history play, *Laharon ke rajhans* (The royal swans on the waves, 1963), which portrays the crisis that the Buddha's call to renunciation brings about in the married life of his younger half-brother, Nanda. The absence of closure in these palimpsestic works, I argue, turns myth and history into figural narratives of uncertainty, incompleteness, and repetition. The ambivalent immersion in the past signaled by the plays of Karnad and Rakesh dominatse modernist drama during the first decade of independence, but it is counterbalanced after 1960 by the powerful arguments for a revisionary urban social realism put forward by playwrights such as Vijay Tendulkar, Mahesh Elkunchwar, and Mahesh Dattani.

In chapter 4, "Modernism, Realism, and the Postcolonial Urban Present," I trace the emergence of experimentally oriented realist drama in the 1950s and 1960s after several decades of disjunction between realist form and content and the consolidation of this strain into the twenty-first century. Unconventional urban-realist plays such as Badal Sircar's *Ebong indrajit* (And Indrajit, Bengali, 1962), Elkunchwar's *Atmakatha* (Autobiography, Marathi, 1988), and Dattani's *Tara* (English, 1989) emphasize individual (gendered) experience, the institution of the family, and sociopolitical identity in the postcolonial urban present; but they also merge realism with fantasy, nightmare, nostalgia, and the absurd to give modernist expression to drives that lie submerged under the mundane surface of urban life. Significantly, in a distinctive subset of realist drama contemporaneous with the drama of social existence, other playwrights (notably G. P. Deshpande, Mahasweta Devi, and Datta Bhagat) manipulate the conventions of realism in similar ways to create overtly political narratives about the personal and social cost of radical resistance and activism. Space constraints prevent me from analyzing this variation closely, but in its totality modernist realism encapsulates the family romance, challenges to patriarchy, gender conflicts, frustrated desire, and the relationship of the personal to the political across a very broad experiential and ideological spectrum.

Chapter 5, "Modernism and Tradition," discusses the paradoxical fashioning of modernist form and affect through nonmodern (often folkloric) subject matter and nonverbal presentational styles that are flamboyantly antirealist and "traditional" in a very different way from T. S. Eliot's classic literary-critical formulation in "Tradition and the Individual Talent" (1919). Plays such as Shanta Gandhi's *Jasma odan* (Hindi, 1968), Karnad's *Hayavadana* (Horse-head, Kannada, 1971), Tendulkar's *Ghashiram kotwal* (Constable Ghashiram, Marathi, 1972), Chandrashekhar Kambar's *Jokumaraswami* and *Samba-shiva prahasana* (Samba and Shiva, a farce, Kannada, 1972 and 1985), and Habib Tanvir's *Charandas chor* (Charandas the thief, Chhattisgarhi, 1974) are considered iconic examples of the Theatre of Roots, which calls for a rejection of all forms of Western influence on Indian theater and a dehistoricized return to classical aesthetics and indigenous performance practices. The "traditionalism" of these postindependence plays, however, is thoroughly embedded in a historicized present: they use tradition for radically subversive explorations of selfhood and identity, feminine desire, social hierarchy, and the will to power in coercive politics. In a form very different from realist drama but through a consciousness responding to the same postcolonial conditions, seemingly traditionalist plays in fact constitute a *parallel modernist* archive of subaltern resistance to systems of oppression.

Chapter 6, "Conclusion: Cosmo-Modernism and Theater in Retrospect," draws the discussion to a close by revisiting and selectively elaborating on the key features of modernist theory and practice in postindependence Indian drama and theater: connection to the continuities of Indian literary culture through multilingual literacy; transregional and transnational affiliations that represent time-and-place-specific forms of cosmopolitanism; the density of cosmo-modernist authorial careers; the playwright-director relationship; and the role of translation in all its forms. I suggest that as modernist paradigms weakened in the 1990s with the passage of time and the sociocultural effects of a neoliberal political economy, they were followed by the antithetical energies of intensifying cultural activism, on the one hand, and the regressive antimodernity stance of official cultural policy, on the other, relegating a potentially "postmodern" reaction very much to the periphery. However, in a reconstructive scholarly perspective (such as mine) these changes do not diminish the force of the modernist "canon," and the qualities of canonicity should invite not facile forms of dismissal but circumspect understanding of the works in relation to twentieth-century Indian drama and theater history in all of its national and transnational complexity.

Two aspects of the postindependence modernist enterprise need especially careful contextualization because they involve modernism's relation to contestations over gender, subalternity, social inequity, and political marginalization that have acquired topical urgency in the practice and reception of contemporary theater. First, women contribute to modernist theater substantially as performers and to a notable extent as directors, but when comparing them to their male counterparts, women were virtually absent as "authors" until the 1980s. This particular model of authorship implies the proprietary creation of dramatic works that appear in print, negotiate a materially precarious performance economy in various ways, and acquire more or less robust performance histories in the original language of composition and in translation. All the major modernist playwrights I discuss in this book belong to this authorial paradigm, and all of them are male. Moreover, the theater form is the most extreme example of this gender imbalance and continues historical trends: Tutun Mukherjee's anthology of modern Indian plays by women, covering the nineteenth and twentieth centuries, contains a *total* of eighteen plays, and only four of these were written by women belonging to the period before independence.[39] In contrast, over the same time period women were increasingly prominent in the artistic fields of dance, music, film, and television and emerged as significant writers of fiction, nonfiction, and poetry, among other literary genres. In the past three decades a notable number of new women playwrights *have* joined the ranks of proprietary authorship, but the historically unprecedented revolution in "women's theater" now underway in India has become possible because the creative focus has shifted to auteurship, devised and collaborative work, women's collectives, feminist activism, and performance art.[40] The role women have played as actors, directors, and, most important, as dramatic characters in modernist Indian drama and theater informs my discussion of gender issues throughout this book. But the dominance of male playwrights in modern (and not just modernist) Indian theater is a historical circumstance that cannot be retrospectively undone: in a body of work that even now has little transnational recognition, the male strain needs appropriate attention instead of being set aside because of the asymmetries of authorship. A powerful women's theater movement is incrementally redressing the imbalance.

Second, the cosmopolitanism that major playwrights bring to their craft and their public selves complicates their politics and the political content of their work. Personal identity in India is deeply marked not only by gender and class but by caste, religion, region, and language; and it is natural to speculate about how these categories inform authorial identity, the content of drama, and engagement with the public sphere. The "personal experience" of Dharamvir Bharati, a Hindi-speaking author from the Kayastha subcaste, born and brought up in conditions of economic precarity in the historic northern city of Allahabad, would of course be substantially different from that of Girish Karnad, a Kannada-speaking author who grew up in a middle-class Saraswat Brahman family in the small Karnataka town of Sirsi in the south; and both of these Hindu authors would be expected to present strong contrasts with Badal Sircar, a Bengali-speaking native of Calcutta whose family converted to Christianity in the late nineteenth century. Yet these markers of identity are not central to the aesthetics, thematics, and politics of their plays, not because of spurious efforts at erasure but because of deeply rooted, instinctive modernist drives toward impersonality, omnitemporality, and connectedness to the world at large. In *Andha yug* (Blind epoch, 1954), Bharati uses the end of the *Mahabharata* war in the eponymous Sanskrit epic for a poetic meditation on India's civilizational legacy of suffering and destruction but invites the reader/viewer to interpret the action as a "cosmo-modernist history of mankind." Karnad's *Tughlaq* (1964) has been regarded since its first appearance as an uncannily prophetic enactment of an unresolvable historical problem: the antagonism between Hinduism and Islam on the subcontinent, which in turn points to the volatile relationship between religion and politics in modern democratic polities. But the politics of the play are neither topical nor activist; instead, for sixty years the parallels it establishes between fourteenth- and twentieth-century India have created an open-ended hermeneutic capable of accommodating every new phase in the country's ongoing crisis of governability.

As mentioned earlier, modernist plays based on "traditional" narratives (especially folklore) paradoxically embody the strongest critiques of class, caste, and gender, which are also conspicuous themes in modernist forms of realism that focus on urban and rural spaces.[41] The prominent political playwright G. P. Deshpande, a professional China scholar affiliated with the Communist Party-Marxist (and in terms of "identity" a Marathi-speaking brahman from the small town of Rahimatpur in the western state of Maharashtra), uses the form of the family romance or the Shavian drama of ideas to embody his left-wing icons in plays such as *Uddhwasta dharmashala* (The ruined sanctuary, 1974) and *Ek vajoon gela ahe* (It's Past One O' Clock, 1983). However, the formative features of modernism and modernist self-fashioning discussed in chapter 2, as well as the analyses of major plays and playwrights in this book, indicate that most of the authors I consider do not exemplify easily definable "dominant" or "subaltern" positions. Their work represents, instead, a strain distinct from the activist theaters that address widespread problems of inequity and discrimination, often in various forms of street theater—the mistreatment of women, for instance, or the continued oppression of formerly "untouchable" Dalit communities. Pointing out this separation does not imply any judgments of value but acknowledges the difference between the modernist corpus concentrated in the 1950–1990 period that is my primary focus and the theaters of protest and resistance that have gained tremendous momentum since the 1980s.

Following these lines of demarcation, the works for the theater analyzed in my sequence of chapters involve Hindi, Bengali, Kannada, Marathi, Chhattisgarhi, and English as the original languages of composition; languages such as Gujarati, Malayalam, and Manipuri as important points of comparison; and English as the "leveling" language of theory, criticism, and translation. Throughout my analysis, the plays' textual modes of existence (whatever their scope) are connected to their staging and reception in a noncommercial performance economy. From chapter 2 onward, I also deal in depth with primary Indian-languages materials—theoretical, critical, and creative—that highlight authors and works that are largely unknown outside India. This method of recuperation and self-representation is a fundamental feature of my project, which seeks to connect major modernist Indian playwrights and other theater professionals appropriately to the evolving conversation on global modernisms. Functioning within a uniquely complex, multilingual, postcolonial environment, these artists collectively offer perspectives on the relation of modernity to modernism; of the aesthetic to the social and the political; of language to place; and of modernist form to content that should leave their mark on a reconfigured map of late-twentieth-century modernisms.

Chapter One

MODERNISM, INDIA, AND THE AXIS OF LANGUAGE

The most familiar use of the term "axis" in relation to language appears in the disciplinary study of syntagms and paradigms in linguistics, which was given its authoritative twentieth-century form by the structuralist method of Ferdinand de Saussure. In the syntagmatic axis, which functions horizontally, "sequences of words are formed by combining them in a recognized order," and the "syntagmatic dimension is therefore the 'linear' aspect of language."[1] A particular arrangement of words in grammatical order also creates a particular meaning: in any given sentence, a different syntactic arrangement—even of the same words—would potentially either violate the grammar of that language or create a different meaning. The paradigmatic axis, which operates vertically, consists of "a set of linguistic or other units that can be substituted for each other in the same position within a sequence or structure. A paradigm in this sense may be constituted by all words sharing the same grammatical function, since the substitution of one for another does not disturb the syntax of a sentence."[2] In a broader sense, the syntagmatic aspect of language involves the structural relationship of its elements governed by its particular grammar, whereas the paradigmatic aspect brings in the full extent of its lexical resources. Both aspects pertain to the function of language as a system of communication aimed at the successful creation of meaning, but syntagmatic relations have a closer connection to semantics and have therefore tended to be more dominant in the discipline of linguistics than paradigmatic relations.

My reference to the "axis of language" in this book does not invoke the technical meaning of linguistic axes in any literal way—but it *can* signify figuratively that as an expressive medium every language carries with it a cultural history, a complex of qualities, and a network of relationships that constitute its creative grammar, and that these need to be considered as integral aspects of its expressive potentialities. In the study of global literary and theatrical modernisms, the languages of composition, reception, and interpretation also function as distinct entities that determine the accessibility and visibility of entire bodies of work. Taken together, these properties of language have created a "hierarchy of access" in modernist studies that has been difficult to negotiate or transcend despite the fundamental reconfigurations of the past thirty years. At the apex of the hierarchy is English—as the language of original composition *and* of criticism—and the effects of this dominance on Indian modernist production have been predictable. Anglophone Indian and Indian diasporic fiction and poetry, discussed in Anglophone criticism, have had the greatest visibility and have been included in influential discussions of topics such as cosmopolitan modernisms "beyond the nation," "postcolonial modernity," "Caliban's modernity," "metageographies of modernist fiction," "transnational reading," "extravagant postcolonialism," "postcolonialism and globalism," and "cultural parataxis," in addition, of course, to sweeping surveys of global modernism.[3] Modernist works in other Indian languages that have been translated into English or that are discussed in Anglophone criticism constitute the second tier. This book belongs in this category, along with books and essays dealing with modernist fiction, poetry, and drama originally written in Hindi, Urdu, Marathi, Bengali, Gujarati, Kannada, Tamil, and Malayalam, to name the leading literary languages.[4] The third and fourth tiers consist, respectively, of works in Indian languages that are translated into or receive criticism in languages other than English, or remain in the original language of composition and are discussed mainly or exclusively in that medium. The globally operating axis of language prevents works in these last two categories from appearing in *any* transregional, let alone transnational, perspectives on modernism that would make them accessible or "readable," literally and figuratively.

MODERNISM, INDIA, AND THE AXIS OF LANGUAGE

This chapter, and the book as a whole, engages with this figuratively conceived axis by considering the methods and outcomes of a comprehensive theoretical and interpretive focus on Indian languages as written and orally performed modernist media. To underscore the critical disparity between the arts of language and other forms of modernist expression, I approach this discussion through a series of revealing contrasts: Indian modernisms that do not involve language as the essential medium (visual art, dance, and architecture, for instance) or that combine language with another medium (film and other popular/mass cultural forms) have been *conspicuously* easier to define, theorize, and assimilate to transnational critical models in modernist studies. In this respect, the frequent diversion from written to visual and plastic forms in works of criticism which seek to place Indian modernisms in a global context simply continues a trend that has been evident in studies of Indian modernism for some time. Scholarly and critical arguments on this subject are qualitatively more confident and articulate when they deal either with Anglophone writing or with forms that lie more or less outside the ambit of language. The hierarchical advantages of English vis-à-vis other Indian languages in literary-theatrical contexts are addressed in the introduction—the media of film, painting, and architecture offer other notable points of divergence from language-based arts in general.[5]

DEFINING MODERNISMS OUTSIDE THE LANGUAGE AXIS: SOME CONTRASTS

Like modern Indian theater, Indian cinema was created from the beginning (1913–) in major regional languages such as Bengali, Marathi, Tamil, and Telugu, and on a massive scale in the majority language, Hindi. Yet film is a fascinating counterpoint to literature and theater because, in transnational perspectives, its visual and technical dimensions overcome the constraints imposed by the verbal dimension, and the convention of subtitles provides an "immediate" solution to the problem of linguistic access. Indian as well as international film scholars and critics have thus discussed with comparative ease the influence of European filmmakers such as Jean Renoir and Vittorio de Sica on the art and parallel cinema of Satyajit Ray and Ritwik Ghatak, both of whom made films in Bengali. More unexpectedly, even mainstream commercial Hindi films leaning toward romance and melodrama have supported the systematic association of actor-director Raj

FIGURE 1.1 Raj Kapoor in a still from the film "Mera Naam Joker" (My Name is Joker), 1970.

Kapoor with De Sica and Charlie Chaplin (figs. 1.1 and 1.2), and of actor-director Guru Dutt with Orson Welles and German expressionism.

The closest comparisons involve Guru Dutt's 1959 film *Kagaz ke phool* (Paper flowers) and the work that inspired it directly in terms of cinematography, set design, lighting, characterization, atmosphere, and tone—Welles's wartime masterpiece, *Citizen Kane* (1941). The modernist resemblances between the two works function at the levels of style and signification rather than plot: *Kagaz ke phool* is also a metacinematic film about films, but it presents a more conventionally "tragic" narrative about a successful film director, Suresh Sinha, whose career ends in alcoholism, failure, and death because of his rich wife's contempt for the film medium and the stigma of his love for a young actress whom he discovers but cannot allow into his life because of social and legal constraints. Visually, *Kagaz ke phool* fills the screen with massive material structures reminiscent of Welles's Xanadu, and uses the same expressive array of wide-angle, high-contrast frames, punctuated by the chiaroscuro effects and probing close-ups associated with film

FIGURE 1.2 Charlie Chaplin with a doll representing his tramp persona, 1917. Photo credit: Alamy.

FIGURE 1.3 Guru Dutt as Suresh Sinha in a still from "Kagaz ke Phool" (Paper Flowers), 1959.

noir. At a micro level, Dutt the director seems determined to make Dutt the actor interchangeable with Charles Foster Kane (figs. 1.3 and 1.4). Although roses have no particular symbolic significance within *Kagaz ke phool* (beyond the invocation of flowers in the title), in the publicity poster a large red rose (not a rosebud) appears beside the intense faces of the two lead characters in an overt act of citation (fig. 1.5). At the macro level, Wellesian modernism enables Dutt to disrupt the conventional narratives of ideal domesticity and fulfilled love in popular Indian cinema in ways that have made *Kagaz ke phool* a cult classic, and a work ranked at number 160 in a 2002 *Sight and Sound* poll of the greatest films of all time.

Among representational forms, it is in the field of visual art that Indian modernism has had its most substantial critical exposition. There is nothing so far in studies of literary modernism to compare with the clarity of focus and content that appears in studies of modernist art by Geeta Kapur and Partha Mitter. "The characteristic feature of Indian modernism, as perhaps of many postcolonial modernisms," Kapur notes, "may be that it is manifestly social and historical, and hence not of much interest to 'western modernism in its late phase.' But we should see our trajectories crisscrossing the western mainstream and, in their very disalignment from it, making up the ground that restructures the international.... We should reperiodize the modern in terms of our own historical experience and mark our modernisms so that we may enter the postmodern at least potentially on our own terms."[6] Kapur brings this perspective to bear on the films of Ghatak and Ray as well as on major painters, from Amrita Sher-Gil and Jamini Roy in

FIGURE 1.4 Orson Welles as Charles Foster Kane and Joseph Cotten as Jedediah Leland in a still from "Citizen Kane," 1941.

FIGURE 1.5 Guru Dutt and Waheeda Rehman on the publicity poster for "Kagaz ke Phool." Photo credit: Alamy.

FIGURE 1.6 Pablo Picasso, "Guernica," oil on canvas, 1937. https://en.wikipedia.org/wiki/Guernica_%28Picasso%29

the 1930s to F. N. Souza and M. F. Husain in the 1950s. Mitter marks the 1922 Bauhaus exhibition in Calcutta as the beginning of the avant-garde movement in India, which paradoxically made modernism in art an expression of anticolonial resistance, especially through a primitivist embrace of rural subjects. He also argues that during the 1920s and 1930s modernism and its obverse, naturalism, came together in a "common distaste for history painting and the master narrative of nationalism that had obsessed the previous generation."[7] Then after independence, Calcutta and Bombay served as "virtual cosmopolises" where artists could practice a visibly international art without the stigma of "derivativeness."[8] This relationship is vividly evident in a juxtaposition of Picasso's *Guernica* with M. F. Hussain's quasi-cubist horses, and Mitter makes it a point to argue at the outset that such signs of influence do not turn an Indian painter into a Picasso *manqué* (figs. 1.6 and 1.7).

Finally, the transnational dimension of modernist forms in India is perhaps most clearly manifested in architecture and the built environment. The decisive event in this respect was Prime Minister Jawaharlal Nehru's invitation to Le Corbusier to design the city of Chandigarh as a new capital for the state of Punjab, which had lost its old capital of Lahore to Partition in 1947. During a 1952 site visit, Nehru described Chandigarh as "a new town, symbolic of the freedom of India, unfettered by the traditions of the past—an expression of the nation's faith in the future,"[9] and in 2016 the entire city was declared a UNESCO World Heritage Site (fig. 1.8).

FIGURE 1.7 M. F. Hussain, "Horses," oil on canvas, c. 1970. Photo credit: Sotheby's, London.

FIGURE 1.8 Palace of Assembly, designed by Le Corbusier for the Capitol Complex, Chandigarh, inaugurated in 1964. https://en.wikipedia.org/wiki/Palace_of_Assembly#/media/File:Palace_of_Assembly_Chandigarh_2006.jpg

FIGURE 1.9 Filip Dujardin, "Untitled," from the series "Fictions," 2007. Photo credit: Filip Dujardin.

Chandigarh's rectangular grid and mass concrete construction into fifty-six sectors have clearly had uneven success in the climatic and social conditions of north India. But in selective urban sites, major postindependence architects such as Charles Correa and Satish Gujaral have made Corbusier's modernist legacy quite spectacularly visible. Corbusier had theorized that "white concrete monoliths filled with cells of humane and effortless space would solve the quandary of twentieth-century urban sprawl."[10] The Belgian photographer Filip Dujardin's "fictional photography" *imagines* a structure designed according to these aesthetic principles, whereas Charles Correa's Kanchanjunga Apartment Building in Mumbai actualizes the conception, for the precise reason stated by Corbusier (figs. 1.9 and 1.10).

MODERNISM, INDIA, AND THE AXIS OF LANGUAGE

FIGURE 1.10 Kanchanjunga Apartments, designed by Charles Correa, Bombay/Mumbai, 1983. Photo by Peter Serenyi. https://www.reddit.com/r/brutalism/comments/j14p0f/kanchenjunga_apartments_designed_by_architect/?rdt=33546

In comparison with the arts of language, architecture also appears to be a field in which the transcultural and the intracultural do not appear in predetermined, polarized, hierarchical relations. Transcultural modernism in architecture sounds similar to its contemporary literary-critical equivalent in that it does not build, as Marion von Osten notes in her introduction to a collection on the subject, "on the notion of modernism as having moved from the North to the South—or from the West to the rest of the world." Instead, it emphasizes the "exchanges and interrelations among international and local actors and concepts, a perspective in which 'modernity' is not passively received, but is a concept in circulation, moving in several different directions at once, subject to constant renegotiation and reinterpretation."[11] Equally important, when applied to architecture, the antithetical concept of the "vernacular" is not reductive, patronizing, or deterministic (fig. 1.11). Michael Meister argues that "a 'vernacular' uses available materials, is built by local craftsmen, and serves a community . . . but new vernaculars can be born, created, defined. . . . The strength of vernacular is that it can always be modern."[12] Applied mainly to structures that respond to local resources, climatic conditions, economies, and cultural aspirations, in India the idea of vernacular architecture encompasses everything from premodern temple design to low-cost housing in small towns.

The arguments I have made about film, painting, and architecture are also more or less applicable to photography, music, and dance. When we turn from this succession of plastic, visual, and audiovisual forms to the vectors of Indian multi*lingualism* and multi*literacy*, we lose the enabling mnemonic of line, material, spatial configuration, corporeality, sound, color, and image and confront the resistance that language-based arts (literature and theater) offer to comparable attempts at clear critical articulation. An informed, nuanced, "from the inside out" approach to a large

FIGURE 1.11 "Tropical modernism meets vernacular charm in this striking Himalayan refuge." The Kumaon, Almora, Uttarakhand. Photo by Akshay Sharma. https://homeworlddesign.com/kumaon-hotel-nestled-rugged-mountainside-kasar-devi-india/

literary-performative field is therefore vital for bringing Indian-language modernisms into the global ambit from which they have been excluded so far because of their non-Europhone matrices. The critical challenge to modernist studies in this respect is a challenge to Indian modernist studies as well: if modernism is a global movement with local features, it is also a pan-Indian movement that can become fully visible only when scholars move away from their preoccupation with individual regionally oriented languages and consider the transregional and transnational networks in which modernist practices are embedded.

THE LANGUAGES OF MODERNISM IN INDIA: HISTORY, PLURALITY, AESTHETICS, POLITICS

The instrumental role of language in Indian modernisms and the effects of multilingualism can be understood only in relation to the singular history and geography of languages on the subcontinent. India has no "national language." Hindi and English are the two "official languages of the Union" in which the activities of the central government can be conducted; they are also the two pan-Indian link languages, with a total of 528 million and 129 million speakers, respectively. In addition, the Eighth Schedule to the Indian Constitution recognizes twenty-two "official languages of the Republic of India," most of which are the majority languages of specific regions and correspond more or less closely to the geographical and political boundaries of individual states. Inclusion in the Schedule entitles languages to government support of the kind that is meant to enable them to "grow rapidly in richness and become effective means of communicating modern knowledge."[13] However, the current Schedule includes the dead classical language, Sanskrit, and the majority language, Hindi, but not English—a contradiction that can be resolved only on the basis of a continuing distinction between "indigenous" and "foreign" languages. The common geographical representation of contemporary Indian languages appears on the map in figure 1.12, which differs from the Eighth Schedule in omitting Bodo, Dogri, Maithili, Santhali, Sindhi, and Urdu, and in adding Ao, Khasi and Gao, Mizo, and Nissi/Daffla, the languages of the northeastern region.

The information provided in this figure contains several notable features. The map represents three major language families: the Indo-European in the north, the Dravidian in the south, and the Tibeto-Burman in the

MAP OF MAJOR LANGUAGES IN INDIA

FIGURE 1.12 Map of Indian Languages. https://www.slideshare.net/slideshow/languages-of-india-47181346/47181346

northeast. Hindi, along with its major and minor dialects, is the most widespread Indo-European language, occupying about half the subcontinent; but seven other major languages belong to the same family—Kashmiri, Panjabi, Gujarati, Marathi, Bengali, Oriya, and Assamese. However, only two of these—Hindi and Marathi—share the same Devanagari script that also belongs to the classical language, Sanskrit. The remaining languages have scripts that display family resemblances but are otherwise autonomous. Among the four major Dravidian languages, the scripts for Telugu and Kannada are similar but not identical, whereas Tamil and Malayalam are fully distinct. The four main Tibeto-Burman languages of the northeast embody a substantially different history and culture from the rest of the subcontinent and are also geographically isolated.

This map was affected to varying degrees by the Islamic conquest of the subcontinent after 1200 CE and by British colonialism after the late-eighteenth century. Islam brought in Arabic and Persian, and Persian was the court language that mingled with Hindi to form Urdu, both a spoken and a literary language; Urdu in turn mingled with Hindi to form Hindustani, which is the spoken and written language of both urban North India and Pakistan. However, Urdu is omitted from the map because it is not specific to any one region within India, whereas it is the national language of Pakistan. English is also absent despite its official status and pervasive national presence—it is everywhere and nowhere.

The scale of linguistic complexity embodied by this plurality of languages can be gauged by the number of speakers in each language, who then serve as potential receptors for all cultural activity in that language—oral, written, and performed. Table 1.1 represents these figures in descending order. The first ten languages in table 1.1 appear among the top thirty languages in the world. There are, in fact, thirteen South Asian languages in the top thirty, so almost 50 percent of the world's leading languages in terms of demographic spread are in South Asia. With the exception of Sanskrit, the dead classical language, speakers in the remaining languages range from 1.8 million to 528 million, counting those who regard a given language as their "mother tongue" or "first language": for most languages the total number of speakers is significantly larger because they function as second or third languages both within and outside their respective regions.[14] As mentioned previously, none of these languages has the official status of a "national" language, but with a few exceptions the number of speakers also indicates that these are not "minor" languages.

In an ethnolinguistic perspective, the multilingualism resulting from this profusion of languages is unique both in its premodern and modern forms because it is geographically contained, historically continuous, chronologically simultaneous, and sustained by the incessant activity of translation.

TABLE 1.1
Number of speakers in major Indian languages (2011 census)

Hindi and its variants	528 million
Bengali	97 million
Marathi	83 million
Telugu	81 million
Tamil	69 million
Gujarati	55 million
Urdu	50 million
Kannada	44 million
Oriya	37 million
Malayalam	34 million
Panjabi	33 million
Assamese	15.3 million
Santhali	7.3 million
Kashmiri	6.8 million
Sindhi	2.7 million
Konkani	2.25 million
Manipuri	1.8 million

India effectively achieves as a subcontinental region what Europe achieves as a continent—the gradual emergence of modern languages from shared classical origins over more than a millennium of evolution and change, with the multiple languages being connected by systemic similarities and many forms of cultural cross-fertilization. The difference between the two geographies is that major individual European languages become identified with emergent nation-states, whereas most Indian languages are identified with specific regions within the subcontinent. Languages such as Hindi, Bengali, Marathi, and Kannada, however, have a transregional presence in India that corresponds to the transnational presence of languages such as English, French, and German in Europe. Multilingual speakers, internal diasporas, and populations on the move also expand the regional compass of a given language over time.

The singularity of Indian multilingualism is underscored further by its difference from the forms of linguistic plurality that have recently received increasing attention in Western criticism. At the literary-textual level, the Western exemplars include the presence of multiple languages in modernist classics such as *The Waste Land, Ulysses,* and *Finnegans Wake,* and the variety of language experiments by authors such as Katherine Mansfield, Beckett, and Jean Rhys. At the sociocultural level, they involve the recognition of "minority" languages within a cultural field dominated by a majority/national language (native American languages and Spanish in the primarily Anglophone United States, for example), or the heteroglossia that results from the presence of many immigrant communities and the preservation of their native languages in the diaspora (Greek, Polish, Arabic, and Hmong in the United States). In contrast, Indian multilingualism denotes *not the presence of many languages in a single work* but *the simultaneous presence of works in many languages*, and the translation of any given work potentially into every other Indian literary language, including English. Hence this multilingualism does not *depend* on the activity of translation, but as a later section in this chapter demonstrates, translation is in practice the primary engine of national and transnational mobility for Indian-language writing, including works for the theater. In sociocultural terms, the diversity of Indian languages does not depend on the phenomena of migrancy and racial difference, and the majority/minority relation is also fundamentally different from that of predominantly monolingual cultures in the West and elsewhere. For example, Hindi can be described as India's "majority" language, but each linguistically defined region within the country has its own majority language as well.

The concurrent plurality of languages in India thus creates a unique expressive culture that Sheldon Pollock describes as "a story of complex creativity and textual devotion with few parallels in history" because an unbroken tradition of multilingual literacy has embodied and preserved "the experience of South Asian peoples" for more than two millennia.[15] What, then, are the implications of this history for a *modernist* hermeneutic, and what are the distinctive qualities that Indian languages bring to a planetary modernism? In the broadest frame, modernism is the revisionary postcolonial phase at which literature and performance arrive after diverse languages with fully developed precolonial literary histories have negotiated the inexorable cultural transformations of colonial modernity and modernization. A long premodern history of continuous development through orality, writing, and transregional circulation within the subcontinent (c. 900–1800 CE) is followed by a process of rapid modernization during the British colonial period (c. 1810–1930). In the mid-twentieth century (especially 1940–1960), the intensifying cultural-political ferment of anticolonial nationalism and postindependence disenchantment triggers the qualities of rupture, rebellion, and experiment that connect Indian modernisms to transnational modernist formations. Although print arrived belatedly in India, only around 1800, by 1860 the country had the largest multilingual print culture outside Europe—a development that turns listeners into readers and significantly alters the earlier interdependencies and continuities of orality and writing. Large-scale publication in turn shapes authorship as an institution of modern print culture in textual as well as performative genres, preparing the ground not only for proprietary authorship on the Western model (as noted in the introduction) but also for the "autonomy of the aesthetic" that is a prominent feature of Indian modernisms. Because multilingual circulation is a fundamental attribute of Indian literary culture, intracultural and intercultural translation also become constitutive elements of the modernist repertoire—a fertile testing ground for Mao and Walkowitz's claim that Anglophone modernist studies has moved toward "a greater acknowledgment of the role of translation and multilingual circulation in the development of national and micronational literary histories."[16]

Shaped by the literary culture outlined previously, the place of India's multilingual modernist corpus within the networks of postcolonial, transnational, planetary, or global modernisms cannot be determined by easy reference to concepts such as influence, imitation, indigenization, or transculturation, especially when the writing takes place at least initially outside the ambit of global English. The Euro-American modernist canon circulates extensively in India, in the original and in translation, but the modernist turn *within* each language is propelled as much by a logic internal to its own literary-political history as by "secondary stimuli from outside."[17] Western modernisms also have multiple, reciprocal connections with non-Western aesthetic and cultural practices that are certainly synchronous with the larger histories of colonialism and decolonization but that cannot be contained within a simplistic narrative of dominance and subalternity.[18] In short, what happened in major languages such as Hindi and Bengali between about 1940 and 1980 was as dependent on the modern history of those and other Indian languages as on influences from the literary world at large. The poet Amiya Dev's argument about Bengali is an apt example. Modernism, he notes, was not just another instance of Western impact on

Bengali writing because "what mattered immediately was how to come to terms with Rabindranath [Tagore] and not be overwhelmed by his pervasive presence.... Bengali Modernism was not Western Modernism in Bengali dress; it was Bengali writing after Rabindranath in Modern dress."[19] This account by a "Bengali insider" provides further support for the view that Tagore triggered the modernist iconoclasm of the 1920s because he had come to symbolize the somewhat "sweet and stale" pursuits of "cultural nationalism, romantic love, nature mysticism, metaphysical leanings and the ideal of nation-building."[20]

The comments by Dev and Anantha Murthy point to an intrinsic and "leveling" feature of Indian modernist studies: whether the objective is to theorize modernism as a pan-Indian movement or to focus on modernist practices in a specific language, criticism inevitably becomes anchored in the past, present, and future of one or more languages. Vasudha Dalmia's discussion of Mohan Rakesh's "modernist quest" foregrounds Hindi, and Jennifer Dubrow notes the refraction of modern Urdu literary culture through the idea of "cosmopolitan dreams."[21] These studies are metonyms for an entire body of criticism in which the name of an Indian language precedes the noun "modernism" to signify the creative medium that has been selected for discussion. Among more inclusive approaches, a collection that aims to "identify common patterns in the original growth of the [modernist] movement as evidenced in the different literatures" settles on Bengali, Hindi, Kannada, and Malayalam as case studies, because in these languages the "Modern Movement altered the mode of perception in a forceful and radical way."[22] Similarly, Vinay Dharwadker's discussion of modernism's "four phases" draws principally on the literary histories of Bengali, Hindi, Urdu, Marathi, Panjabi, and English; and the high-metropolitan bilingual literary culture of Marathi and English during a very distinctive phase in postindependence poetry constitutes the "Bombay modern" in Anjali Nerlekar's formulation.[23] In their respective ways and to varying degrees, these arguments connect modernism to multilingual modernity and Indian literary-cultural history, but the very strength of the connection calls for a reevaluation of some persistent misconceptions in mainstream literary studies about the status of Indian languages, not just as modernist but as literary and performative media within the global literary economy.

INDIAN LANGUAGES AS EXPRESSIVE MEDIA: DISMANTLING "VERNACULAR" AND "CENTER-PERIPHERY" MODELS

The rootedness of Indian multilingualism in a long premodern past creates qualities that challenge the conventional vocabulary of hierarchical relations between the West and the rest that has been questioned, but not effectively dislodged, in various theoretical frameworks, including those of present-day modernist studies. Among the conspicuous signs of this ahistorical thinking are two assumptions that are especially misguided in relation to India: that in the hands of Indian writers, both English and the modern Indian languages embody "vernacular" culture and experience, and that the postcolony continues to represent a "periphery" in relation to an ex-imperial "center." Both positions imply an unreflective "demotion" of contemporary Indian languages as spoken, written, and expressive media that has to be challenged because it is inconsistent with their state of development and cultural reach.

The terminology of modernist studies follows a general trend that makes the term "vernacular" virtually inescapable in discussions of Indian cultural forms, regardless of the specificities of language, genre, or medium. In discussing the Indian photographer Raghubir Singh and the novelist Amitav Ghosh, for instance, Ariela Freedman returns compulsively to the idea of "vernacular" art: Singh attempts to create a "modernist Indian vernacular in photography," and "Singh and Ghosh at once demand the creation of a new vernacular and retain an integral link to the past."[24] Manishita Dass's discussion of the portrayal of modern Indian women in early cinema employs the same terminology and describes the cinematic genre of the "Indian social" as "a distinct brand of vernacular modernism, one that evolved in a complex relation (of adaptation and critique) to American and other foreign films while simultaneously drawing on and reshaping vernacular traditions in theater, literature, print, and visual culture. . . . [T]he early social demonstrates the need for a large-scale archaeology of the genre, its contexts of production and reception, and its relationship to international cinematic trends, vernacular cultural practices, and local trajectories of aesthetic modernism."[25]

In this description, "vernacular" virtually becomes the antithesis of "foreign" and "international," subjecting Indian cultural forms to precisely the kind of parochialization that the new modernist studies has disavowed.

An equally astonishing judgment is offered by Rudrani Gangopadhyay when she describes Ashok Shahane (a cultural polymath in Marathi) and Agyeya (*the* foundational figure in Hindi poetic modernism) as "bridges between multiple vernacular modernisms" because of their work as translators![26]

These are Eurocentric and Anglocentric judgments even when they come from non-European or Indian scholars.[27] Modern Indian languages cannot be separated from their premodern/precolonial trajectories, and in that historical perspective they are neither "vernacular" vehicles for modernism or cosmopolitanism nor merely mediums inhabiting the postcolonial outposts of a now-absent imperium. Rather, they participate in literary-cultural economies that have "classical" origins and a continuous history of evolution over the past millennium, and they constitute expressive and cultural systems that are perceived as metropolitan by very large numbers of native speakers and readers (as table 1.1 indicates). Sanskrit, the classical language in relation to which the modern languages were vernaculars, began its decline in the twelfth century and had become a dead language well before the beginning of the modern period. During the nineteenth century, English followed Persian as the imperial language of a minority ruling class and functioned as the master language in relation to which the indigenous languages could be described for a time as vernaculars. But even during the colonial period, English remained secondary to Indian languages in the cultural sphere, and in the postcolonial period it has come to dominate the fields of education, academic scholarship, journalism, and business but not those of literature, theater, and popular culture: in no sense has English dislodged the modern literary cultures of the major indigenous languages. Conversely, because the term "vernacular" refers to a "native language" or "mother tongue," English can be described as a vernacular in India only in the pejorative *metaphorical* sense of a medium that is inherently secondary to the dominant forms of the West—a judgment starkly at odds with the extraordinary success of Anglophone (mostly diasporic) Indian writers such as Anita Desai, Salman Rushdie, Rohinton Mistry, Amitav Ghosh, and Arundhati Roy in the global literary sphere. In relation to India, English is thus neither a master language nor a vernacular—a state of indeterminacy appropriately in keeping with its paradoxical presence everywhere and nowhere on the subcontinent.

Major Indian languages such as Hindi, Bengali, Marathi, and Kannada are also not vernaculars, for the same reasons that the term is no longer appropriate for modern European languages. The elements of historical progression and synchronic development are similar in both cases: the classical languages (Sanskrit, Greek, Latin) retain their historical and philological priority, but the modern languages achieve autonomy and centrality in their respective geocultural spaces over the course of a millennium and more. As successive chapters in this book demonstrate, leading postcolonial writers in a language such as Hindi, which is the third most commonly spoken language in the world after Mandarin Chinese and English, are not "vernacular" artists but cosmopolitan moderns who are fully cognizant of movements around the world, but also fully committed to an indigenized aesthetic. Their cosmopolitanism thus inheres in their intellectual capaciousness, and in the cultural ambidexterity of their vision. If their medium is not that of the Western imperial metropolis, it is a medium with its own imperial and metropolitan history; and if their modernism is furthest from the Anglo-European center in terms of geography, language, and cultural codes, it is proximate enough in theoretical, aesthetic, and political terms to constitute a distinctive formation within geomodernism.

To acknowledge this complicated genealogy is to unsettle the Eurocentric binarism of center and periphery in a new and especially forceful way: modernism can no longer be approached as a predominantly Western aesthetic, and non-Western modernisms cannot be claimed to be merely derivative or subsidiary versions of hegemonic models. Even during the later nineteenth century, the British colonial state's indifference toward "vernacular" cultural life in India, and the dominance of indigenous narratives in indigenous mediums, sheltered colonial modernity from the reductive effects of mere mimicry. It also placed literary-performative activity outside the primarily Anglophone sphere of colonial control. Nearly two centuries later, the immeasurable expansion in the activities of writing, print, and performance makes contemporary Indian cultural production especially receptive to the destabilization of global hierarchies inherent in the efforts "to locate many centers of modernity across the globe," or to "collapse the margin and center assumptions embedded in the term *modernism* by conjuring instead a web of twentieth-century literary practices, shaped by the circuitry of race, ethnicity, nativism, nationalism, and imperialism in modernity."[28] Studies of Indian postcolonial modernisms thus do not need to be preoccupied with what Simon Gikandi calls "the roles played by ostensible margins in the constitution of cultural centers," or what Walkowitz describes as the "persistent efforts to reimagine the center in terms of peripheries, within and without," especially when European languages are not the original media of composition.[29] Rather, to deal with postcolonial Indian literature and theater adequately as products of multilingual literacy, one has to reimagine the periphery *as* the center and attend to the *internal* processes of modernist self-fashioning.

In a remarkable turn, Immanuel Wallerstein's world-systems theory has been invoked recently in modernist studies because it appears to offer an "objective" model for compartmentalizing the globe when *some* principle of differentiation is needed to explain asymmetries of power. Mark Wollaeger acknowledges, for instance, that the "concepts of center and periphery still operate in many of the essays" in *The Oxford Handbook of Global Modernisms*, "though not in [a] rigidly binary way," and notes that

> world-systems theory provides a materialist account for why the terms 'core,' 'periphery,' and 'semi-periphery' should still matter: they map the unequal distribution of economic power across the globe.... Center-periphery models, moreover, *are not just materialist methods*: continuing interest in center and periphery as tropes has as much to do with cultural processes and strategic defamiliarization.... [A]ttention to the historical experience of 'being at the core or on the periphery' ... aims to open up the potential for *new hierarchies of value* by promoting a fresh vision of the cultural field.[30]

For Moody and Ross, world-systems theory demonstrates that "modernity is a system—a single system—that is constituted through unequal distributions of power and wealth," and the economic-political differences explain the cultural disparities. As "one of the aesthetic modes of the modern world-system," modernism is thus "inherently global," but although "modernists of core and periphery ... participate in a single world-system, they do not do so on equal terms."[31] In both arguments, world-systems theory provides a materialist core around which global aesthetic practices can be ranged hierarchically, with "objectivity" and without Eurocentric "misrepresentation."

The problem with these positions is that Wallerstein's four-volume analysis of the modern world-system *is exclusively materialist* and offers no perspectives on aesthetic culture, in the West or elsewhere. He is concerned with a formation that originated in Europe and the Americas in the sixteenth century and "has always been a *world-economy*. . . . a *capitalist* world-economy."³² Even his concept of "geoculture" refers primarily to "norms and modes of discourse that are widely accepted as legitimate within the world-system"—for instance, the politico-economic culture of liberalism that triumphed during the nineteenth and much of the twentieth centuries. Wallerstein acknowledges the existence of political and cultural heterogeneity as well as some "common cultural patterns" in a world-economy, but "what unifies the structure most is the division of labor which is constituted within it."³³ To approach global modernisms through world-systems theory, then, is to assume the primacy and explanatory power of material over cultural categories in ways that are neither asserted nor supported by the theory itself.

The pitfalls of such a deterministic approach are conspicuous when the focus is on premodern and modern India. In relation to the "European division of labor" that determines the status of individual states within the world-system, India is consigned to the "external arena" in the sixteenth century despite the dynamism of Indian Ocean trading, undergoes "peripheralization" during the high period of colonialism (1750–1850s) and now represents a precarious "semi-peripheral" state that is eager to advance toward the core even as it struggles to avoid regressing back into the periphery.³⁴ Radically at variance with this Eurocentric materialist profile, however, are the rich continuities of subcontinental literary and cultural history over the same time span—the ascendance of classical Sanskrit, the development of modern Indian languages, the formation of Indo-Islamic culture, the pan-Indian *bhakti* movement, the European orientalist canonization of Sanskrit, and the nineteenth-century "Indian Renaissance," which is the direct precursor of twentieth-century Indian modernisms. Historically, India's shifting position in the *world economic system* has no direct relation to the state of its culture, and the country's culture also habitually exceeds its material circumstances and the constraints of capital. Throughout modernity, the "presence of the past" has given a synchronic and culturally instrumental existence to historical periods that were shaped by widely divergent material circumstances, and the cultural forms of the countryside—embedded in premodern and precapitalist agrarian formations—have continued to coexist with urban and intermediary (urban-rural) forms into the twenty-first century. Benedict Anderson's idea of "print capitalism" as a constitutive feature of the modern nation is also still not fully sustainable in India: as Pollock notes, "[p]rint and capitalism only slowly achieved (and according to some contributors, may not yet have achieved) a synergy critical enough to transform the character of literary culture."[35] Specifically, the "high period" of modernism takes shape in the mid-twentieth century under conditions that make cultural capital an uneasy substitute for material capital, and the lack of commercial success in creative fields becomes a mark of artistic integrity! Postindependence urban theater and performance have also developed as largely noncommercial activities, and despite its extraordinary size, even the Indian film industry has not managed to organize itself as a systematic capitalist enterprise on the Western model. For all of these reasons, the ostensibly nonbinary triad of core, semi-periphery, and periphery is no more pertinent to Indian modernity and modernism than the earlier imperialist model of center-periphery relations.

TRANSLATION AND TRANS/NATIONAL MOBILITY

Counterbalancing the cultural politics of vernacularism and anachronous definitions of center and periphery, a focus on language also uncovers the instrumental role of translation in the ontology of Indian modernisms. The circulation of modernist works in translation is largely an *international* phenomenon in the West but an *intranational* process in India because multilingualism has generated active mechanisms of nationwide dissemination and reception since well before the modern period. In both textual and performative terms, drama and theater are also the genres most easily "carried across" from one nation/culture or region to another through translation, adaptation, and transculturation. Translation activity between Indian languages gives contemporary plays a unique mobility within the nation as they are consumed in the original language and in multiple versions, on stage and in print. Translation into English gives the plays greater visibility in print and allows mobility both within and outside the nation. Key aspects of these processes can be gauged respectively from the movements of two contemporary modernist classics—the nationwide circulation of Vijay Tendulkar's *Shantata! court chalu ahe* (Silence! The court is in session, Marathi, 1967), and productions of Mohan Rakesh's *Ashadh ka ek din* (One day in the season of rain, Hindi, 1958)—for audiences in the American Upper Midwest.

Shantata was inspired in part by a conversation Tendulkar overheard on a local train among members of an amateur theater group on their way to performing a mock-trial in the Bombay suburb of Vile Parle, but it also carries echoes of Friedrich Dürenmatt's novel *Die Panne* (A dangerous game, 1956). In its metatheatrical structure, Tendulkar's play-within-the-play is a trial (oddly) of President Lyndon B. Johnson for "producing atomic weapons," but the group get accidentally locked into their small-town rehearsal space, and the "trial" becomes an opportunistic exposé of the private life of a woman member whose financial and sexual independence is resented by the overwhelmingly male community. Tendulkar had drafted the play in 1963, but he completed it in record time for a 1967 production directed by Arvind Deshpande (1932–1987) for Rangayan, the experimental theater group that had launched his playwriting career in the 1950s. The leading role of Leela Benare was the acting debut of Sulabha Deshpande (1937–2016), Arvind's wife and creative partner who went on to become one of the finest stage and screen actresses of her generation, especially in the realist mode. The Rangayan production was described immediately as a landmark in Marathi theater, and Tendulkar won two major awards for the play in 1970—the Kamaladevi Paritoshik from the Bharatiya Natya Sangh (Indian Theater Guild), and the annual playwriting award from the Sangeet Natak Akademi, India's National Performing Arts Academy. Making explicit reference to these forms of literary-theatrical recognition, the first Marathi edition of the play appeared in 1971 from Mauj Prakashan, a leading publisher of literature in this language, followed by a reprint the same year. No subsequent editions or reprints from Mauj are documentable, but Popular Prakashan (another prominent imprint for Marathi) published the play in 2003 and 2022, and it is safe to assume that *Shantata* has remained in print in its original language. However, the play's extraordinary presence in the Indian theater-verse over nearly six decades, in both the original language *and* in multiple translations, captures the process by which print and performance serve as autonomous as well as interdependent modes of multilingual existence for a successful work, securing its status separately and together for readers as well as viewers.[36]

Remarkably, the first production of the play *in translation* predated even the first published Marathi text of 1971. Om Shivpuri and his wife Sudha (née Sharma), both alumni of the National School of Drama (NSD), launched their theater group Dishantar in 1968, and in 1969 their Hindi version of Tendulkar's play, titled *Khamosh! adalat jari hai*, premiered in Delhi, with Sudha Shivpuri as Leela Benare (a role that continues to be regarded as among the most challenging for women actors in India). Dishantar's other major production in 1969 was Mohan Rakesh's new Hindi play, *Adhe adhure* (Incomplete, unfinished), with the Shivpuris again in leading roles, so the pairing with Tendulkar signaled several important emerging patterns. The translation of *Shantata* was undertaken specifically to bring an outstanding new Marathi play from Bombay to Delhi (both metropolitan cultural centers) and to perform it alongside a major new Hindi play for Hindi, Panjabi, and English-speaking audiences in the nation's capital. But the translation, presumably by the Shivpuris, was not published. This version was also likely used for the NSD Repertory production directed by Sudhir Kulkarni in 1978 and the Padatik production directed in Kolkata by Shyamanand Jalan in 2001, with the later productions using the same Hindi title for the play.

In the meantime, the success of the Hindi translation on stage prompted publication in 1983 by Sambhavana Prakashan in the "provincial" town of Hapur (Uttar Pradesh), but this text did not mention a translator. The first translations in Hindi by recognized translators (Sarojini Varma and Padmaja Ghorpade, respectively) appeared from New Delhi–based Vidya Prakashan in 2009, and Vani Prakashan in 2019. B. V. Karanth, another leading NSD alumnus who served as its director from 1977 to 1982, directed a Kannada translation of the play for Kalakunja (Bangalore) in 1969–70, but there is again no record of a corresponding published text. The only other documented translations of the play into Indian languages (excluding English) consist of an Oriya version by Prafulla Chandra Patnaik, published in Bhuvaneshwar by the Orissa Sangeet Natak Akademi in 1978 under the title *Chup! korta chalichi*, and an Urdu version by Abdussattar Dalvi that appeared in Mumbai in 2018, with exactly the same title as the Hindi version. The sparse publication records are at odds with frequent claims in print that *Shantata! court chalu ahe* has been translated into thirteen or sixteen other languages.[37] But this disparity supports the inference that at the height of the theater movement that began in the 1960s successful plays were translated quickly for performance and absorbed into a multilingual theater culture, relegating the print medium to a secondary position. Directors, actors, and audiences shared an urgent commitment to the staging of new works—plays of a kind that had never appeared in India before—and consequently, strong plays in one language had the potential for enriching theater in every other major language. Shared cultural codes also allowed the actual dramatic content to travel with relative ease beyond the borders of region and language.

English, in contrast, functions very differently as the target language of translation in the spheres of both print and performance. The "canonization" of *Shantata* began early in this medium when Oxford University Press (OUP), an extremely selective publisher of contemporary non-Anglophone Indian writing, published Priya Adarkar's translation, titled *Silence! The Court Is in Session* in 1971, as the inaugural title in its New Drama in India series. This stand-alone edition was reprinted in 1978 and 1982; and in 1989, the play was included in *Three Modern Indian Plays* alongside Badal Sircar's *Evam Indrajit* and Girish Karnad's *Tughlaq*. The OUP volume effectively made these three plays paradigmatic of postindependence modernity, which in this case was synonymous with postcolonial modernism. In 1992, OUP gave Tendulkar singular visibility in English by publishing a collection of *Five Plays*, all in Priya Adarkar's translations, and reprinted the volume in 1995, 2004, and 2009. Another volume, which appeared in 2003 under the title *Collected Plays in Translation*, retained the five earlier works and added two others that had generated controversy but became repertory staples in multiple languages—although not in English. As a playwright, Tendulkar is therefore powerfully present in English and benefits fully from the transnational reach of the language, but mainly in relation to readers, teachers, students, scholars, and critics rather than for live audiences, not only within but also outside India. When his plays are performed abroad, mainly for diasporic audiences, the original Marathi text is in much higher demand than any translation. In short, translation and multilingual circulation transform the life of the modernist play, but interlingual translation in languages other than English highlights the mode of performance, whereas translation into English highlights the medium of print.

Yet for audiences abroad who are unfamiliar with Indian languages, translation is the *only* means of access to the drama, in print as well as performance. Under those conditions, the text in translation becomes a radical locus of familiarization, uncovering the cultural legibility of representations produced by what otherwise appears to be a distant social, linguistic, and cultural system. In the case of modernist drama and theater, this shock of recognition is all the more important because as postcolonial and cosmopolitan cultural forms the plays embody a syncretic fusion of intracultural and intercultural elements, and they exist at the intersection of regional, national, and transnational routes of invention and reciprocal influence.

The legibility of Indian-language modernism was confirmed for me by my collaborative translation of Rakesh's *Ashadh ka ek din* (One Day in the Season of Rain), which was produced at Carthage College in Kenosha, Wisconsin, in March 2010, and revived as the culminating event at the forty-eighth Annual Conference on South Asia, held at the University of Wisconsin–Madison in October 2019. The play is a modernist reimagining of the life of Kalidasa, the classical Sanskrit playwright and poet who was a preeminent figure in Indian literary culture for more than a millennium before European Orientalists "discovered" him at the turn of the nineteenth century and elevated him to the canons of world literature. In Rakesh's "portrait of the artist," the young, unknown Kalidasa abandons the provincial sources of his poetic inspiration and his muse/lover Mallika for the sake of metropolitan patronage, but he returns years later in a state of spiritual and artistic crisis, only to discover that the life he is trying to reconnect with has passed him by. This ambivalent portrayal of an arch-canonical literary-cultural figure is Rakesh's first major intervention in the hagiographic narratives surrounding Kalidasa; the second is to place Mallika rather than Kalidasa at the center of the narrative. In the Hindi language of the original play, Rakesh created a brilliant theatrical idiom that could evoke classical antiquity while resonating fully with the modern and postcolonial present. In our English translation, we attempted to recreate as much as possible this quality of a remote past that was also recognizably contemporary.

Both productions of the translation were directed by white male scholar-practitioners of theater—Neil Scharnick, an assistant professor in the Department of Theater at Carthage College and a doctoral student in the Department of Theater and Drama at UW-Madison; and Joshua Thomas Kelly, an actor-director also pursuing doctoral studies in UW-Madison's Interdisciplinary Theater Studies program. The Carthage production had an all-white cast of ten undergraduate Theater majors who needed some guidance in the pronunciation of Indian names and a handful of Indian terms. As cotranslators, Vinay Dharwadker and I needed only one long workshop with the cast and crew during the rehearsal process, and to our surprise, the final text of the translation became the performance text

FIGURE 1.13 Elodie Senetra as Mallika and Stephen Schreiber as Kalidasa in the production of Mohan Rakesh, *One Day in the Season of Rain*, directed by Neil Scharnick, Carthage College, Kenosha, Wisconsin, March 2010. Photo credit: Neil Scharnick.

without a single change. In other words, the shift from page to stage was seamless, notwithstanding the completely new and disparate performance context of the American Upper Midwest. The audience for the play consisted of faculty and students from Carthage and UW-Madison, members of the Kenosha community, and members of the diasporic Indian community from Wisconsin and Illinois, especially the greater Milwaukee and Chicago areas. This production was then chosen for the Regional Kennedy Center American College Theater Festival at Michigan State University in January 2011, and it almost became a finalist for the National Festival in Washington, D.C., reconfirming the theatrical viability of a culturally unfamiliar modernist work in performance (fig. 1.13).

In the 2019 performance in Madison, eight out of ten cast members were white undergraduate and graduate students from the United States and Britain; one leading female role was played by a professional African-American actress who had begun a PhD in Interdisciplinary Theater Studies, and a secondary role was played by an Indian postdoctoral research scientist (fig. 1.14).

FIGURE 1.14 Director Joshua Thomas Kelly (extreme left) with the cast of *One Day in the Season of Rain*, staged reading, University of Wisconsin-Madison, October 2019. Photo credit: Aparna Dharwadker.

The audience consisted of UW faculty and students, but also South Asianists from various disciplines who were attending Madison's annual South Asia Conference. None of the potentially alienating features of the two productions—the non-Western content delivered by Western speakers, the color-blind casting, the Indian costuming, the racially and ethnically diverse audiences—interfered with the transformation of written dialogue into embodied action that was the raison d'être of the two events. Given the centrality of performance in drama's modes of existence, the Carthage and Madison productions of *One Day in the Season of Rain* affirmed both the verbal and the affective transportability of the Indian-language modernist work through the acts of interlingual and intercultural translation.

RECOVERING INDIAN (THEATRICAL) MODERNISMS

My argument so far has focused on two paradoxical features of the global turn in modernist studies—it has ignored Indian-language modernisms for the most part, and yet it has also created for the first time the critical space in which appropriate methods for approaching and interpreting these modernisms might be formulated. A full explication of the history, aesthetics, and politics of the *Indian* version of multilingualism has been necessary to deduce that the current conjuncture of modernist and postcolonial studies in the Western academy offers much more productive frameworks for my field of study than the critical discourse within each Indian language or the disciplinary orientations of area studies. Although there is an ongoing engagement with the idea of modernity and an acute sense of modernist rupture in writing across the major Indian languages from the 1920s onward, the primarily regional compass of most languages (noted previously) promotes mainly *intralingual* and *intraregional* perspectives, rather than the pan-Indian and transnational sweep that is necessary to connect modernist Indian writing to the networks of global modernism. In the West, modern Indian literatures are housed mainly within South Asian area studies, which is again epistemologically inclined toward individual language-worlds, and has continued its orientalist legacy of privileging the classical and premodern periods over the modern.[38] Even an encyclopedic collection like Pollock's *Literary Cultures in History*, intended as a corrective to the marginalization of literary studies within South Asian area studies, produces disjointed views of modernity and modernism because it follows the principle of organizing criticism and analysis by language and region.[39]

The spatiotemporal and linguistic expansion of the new modernist studies—from the early to the later twentieth century, from Euro-America to other parts of the globe, and, ideally, from Europhone to non-Europhone expressive systems—can counterbalance this fragmentation and reorient the study of Indian modernisms more effectively than other methodologies. While adding immeasurably to the forms, times, places, styles, subjectivities, ideologies, and mediums being addressed in present-day Euro-American modernist studies, the new initiatives have also established key theoretical principles through which the non-Western "world" can be approached on its own terms. Extended specifically to India, the fundamental generative concept is that of a resilient "global horizon" that does not impose "strict national or temporal frameworks or even explicit aesthetic programs," and in which the naming of various works "as 'modernist' is less pressing than the need to understand the circuits they share."[40] This idea reappears in Wollaeger's suggestion that modernism in a global frame engenders "a set of criteria, subsets of which are enough to constitute a sense of decentered resemblance," or in Ross and Lindgren's acknowledgment that "disparate temporalities, aesthetic regimes, and definitional schemas" undergird the global mapping of modernism.[41] More elaborately, Friedman's move from "globalism" to "planetarity" dislodges post-Enlightenment Western modernity conclusively as the sine qua non of modernist aesthetics, and uncovers modernisms in the *longue durée*, in widely disparate global locations.[42]

The initiative closest to the content of my book in some respects is the focus on modernism's relation to colonialism and postcolonialism, analyzed without simplistic recourse to concepts such as "derivativeness," "minority," and "marginality." Simon Gikandi notes that "a convergence of political and literary ideologies mark[s] a significant part of the history of modernism and postcolonialism. . . . The archive of early postcolonial writing in Africa, the Caribbean, and India is dominated by and defined by writers whose political or cultural projects were enabled by modernism even when the ideologies of the latter, as was the case with Eliot, were at odds with the project of decolonization. . . . [W]ithout modernism, postcolonial literature as we know it would perhaps not exist."[43] High modernists such as Eliot and Yeats become deeply influential in late colonial/postcolonial contexts despite their Eurocentrism and elitism because of the ideological erasure of their political positions and a preoccupation with literariness on the part of colonially conditioned readers—a move that Gikandi describes as "the great irony of the history of postcolonial literatures."[44] In Indian writing, Western influences are sublimated further by a largely non-Anglophone, multilingual literary/performative economy that estranges global readers from the Indian modernist corpus to a much greater extent than is the case in Afro-Caribbean writing. However, my discussion of the genres of modernism in Indian theater (chapters 3–5) amplifies Gikandi's claims by analyzing the structures of myth, history, realism, traditionalism, and antirealism in post-1950 theater not only as modernist in their rupture with the past but also as postcolonial in their thematics.

As selective and strategic points of reference, new modernist studies and postcolonial studies offer the revisionary frameworks that support the main object of this study—to recover modernist Indian theater at the levels of both theory and practice by locating formative discourses and delineating the major *kinds* of modernist representation that come into view after independence. Chapter 2 traces the evolution of modernist positions over several decades in the mid- to late-twentieth century, locates theoretical and aesthetic principles in the self-reflexive discourses of cosmopolitan authors, and discusses the dynamics of writing and staging modernism in the theater; chapters 3–5 relate theory and circumstance to practice through the structures or modes of myth, history, urban realism, and tradition, relating the Indian works to relevant transnational patterns. These materials and methods diverge from current approaches to "non-Western" or "postcolonial" modernisms in several respects. My focus is not on Anglophone fiction, poetry, or nonfiction but on post-1950 works for the theater in six different languages, including English. Regardless of language, the works I discuss are largely unknown in the West for reasons that are already familiar, even though the Western academy has fostered the development of modern Indian theater studies as a scholarly field to a significant extent since the 1990s. The global audiences available to Anglophone writers, particularly those who inhabit the South Asian diaspora in Europe and North America, are simply out of bounds for the stay-at-home Indian-language playwrights, although their work circulates continuously in multiple languages within India, and in English translations abroad. The most important shift Indian modernisms demand, then, is from the global marketplace of Europhone/English writing to the less visible, but no less significant field of non-European languages drawn into the orbit of modernity. The forms of insider knowledge necessary for this reorientation involve the ontology of Indian languages and belong to the initial stages of geomodernist interpretation; translation into, and criticism in, languages with a global presence have to represent the crucial next steps, so that the rethinking of time, space, hierarchy, and form in modernist studies can also fully encompass India.

Chapter Two

MODERNITY, MODERNISM, AND INDIAN THEATER

The urban theater that takes shape under Anglo-European and local influences in the cities of Calcutta and Bombay after 1860 is, for its own time and place, a "radically modern" institution because its constitutive features are historically unprecedented and culturally transformative. Located firmly in the colonial metropolis, it counterpoints the vast array of traditional, religious, ritualistic, folk, and intermediary performance genres that followed the decline of classical Sanskrit drama after the twelfth century CE and had maintained a varied presence in rural and semi-urban regions for several hundred years. In terms of material organization, this theater's new spatial environment and production technologies incorporate many of the institutional features of European, especially British, theater, becoming a part of what I have called Indian theater's heterogeneous "poetics of modernity."

> Enclosed theater buildings, darkened auditoriums, proscenium stages, painted scenery, props, and mechanical stage apparatuses made their appearance in India for the first time. The borrowed practice of commercial ticket sales tapped into a growing body of educated middle-class viewers who were drawn to the new forms of commodified entertainment, and selectively accepted women on the stage as well as in the audience. The large-scale investment of capital in urban proscenium theaters and touring companies, especially by Bombay's enterprising Parsi community, also led to the first

'professional' establishments (with resident managers, playwrights, actors, musicians, and technicians) that expanded their operations beyond the city to semi-urban, and even rural, areas in particular regions of the country.[1]

As a complex, successful, and fully commercial venture—the only formation of its kind in the global British colonial system—Indian theater of the colonial period is also scrupulously secular, even cosmopolitan, in its effective delinking of performance from religion and from the predominantly intracultural content of precolonial genres.

The modernity of colonial theater has several other systemic dimensions as well. The ambitious theoretical reflections contained in the letters of Michael Madhusudan Dutt (1824–1873) and the essays of Girish Chandra Ghosh (1844–1912), Bhartendu Harishchandra (1850–1885), Rabindranath Tagore (1861–1941), and Jaishankar Prasad (1889–1937) adjudicate the all-powerful legacies of Sanskrit drama and aesthetic theory in an effort to determine their relevance for a rapidly modernizing present.[2] Beginning with Bengali and Marathi, multiple *modern* Indian languages in their urbanized forms become, for the first time, the dominant mediums for creating and sustaining new genres of playwriting and performance. Borrowed European forms (the social-realist play, the history play, political allegory, and so on) are modeled on the Shakespearean five-act play but also accommodate indigenous cultural matter derived from myth, history, legend, folklore, and contemporary sociocultural experience, and this synthesis is opened up in turn to the audiovisual embellishments of dance, music, and spectacle. The theatrical forms resulting from this thorough indigenization of foreign influences are modern without being imitative or derivative. Large-scale translation, adaptation, and transculturation from Sanskrit, English, and other European languages root commercial performance firmly in the processes of interlingual and intercultural exchange. Although performance is drama's primary mode of existence throughout the colonial period, the prolific playwriting of literary icons such as Dutt, Harishchandra, and Tagore connects drama to proprietary authorship and "literariness" in the familiar Western sense, and the steady publication both of closet plays and plays intended for commercial consumption gives drama a visible role in the culture of print. By the turn of the century, "drama" thus emerges "as an institution of colonial modernity with a distinctive textual, performative, and theoretical presence in urban India—differing, of course, in scale and level of development from its Anglo-European correlates, but marking a decisive departure from *all* premodern Indian traditions of performance, classical and postclassical" (*POM*, xxxvi).

The relatively short time span between the effective beginnings of "modern" theater in India (the mid-nineteenth century) and the full-scale "modernist" reaction (the 1940s onward) indicates that the progressive modernization that occurred in England over several hundred years (c. 1580–1870) takes place in Indian theater in the course of a few decades, telescoping time and accelerating the pace of change to an extraordinary extent. This abbreviated history also suggests that one way to chart the transition from modernity to modernism is to separate the features of modernity that are carried forward into the modernist project from those that are reflexively jettisoned. In this bifurcation, urban locations, proscenium staging, Indian-language composition, secular values, and the ubiquity of translation are fully adapted to modernist ends; commercial systems of organization, the theoretical and aesthetic preoccupation with classical tradition, the opportunisms of form (blending realism with dance and music), and the emphasis on commodified entertainment are subjected to stringent criticism and discarded as the dominant models of theater activity. The modernity/modernism relation in urban Indian theater becomes, therefore, a multilayered interplay of continuities and disjunctions, although the modernist rhetoric is one of uncompromising change, and other postcolonial discourses problematize the concepts of modernity, tradition, and contemporaneity further by compulsively revisiting the nature of the relationship between past and present.

In this chapter I address the emergence, discursive amplification, and actualization of the aesthetic-political positions that make Indian-language theater a significant locus of modernism in the long twentieth century. This involves, first, a discussion of the rejection of colonial models *within* the colonial period by major literary authors, and the confirmation of that rejection through a multidimensional activist, ideological, and artistic critique during the 1940s and 1950s. I then focus on three paradigmatic playwrights who practice several literary genres with notable success, and whose authorial self-fashioning establishes some defining qualities of postcolonial modernism in Indian languages. Subsequent sections deal with the conditions under which modernist plays are written, staged, and received in a noncommercial performance economy, and the brief performance history of an already familiar play—Mohan Rakesh's *Ashadh ka ek din*—indicates how these emergent processes work in practice. Throughout the chapter, my analysis is deeply intertextual with the theory and practice of Indian-language modernists for three strategic reasons: as mentioned previously, bringing major non-Western, non-Anglophone authors fully into the purview of global modernisms is a key objective of this book; close attention to their work reveals both the complexity of their authorial positions and the proximity or distance they maintain from more familiar forms of Euromodernism; and the juxtaposition of authors who work contemporaneously in different languages and regions opens up new and precise perspectives on multilingual modernism. In its entirety, this approach establishes that the *definitional* imprecision of the modernity/modernism relation in Indian languages does not prevent modernist positions from becoming fully articulated and translated into theatrical practice after independence. Mohan Rakesh makes several appearances in this otherwise diverse discussion because as a postcolonial modernist he offers an exceptionally coherent and meaningful amalgam of theory, polemic, and practice.

FROM PROTO-MODERNIST ANTITHEATRICALISM TO MODERNIST ICONOCLASM

The singular history of modern Indian theater during the colonial period consists in the establishment of theater as a secular, commercial, and urban institution for the very first time, and then the dismantling of these structures under the aesthetic-political imperatives of political independence and new nationhood. Between about 1870 and the late 1930s, proscenium theaters functioned as successful profit-making ventures in the cities of Calcutta and Bombay, and urban companies toured various parts of the country with enough regularity for theater to become a "nationally" visible commodity. But from the beginning and for a variety of reasons, these new systems also had the effect of separating "theater as commercialized entertainment" from highbrow "literary" drama as well as obscure "closet" plays that were not intended for performance at all. The proliferation of closet works by unknown authors was a sign of excitement about the newly rediscovered drama form, and of the desire to exploit print as a relatively accessible medium in comparison with the material complexities of staging. In a less pragmatic vein, the vocal opposition to popular commercial theater on the part of major poet-playwrights such as Bhartendu Harishchandra, Tagore, and Prasad can be viewed as a carefully theorized, "protomodernist" antitheatricalism that prefigured the sustained and successful critiques of the mid-twentieth century.[3]

Three representative essays by these colonial-era playwrights can serve to clarify their basic positions: the 1883 minitreatise titled "*Natak*" (Drama) by Harishchandra, Tagore's 1913 essay titled "*Rangmanch*" (translated as "The Theatre"), and Jaishankar Prasad's "*Rangmanch*" (translated as "The Stage," 1936). Written over more than fifty years in two different languages, Hindi and Bengali, the essays have similarities that reflect the "serious" modern Indian mindset in relation to the genre of drama. All three writers use classical Sanskrit theater as a touchstone because, as Prasad puts it, "the ancient stages developed in accordance with the principles of literary composition (*kavya*), and literary works were not compelled to accept the rule-bound nature of the stage" (*POM*, 143). For all three, poetry is the privileged creative medium and the heart of drama. Bharatendu persistently uses the verb "to make" to describe the act of playwriting, and refers to an individual play as a "*grantha*"—that is, a text, tome, or volume that has its primary existence in the world of print. Tagore begins by rejecting Wagner's idea of the unified art work because "the muse rules in full splendour where she rules alone. If she has to share the household with a co-wife, her stature is bound to be diminished, especially if the other wife's presence happens to be strong" (*POM*, 70). He then rejects the idea that drama is a "less independent" or an intrinsically collaborative art, because "good poetry wait[s] for no one but the sensitive reader" (*POM*, 70). From here it is only a short distance to the positions that the "art of acting," not drama, is "dependent on others for shelter"; that "a play which compromises itself in the interests of performance" is an object of derision; and that poetic drama can do its work by appealing to the spectator's imagination because "the stage is cramped but the poetry is not" (*POM*, 71–72). In a similar way, Prasad describes the idea that plays should be written for the stage as a "serious misapprehension about the theater. The greater effort, which is also more practicable, should be to provide a stage for drama" (*POM*, 146).

The antitheatricalism of these judgments is both pointed and precise because all three authors have a common object of attack in the Parsi theater, the profit-driven hodge-podge of melodrama, spectacle, and musical entertainment that was nonetheless the only *nationally* visible theater formation of the colonial period. Harishchandra reports an incident where two friends, one British and the other Indian, fled from a Parsi theater performance of Kalidasa's classic play, *Shakuntala*, because they could not bear to see the poet slaughtered by hack actors. Tagore uses the same play to argue that the Sanskrit definition of drama as *drishya kavya* ("visually presented and experienced poetry") refers to the mind's eye, and not to "the wretched wooden planks" that insult the poet, the actor, and the audience's imagination whenever there is an attempt to "represent reality" on the stage (*POM*, 72). Realism for Tagore is a sign of the European appetite for "the truth of material fact," but on the Indian stage this mode produces only "expensive rubbish" that the country cannot afford and does not need because of its own ecological performance traditions (*POM*, 72, 73). Prasad describes the Parsi stage as a "horrifying" spectacle and attacks it for what he calls the unseemly practice of casting men in female roles. Unlike the two earlier authors, he is also historically well-positioned to criticize Ibsen and Ibsenism for confining drama to a prosaic present, and cautions that "the new Western inspirations should not become our only guide-posts" (*POM*, 146). Finally, since Prasad's professed goal is the "ascent of the Hindi stage," unlike Tagore he acknowledges the collaborative nature of performance and looks ahead to a time when like-minded poets, actors, and directors can work together to create a new theater.

The two decades following Prasad's essay are singular in Indian theater history not only because the much-maligned colonial commercial superstructure came to an end (in part because of the arrival of talking cinema in 1931) but also because serious theater was delinked from commercialized performance by a process that has yet to be reversed. Antitheatricalism had powerful material consequences for the institution of modern urban theater for which materialist explanations alone are not sufficient. For example, the nuts-and-bolts explanation could be that films supplanted Parsi theater and other market-driven forms rather quickly in the 1930s because they yoked capital more efficiently to mechanically reproducible mass entertainment and had superior technological means for negotiating realism and spectacle. But it was the extended ideological critique of colonial theater from left-activist, bourgeois-nationalist, *and* modernist positions that turned this apparently natural decline into an occasion for the radical reimagining of urban theater.

The first serious critique of colonial practices came from the Indian People's Theatre Association (IPTA), which was launched in May 1943 as the antifascist, anti-imperialist cultural wing of the Communist Party of India. The First Bulletin of the organization declared that art and literature could have a future only if they expressed and inspired "the people's struggles for freedom and culture"—a test that writers and artists of the previous century had failed signally.[4] In particular, IPTA manifestoes described urban drama of the previous half century as having fallen to "some of the lowest depths of degeneration" because of its dependence on inane middle-class conventionality or its escape into "bad history and senseless mythology" (Pradhan, vol. 1, 134, 136). An important part of the IPTA's activist program was therefore to revive the traditional, folk, and intermediary performance genres that nineteenth-century urban practitioners had rejected as debased and corrupt but that now appeared to have several self-evident advantages. Forms such as Jatra and Tamasha were culturally indigenous, antirealistic, or nonrealistic in terms of presentational style, rural or semi-rural in terms of primary location, and capable of mass appeal—in short, antithetical in every respect to the bourgeois urban forms the IPTA intended to displace. Rooting itself in the "significant facts, aspirations, and struggles of our people," the movement also asserted its commitment to a "national" perspective: "the IPTA in its dramatic works, while always keen to imbibe healthy influences from abroad, must strive to see that its work is rooted in the national tradition. All cosmopolitan tendencies, which have no relevance to our living conditions, must be opposed" (Pradhan, vol. 2, 162).

The first decade of the IPTA's existence was transformative for theater, but as it declined rapidly in the 1950s because of conflicts with the Nehruvian democratic-socialist state the cultural bureaucracy of that very state stepped in to mediate a second phase of decommercialization, this time in the name of a resurgent Indianness that was bourgeois and cultural-nationalist, not populist, in orientation. At the five-day Drama Seminar organized by the newly formed Sangeet Natak Akademi (the National Performing Arts Academy) in April 1956, the unsuitability of colonial practices to a new national theater culture and the need to rescue theater from the marketplace were two major topics. Influential discussants like the novelist Mulk Raj Anand and the actor Balraj Sahni argued that the enclosed auditorium, the proscenium stage, commercial ticket sales, and naturalist staging were all imperialist impositions alien to Indian habits of performance and spectatorship. The association of drama with theater companies was also a deterrent to serious playwriting and had caused a serious shortage of reputable playwrights and "good actable plays" after independence. To create a conceptual basis for their positions, the seminar participants chose to redefine the concepts of "professional" and "amateur" practice. The term "professional," a synonym for "commercial," signaled a theater that was nonserious, superficial, inartistic, or merely popular, and hence not worth preserving. The counter term, "amateur," denoted aesthetic and thematic seriousness, artistic boldness, and a long-term commitment to the art. The consensus was that in a decolonizing culture the "future hope for the establishment of a national theater and dramatic renaissance" lay in the "encouragement and promotion" of amateur theater that would be sustained by talented individuals, a national network of state-supported arts institutions, and corporate philanthropy.[5] These utopian conceptions never gained enough momentum to produce a program of action, but the sheer discursive gravity of the seminar gave cultural administrators and policy makers in the new nation's bureaucracy an ideological platform that could not be challenged in any marketplace.

In hindsight, the activities of the IPTA and the Drama Seminar can be viewed as ideologically disparate but ultimately provisional "space-clearing gestures" that prefigure the radical modernist overhaul of the early postindependence decades. Gathering momentum during the 1940s and arriving at its formative pan-Indian phase in the 1950s, modernism registers a decisive rupture from the "travestic" forms of colonial modernity, which in turn had marked a break from precolonial "tradition" over the course of the nineteenth century. Compelled to frame a response to their precursors rather than to foreign models, leading playwrights in languages such as Bengali, Marathi, Hindi, Kannada, and Gujarati dissociated themselves explicitly or implicitly from all the dominant formations of the previous hundred years: the commercial urban stages of Calcutta and Bombay, the unstageable literary drama of Harishchandra, Tagore, and Prasad, the extra-theatrical corpus of closet plays, the nationwide left-wing populism of the IPTA, and the dictates of the new nation-state about how "the future Indian drama" could contribute to postcolonial cultural reconstruction. Gathered together into a conscious or unconscious community, these playwrights also followed what Fredric Jameson calls the "full-blown ideology of modernism"–"that moment in which the modern . . . [is] theorized and conceptually named and identified in terms of the autonomy of the aesthetic."[6] Extending the principle of aesthetic autonomy to drama (the aggregation of texts) as well as theater (institutionalized performance), modernism reconciled colonial-era antagonisms by managing to bring "highbrow" or "literary" plays successfully onto urban stages.

The impact of these reorientations on the cultures of playwriting and performance is foundational. With no historical avant-garde of their own to embrace or oppose, numerous mid-twentieth-century Indian playwrights come to embody the qualities of "writerliness" by focusing their revisionary energies primarily on three objects: the author, the work, and the labor that author and work perform together in the world. In one direction, modernist aesthetics enable playwrights to assert the primacy of authorship, form, and language, so that the writing of plays becomes a "private" textual act dissociable in principle (though not in practice) from public performance, and drama appears as a literary construct with a secure existence in print. In the other direction, textuality and print are fully and painstakingly assimilated to a volatile, noncommercial performance economy. Serious playwriting in this period reveals either an *unconscious* attraction to the drama form on the part of playwrights who have no overt concern with performance, or a *conscious* commitment to drama on the part of those who both desire and expect performance, but not with any certainty. The availability of stable institutional structures and "performative circumstances" is thus not necessary to the formation of a postcolonial modernist repertoire. But instead of producing closet plays, these conditions produced major works that became contemporary stage classics even in the absence of a functioning marketplace, and they were performed successfully in multiple languages in India and around the world. The paradoxical processes create authorial personae, dramatic oeuvres, and performance histories of a kind that did not exist in modern Indian theater before the 1950s. Even at the beginning of their respective careers, major modernist playwrights such as Dharamvir Bharati, Mohan Rakesh, Badal Sircar, Girish Karnad, and Vijay Tendulkar seem to be fully formed *authors*, although being acutely aware that they are not part of any ongoing *theatrical* tradition. The arc of their careers in the theater delineates how they help to create, on their own terms, the performance culture that their brand of modernism demands.

The next two sections substantiate these claims by focusing, respectively, on the self-positioning of three leading cosmopolitan modernists, and on the processes of deferral and actualization that undergird the "performance of modernism" on urban stages. Worth noting here are some broad perspectives on modernism that come into play as writers and theater professionals of all kinds struggle to find adequate means of artistic self-expression in the new sociopolitical and cultural environment of a newly independent nation. First, in India modernism and the postcolonial are not mutually opposed, and the end of modernist aesthetics is not a precondition for the emergence of postcolonial literature. On the contrary, what is chronologically "postcolonial" is often qualitatively and aesthetically "modernist," and this implies not a derivative dependence on European political and cultural influences but an extended revamping of the narrative-aesthetic resources of the modern Indian languages, individually and collectively. Like colonial playwrights, the postcolonial modernists turn obsessively to Indian myth and history, but mainly to de-idealize the past and suggest its analogous relation to an imperfect present. The plays they set in the present are mainly realist portraits of the modern urban individual caught in the nexus of familial claims and societal norms. As becomes clear in the discussion of works by Girish Karnad, Mohan Rakesh, Badal Sircar, Mahesh Elkunchwar, and Mahesh Dattani in chapters 3 and 4, both settings produce deromanticized and deeply ambivalent views of the nation and national culture. Second, postcolonial modernists in India are not concerned primarily with colonialism or "writing back" to the empire; instead, they often refract a troubled present through a *pre*colonial past—in Tendulkar's *Ghashiram kotwal* (Constable Ghashiram, Marathi, 1972), for instance, late-eighteenth-century Maratha history becomes the narrative basis for exposing the divisive and violent late-twentieth-century politics of caste, religion, region, and language. Other thematic and artistic preoccupations associated with the modernist turn include the negation of transcendence; the pursuit of individuality, ordinariness, and authenticity; the appearance of an articulate, self-reflexive, non-self-censoring authorial voice; an apolitical politicality that relentlessly critiques the nation-state; and a cosmopolitan sense of connection with the world that is always aware of its own historical positioning within modernity. In the Western perspective Indian theater may be "othered" by linguistic and cultural difference, but it is recuperated for modernism by the deep philosophical, existential, and aesthetic connections to the world at large that cosmopolitan Indian modernists bring to bear on the literary cultures they inherit, creating their own variations on "modernism beyond the nation" as theorized by scholars such as Berman, Walkowitz, and Rabaté.[7] This is not a shallow, belated, derivative, or "abstract" modernism: its defining qualities are fully manifest in the thought of the three playwrights profiled in the next section, and in the plays discussed throughout the second part of this study.

Finally, it is important to reiterate the historical particularity and oppositional tension of the modernity-modernism relation in Indian expressive culture of both the colonial and the postcolonial periods, especially because it diverges from ongoing Western usage and some provocative recent conceptualizations of the space-time of modernism. In general, Western criticism does not support a conceptually precise distinction between "modern" and "modernist" in relation to post-Enlightenment modernity, and Susan Friedman's radical take on the familiar definition of modernism as the "aesthetic dimension of modernity" delinks modernism from Eurocentric conceptions of modernity, conventional twentieth-century periodizations, and the constraints of any particular geography or chronology.[8] The Indian modernisms I am concerned with, however, constitute the aesthetic dimension of a complex post/colonial modernity that follows tangled lines of development from the late-nineteenth to the early-twenty-first centuries, and the specific historical rupture between colonial and postcolonial praxes is integral to their emergence. The historical perspective also underscores the unprecedented nature of sociocultural and political conditions that joined together for the first time on the subcontinent to engender the particular modernisms I want to highlight—British colonialism, the arrival and development of print culture, the increase in literacy, the engagement with the Western canon through education and large-scale translation, the emergence of proprietary authorship, the interpenetration of English with modern Indian languages, the achievement of political independence and modern nationhood, the rejection of colonial aesthetics at the levels of form and language, anticommercialism in performative genres like theater, and the cosmopolitan investment in the world, to name some key elements. This is in many ways the kind of singular and linear chronology of modernism that Friedman argues against; but the linearity in this case is not dictated by Western models, and it is essential for bringing specific *Indian modernist* practices into focus.

MODERNIST SELF-FASHIONING IN THE POSTCOLONY: DHARAMVIR BHARATI, MOHAN RAKESH, AND VIJAY TENDULKAR

The discussion of three leading postindependence authors in this section highlights the qualities, positions, and choices that define their modernism, providing definitional precision in a transnational frame, especially for readers unfamiliar with their work. The broadest similarity between the three figures is the enormous range and depth of their writerly output—they are playwrights, novelists, short story writers, travel writers, memoirists, translators, theorists, essayists, critics, literary journalists, diarists, and correspondents.[9] Bharati was also a poet, and as the editor of the Hindi weekly *Dharmayug* from 1960 to 1987, he was one of the most influential literary editors of the late twentieth century. Rakesh was a key figure in the *nai kahani* (new story) and *naya upanyas* (new novel) movements in Hindi that began in the 1950s. Tendulkar's creative medium was Marathi, but he was professionally a political journalist in English, the most important screenwriter for the parallel cinema and middle cinema movements in Hindi and Marathi (1970s–1980s), and a screenwriter for television in all three languages. The modernist dramaturgy of these playwrights is therefore one (integral) part of an expansive oeuvre that makes them seminal members of postcolonial literary culture. In the discussion that follows, I refer extensively to their self-reflexive writing (in my own translations) so their voices become accessible to a wider readership and their modernisms acquire a new habitation in the medium of English.

Bharati: The Cosmo-Modernist Paradigm

Dharamvir Bharati published his first collection of five plays, *Nadi pyasi thi* (The river was thirsty) in early 1954, and later that same year produced *Andha yug* (Blind epoch), the condensed, cosmo-modernist verse epic based on the *Mahabharata* that is arguably the first significant new postindependence play in any Indian language. He did not publish any other plays for the rest of his career, but the ambitious range and careful self-positioning in his theoretical and critical writing of the 1950s and 1960s opened a singular space for the Indian-language author within the discourses of modernity and modernism. As noted previously, three of the nine volumes in the *Dharmavira bharati granthavali* (The collected works of Dharamvir Bharati) consist of essays (vol. 4), literary criticism (vol. 5), and research writing (vol. 9). One prominent theme in these works is the consciousness of new beginnings in a crisis-ridden and transitioning world, appearing in such essays as "Old idols, new ideals," "Non-belief," "The new poetics," "Crisis and the new direction," "Asian modernity and the hula-hoop," and "Modernity, or the sense of crisis" (all included in vol. 4). Another recurrent interest is the writer's relationship to the political sphere, addressed in "The state and the stage," "Political destiny and the Indian writer," and "The politics of apoliticality." The founding of the Progressive Writers Association in 1936, followed by the IPTA in 1943, had given great prominence to progressive beliefs and qualities in Indian cultural discourse for two decades. However, part 1 of volume 5, which contains Bharati's literary criticism, is titled "Progressivism: a critique," and it juxtaposes his belief in the value of the individual and the artist's refusal to be "anyone's mental slave" with what he regards as the failure of artistic elements in progressive literature. Another cluster in this volume takes up "Human values and literature," and combines modernist alienation with romantic-idealist disenchantment in the essays "The erosion of human elements," "Ruins of the inner spirit," and "Choked creativity: the impotent hero and social unreality." At a considerable distance from this level of generality, some of Bharati's most trenchant criticism is directed at the politics of language in India—what he perceives as the continuing imperialism of English and the consequent erosion of Indian languages, especially Hindi.

Bharati's thought can therefore be characterized as a simultaneous engagement with the global, the national, the regional, and occasionally the local. At the level of maximum generalization, he acknowledges the existence of earlier modernities but defines "our" modernity as a historically unprecedented condition of crisis in terms that are worth quoting at length for their deeply internalized sense of humanity's shared destiny in "our times":

> Every age has been a modern age in its own time, but no age has been so conscious of its own modernity as the present age. . . . There have been many times in history when periods and cultures have been jolted by their living present. . . .The more intense this disharmony [between the past and the present], the deeper the sense of crisis, and the more swiftly the attention

of that age has been fixed on its present. For this reason, it would perhaps not be an overstatement to say that in history, a sense of crisis and a sense of modernity have often emerged at the same time, like two aspects of the same historical experience.... That is why when we find our times intensely alert towards their modernity, we can easily deduce that today's crisis is deeper, more pervasive in the areas of religion, philosophy, knowledge, art, and language than any other age has ever experienced.

.... It's not only that this age is more intensely aware of its own modernity than any previous age, but that it is negotiating the sense of modernity ... as no other age had ever done before. To have such a deep awareness of cultural crisis, such anarchy and erosion of values, and yet to know that this turn in history is the most important one for human destiny, and that the decisions we take—right or wrong—will determine the direction of humanity for ever—these are aspects of the sense of modernity that had not emerged in history until now.[10]

What a terrifying desert the present age has proved to be for human consciousness, and how full it has been of distracting mirages—philosophical materialism, which reduces man to matter; capitalism, which takes away economic conveniences and reduces humans to frustrated pygmies; so-called collectivism, which robs human beings of intellectual freedom and turns them into slavish adherents of personality cults.... Philosophers, scientists, social thinkers—all are alert today to this pervasive crisis, and are looking in their respective spheres for ways to redress it.[11]

What Bharati calls the "new aesthetic" in literature is the writer's response to this challenge, and if "the traditionalist is shocked by the new literature.... there's nothing new about that. This is what has always happened" ("Cactus," *DBG*, vol. 4, 70–71). The "new writer" also dispenses with facile notions of beauty—what is outdated has to be discarded, and what was proscribed earlier can be brought in if it awakens a "new sensibility" in the reader and reflects an "encompassing relation" to the writer's time ("Cactus," *DBG*, vol. 4, 69–70).

Turning his attention to the "false valuation of modernity" he views as a pan-Asian problem ("from Calcutta to Tokyo"), Bharati interprets it as "a residue of mental slavery ... left behind in the colonial spaces overrun by imperialism," and criticizes responses at both extremes of the postcolonial reaction: "The fanatic who rejects everything new because he assumes it comes from the West, and the discontented 'modern' who considers himself an orphan in Asia and makes pathetic overtures to the West—both are equally victims of a false system of values generated by mental slavery. In their extreme forms, both these viewpoints are merely self-destructive" ("Asian modernity and the hula-hoop," *DBG*, vol. 4, 442). Bharati's deepest disillusionment, however, centers on the state of his own country and culture, especially what he regards as the betrayal of every promise associated with independence: "We have just passed through a phase of national life which makes it hard to understand how the brilliant tradition of sacrifice, discipline, dedication, selflessness, devotion, truth, and surrender . . . was suddenly transformed into this emptiness, degeneracy, impotence, escapism, delusion, and pathetic unreason. . . . As soon as the time of struggle ended and the time to rule arrived . . . the imbalance and folly inherent in this whole arrangement became clearly visible" ("Indian towers of ivory," *DBG*, vol. 5, 234, 239).

What has risen up against the new "arrangement" (read: the Nehruvian postcolonial state) is "the voice of the embattled, vibrant modern Indian sensibility that had revolted against the defeatism and decline endemic in Indian society for centuries" ("The middle class ocean and the old fisherman," *DBG*, vol. 4, 375–76). Bharati sees this revolt as "a very good sign" because it is opposed to "the circuits of hollowness, passivity, mental slavery, and moral bankruptcy, to the counterrevolution that began after independence. . . . It is this state of agitation that propels it through that deadly maze of false, inert spirituality in which tired and spent minds often seek shelter in the name of Indianness" (*DBG*, vol. 4, 375–76).

As an embodiment of this "modern Indian sensibility," it is the mid-twentieth-century writer who most effectively confronts "the old understanding, the old consciousness, the old viewpoints" with a "new vision," although the two are irreconcilable: "This new sense of the times is bent upon rapidly destroying the fading haloes, the pretenses to divinity, the old self-deceptions, the false masks. In their place, with great firmness it has begun to valorize the ordinary individual . . . in poetry, in fiction, in criticism, in consciousness and sensation. The new vision is related to an entirely different set of standards, different contexts, a different vocabulary, a different temper. So much so that it feels as though we speak two different languages, live in two different worlds" ("Indian towers of ivory," *DBG*, vol. 5, 241–42).

Ironically, what impedes the resolute writer in Bharati's view is the "divide-and-rule policy" behind the presence of English in India, which is "trying its utmost to poison the atmosphere for all the Indian languages, not only at the governmental but also the literary and cultural levels. Remove English from the middle and then see how well the interconnections between the Indian languages flourish! And Hindi will be the most capable medium for that" ("Sitting on the fence," *DBG*, vol. 4, 136). Elsewhere he describes the forms of knowledge embodied in the English language as grotesque and "unpatriotic" and warns that the failure to keep English in check will do lasting damage to Asian cultures.

In their sweeping generalizations, Bharati's metanarratives of decline and crisis may occasionally create the same kind of skepticism as the positivist narratives of cultural superiority and progress he sets out to dispute. But as an iconoclastic author, ethical thinker, polemicist, scholar, and world citizen, he is an Indian poster child for what Douglas Mao and Rebecca Walkowitz have termed "bad modernism." Conforming remarkably to the latter's definition of "badness," in world-encompassing terms Bharati is opposed to positivist thinking, facile quests for popularity, the "uncritical endorsement" of tradition, and complacency about the state of society and the world; with India in mind, he challenges his audience, rejects bourgeois and capitalist values, and criticizes mass culture.[12] Due to space constraints Bharati's drama does not figure prominently in this book, but among the writers of his formative generation his thought has the widest cosmopolitical reach.[13]

Rakesh: The World, the Text, and the Playwright

Mohan Rakesh was born a year before Bharati, practices an equally astonishing number of genres, and is an even more provocative authorial presence in the same language—Hindi. He is also a much more prolific and seminal twentieth-century playwright and engages deeply with the drama and theater of his time. Indeed, in a theater culture where playwrights offer frequent but not systematic commentary on their craft, Rakesh's reflections on drama and theater over the course of a controversial career make up an extraordinary archive, especially in light of his premature death at the age of forty-seven in 1972. Collected posthumously, most recently in a convenient single volume titled *Natya-vimarsha* (Meditations on theater,

2003), the writings vary in form, subject, and occasion but are linked by a cosmopolitan sensibility that, like Bharati's, moves fluidly between the personal/local, the regional, the national, and the international. In his prefaces and a handful of personal essays, Rakesh focuses specifically on the Hindi stage and his own position within the traditions of Hindi and Indian theater. But the general questions to which he returns repeatedly—the nature of modernity, the relevance of Western to Indian practices, the relation of words and language to theater, and drama's relation to technology and the technological media of film and radio—are invariably formulated in the context of world theater, especially modern Western theater. Authors such as Chekhov, Gorky, Kafka, Woolf, Eliot, Spender, Sartre, Camus, Hemingway, Brecht, Beckett, and Pinter appear in the essays as strategic points of reference for arguments about criticism, authorship, form, sexuality, the inbuilt obsolescence of avant-garde experiments in theater, and so on. Complementing the essays are a series of public and polemical forums for Rakesh's ideas: the 1966 "East-West Seminar" in Bombay, a conversation with the Soviet playwright Aleksei Arbuzov (date unavailable), a long interview with Carlo Coppola (recorded in 1968 and published in 1973), and a national "Roundtable on the Contemporary Relevance of Traditional Theatre," organized by the Sangeet Natak Akademi in 1971. His most complex intercultural experience came in 1970–71, when he visited Geneva, Moscow, Vienna, Prague, Munich, Paris, London, East and West Berlin, Copenhagen, Stockholm, and Helsinki to gather materials for his Nehru Fellowship project titled "The Dramatic Word." At the time of his death, Rakesh was preparing to visit Southeast Asia and the United States for further research, and he left behind an outline of the project in English that forms an appendix to *Natya-vimarsha.*

In view of this internationalism, Rakesh's modernity could be regarded as an effect of his engagement with what Eugenio Barba calls, in a different context, "the common borders of the profession of theater."[14] But his modernist positions, much more than Bharati's, are pointedly and consistently related to the sense of a radical rupture between the "old" and the "new" in mid-twentieth-century *Indian-language writing*—a break that is generational as well as historical because it coincides with the transition from colonial to postcolonial temporalities. Rakesh regards the event of Partition in 1947 as the beginning of a crisis that enveloped the generation of writers who came to maturity in the 1954 to 1964 period, giving this decade the same transformative role that the 1910s performed in Anglo-modernism. The immediate context of much of his theorizing is the emergence of the "new short story/novel" and the "new poetry" in Hindi, but the crucial general stance is a sense of absolute and irreconcilable difference from the preindependence generation, proclaimed in an essay appropriately titled "*Imaratein tutane par*" ("On the collapse of structures"):

> A new era does not begin in literature until the consciousness of the age has been converted into certain convictions and uncertainties. As long as some entrenched ideas continue to propel consciousness, the earlier age that is in decline does not come to an end. In the years after Partition, the clash between the outgoing and incoming eras has been constantly evident. . . . In this kind of battle, there are no grounds for give-and-take. . . . In the clash between an emerging consciousness and a collapsing traditionalism, any talk of a compromise, of "taking the good and rejecting the bad in both" seems pointless and unfounded. This is not a crisis of relative achievements, about what is good in one or the other, but of two radically opposite visions that cannot be reconciled under any circumstances.[15]

This sense of mutual antagonism appears unfailingly whenever Rakesh takes up generational relations among Hindi authors. Tongue firmly in cheek, he describes the phony complacency with which the old establishment has decided to label the new writing nonsensical, half-baked, and merely fashionable, so that it poses no threat to the edifice of Hindi literature. "The new writers," Rakesh asserts, "have no complaint at all that the critics of the older generation did not offer them recognition; rather, it's the critics who complain about the new people not wanting recognition from them. . . . They've not given themselves time to ponder why a generation that has no intellectual compatibility with them, whose creative values do not match their critical values, would place any importance on their validation, especially when they have placed the bar of convention across their own receptivity?" (*BK*, 79).

The embeddedness of these arguments in the particularities of modern Hindi writing is self-evident, but throughout his career Rakesh also asserted the need to conceptualize a transregional Indian modernity independent of Western models. In an essay intriguingly titled "*Samajik-asamajik*"

(Social-antisocial), he complains that the debate about modernity and the new sensibility in India has always been dependent on extrinsic concepts of modernity, although there is no genuine relation between the two. Consequently, when derivative ideas are used to evaluate literary experiments at home, "either those ideas seem superficial and unfounded, or all of our literature begins to look shallow and backward" (*BK*, 85). In the mimetic genre of theater, there is an even greater need to avoid replicating the modes of developed nations because such imitations create a false sense of avant-gardism without accomplishing anything real. Elsewhere, Rakesh mocks those for whom "real life can only be lived outside this country, new literary experiments are possible only in other languages, the problems of the age are born only in the Atlantic and Pacific continents, and the true touch of modernity can be felt only in the air of Europe and America" (*BK*, 109). His unease is in line with Partha Chatterjee's argument that "modernity was a contextually located and enormously contested idea" in India because "in the world arena of modernity, we are outcastes, untouchables," while in the Indian arena writers were not able to subscribe to any uniform concept of modernity "irrespective of geography, time, environment or social conditions."[16] "Ours is the modernity of the once-colonized," Chatterjee observes, and his enabling move is to derive the particular from the universal: "if there is any universal or universally applicable definition of modernity, it is this: that by teaching us to employ the methods of reason, universal modernity enables us to identify our own particular modernity."[17] Rakesh's particular modernity demands that Indian-language theater first give adequate expression to the existence around it, and only then approach the national and the global.

Conversely, with immediate everyday experience as his main focus, Rakesh also sees no incompatibility between modernity and the categories of "Indianness" and "intrinsic tradition" that were valorized after independence. In an essay whose title can be translated as "The elements of modernity versus the elements of Indianness," he poses his arguments on this subject as a set of questions: "What is this Indianness? Is Indian tradition an inert static substance or an endlessly amplifying current? Is it necessarily antithetical to so-called modernity? Is this modernity a necessary demand of history or merely a charade to fill our own inner void with mawkish foreign imitations? And above all, is there an opposition between universality and national traditions in the realm of art?"[18]

Like Bharati, Rakesh therefore rejects a shallow dependence on the West as well as appeals to intrinsic tradition and essential Indianness. What he does formulate is a powerful argument for an indigenized (not vernacular) modernism that can deal with the sprawling chaos of contemporary Indian life without resorting to either derivativeness or dogmatic revivalism. The traditions of living, he argues, have precedence over the traditions of art, and the issue of tradition has to be considered in relation to the life of the people, not only in relation to literature.

Rakesh's modernism in the theater consists, then, in a rupture from the "modern" practices of the previous century, a revaluation of the playwright as artist, a focus on the word as the defining element in drama, and an unsentimental approach to the nation's past and present. His distaste for and alienation from colonial theater formations are made explicit in his criticism. Parsi theater in his view was a ridiculous spectacle modeled on second-rate Western theater that could create only a "low and rotten" legacy for theater in Hindi. Harishchandra was a pioneer who failed due to limited means and the absence of support, whereas Prasad "broke away from the Parsi company traditions, but neither advanced Bhartendu's tradition nor created any sign of a new tradition in theater."[19] Both literary playwrights separated "drama-as-verbal-text" from "theater-as-popular-performance," but the effect especially of Prasad's refined language, thematic gravity, and literary perfection was such that "the very consciousness of the relationship between drama and the stage disappeared" from the playwright's craft (*NV*, 38).

Imagining a future in which "drama" and "theater" can achieve parity is therefore a crucial move for Rakesh, and his revisionary aesthetic places the playwright-artist at the center of both activities. A 1966 English essay titled "Looking Around as a Playwright" sets the tone by describing the act of writing as the expression of an irrepressible urge and a psychic struggle:

> What concerns me most is my desire to write, or to put it more aptly, my inability to help writing plays. The forces inside and outside me create a sort of compulsion. . . . to express and communicate something that is by its own nature dramatic. . . . I find myself under the sway of this something happening to me as well as around me; something that is a force, a conflict and a terrible irony. At every step it strikes me down, but again lifts me to my feet—by that contradicting and negating itself. What is this great 'something'? I do not know. It is in the air, in the age, in me. I know it is there, but cannot give it a name. Maybe I want to write drama because I cannot give it a name.[20]

To persistent questions about why he chooses to write about certain things and not others, Rakesh's response is that "I cannot write, or try to write, like anyone else, because I am not anyone else. I write [in] a particular way . . . because I find facility in writing that way."[21] The importance of "writing" also leads him to question the claim that theater, like film, is a "director's medium": he is vitally invested in performance, but for him the dramatic text also exists apart from the staging process, and regarding the director as the sole orchestrator of the performance event is to create an artistic void in theater. Rakesh's arguments about the ideal conditions for translating text into performance are discussed further in the next section, but it is worth noting here that there is no discursive or creative context in which he is willing to cede the priority of the playwright as author, and of drama as text.

This textualist conception is also inseparable from the instrumental role of language in theater, embodied in what Rakesh persistently calls "the dramatic word." "The problem of wrestling with language for the sake of expression," he comments, "comes before every writer—that is, before every alert and sensitive writer," because the attempt to articulate feeling is always "incomplete." Language is also for Rakesh both a "primitive" and a "finite" instrument, and the "graphs of sensation" are so complex that the act of writing always leaves behind a residual anguish about what has remained unsaid (*BK*, 71). Much of this struggle for expression evokes the well-known passage in the final movement of T. S. Eliot's "Burnt Norton": "Words strain, / Crack, and sometimes break, under the burden, / Under the tension, slip, slide, perish, / Decay with imprecision, will not stay in place / Will not stay still."[22] But this writerly conflict symptomatic of high modernism does not preclude Rakesh's firm, even stubborn insistence on language as the sine qua non of drama, especially in the postcinema age. In a conversation with the Soviet playwright Aleksei Arbuzov (titled "*Rangmanch aur shabda*" [Theater and the word]), he argues that drama and theater have to be regarded as primarily verbal-aural rather than visual forms because in mimetic terms aurality is what separates drama from film: "the fundamental difference between the two mediums is that in one, the visual expectation gives birth to the word, and in the other, the verbal expectation gives birth to the scene" (*NV*, 65). Words and images are certainly interdependent in both media, but the word is central to drama, and the image to film.

Rakesh clarifies, however, that word-centeredness in theater does not enforce "literariness"—words do not have to achieve literary effects but the resonances appropriate to a particular dramatic structure. He is also predictably unfazed by the charge that his thinking may be determined by "drama" rather than other forms of theater because his "prime concern," he declares, "is with this form of theater only."[23] For Rakesh, a rejection of the word would eventually challenge the very existence of "dramatic theater" because "all efforts to expand the visual possibilities of theater through technological legerdemain eventually only underscore its limitations and vulnerability in comparison with film" (*NV*, 68). In the exchange with Arbuzov, he also resists the suggestion that the issues of word and language may have a disproportionate significance in postindependence India because "in a broader perspective they are also the fundamental questions for theater everywhere" (*NV*, 70). To sum up, Rakesh locates the uniqueness of theater not in its mimetic qualities (which it shares with film) or even in the fact of live performance but in the creation of a living idiom for the stage, which he describes as the playwright's particular challenge.

Finally, Rakesh is led by the shape of his own theatrical career to reconcile the principle of modernity with the historical matter from antiquity that formed the basis of two of the three full-length plays published in his lifetime. The first play, *Ashadh ka ek din* (see chapter 1), used the figure of Kalidasa to offer its ironic portrait of the artist caught between the provincial sources of his poetic inspiration and the ambiguous attractions of metropolitan patronage. The second play, *Laharon ke rajhans* (The royal swans on the waves, 1963), symbolically evoked the tension and malaise in the palace of the Buddha's stepbrother, Nanda, as Nanda inexorably loses interest in a life of married luxury with his wife, Sundari, and sets out at the end to seek the eightfold path of enlightenment. In the case of Kalidasa, Rakesh was accused of passing off fiction as "history" for the sole purpose of debasing the symbol of Indian literary greatness. But after the success of *Laharon ke rajhans* he was also accused of turning his back on an unmanageable present by retreating into a pristine past.

Rakesh's rejoinders to the criticism leveled at him are part of my discussion of myth and history as narrative sources for modernist drama, and *Laharon ke rajhans* as one of the "palimpsests of the past" (see chapter 3), so his relationship to the remote Indian past will come in for further consideration. But in a compensatory move, in his third full-length play, *Adhe adhure* (Incomplete, unfinished, 1969), he "tried to grasp the realities of the life around me in a straightforward way, and tried to search for a language that would be the language of ordinary conversation and accessible to the largest numbers of spectators" (*NV*, 155). The play was hailed immediately as a classic of the nuclear family's material and emotional collapse within the circumscribed space of the contemporary urban middle-class home. Its status as a modernist tour de force—as a work that carefully matches Rakesh's aesthetic with an arch-contemporary setting—rests on its particular integration of form and content, theme and treatment. It takes up a "foundational discourse" of modern drama—the representation of home as a place of victimage from which the protagonist struggles to escape for the sake of autonomy and selfhood—and transforms it through a stylized, indigenized realism that poignantly captures the conjuncture of failed ambitions, spaces, and relationships in the postcolonial metropole. Furthermore, just as Rakesh's first two plays intervene in the postindependence preoccupation with myth and history, his innovations in *Adhe adhure* consolidate the forms of modernist realism in postindependence theater.

Tendulkar: The Private, the Social, and the Public

The Marathi playwright Vijay Tendulkar (1928–2008) is another iconic postindependence figure whose work can be positioned productively in relation to global modernisms, but his styles of introspection and connection to the world are substantially different from those of Bharati or Rakesh. Like Rakesh, he offers systematic reflections on drama and theater in volumes such as *Natak ani mi* (The theater and I, 1997) and *The Play Is the Thing* (also 1997), and in self-reflexive essays such as "*Majhe lekhan kashasathi*" (What is my writing for?, 1988) and "A Testament" (1992). However, Tendulkar's theory and criticism do not have the ambitious planetary sweep of Bharati and Rakesh: he focuses mainly on his own practice, the work of other playwrights in Marathi, and selectively on writing in other Indian languages rather than on the global crisis of modernity, the East/West problem, or the imperatives of decolonization. A second point of difference is that he practices multiple prose genres as do Rakesh and Bharati, but his main output is in and for the theater—nearly fifty full-length and one-act plays (some more experimental than others) that explore the interpenetration of the domestic, the social, and the political in contemporary urban settings in India, employing the mode of social realism.[24] Tendulkar's screenplays for films such as *Nishant* (Night's end, 1975), *Manthan* (The churning, 1976), and *Akrosh* (Rage, 1980) extend a gritty realism to the problems of caste and class exploitation in the countryside, making him the foremost (and still unequaled) crossover from theater to parallel cinema. Finally, Tendulkar maintains that a writer for the theater can succeed only through firsthand experience *of* the theater. From the beginning, his career as a playwright, unlike that of Bharati or Rakesh, involved close collaboration with two key experimental theater groups in Marathi—Vijaya Mehta's Rangayan, which brought his early work onto the stage, and Awishkar, which he cofounded with the acting duo of Arvind and Sulabha Deshpande in 1974. As the title of this section suggests, Tendulkar's portrait of the artist is thus uniquely balanced between the personal, the social, and the public as he negotiates the genres of drama, theater, and performance.

At the beginning of the three Shri Ram Memorial Lectures published as *The Play Is the Thing* (1997), Tendulkar repeats two claims that have appeared in his essays, lectures, addresses to the reader, and reminiscences for half a century: "more than a playwright I consider myself to be a writer"; and, "I love to indulge in the physical process of writing. I enjoy this process even when there is nothing to be said."[25] In the short essay "*Majhe lekhan kashasathhi?*," which has the quality of a condensed artistic autobiography, Tendulkar describes writing as an activity that was embedded in his consciousness from early boyhood, but developed into a compensatory obsession in adolescence around the time the Quit India movement of 1942 disrupted his education. Separated from friends and alienated from family members, he turned to words in desperation and "wrote with a singular concentration. Wrote anything, anyhow. Wrote without thinking about what it would lead to. In the isolation of my mind, I had secured the companionship of writing."[26] In the decades that followed, as Tendulkar moved frenetically between the worlds of theater, cinema, political journalism, long and short fiction, children's theater, and television, there was no time to ask what the writing was *for*: "I wrote like a man seized by a fever, whose head was full of the hallucinatory clamor of many stories. I kept myself alive, and kept writing. There were no boundaries left to separate writing from living. Like breathing, seeing, and speaking, writing had become a law of the body."[27] Such a visceral connection to his vocation does not preclude times of frustration, disappointment, and even rage at unreceptive audiences, but his discontent never translates into a rejection of the writer's life because "at the very next moment I realize that this is not possible. Not possible at all. Just as one cannot breathe in and out at a distance from one's body, or separate oneself from the assault of anxieties while remaining alive, I cannot detach myself from this process of writing. I and it are one. As with Siamese twins, this is a bond from birth to death. It will break only on one day . . . forever."[28]

The intuitive nature of Tendulkar's authorial life leads "naturally" to the view that creativity is not a matter of deliberate calculation, rational control, or soothing sublimations but is an ungovernable impulse that takes the writer in unexpected, even unwanted directions. Writing, he observes impressionistically, is the "result of grief over something, anger at something, joy about something in life," and it "begins not from an idea but from an experience, mine or somebody else's which then becomes mine."[29] In one of his most public self-reflections—the 1994 acceptance speech for the Saraswati Samman (a major Indian literary prize)—Tendulkar acknowledges that his work has often been an assault on social norms, but he has never apologized for his choices because "I could not have written anything other than what I wrote. . . . I could not have done anything other than writing."[30] Characteristically, Tendulkar's major collection of writings on theater in Marathi, *Natak ani mi*, posits his own complicated selfhood as the focal point in relation to which the public and the collaborative medium of theater unfolds. His many declarations of artistic independence as a theater professional may strike us as unusually intense, even "romantic," but they differ only in degree, not in kind, from the modernist self-positioning of major playwrights in every theatrically active language, including Bharati and Rakesh in Hindi, Girish Karnad in Kannada, Mahesh Elkunchwar in Marathi, Mohit Chattopadhyay in Bengali, Madhu Rye in Gujarati, and Mahesh Dattani in English.

This emphasis on the personal and the intimate is reconciled in interesting ways with the high modernist principles of "impersonality" and "depersonalization" in Tendulkar's thought as well as craft. In an essay strategically titled "A Testament," he produces his own version of T. S. Eliot's separation between "the man who suffers and the mind which creates" by positing a distinction between his "social being" and his "creative self."

> As an individual—rather as a social being—I feel deeply involved in the present state of my society. . . . But when I look back at what I have written during these years, and what I have been doing as a conscious social being, I find

that my writing reflects a mind which is distinctly different from the mind which acts in real life as a socially aware person.

As a writer I now find myself persistently inquisitive, nonconformist, ruthlessly cold and brutal as compared to the other committed and human me. The writer me is more analytical than emotionally committed one way or the other. The writer me raises inconvenient questions instead of choosing his side and passionately claiming thereafter that it is always the right one. The writer me refuses to provide—or go by—new or old solutions. . . .

As a social being I am against all exploitation, and I passionately feel all exploitation must end. As a writer I feel fascinated by the violent exploited-exploiter relationship, and obsessively delve deep into it instead of taking a position against it. That takes me to a point where I feel that relationship is eternal, a fact of life however cruel, and will never end. (*POM*, 278–80)

The creative self, passionate about creativity, is detached and unsentimental in its social vision, whereas the social self is idealistic. The plays, in turn, deal so extensively with the minutiae of lower- and middle-class urban life in a dystopian postcolonial present that they transcend the boundaries of their region and have earned Tendulkar the status of postindependence India's first "national" playwright.

An equally important, complementary arena for the sublimation of the self is the theater itself. Tendulkar defines a playwright as "one who is willing to devote his prime years to learn and internalize this demanding art," and a play as "a performing art and not literature. Unless you learn the techniques of enactment . . . and internalize them fully, you will not be able to write a good playable play with a content of its own" (*PTT*, 1, 18). Because of his father's involvement with amateur groups that still used cross-dressed actors in the 1930s, he was exposed early to the "mystique of the theater" and developed what he calls a "subconscious and unquenched desire to explore by myself the magic and the beauty of this form" (*PTT*, 9). At the beginning of the essay "*Majhe natyashikshana*" (My theater education), Tendulkar notes that he learned the craft of theater by following a series of pragmatic imperatives: "Read the celebrated foreign plays. Watch the plays around us, both good and bad. Plunge headlong into one's own plays and see what happens. Improve oneself through one's mistakes. Engage in discussions with others like oneself. This is primarily how my own theater education took place."[31] Once he had begun writing seriously, the rehearsal hall became the crucial place for learning by trial and error. It was while watching the rehearsals for a Marathi production of Ionesco's *The Chairs*, for instance, that Tendulkar "sensed a calculated and measured structure under its absurdist surface and then in the rehearsals that followed I realized fully the exciting and innovative theatricality of the masterpiece with its theme of boredom" (*PTT*, 17). Tendulkar's work for the theater thus depends vitally on the experience of spectatorship, and represents, in the postindependence field, a singularly unconventional balance between the private writerly self and the public world of the stage within the boundaries of a modernist aesthetic.

THE PERFORMANCE OF MODERNISM: DEFERRAL AND ACTUALIZATION

The decommercialization of urban theater in the mid-twentieth century, and the formation of what I have described elsewhere as a "new national" canon over the next four decades, are two contradictory but equally real events indicating that in contemporary India the relationship between drama and theater, text and performance, differs markedly from Western models in which an extensive network of commercial or state-supported theaters exists to organize the regular staging of new and old works.[32] As noted previously, after 1950 some playwrights created major works without any sense of connection with a theater tradition, and others were actively interested in performance but struggled to devise the conditions under which their work could reach the stage. Despite these handicaps, there is continuous theater activity from the early 1950s onward, and a large number of new plays acquire dense, multilingual performance histories because of the determined collaborative effort of directors, actors, and other theater professionals who occupy a range of material and institutional positions. In my view, these (once again) paradoxical outcomes are possible because the basic constituent elements of theater practice—choice of plays, directing methods, acting styles, performance spaces, mise-en-scènes, audiovisual design features, and audience outreach/reception—are also informed to a large extent by modernist aesthetics, with only certain forms of activist, propagandist, and avant-garde theater lying clearly beyond this pale.

In the absence of a theatrical marketplace, I suggest, therefore, that the performance of modernism in postindependence India involves two mechanisms—a process of *deferral*, in which major modernist plays are written with no specific expectation or certainty of performance; and a process of *actualization*, in which a variety of institutional structures emerge to ensure nationwide circulation and multilingual performance for the modernist oeuvre, again without any predictable regularity. The erratic nature of theater work is most starkly evident in the early decades of independence when the new systems are taking shape, but with a few exceptions, irregularity continues to be a defining feature of urban stages, exercising long-term effects on the possibilities of performance.

Performance Deferred: The Divergence of "Drama" and "Theater"

The postindependence disconnection between the writing/publication of major plays and the possibility of their enactment takes a number of different forms that are most vividly described by the playwrights themselves. I focus here on three key figures—Rakesh, who appeared in the previous section as a paradigmatic self-fashioning modernist; Girish Karnad (1938–2019), who claimed a primary identity as playwright despite an active lifelong career as actor, director, and screenwriter for film and television; and Mahesh Elkunchwar (born in 1939), who is now among the last few living members of the first generation of postindependence playwrights. Between them, these authors represent three major theatrical languages—Hindi, Kannada, and Marathi—and three distinct regions—Delhi and the Hindi belt in the north; the west-central state of Maharashtra, which includes the theatrically vital metropolis of Bombay/Mumbai; and Karnataka, one of the four major southern states and another active site of theater activity. The similarities between their predicaments underscore the "national" scope of the problems they describe, which in turn affects numerous other contemporaries as well. But it is also important to reiterate that despite these conditions none of the playwrights I discuss has produced any closet drama.

Mohan Rakesh's short prefaces to the first two editions of his first play, *Ashadh ka ek din*, are like early diagrams of the initial separation of postindependence drama from the circuits of performance. The first preface makes three critical assertions—drama in Hindi has no living connection with any particular theatrical tradition; the achievements of Western theater, however considerable, cannot redress this lack because they are unconnected with the rhythms of life in India; and the development of the Hindi stage cannot depend on the intervention of governmental or semigovernmental institutions. "The question is not merely one of economic convenience but also of a certain cultural vision," Rakesh argues, and the Hindi theater will have to emerge naturally from its own environment if it is to express the "desires and aspirations of its audience."[33] Rakesh considers "theatrical experimentation" on the part of the playwright the stimulus that will bring "the constitutive features of this stage ... to life," and notes optimistically that "it will continue in the hands of capable actors and directors" (*ODSR*, 220). He also hopes that his play would "contribute something towards the *search for those possibilities* (*ODSR*, 220; emphasis added). In this theater culture, everything is therefore latent; nothing has been achieved or actualized. The second preface reinforces the idea of deferral by recording that despite the efforts of some "friends" in the cities of Delhi and Lucknow there are no concrete prospects for a production of *Ashadh*. Rakesh's preference would have been to publish the play after it had received a major production because the text could then reflect the lessons of rehearsals and the eventual staging. But given the contingent responses to his play, he is pragmatic enough to acknowledge that "it will take us some years to get to that stage" (*ODSR*, 221).[34] His disappointment is made more poignant by a comment in a letter of August 7, 1958, to his close friend and mentor, the Hindi writer Upendranath Ashk: "I've written the play strictly for the stage, so I'd ... like to know your thoughts about its actability" (*ODSR*, 222).

Rakesh's preeminence in the discourse of modernist deferral is strengthened by the clarity with which he defines the qualities of the kind of urban theater he *would* like to see taking shape in postindependence India. The criticism he published in the 1960s elaborates on three crucial concerns. First, theater should cultivate its distinctive characteristics and maximize its own potential, instead of getting caught up in a game of technical one-upmanship with the medium of film that it is bound to lose. In the essay titled "Theater Without Walls," Rakesh argues that the "overelaboration of technical devices and an increasing dependence on them, in the given conditions here, is more likely to retard the growth of theater and confine it to a groove that may not let it expand into new shapes through its own dynamism."[35] Having defined language and a stage "idiom" that speaks to its own time as the heart of the new theater, he also views this approach as a solution to the problem of resources: "A technically well-appointed and complex theater is certainly one direction of development, but there is a second course different from it, and that is the course I feel our experimental theater can follow. This direction is one of enhancing the verbal and human dimension of theater—in other words, of being able to perform the most complex experiments with minimal resources. It is here that the place of the literary craftsman becomes important in theater—far more important than we have been able to grasp so far" (*POM*, 237).

Second, if the Hindi stage is really to represent the "cultural desires and aspirations" of its immediate audience, it has to stop engaging in pretentious but shallow avant-garde gestures derived from the West. In "*Natakkar aur rangamanch*" (The Playwright and the Stage), Rakesh explains how his aspirational goals separate him from the "mimic men" of his generation: "[Their] vision is concerned with giving the stage a 'new' and 'modern' look from the outside, and not with searching for a theatre within our personal lives and circumstances. For that quest we need a deep understanding of our life and environment—a clear recognition of the theatrical possibilities of the assaults and counter-assaults on our sensibilities. Only this quest can lead us in the direction of really new experiments, and *give shape to that stagecraft with which even we have not yet become acquainted*" (*POM*, 236–37; emphasis added). Clearly, two decades after independence and a decade after his first play, Rakesh is still imagining a *future* theater craft, reflecting the slow progress of productive artistic partnerships between playwrights and theater-makers in even the most theatrically active cities.

The third major problem with the nascent theater culture is addressed in the same essay: "in our country, especially in Hindi, there's simply no well-organized theatre of the kind of which the playwright may be imagined as an integral part; and . . . the intellectual framework for such an imagining has also remained quite undeveloped until now" (*POM*, 234). Rakesh finds unacceptable a situation in which the living playwright is merely a guest or an alien presence outside the dynamics of the rehearsal process, or in which the two intimately connected spheres of experiment—text and performance—remain disjunct. His ideal vision for the future is therefore of a "playwright's theatre" that is based on close collaboration between the playwright, the director, and the actors but that "accept[s] the playwright as the focal point of the theatrical imagination" (*POM*, 237). Although the problem of deferral belongs squarely to the sphere of *theater, not drama*, Rakesh is passionate in his belief that playwrights can find real fulfillment only if they work proactively to participate in, and bring about, the performance event.

Unlike Rakesh, who came to playwriting after postsecondary degrees in Hindi, English, and Sanskrit literature and a particular interest in the Sanskrit poet-playwright Kalidasa, Girish Karnad was a master's student in Statistics at Bombay University when he experienced a moment of epiphany while watching Ebrahim Alkazi's production of August Strindberg's naturalist classic, *Miss Julie*. Recalling "the power and violence I experienced that day" in an essay titled "Theater in India," Karnad connects the new psychology of the play to the new stage technology that included technical devices like dimmers. "The two together defined a stage that was like nothing we had known or suspected," he notes: "I have often wondered whether it wasn't that evening that, without being actually aware of it, I decided I wanted to be a playwright."[36]

Karnad's first play, *Yayati* (1961), was written two years after this experience, during a time of emotional turmoil as he prepared to leave India on a Rhodes Scholarship to study philosophy, politics, and economics at Oxford. Both the subject of the play—an episode in the classical Sanskrit epic, the *Mahabharata*—and its language—Kannada rather than English—took him by surprise because his "modern" neocolonial education had steered him toward poetry in English as a vocation. A more serious crisis, however, was the forced choice of a form that had been available to him only at a textual level, and at a considerable cultural distance: "Oddly enough the play owed its form . . . to Western playwrights whom until then I had only read in print: Anouilh (his *Antigone* particularly) and also Sartre, O'Neill, and the Greeks. That is, at the most intense moment of self-expression, while my past had come to my aid with a ready-made narrative within which I could contain and explore my insecurities, there had been no dramatic structure in my own tradition to which I could relate myself."[37]

The source of the crisis, as Karnad acknowledged, was that "to my generation, a hundred crowded years of urban theatre seemed to have left almost nothing to hang on to, to take off from. And where was one to begin again?"[38] He saw the same question being posed by the 1950s masterpiece, Dharamvir Bharati's *Andha yug* (1954), which was "actually written for the radio, as a play for voices. It was as if, at the time of conceiving the play, the playwright could imagine no stage on which to place it."[39] Indeed, Bharati's play received its first production, and established its credentials as "genuine theatre," only when the upcoming director Satyadev Dubey took it up as a challenge in 1962. The makeshift "stage" for this production, which is now recognized as a landmark event in Indian theater, was the rooftop of director Ebrahim Alkazi's apartment building in Bombay's Kamballa Hill area.

Karnad's second play, *Tughlaq*, was also written at Oxford, in response to a challenge by the critic Kirtinath Kurtkoti that there were no good modern historical plays in Kannada. The subject of the play, Delhi's fourteenth-century Muslim sultan Muhammad bin Tughlaq, was discovered in a textbook of Indian history in the Bodleian Library, and this time Karnad adapted the conventions of the obsolete Parsi commercial stage because he discounted the possibility of performance altogether: "No one had thought of putting *Yayati* on the stage. I thought my second play would meet the same fate. Why not write a play on a grand scale? A play involving about fifty characters!"[40] Karnad was particularly attracted by the careful social hierarchy Parsi theater maintained in its historical-political extravaganzas through the spatial alternation of "deep" and "shallow" scenes on the proscenium stage. But he found the distinctions dissolving under the weight of his postcolonial thematic, which in part conjures the historically unprecedented exercise of political rights by a massive urban-rural Indian electorate after independence. The monumental production of the play in 1974, again by Alkazi, abandoned the nod to Parsi theater and the conventional stage altogether and placed the action on the ramparts of the Purana Qila (Old Fort), a sixteenth century monument on the banks of the Yamuna River in New Delhi. Interestingly, Karnad's artistic and geographical disengagement from Indian theater in *Yayati* and *Tughlaq* was redressed by the theater itself. The unexpectedly strong reception of both plays in print and performance during the 1960s led the author to rethink his relationship with drama and committed him to playwriting as the principal vocation in a long artistic career that included the mediums of film and television. But unlike Rakesh and Tendulkar, Karnad's authorial reflections were not "self"-centered, and despite his work as a director in the other media, he did not offer theoretical or polemical arguments about the direction he wanted an emergent postindependence theater to take.

Mahesh Elkunchwar offers yet another contrast to both Rakesh and Karnad. Belonging to a brahman family that was part of the land-owning *wada* culture in the northeastern Vidarbha region of Maharashtra, he came of age in the city of Nagpur, which was entirely lacking in any regular theater activity during that period. He was, instead, an aficionado of new wave European cinema, Hollywood, and classical music, until *his* accidental encounter in 1965 with a touring production of Vijay Tendulkar's play, *Mi jinkalo! mi haralo!* (I won, I lost, 1963), which a friend persuaded him to try out because tickets to the film they had set out to see were sold out: "What I went through is what is called an *'electrifying experience'*. . . . And at that very moment, doors somewhere inside me of which I was unaware until then began to open rapidly, one after the other. For no reason, I began to feel the confidence and conviction that this is something I must do, that this would agree with me" (*POM*, 376).

The first attempts at playwriting, however, were a failure, and even after Elkunchwar began producing work that he found satisfactory, he did not think of performance as a concrete possibility: his first seven plays were published in the leading Marathi literary magazine *Satyakatha*, reaching a highbrow *readership*. Another accident brought the published plays to the attention of Vijaya Mehta, the accomplished woman director who had also brought Tendulkar's early plays to the stage, and according to Elkunchwar, "it was only when Vijayabai did my one-act plays for Rangayan that I discovered for the first time they were also worthy of performance" (*POM*, 377).

The effect of this affirmation—the "new knowledge that what I wrote could come onto the stage and even stand on its own"—was to generate a succession of ambitious plays in which Elkunchwar skirted the ideologically driven contemporary interest in folk forms, "Indianness," and politically "committed" work, and appeared instead in the vanguard of an experimentally driven urban realism. His lifelong modernist commitment has been to the process of *writing*, and to the creation of plays that connect authentically with his own temperament and experience, so that the sociopolitical subtext of his drama is rooted in the deeply personal. Although his major plays have acquired dense performance histories, like Karnad he has little to say about theater as an institution, and his criticism is almost confessional in its introspections rather than overtly theoretical or polemical. In many of these respects, Elkunchwar's self-positioning is surprisingly close to that of his idol Tendulkar, although the latter's association with Rangayan and Awishkar would seem to place him in the opposite category of authors whose playwriting is an extension of their direct involvement with the theater. Yet, as noted previously, Tendulkar also regards writing as a compulsive, self-sufficient act, disengaged from the obligation to "say anything." Rakesh, Karnad, and Elkunchwar exemplify three different yet similar versions of the process by which major modernist careers in the theater are launched in paradoxical disjunction from any form of institutionalized theater activity. It is worth noting in conclusion that this "accidental" quality of authorship extends to a number of other leading playwrights. Badal Sircar (1925–2011) was trained as an architect and urban planner in Calcutta and wrote his first groundbreaking plays while on a multiyear professional assignment in Nigeria. Satish Alekar (1949–) was born into a prominent political family and was a biochemist by profession until he took early retirement at the age of fifty to direct the Lalit Kala Kendra (Performing arts center) at Pune University. G. P. Deshpande (1938–2013), one of the two most prominent political playwrights of his generation, was a professor of political science and a scholar of China with a lifelong career at Jawaharlal Nehru University in New Delhi. Indira Parthasarathy (born 1930) and Chandrashekhar Kambar (born 1937) were also academics in the cities of Chennai and Bangalore, respectively. The next section deals with the multifaceted processes of theatricalization that began in the 1950s and turned (modernist) drama into theater, but what sets these processes into motion is an extraordinary constellation of authors who create, obsessively and "unexpectedly," the plays that need actualization.

Performance Realized: "Drama" as "Theater"

MAKING THEATER OUTSIDE THE MARKETPLACE: ARTISTS AND INSTITUTIONS

The numerous means by which a substantial body of important new drama becomes part of a culture of urban performance in late-twentieth-century India bring into play the full dynamics of a postindependence theatrical field struggling to replace the dismantled colonial marketplace. This modernist reconciliation of artistic quality and stageability is markedly different from the proto-modernist antitheatricalism of colonial literary playwrights such as Tagore, Harishchandra, and Prasad, which echoes Euromodernist efforts to bypass the compromising effects of live performance and preserve the "true" nature of (poetic) drama. In contrast, postindependence theater artists, including the modernists, are opposed not to *theater* and *theatricality* per se but to the imperatives of *commercialism*, which they see as prejudicial to their art. One of their key objectives is to bridge the gap between literariness and performability, so they reject the "theater-for-lowbrow-entertainment" model entirely, but they also either critique or ignore their "highbrow" colonial-era precursors. Interestingly, the demise of colonial institutions and the inability of postindependence theater to reorganize itself as a capitalized "industry" accomplishes *by default* the goal of keeping theater away from the profit motive, but the institutional transition is also accompanied by fully articulated modernist positions.

The process of reorientation begins in the 1940s with the IPTA's populist politics and the bourgeois-nationalist vision of state-supported theaters developed by policy makers such as Kamaladevi Chattopadhyay, with the 1956 Drama Seminar registering a decisive discursive shift toward the second model. Mulk Raj Anand, one of the leading modernists in Anglophone Indian fiction, argues in this forum that "we cannot follow the Western system of founding a chain of grandiose closed theatres in India, in blind imitation of the West and merely mount plays in those theatres according to the commercial techniques discarded by the most advanced experts in Europe."[41] Sombhu Mitra provides the practitioner's version of Anand's modernist argument by noting that "in our country, the professional stage has not been able to fulfil its mission satisfactorily.... In order, therefore, to establish a good theatre tradition in our country, it would be necessary to create the conditions in which the amateur theatre movement may survive, may grow."[42] In a paper setting out in detail the artistic training of the actor, Ebrahim Alkazi, soon to be the transformative second director of the National School of Drama, claims that "there is only one legitimate type of modern theatre. And that is what is known as *avant-garde* theatre, which, I assert, is the very 'nature' of theatre.... [T]he state to which the actor should aspire is that of the poet, the lover and the fool."[43]

Seven decades after this modernist commitment to seriousness, artistic quality, experimentation, and ingenuity in theater, we are in a position to grasp how a geographically dispersed and multilingual but noncommercial field of theater practice manages to survive, and occasionally even thrive. The institutional structures, material arrangements, and patterns of interpersonal connection instrumental to postindependence theater as an operational terrain fall into several categories. The most important of these is the theater group, organization, or company founded by an actor-director who remains connected with it for an extended period of time (usually for three or four decades), providing artistic leadership and shepherding resources. Sombhu Mitra's group Bohurupee in Calcutta (formed in 1949), and Ebrahim Alkazi's Theater Group in Bombay (formed in 1951), become pioneering models that are replicated in metropolitan and provincial urban locations around the country, and the goal common to all of these ventures is to offer professional quality theater despite the absence of regular sources of material support. In a smaller subset of this arrangement, the founding figure is a major playwright in addition to being an actor and director, and so the group becomes the primary conduit for their authorial output as well. This variation includes Habib Tanvir and Naya Theater (Delhi), Utpal Dutt and the People's Little Theater (Calcutta), Badal Sircar and Satabdi (Calcutta), K. N. Panikkar and Sopanam (Trivandrum), Ratan Thiyam and the Chorus Repertory Theater (Imphal), and Mahesh Dattani and Playpen (Bangalore). In both instances, the economics of theater production is in a constant state of precarity. Groups survive through private and corporate funding, ticket sales, and subsidized theater spaces; there is no regular annual season; rehearsal space is difficult to arrange and afford; actors are not always paid; and audiences are small although often stable and supportive of the work of particular directors and groups.[44]

The simultaneously impossible and indispensable existence of these groups and organizations from the viewpoint of an artistically fulfilling theater is summed up poignantly by Sombhu Mitra: "[B]ehind the country-wide renaissance for theatre, the main driving force is that of a few actors and actresses who are crazy about the theatre. Their madness for theatre is so intense and deep-rooted that on the one hand the nerve shattering race for earning a livelihood, and on the other hand, the irresistible desire to stage good plays and the unending blind meaningless obstacles in the fulfilment of that desire continuously try to batter them down, but never completely succeed."[45] In the 1970s, Badal Sircar offers a less flamboyant but equally resolute model of collaborative theater activity in his individualized definition of the "group theatre," which "rests on the resolution that theatre will neither be a commodity nor a mere pastime. Most of those who come to this theatre are not well off but they do not look to theatre either as a profession or as a means to earn money" (*POM*, 288). The usual practice of ticket sales is therefore replaced by the principle of low-cost voluntary membership for those who can afford it, and free access to theater for those who cannot.

Mitra and Sircar pinpoint the tensions I perceive as fundamentally generative for the performance of modernism in postindependence India, especially because their goals also create the right conditions under which modernist playwrights develop lifelong creative partnerships with one or more directors, often with very little expectation of financial return. The link between Tendulkar/Elkunchwar and Vijaya Mehta/Rangayan has already been mentioned. Similarly crucial relationships developed between Rakesh and Shyamanand Jalan in Calcutta, Karnad and Satyadev Dubey in Bombay, or Mahesh Dattani and Alyque Padamsee, also in Bombay, and these relationships are again symptomatic of the process by which the work of many other playwrights reaches the stage. Director-led groups fuel the determination that plays *have* to be brought onto the stage, but in the "right" way, with due regard for the artistry, talent, and integrity of all those involved in the production process. In addition, they carry out a major modernizing project by bringing world drama in translation to the urban Indian stage, and at the same time ensure the transregional circulation of new Indian plays, both in the original language and in translation.[46]

There are three major alternatives to the director/group model of theatrical actualization: state-supported institutions of theater training and patronage such as the National School of Drama (NSD) and the Sangeet Natak Akademi (SNA); private and public cultural organizations such as the Shri Ram Centre for Art and Culture in New Delhi and the National Centre for the Performing Arts and Prithvi Theatre in Bombay/Mumbai; and corporate sponsors such as the Tata and Mahindra companies. NSD supported the legendary careers of its two outstanding directors, Ebrahim Alkazi and B. V. Karanth, from 1962 to 1983, and has facilitated the directing work of numerous theatrically prominent faculty members, including Ram Gopal Bajaj, Devendra Raj Ankur, Anuradha Kapur, Tripurari Sharma, Kirti Jain, Robin Das, and K. Rajendran. Since its inception in 1999, the school's Bharat Rang Mahotsav (India theater festival) has also become the largest state-supported annual forum showcasing national and international theater. SNA supports the performing arts through its main office in New Delhi and branches in various states, offering fellowships, grants, awards, production subsidies, and festivals at the regional and national levels. The recipients of its most prestigious fellowship for theater, the Ratan Sadasyata (Diamond Membership), make up a virtual modernist constellation, and its fifteen-day Nehru Centenary Theatre Festival, held from September 3–17, 1989, could be described as the most high-profile modernist showcase of the late-twentieth century.[47] Among private organizations, the Shri Ram Centre has had an active Repertory Company since the 1960s, and Prithvi Theatre promotes specific playwrights and directors while providing affordable performance space to theater groups at large. Leading theater organizations such as Nandikar in Calcutta, Ranga Shankara in Bangalore, and Ninasam in Heggodu periodically organize theater festivals that showcase old and new work. Multinational companies, industrial houses, large businesses, and philanthropic organizations underwrite festivals and events of all shapes and sizes, and the privately endowed Mahindra Awards for Excellence in Theatre, which provide full financial support for the selected productions, have become a highly anticipated annual event. From the 1950s onward, multilingual and multiregional Indian theater therefore has offered a singular postcolonial perspective on the actualization of modernism in performance, sustained through artistic collaboration, private patronage, and government action.[48]

RECEIVING THEATER OUTSIDE THE MARKETPLACE: AUDIENCES ACROSS THE NATION

The final participants in a fluid postindependence performance culture are urban theater audiences, who in the modern Indian context display a number of unusual characteristics. Colonial theater institutions were devoted overwhelmingly to the entertainment for profit model, and playwrights who disapproved of this approach kept away from the commercial stage, so colonial audiences could be described broadly as "popular" and more or less "middlebrow." When this model ended in the 1940s and the new structures described earlier in this section began to take shape, audiences bifurcated into two observable streams. Theater as a form of popular entertainment continued, albeit on a smaller scale, in metropolitan locations such as Calcutta, Bombay, Delhi, Madras, Pune, Trivandrum, Bangalore, and Hyderabad, in languages such as Bengali, Marathi, Gujarati, Hindi, Panjabi, Tamil, Malayalam, Kannada, and Telugu; indeed, on a limited and erratic scale theater is still able to operate as a "business" in these locations. Spectatorship in a radically altered postindependence theater field, however, has involved a relatively small, primarily metropolitan audience shaped by a cosmopolitan education; a middle-to-upper class identity; an interest in the theater form; commitment to new Indian plays in their original languages and in translation; loyalty to the work of specific groups, directors, and performers; and interest in the repertoire of Western and world theater that was also being made available by the new generation of practitioners. The two constituencies overlap to some extent but also remain distinct because a portion of the membership in each category adheres exclusively to its own preferences. Since the 1950s, however, urban theater viewers of *all* kinds have formed a minuscule subset of the massive audience for proliferating popular and mass-cultural forms—film, television, video, and now the new electronic media. In addition, the audience's metropolitan/urban location has made it vulnerable to the rising problems of overpopulation, crowding, pollution, unmanageable traffic, expensive transportation, and high living costs, leading to a perceptible decline in theater attendance. As Girish Karnad noted presciently, theater audiences "all but disappeared, even in cities like Bombay," when Indian television discovered the soap opera genre in the mid-1980s, and the mass-cultural media are also now in active competition with each other.

> Ultimately all resources are limited, especially those that support the entertainment industry. There are more films made every year. There are more television channels. But they are all aimed at the same audience—mainly the urban middle class. And here, even apart from the competition between different media, what has queered the pitch is inflation. Bombay and Calcutta at least have cheap, reasonably efficient city transportation. But in Bangalore if a young couple want to go to the movies, they have to spend something like 75 rupees, excluding the tickets. No middle-class couple can keep that going. They prefer to rent a videotape for ten rupees and invite the neighbours over for a social evening.[49]

Despite the practical difficulties of access and affordability, however, there is unquestionably an audience for live urban theater in present-day India, and a significant proportion of it consists of "serious theater aficionados," or, to adapt Sombhu Mitra's vivid phrase, of viewers who are "crazy about the theatre."

In relation to this small, embattled, but persistent collectivity of spectators, a few initiatives in different parts of the country are worth noting for their boldness and lasting influence. After his return from London's Royal Academy of Dramatic Art in 1950, Alkazi's drive as founder-member of pioneering theater groups, artistic director, and national-level theater administrator was inseparable from his efforts to create and sustain audiences because effective communication between artists and those who experienced their work was "the real test of theatre" for him.[50] During his management of Theatre Group and Theatre Unit in Bombay (1950–1962), the emphasis was on Western theater in English and in English translation (T. S. Eliot, Sartre, Beckett, Ibsen, Strindberg, Shakespeare, Sophocles, Euripides), and the two organizations gradually "built up an audience of something like 3,000 persons who we could be reasonably sure would see any kind of play regardless of style, character, or quality [sic]."[51] After he moved to Delhi in 1962 as director of the National School of Drama, Alkazi's artistic goals underwent a strategic transformation. He identified the Hindi-speaking middle-class population—"a very important factor in Delhi society"—as his target audience, and he mounted landmark productions of vital new Hindi plays (by Rakesh, Bharati, and Laxmi Narayan Lal) as well as other Indian and foreign plays in *Hindi* translation (including works by Balwant Gargi, Vasant Kanetkar, Karnad, Sircar, Buchner, Strindberg, Lorca, Anouilh, Beckett, Osborne, Molière, Euripides, and of course Shakespeare).[52] In 1964 Alkazi established the NSD Repertory Company as the only continuously active professional organization of its kind in Delhi (a role it continues to fulfill today), and in addition to annual local seasons that offered Delhi audiences affordable theater of unprecedented quality, the company established a national schedule of touring productions to replicate the same experience in other parts of the country. His access to the cultural bureaucracy in Delhi also enabled him to mount open-air productions in some of Delhi's most famous archeological and historical monuments—the Old Fort (Purana Qila), Ferozeshah Kotla, and Talkatora Gardens. Alkazi's productions of *Tughlaq*, *Andha yug*, and *King Lear* in these venues (1964–1974) combined artistic value, accessibility, and historical importance in ways that marked a turning point in the experience of spectatorship in Delhi, and it made him the preeminent Indian practitioner of an urban, urbane, cosmopolitan modernism.[53]

In the east-central part of Karnataka, K. V. Subbanna (1932–2005) undertook a radically different experiment in theater/audience dynamics by establishing Ninasam (Nilakanteshwara Natya Seva Sangh) in 1949, in the isolated village of Heggodu, as a cultural organization "dedicated... to making accessible to its society the best of world art, literature, culture, and knowledge."[54] Like the NSD but completely outside the circle of government patronage, Ninasam was designed as an institution of rigorous theater training and practice, with Kannada, the state's majority language, as the *exclusive* medium for productions of regional, national, and world theater. Between 1953 and 1995 Subbanna translated and/or directed classical Sanskrit plays by Kalidasa, Mahendra Vikram Varman, and Vishakhadutt; modern and contemporary Indian plays by D. L. Roy, Tagore, Tendulkar, and Chandrashekhar Kambar; and an array of Western classics by Shakespeare, Molière, Gogol, and Brecht. In addition, a large number of other directors associated with Ninasam contributed notably to each of these categories, and collectively they created the most diverse and substantial body of directing work by a single private institution in the postindependence period.[55] The immediate consumers of these all-embracing initiatives were members of the small rural community in Heggodu (numbering 421 in the 2011 census!) and the comparatively larger provincial towns of Sagar and Shimoga, which even in 2024 had a combined population of 450,000. In 1985 Ninasam Tirugata was launched as a touring repertory company to counteract the limitations of both "popular" and "highbrow" theater in the state; taking three major plays from the Indian and Western traditions and one children's play annually to multiple venues in Karnataka, by 2001 the company had mounted 2,330 shows and reached a total audience of more than 1.5 million. The organization's approach to reception is summed up in Subbanna's belief that "theatre cannot survive without a community—so long as you are in touch with the needs of a community, your theatre will live; if not, it will atrophy and die."[56] In the context of Heggodu, however, this conception of "community" has a revolutionary aspect because it reverses the relations of power between metropolis and village. Theater activities at Ninasam oscillate continuously between the local and the global for their rural and semi-rural audiences, supporting the claim that the organization has "developed into the authentic voice of a people engaged in exploring an alternative model of modern civilization."[57]

Based in the eastern metropolis of Calcutta and using Bengali as his medium, Badal Sircar offered a provocative counterpoint to both Alkazi and Subbanna by theorizing a "Theatre of Synthesis—a Third Theatre" that could address the "unfortunate dichotomy between urban and rural life, expressed in disparities in economic standards, services, educational levels and cultural development" (*POM*, 282). The disjunction was in his view a pervasive effect of colonialism: the state's political economy gave priority to city over village, and by attempting to replicate contemporaneous Anglo-European models, colonial urban theater disrupted earlier performance traditions in which there was no strict separation between performers and audiences, in urban as well as rural locations. After creating unorthodox but notably successful plays for the proscenium for fifteen years (1956–1970), in 1973 Sircar defined live contact between actors and spectators as the essence of theater (which also separated this form categorically from the medium of film) and placed the two interactive communities side-by-side in a variety of performance spaces. Relying primarily on the performer's body to invest a spare text with meaning, he devised experimental works that could be performed both indoors and outdoors, and succeeded with both city and village audiences. Finally, the Third Theatre was either inexpensive or completely free for the viewer, so that it effectively neutralized the persistent problems of affordability and access posed by theater. Free weekend performances of plays such as *Spartacus* (1972) and *Michhil* (Procession, 1974) for several thousand spectators in Calcutta's Surendranath Park, and the mobility of plays such as *Bhoma* (1976) and *Bashi khabar* (Stale News, 1978) across the Bengal countryside embody Sircar's singular approach to audience development as the removal of hindrances and the bridging of cultural differences. Considered together, Alkazi, Subbanna, and Sircar underscore the enormous diversity of those who consume modernism-in-performance, placing in perspective the single "case study" that concludes this chapter.

Ashadh ka ek din: A Brief Performance History

Rakesh's iconic first play served in the previous chapter to exemplify the transnational legibility of modernist theater in translation; its performance history also tellingly captures the chain of circumstances through which the postcolonial modernist text participates in the complicated processes of deferral and actualization characterizing India's contemporary urban performance culture. According to the entry for February 6, 1959, in Rakesh's diary, *Ashadh* received its first performance in early January at the annual political convention of the Congress Party in Nagpur (a report that was unconfirmed) and won several awards at a Drama Festival on January 21, but it also antagonized various influential intellectuals because it had ostensibly belittled Kalidasa, the symbol of Indian literary greatness (*ODSR*, 218). (Rakesh's exasperated comment in his diary about these events: "What people!") Notwithstanding the attacks, later that year *Ashadh* received the Sangeet Natak Akademi award for the best play of 1958, an event that brought it national attention but underscored the fact that it had not yet received a notable production. In a diary entry for September 21, 1959, Rakesh confessed that the idea of producing the play himself had become an overpowering obsession, but he "gave it up finally—writing is the foremost thing, nothing else is" (*ODSR*, 219). But when *Ashadh* was broadcast on All India Radio as a "national play" on October 22, 1959, showcasing it for a national audience and adding another stamp of governmental approval, Rakesh noted that he "felt like committing suicide after listening to it. And I feel like destroying all that I have written" (*ODSR*, 219).

The premier stage production of the play took place in 1960, not in Delhi or any other city in the northern Hindi belt but in Calcutta where the majority language is Bengali. The director was Shyamanand Jalan, a successful lawyer, actor, and theater enthusiast who had become associated with the fledgling group Anamika and had taken on the task of promoting Hindi theater in a Bengali-speaking city. Curiously, the standard edition of Rakesh's *Collected Plays* includes comments on *Ashadh* by several directors and actors, but none by Jalan, who was the first to give Rakesh a stage presence that matched the modernist iconoclasm of his work.[58] With the Calcutta production serving as the important debut event, *Ashadh* moved to a second crucial performance context in 1962 when it became the first contemporary Indian play directed by Alkazi, who had just begun his tenure as director of the National School of Drama. The leading roles of Kalidasa and his muse Mallika were played by Om Shivpuri and Sudha Sharma (mentioned earlier in connection with their 1969 Hindi production of Tendulkar's *Shantata!*), who became celebrated NSD alumni and launched the group Dishantar in 1968. In 1973 they revived *Ashadh* in another major production, creating a lasting identification as

FIGURE 2.1 Om Shivpuri as Kalidasa and Sudha Sharma (later Shivpuri) as Mallika in *Ashadh ka ek din*, directed by Ebrahim Alkazi, National School of Drama, New Delhi, 1962. Photo credit: NSD Repertory Company.

well as tension between their stage roles and real selves because what the play enacts is the stark *impossibility* of the union of Kalidasa and Mallika (fig. 2.1) Sudha (Sharma) Shivpuri recaptures the poignancy of that identification in a 1992 memoir: "Today, when Mohan Rakesh is no longer with us and his Kalidasa has also left me alone and gone away, become disengaged from life, I remember [the] lines from *Ashadh ka ek din* and console myself" (*ODSR*, 45).

The status that Jalan, Alkazi, and the Shivpuris secured for *Ashadh* as a contemporary modernist classic in the postindependence repertory was consolidated over two decades by major Hindi productions directed by Satyadev Dubey (Bombay, 1964), Mohan Maharishi (Jaipur, 1968 and Delhi, 1970), Amal Allana (Delhi, 1981), and Rajinder Nath (Delhi, 1983). Joy Michael brought the play to Mary Washington College (Virginia) in 1968, in its first English translation; Faisal Alkazi (Delhi, 1971), Alyque Padamsee (Bombay, 1972), and Gowri Ramnarayan (Chennai, 2010 and 2020) are other directors who have mounted it in English (Ramnarayan was also the translator/adapter of her version). B. V. Karanth (date unknown) and Akshara K. V. (Heggodu, 1991) produced the play in Kannada, and Ratan

Thiyam, one of the leading figures in the "Theatre of Roots" movement, produced it in Manipuri (date unknown). Atul Pethe's Marathi production was part of the NSD's Bharat Rang Mahotsav in January 2015, giving *Ashadh* one of its most visible international presentations. Outside these professional but uniformly noncommercial circuits, the play is too much of a repertory staple for college, university, and community productions, across India and in the global Indian diaspora, for extensive documentation to be feasible (the two US productions of my collaborative English translation, discussed in chapter 1, are part of this pervasive presence).[59] The performance trajectories of Rakesh's modernist *kunstlerroman* (tracing the tensions between poet and muse, court and country, time and desire) have therefore crossed the boundaries of region, nation, and language for more than six decades and remain invitingly open; they also bring into focus the full architecture and reach of urban India's contemporary performance culture, which underwrites the staging of all the works discussed in part 2 of this book.

PART II
Writing and Staging Modernism

Chapter Three

PALIMPSESTS OF THE PAST

Myth, history, and sometimes "mythistory" appear conspicuously in twentieth-century modernist writing as culturally resonant narratives that are refashioned in the present, and the most visible examples of this aesthetic and political orientation have come from the Euro-American authorial line. As a singular work of fiction, Joyce's *Ulysses* retrieves archetypes deeply rooted in cultural memory and places them within time and history to reconfigure modern experience at the individual, communal, national, and "universal" levels. In a different creative register, modernist versions of a nation's "founding myths"—which imply that the "soul" of a nation cannot be contained by mere history—place collective racial memory and shared political-cultural experience at the center, with a romantic slant (in Yeats) or a critical edge (in Synge and McDiarmid).[1] As the source of available knowledge about the past, history-as-subject brings its own range of representational possibilities to modernism. It registers opposition to the "Hegelianized sense of history that had become the West's mythology and self-justification" (in Brecht's *Edward II*); views the present as a repetition of "past atrocity" (in Graham Greene's *Ministry of Fear*); or becomes, antithetically, the means of connecting with a healing and redemptive past (in William Carlos Williams's *Paterson* and Hart Crane's *The Bridge*).[2] The acts of retrospection have multiple facets, but one of their corollary effects is an assessment of the state of society and culture in the present. They also reveal how immersion in earlier, often remote, events and archetypes can be reconciled with modernism's radical contemporaneity, and how "tradition" can inform aesthetic forms that are intentionally experimental, iconoclastic, and often explicitly antitraditional.

The drama form is an especially fertile medium for re-presenting the past because it has drawn on myth and history as narrative resources from the beginning, and its verisimilitude creates unique correspondences between characters and events transported across space and time. In twentieth-century modernist drama, Aeschylus's *Oresteia* is reinscribed as O'Neill's *Mourning Becomes Electra* (1931), swapping the American civil war for the Trojan saga, and New England for Argos. Sophocles' Antigone reappears in Anouilh's *Antigone* (1944) as an obstinate idealist, invoking the French Resistance against Nazi occupation in her determination to sacrifice herself despite Creon's cynical attempts at dissuasion. Among "history plays," Shakespeare's fatally irresistible Cleopatra becomes Shaw's defiant sixteen-year-old girl in *Caesar and Cleopatra* (1906), a secondary character in another ironic comedy that predicts the coming imperialist war. Ibsen's nationalistic tribute to Norwegian history in the verse tragedy *Brand* (1867) has an antiheroic counterpoint in Arthur Miller's *The Crucible* (1953), which re-presents the Salem Witch Trials of 1692–93 as a "national" allegory of ideological entrapment during the McCarthy era. Beginning in the 1950s, postcolonial Anglophone drama takes the topoi of myth and history in stunning new directions, in part by employing poetry as its medium. Yoruba mythology and history form the core of Soyinka's plays set during the colonial period (*The Lion and the Jewel*, 1959; *Death and the King's Horseman*, 1975) and at the postcolonial moment of the nation's "birth" (*A Dance of the Forests*, 1960), whereas *The Bacchae: A Communion Rite* (1973) substitutes the Yoruba god Ogun for Dionysus in Soyinka's revision of Euripides's tragedy. Ngugi wa Thiong'o's *The Trial of Dedan Kimathi* (1974) renders the title character as a Christ figure to rewrite the history of the anticolonial Mau Mau rebellion in Kenya but also extends its critique to repressive postcolonial regimes. Derek Walcott counters the notion of the Caribbean as a region "without history" in his *Haitian Trilogy*, which combines the early plays *Henri Christophe* (1949) and *Drums and Colours* (1958) with a later work, *The Haitian Earth* (1984). Turning to a different mythology, *The Odyssey: A Stage Version* (1993) complements *Omeros* (1990), Walcott's poetic epic of the "new Aegean," and both together accommodate the entire Homeric tradition to the Caribbean.

Against this backdrop of sustained Western and postcolonial modernist engagements with past legacies, modern Indian drama and theater present the now familiar pattern of a substantial comparable output that is absent not only from transnational critical frameworks but from national ones as well. The succession of heroic figures in India's long classical/postclassical history, the civilizational centrality of mythology, the traditions of multilingual literacy, and the efficient modes of oral and written transmission intersect with the processes of colonialism in such a way that myth and history in fact become the leading narrative sources for colonial theater. This pattern continues after independence, but with radical changes in form, structure, authorial stance, and tone, which record with unusual clarity the shift in drama from "modern" to "modernist" aesthetics and politics. There are still no *transregional* discussions, however, of colonial theater's immersion in the past, and significant commentary on the postcolonial turn has come primarily from playwrights, not the receivers of their work.[3] As materials for modern/ist Indian drama, myth and history therefore need the kind of contextualization that addresses the power of cultural archetypes and the epistemological issues surrounding a culture's knowledge of its own past in colonial and postcolonial settings. With this objective, in the next section I discuss the particular traits of Indian mythology and history that shape their theatrical use and underscore the differences between colonial and postcolonial playwriting. In later sections, I define "palimpsestic modernism" as a distinctive set of qualities in drama that engages with myth and history, and I analyze two palimpsestic plays—*Yayati* (1961) by Girish Karnad and *Laharon ke rajhans* (1963) by Mohan Rakesh—as notable postindependence variants of the type.

MYTH, HISTORY, AND INDIAN MODERNISMS

Mythology and History in Culture

In Indian cultural forms, the narratives of myth take precedence over those of history because of several culture-specific features of Indian mythology that determine its place in modern society, literature, and theater. First, contrary to current Hindu fundamentalist claims, *India* is not synonymous with Hinduism; but for complex historical reasons, Indian *mythology is* largely synonymous with Hindu mythology—a claim that needs explanation because of India's religio-cultural diversity and constitutional secularism. As the first major indigenous religion that emerged on the subcontinent around 1000 BCE and currently has about eight hundred million followers, Hinduism is a nonproselytizing, polytheistic faith that has never encountered the kind of historical rupture that separated Graeco-Roman antiquity from the Judaeo-Christian tradition, and Judaism from Christianity. The three largest "minority" faiths in India—Islam (204 million), Christianity (27. 8 million), and Sikhism (20. 8 million)—are monotheistic, proselytizing "religions of the book" with powerful historical dimensions, and Islam forbids anthropomorphic representation in iconography and performance. The other minority religions—Buddhism (8.5 million) and Jainism (4.5 million)—have a distinct theological, cultural, and iconographic presence, but they have demographically represented a small fraction of the total Indian population. Hinduism is therefore dominant not only in terms of numbers but as the only indigenous religion in the country with a powerful and continuous mythology that has penetrated the full spectrum of literary and performative genres for nearly three millennia. Colonial and postcolonial authors have given the mythic narratives radical new forms since the mid-nineteenth century, but the narratives have been culturally active and readily available to them, instead of needing retrieval through philology and allegoresis, or through the scientific disciplines of anthropology and psychology.[4] Equally notable, this indigenous cultural framework was not undermined but reinforced during the British colonial period by European orientalist scholarship and the philologically grounded discipline of Indology, in stark contrast with the hostility toward precolonial cultures in imperial and settler colonies elsewhere. Orientalism certainly revalorizes India's classical past for Indians, but its principal function is to retrieve this iconic past for the West.

Second, Hindu mythology is also the foundation of Hindu theology and religious practice, so myth is continuous with religion instead of being an alien or antithetical resource. The Hindu components of Max Mueller's fifty-volume compendium of "sacred books of the east"—Vedas, Upanishads, Puranas, spiritual discourses, codified laws, didactic homilies, and so on—are grouped under the title "Vedic Brahmanic System" and function simultaneously as mythology, religion, codes of social organization, and poetry. In the Hindu trinity, Brahma the creator is formless, but Vishnu the preserver and Shiva the destroyer anchor the two principal devotional traditions in Hinduism (Vaishnavism and Shaivism) and maintain a monumental presence in forms of religious worship, iconography, and the full range of cultural forms transmitted through orality, writing, print, and performance. Furthermore, the nine incarnations of Vishnu include the two most powerful deities in the Vaishnava tradition of worship: Rama, hero of the Sanskrit epic *Ramayana*, and Krishna, the child-god who in his mature adult form is also the only divine presence in the *Mahabharata*, the world's longest epic poem. Again, Rama and Krishna function simultaneously as gods, mythic symbols, and epic heroes in overlapping cultural practices that do not need to maintain clear distinctions between religious belief, ritual, and aesthetic expression. The *Bhagavad-gita*, which contains Krishna's epic discourse to his protégé Arjun on the Mahabharata battlefield, is also considered a profound meditation on the nature of human action in its own right and is valued as a philosophical text by agnostics and atheists.[5]

Third, like its Greek and Roman equivalents, Hindu mythology has had a special relationship with the drama form since the classical Sanskrit period. Of the thirteen plays by Bhasa, the earliest extant playwright (second century CE), six are based on episodes in the *Mahabharata* and two are based on the *Ramayana*. The *Mahabharata* is also the narrative source for Kalidasa's iconic play, *Shakuntala*, which entered the canons of world literature following its translation into English by Sir William Jones in 1789. The decline of Sanskrit drama after the twelfth century CE disrupts the use of epic matter in literary drama for several centuries, channeling the narratives into a pan-Indian circuitry of traditional, religious, folk, popular, and intermediary performance genres. But the practice reappears in the mid-nineteenth century when urban theater emerges as a *secular* form under Anglo-European and local influences, initially in Calcutta and Bombay, and later in other major cities around the country. Hence the first two significant plays in Bengali, *Bhadrarjuna* (Subhadra and Arjun, 1852) by Tara Charan Shikdar and *Sharmishtha* (1858) by Michael Madhusudan Dutt, are based on episodes in the *Mahabharata*. The first modern performance in Marathi, Vishnudas Bhave's *Sita swayamvar* (1843), is based on the episode in the *Ramayana* where Sita, the daughter of King Janak, freely chooses Rama as her husband from among a gathering of suitors at her father's court.[6] Dinabandhu Mitra's *Nil-darpan* (The indigo mirror, Bengali, 1860), the first major "political" play critical of the colonial government's agrarian policies, elevates the members of its contemporary Bengali family by modeling them on idealized figures in the *Ramayana*, while the brutal West Indian planters evoke Ravana, the demon king of Lanka whose defeat in war by Rama signifies the epic victory of good over evil.[7] Other colonial-era plays based on the *Mahabharata* include Subramania Bharati's *Panchali shapatham* (Panchali's vow, Tamil, 1912), Tagore's *Chitra* (Bengali, 1914), Krishnaji Prabhakar Khadilkar's *Draupadi* (Marathi, 1928), and, notably, Khadilkar's *Kichaka-vadha* (The slaying of Kichaka), which became the most sensational example of theatrical anticolonialism and colonial censorship when it appeared on the Bombay theater scene in 1907.[8] It is possible to argue, then, that within the vast network of oral, written, printed, and performative genres for which the Hindu epics and other forms of mythology function as ur-sources at any given historical moment, urban literary drama represents a subtradition that serves a distinctive purpose both in relation to anticolonial nationalism and postcolonial counter-nationalism. This renewed presence of the past can be conceptualized as a form of "cultural recursiveness" that restores myth as the basis of drama in the mid-nineteenth century, and it has created not only a continuous but a continually expanding strain in theater since then.

As the narrative source of literature and drama, history is as prominent as myth in modern and modernist Indian writing, but its use also raises particular epistemological issues that are inextricable from the fictional representations. Judged by the standards of Western rationalist historiography, "history," "historicity," "historical experience," "historical consciousness," and "the historical sense" have all been, and continue to be, deeply contested concepts in India. Reflecting on the theoretical, conceptual, and historico-political reasons for this crisis of history writing, I argued in a 2010 essay that

> [t]o a large extent the crisis is a product of cultural difference: it registers the conflicts between Indian and Western, intrinsic and extrinsic ideas of time and history that were inevitable under the asymmetrical power relations of colonialism between the late-eighteenth and the early-twentieth centuries. Indian concepts of time invoke monumental and repetitive cycles that seem disconnected from individual consciousness or a concrete temporal existence, and indigenous ideas of history do not differentiate sufficiently between documented fact, poetic figuration, and mythic narrative, thus

making the historicity of human agents indeterminable. Nineteenth-century European philosophers and historians used these "irrational" concepts, and the differences between Western and Indian social-political formations, to claim that India "had no history" either as the experience of an existence in time or as the textualized record of that experience.[9]

During the nineteenth and early-twentieth centuries, "Indian history" was thus either dismissed on the (Hegelian) grounds that India lacked the qualities of a world-historical culture, or it was practiced as a largely British-colonialist enterprise, aimed at justifying the superiority and magnanimity of British rule. In the postcolonial period, a sophisticated rethinking of Western and Indian models of historiography has thoroughly professionalized the academic discipline of history, and revisionist historians (notably the Subaltern Studies collective) have undertaken an "Indian historiography of India" that systematically critiques and displaces Hegelian-idealist and colonialist historiography. Subaltern historians are committed in equal measure to the parallel tasks of rescuing history from orientalist and bourgeois-nationalist aggrandizements, a project to which postcolonial modernist writers have contributed in remarkably complementary ways.

Unlike the primal resonances of myth, therefore, the use of history as a narrative source in modern Indian theater inevitably brings up a range of epistemological and ideological issues alongside cultural and aesthetic considerations. Portrayals of even the most iconic figures from classical, postclassical, and premodern history have to be accompanied by the acknowledgment, implicit or explicit, that much of the "knowledge" about these figures is conjectural and uncertain, that there are no contemporaneous or continuous historical records relating to them that can be used for verification, and that their "lives" are as much aggregations of hearsay, legend, and lore as of facts. This is the area of starkest contrast with the West, where a connection between history as lived experience and historiography as its written or published record has been maintained over the longue durée. At least since the early modern period, the interpretation of Western historical fictions has involved one or more historical "sources," their intertextual connection to the work of fiction, the audience's knowledge of, and attitudes toward, the history being represented, and the relevance of the fictional work to its own time. These *relationships* continue to exist even when the presumed authority and objectivity of written history are deconstructed, in the discourses of poststructuralism and postmodernism, for instance. In India, the absence of systematic or continuous historiography disrupts every one of the established relationships and raises a series of questions that thoroughly problematize the constitutive (Western) elements of the genre. Is there a verifiable basis or source for the historical fiction? What is its validity or veracity as "knowledge about the past," and what are its ideological implications? How familiar is the "history" to the audience, and what are the author's intentions with respect to the audience's knowledge, attitudes, and expectations? In view of these uncertainties, what conviction does the fictionalized history carry, and how effectively does it connect with the present? Because representations of history in India routinely call into question the existence and epistemological status of source narratives and their modes of transmission, such fictions potentially intervene in the discourse of history not only as aesthetic constructs but as alternative, or even primary, forms of knowledge about the past.

Myth and History: From Colonial Heroics to Postcolonial Ironies

The mythic and historical narratives that pervade modern Indian culture present distinctly different issues of origin, transmission, aesthetic form, and affect (from each other) as they respectively evolve over time. However, they are similar in one key respect: they participate equally in the qualitative shift from colonial (heroic) to postcolonial (satiric and ironic) perceptions of the past, registering a decisive mid-twentieth-century rupture that is generative for modernism. Colonial attitudes are shaped by the orientalist enchantment with India's "classical" age (second to twelfth century CE), the Indian intelligentsia's investment in a nationwide cultural renaissance (similar to the Celtic revival), and the ideology of anticolonial nationalism (especially after the 1880s). All the myth-based plays of the colonial era mentioned in the previous section, for instance, aim to revive the memory of a fabled past to counterbalance a humiliating present, appeal to the audience's cultural pride, and seek to rouse its members to action. The same is true of history, which is used to re-present figures from a more or less distant past as reminders of past glory and as models for the present. Examples include Girish Chandra Ghosh's *Chaitanya-lila* (Bengali, 1884), about the fifteenth-century mystic Chaitanya Mahaprabhu; D. L. Roy's Bengali *Rana pratap singh* (1905) and *Mevar patan* (The fall of Mevar, 1908), about the legendary seventeenth-century king of the Mevar region (now in south-central Rajasthan) and his hapless successor; and, especially, Jaishankar Prasad's sequence of five Hindi plays that self-reflexively announce themselves as "*aitihasik natak*" (historical drama) and use outstanding imperial figures from the "golden age" of Hinduism (fifth century BCE to seventh century CE) as their protagonists.[10] A small subset of colonial history plays denigrate more recent figures who can be blamed for India's capitulation to the British in the mid-eighteenth century. Ghosh's *Siraj-ud-daula* (1905), for instance, portrays the doomed Nawab of Bengal who was betrayed at the 1757 battle of Plassey against Robert Clive by his treacherous minister Mir Jafar, and gave the British their first military foothold in India. Aside from these exceptions, plays about the past are celebratory if not propagandist in tone well into the 1930s, designed to remind the audience of India's civilizational greatness.

Within a decade of independence, however, myth and history move to a new, powerful, and clearly contestatory phase as materials for modernist plays, which maintain a steady presence after 1954 and are most conspicuous from the 1960s to the 1980s. As mentioned previously, the *Mahabharata* ceases to be the source of heroic archetypes and becomes the epic of ambivalence, foregrounding problems of moral indeterminacy, victimage, and injustice by focusing on antiheroes, outsiders, and scapegoats. Richly varied in form, the repertoire of major post-1950 *Mahabharata* plays includes a condensed verse epic (Dharamvir Bharati's *Andha yug* [Blind epoch, Hindi, 1954]); full-length prose plays (Adya Rangacharya's *Kelu janmejaya* [Listen, Janmejaya, Kannada, 1960], Girish Karnad's *Yayati* [Kannada, 1961], and Shankar Shesh's *Ek aur dronacharya* [Another Dronacharya, Hindi, 1978]); highly stylized forms of "total theater" (Habib Tanvir's *Duryodhana* [Chhattisgarhi, 1979], and Ratan Thiyam's *Chakravyuha* [Battle formation, Manipuri, 1984]); classics in revival (K. N. Panikkar's prolific Sanskrit productions of Bhasa's *Mahabharata* plays, 1978–c. 2010); and virtuoso feminist performance (Saoli Mitra's *Nathabati anathbat* [Five lords, yet none a protector, Bengali, 1983]). As postindependence intertexts of the *Mahabharata* created by playwrights active in urban theater, these works constitute the literary-performative dimension not of "nationalist ideology" but of an ideology that simultaneously acknowledges and questions the power of the past in the mythology of the new nation. They bear out S. L. Bhyrappa's view that "the *Mahabharata* is an irresistible theme for an Indian writer," but needs to be understood afresh, with a "twentieth-century mind."[11] The violent end of Duryodhana, the sacrifices of Eklavya, Abhimanyu, and Karna, and the dishonor of Draupadi have become especially poignant mythemes in theatrical works that undermine Hindu-patriarchal claims of morality and ethical conduct and use a modernist poetic register to portray instead a civilizational wasteland of blindness, suffering, and death.

The older and shorter Sanskrit epic, the *Ramayana*, lacks a comparable profile in modernist theater for two main reasons: its preoccupation with an ideal king (Rama) who is an incarnation of the god Vishnu and an object of daily worship in Hindu religious practice leaves much less room for modes of critique; and the much more unified heroic narrative lends itself to a vast and continuously active network of performance genres that range from solo recitation, shadow puppetry, and folk enactments to dance drama, musical drama, traditional forms such as Kutiyattam and Kathakali, and the nationwide, elite/popular, annual reenactment known as the Ramlila. Sita as the unjustly abandoned wife and Ravana as the demon/ized non-Aryan king of Lanka enable contestations based on gender and caste, but a cluster of plays dealing with the figure of Shambuka—among them Kuvempu's *Shudra tapasvi* (The low-caste ascetic, Kannada, 1944), and two Hindi plays titled *Shambuk vadh* (The slaying of Shambuk) by Periyar Lalai Singh (1962) and Brijesh (2006)—represent a robust dramatic subtradition in which Rama's slaying of Shambuka for violating caste hierarchies vividly exposes the injustices of the caste system. In addition to these pan-Indian sagas, contemporary playwrights draw on local and regional mythologies for material, as in Chandrashekhar Kambar's *Siri sampige* (Kannada), K. N. Panikkar's *Koyma* (The right to rule, Malayalam), and Thiyam's *Lengshonnei* (a localized Manipuri version of *Antigone*), all first performed in 1986. Acknowledging the presence of myth in day-to-day life at the philosophical, spiritual, emotional, and experiential levels, the entire spectrum of postcolonial engagements with epic matter reflects an iconoclastic consciousness that disrupts received meanings and undermines various structures of authority.

History is an equally prolific narrative source in postindependence modernist drama, and the deromanticizing impulse is sharper because the protagonists are "real," usually iconic figures along a temporal continuum that stretches from antiquity to the recent past. Rakesh's *Ashadh ka ek din* presents Kalidasa, the arch-canonical Sanskrit playwright-poet, as an antihero, and *Laharon ke rajhans* turns the Buddha's call for renunciation into an unresolvable human dilemma confronted by members of his own family. Girish Karnad's four major history plays, the first three written originally in Kannada and the last one in English, pivot between premodern and early colonial times. *Tughlaq* (1964) retrieves the ambivalent figure of a visionary fourteenth-century Muslim Sultan of Delhi whose reign ended in chaos; *Talé-danda* (Death by decapitation, 1989) deals with the violent failure of a twelfth-century anticaste movement in the Karnataka region; *The Dreams of Tipu Sultan* (1997) uses the life and death of the powerful ruler of Mysore to suggest that the British territorial conquest of India (1757–1818) was aided greatly by the absence of a "national idea" among the Indian ruling class; and *Crossing to Talikota* (2019) revisits the sixteenth-century fall of the powerful Vijaynagara empire in the south by focusing on figures overlooked in history. G. P. Deshpande's *Chanakya vishnugupta* (Marathi, 1988) goes back to Hindu antiquity to portray the nation-building ambitions of the (in)famous preceptor at Chandragupta Maurya's court (fourth century BCE) who wrote the classic treatise on political economy, the *Artha-shastra*. Indira Parthasarathy's *Aurangzeb* (Tamil, 1974) portrays the seventeenth-century Mughal emperor Shahjahan, builder of the Taj Mahal, as an abject, imprisoned father unable to prevent the murder of his eldest son in a fratricidal war of succession, and *Ramanujar* (Tamil, 1997) seeks to rescue the Hindu philosopher Ramanuja (1017–1137 CE) from "a prison of the establishment."[12] Interestingly, colonial history is dramatized only occasionally, in plays such as Utpal Dutt's *Mahavidroh* (The great rebellion, Bengali, 1973/1985) and Gurcharan Das's *Larins sahib* (English, 2001), but it is possible to make a general claim that post-1950 history plays collectively and substantively reenact the history of the subcontinent.

The modernist aesthetics of postindependence performances of myth and history have come gradually into focus in the foregoing discussion. The dominant quality of plays in both categories is an ironic, sometimes iconoclastic revaluation of past legacies in an ancient and irreducibly complex culture that has undergone uneven modernization under colonialism and has arrived at an uncertain postcolonial nationhood. Political independence engenders a strong sense of new cultural beginnings among modernist writers, but they negotiate their art firmly outside the self-aggrandizing frameworks of cultural nationalism. The plays that engage with myth are formally very diverse, adapting "traditional" as well as "modern" styles of presentation, and the thematic emphasis is on wrenching familiar archetypes away from established meanings. The history plays, in contrast, usually follow the conventions of realism in terms of temporal structure and characterization, although the mise-en-scène is often unconventional, and some plays, such as Das's *Mira* (English, 1970) and Karnad's *Dreams of Tipu Sultan*, resort to metatheater. The destabilizing modernist urge, however, is always present: playwrights collectively refashion not only historical narrative but historicity itself, making theatrical representation in part an epistemological, ideological, and aesthetic counterpoint to institutionalized history. As the authors Rakesh, Karnad, and Parthasarathy theorize the "history play," they posit new relations between history and historical fictions and demarcate the space that fiction offers for fresh thematizations and reconfigured relations of power. Finally, beyond the boundaries of region, nation, and any one genre or form, the cosmopolitan sphere of modernist practices in Euro-American literature and theater is an intertextual presence in the entire Indian corpus—a connection that reveals itself in the discussion of individual plays and genres throughout this book.

PALIMPSESTIC MODERNISM: TWO VARIATIONS

The basic features of "mainstream" drama have remained remarkably consistent over two millennia, in the West and elsewhere, because it is a dialogic, durationally limited form, written and performed most often (even now) as the two hours' traffic upon the stage. In print and in performance, plays resemble each other to a much greater extent than poems and novels resemble other poems and novels. When two or more plays use the same narrative basis, especially one derived from myth or history (a frequent practice), the later versions are uniquely palimpsestic because they are superposed on a source text that is more or less similar to them in its dialogic and durational qualities, and their intertextuality highlights the elements of rewriting, reinscription, and revision. *Mourning Becomes Electra* is a palimpsest of the *Oresteia* in this sense, just as every new theatrical version of *Antigone* is a palimpsest of all earlier theatrical versions. Adina Ciugureanu's comments on Pound and Eliot's conception of history as a "modernist palimpsest" are also useful here as a gloss on the significance of connecting the past with the present: freed of its nineteenth-century positivistic strains, history becomes a means of "restoring experience from the past [so that it] becomes analogous to . . . immediate experience in the present; the task of the artist is, therefore, to resurrect the past by making it new, to revitalize the dead voices through interpolation, adaptation, translation, juxtaposition and new composition."[13] These insights can be geoculturally expanded to explain why and how the end of the Mahabharata war in *Andha yug* invokes the carnage of two world wars and the Partition of 1947, or why *Tughlaq* uses passages from a chronicle written by the titular Sultan's court historian to suggest parallels between fourteenth- and twentieth-century India. The differences from Ciuguraneau's formulation are that in India myth is not an accumulation of "dead voices" but a part of daily experience, keeping collective memory and civilizational values alive in ways that writers can access readily, whereas the discourse of history is a mishmash of gaps, ruptures, and misrepresentations that give contemporary historical fictions a fundamentally compensatory and corrective function.

The two plays on which I focus in this chapter—Girish Karnad's *Yayati* and Mohan Rakesh's *Laharon ke rajhans*—are modernist palimpsests embodying the specifically dramatic features I have outlined. *Yayati* is based on a well-known myth in book 1 of the *Mahabharata*, and has a suggestive intertext in the first significant full-length Bengali play of the modern period: Michael Madhusudan Dutt's *Sharmishtha natak* (1858), promptly translated by the author into English under the title *Sermista: A Play in Five Acts* (1859). The same source myth reappears in many other twentieth-century works, some of them also titled *Yayati*, such as the plays by Pammala Sambandha Mudaliar (Tamil, 1914) and Govind Ballabh Pant (Hindi, 1951), as well as the notable novel by V. S. Khandekar (Marathi, 1959). Consciously or unconsciously, Karnad is therefore engaging in 1961 with a steady succession of pretexts. The layering of texts and meanings in *Laharon ke rajhans* is more complex. The Buddha is a foundational figure in Indian and world history, and a fictional representation effectively invokes all that he symbolizes in terms of religious, theological, social, and personal transformation, in his own time and in ours. Rakesh, however, chooses as his principal textual source the second century Sanskrit epic poem *Saundarananda* (Handsome Nanda) by the Buddhist monk Ashvaghosha, in which the Buddha rescues his hedonistic younger brother, Nanda, from the world of sensory pleasures and secures his spiritual liberation. Rakesh thus approaches history through poetry and invents a substantially new narrative and symbolic structure for his dramatic fictions about the monumental past events.

I want to extend the definition of palimpsestic modernism beyond these overt intertextual relationships, however, by analyzing a quality of *self-reflexive* recursiveness—a return of the text upon itself—that characterizes both plays. Caught up in a seemingly open-ended process of composition, each author circles back not only to an original source and its earlier aesthetic representations but compulsively, over several decades, to his own earlier dramatic figurations, regarding the play even at the end of the struggle as unsatisfactory and unfinished. The modernist trope in both instances is that of repetition, and the process denotes uncertainty, anxiety, and the lack of closure.

Yayati was published in Kannada in 1961, translated within a few years into Hindi, Marathi, and Bengali, and performed in these and other regional languages, but Karnad's ambivalence about the play took decades to resolve itself. With one exception, he translated more or less promptly into English every play he wrote originally in Kannada, but he passed over *Yayati* because of uncertainties about its artistic quality. He also did not authorize Priya Adarkar's "excellent" English translation for publication, although translations of the play in several other languages had already appeared in print. In 2005 Karnad omitted *Yayati* from the standard two-volume edition of his *Collected Plays*, clearly unwilling to authorize, especially in the potentially global medium of English, a work with which he "felt uncomfortable and decided to treat . . . as part of my juvenilia."[14] During this period of time, leading directors such as Satyadev Dubey, Shriram Lagoo, Kumar Roy, and Arundhati Raja were drawn to the play's precocious philosophical texture, and mounted very successful productions: Karnad himself described as "magnificent" Dubey's 1967 Hindi production for the Indian National Theater, which had front-rank actors such as Amrish Puri, Tarla Mehta, Sunila Pradhan, Sulabha Deshpande, and Dubey in leading roles. *Yayati* finally appeared as an individual volume in Karnad's own English translation in 2008, forty-seven years after its initial publication, with both a preface and an afterword explaining its troubled genesis and progress. Without any further changes, this version was included in volume 3 of the *Collected Plays* in 2017, two years before the author's death.

Yayati therefore marks in a singular way both the beginning and the end of Karnad's career as a playwright. In one perspective it is a play from 1961, representing myth as the primary subject matter, Kannada as the language of original composition, and Karnad's disconnection from the theater world as the determining condition of its dramaturgical structure. But in another perspective it is a play from 2008, rewritten in both English and Kannada in light of the insights, suggestions, and critical comments offered by "professionals who have actually staged it," not to mention the authorial experience Karnad could bring to bear on it after more than four decades of playwriting (*Yayati*, vii). For readers (like me) who cannot access the Kannada text and are limited to the English version, there is an inscrutable quality about the relationships between the Sanskrit source, the original Kannada text of 1961, its unpublished translation by Adarkar, and Karnad's revisions to the 1961 Kannada version during the process of his own translation in 2007–8. Karnad's cryptic glosses on the stages of reconceptualization are also contradictory. In the preface to the 2008 translation, he notes that at the age of sixty-nine he has resisted the temptation to make changes in a play he had written at the age of twenty-two, except to incorporate a few suggestions that directors such as Dubey, Lagoo, and C. R. Simha had made when they produced the work. But in the short note to *Yayati* in volume 3 of the *Collected Plays* (2017), he states that he has "continued to feel dissatisfied with the original text," and rewritten the play "incorporating many of [the] insights and suggestions" from those theater professionals.[15] The play's anomalously long trek toward publication in English points to Karnad's fastidiousness as an author and translator, and uncovers the circularity that sometimes interrupts the linear progression of literary and theatrical careers. But it also brings up contingencies of bilingual authorship, authorial process, form, meaning, and the text-performance relation that are not present in any earlier myth-based play from the modern period, and make *Yayati* a paradoxical early/late work of modernism in the postindependence corpus.

In Rakesh's *Laharon ke rajhans*, the instability surrounding the "historical" characters and story lines is far more tortuous, even tortured. In the preface to the 1968 edition of the play he admits that "the process of its being written and changed over and over again is so long that I'm embarrassed to even talk about it."[16] Taking *Saundarananda* as his primary source, Rakesh first produced a short story in the late 1940s that did not make it past the manuscript stage (and is now lost). In 1949 the story became a radio play titled *Sundari* that was broadcast in Bombay, creating such disappointment and regret in the author that he resolved to forget he had ever written it (the text does not appear in Rakesh's collected works). Eight years later, the discarded work evolved into a longer radio play titled *Raat bitane tak* (Until the night ends) that was successfully directed by Ramesh Pal and broadcast in Delhi, but confirmed for Rakesh his faulty portrayal of Nanda, the leading male character. The first attempt at a full-length stage play based on the same narrative came in 1957, only to be preempted by *Ashadh ka ek din*, which was written in March–April 1958 and established the author as a leading contemporary playwright in India. When Rakesh turned again to *Laharon ke rajhans*, two versions were left unfinished in 1960 and 1961 due to "personal circumstances," but a combination of the older text and new writing enabled him to complete the script during ten days in April 1963, leading to the first published edition later that year. Then in 1966, Rakesh's extensive collaboration with the Calcutta-based director-actor Shyamanand Jalan and his group Anamika led to a thorough revision of Act 3, and after his return to Delhi Rakesh rewrote the entire play to make the first two acts consistent with the third.

The revised script formed the basis of a January 1967 production directed by Om Shivpuri, and it was published with yet more revisions in 1968 as the second edition of the play, generating mixed responses from theater professionals and readers. The preface acknowledges that after twenty years of obsessive reworking the drama was not finished but abandoned; Rakesh's despairing authorial comment is that "there is something that should have been in this play, and is not. What that is, is not clear in my mind" (*MRR*, vol. 3, 98). Ashvaghosha's poem is about the agonizing but eventually successful conversion of Nanda from a life of sensual self-indulgence to asceticism despite every effort at dissuasion by his equally sensual wife Sundari. Rakesh focuses on the anomy and mounting desperation of the conjugal relationship between Nanda and Sundari, but in a telling example of modernist aporia, he is unable to resolve in any decisive way the power contests between them. *Yayati* and *Laharon ke rajhans* thus become modernist palimpsests of an even denser kind because of persistent revision, with the past-present relation established by the narratives of myth and history being readjusted overtly or covertly with each new iteration.

MICHAEL MADHUSUDAN DUTT'S *SHARMISHTHA* (1858) AND GIRISH KARNAD''S *YAYATI* (1961): MYTH, MODERNITY, MODERNISM

In the "Adiparvan" (book 1 of the *Mahabharata*), the section titled "Yayati" is just over four hundred verses long, and it establishes the title character as a "mighty" and "invincible" descendent of the Kuru dynasty who had already achieved greatness as a king when he first encounters the eminent sage Shukracharya's daughter Devayani and her nemesis, princess Sharmishtha, in the Asura kingdom of Vrishparvan. The story appears to be anchored in a series of transgressions involving caste and gender. When Sharmishtha throws Devayani into a dry well after a quarrel, Devayani uses Shukracharya's brahman supremacy to demand that Sharmishtha become her slave. After Yayati rescues Devayani from the well, *she* proposes marriage to him, although unions between the kshatriya (warrior) and brahman (priestly) castes are taboo, and again Shukracharya allows the "miscegenation" because of his love for his daughter. Sharmishtha follows Devayani to Yayati's palace and feels justified in wooing the king when her womanly "season" arrives, because he owns her by virtue of being her mistress's husband. Devayani's rage at this infidelity, in turn, has more to do with the idea of being slighted by her slave and rival rather than with the rights of a kshatriya queen. Shukracharya responds by cursing Yayati with premature old age, but immediately adds the proviso that the king can retain his youth if someone else assumes the curse. The epic does not question Yayati's illicit desire for Sharmishtha, or criticize his motives when he demands that one of his sons should make the sacrifice because he himself is "not yet sated of youth."[17] On the contrary, Yayati curses his four older sons for refusing the challenge because "the strict do not deem him a son who is contrary to his father," and he blesses his youngest son Puru for accepting it. After a thousand years, Yayati assumes his old age again and gives the kingdom to Puru, because "like a true son, Puru did my pleasure."[18] The myth validates the father's authority and the son's obedience, reinforcing the counter-oedipal logic of filial relations in Hindu mythology.

Michael Madhusudan Dutt's Bengali and English versions of this narrative (1858–59) capture brilliantly the dynamics of myth-as-subject close to the very beginning of modern urban drama in India, and Karnad's Kannada and English versions (1961–2008) register the idiosyncrasies of that tradition a century later. The *Mahabharata* as Sanskrit epic, and the *natak* as the preeminent Sanskrit dramatic form, had maintained a continuous existence in Indian literary culture since their appearance nearly two millennia earlier. But the orientalist valorization of the classical period, the influx of European cultural influences, and the interest in urban theater as a secular cultural institution provided Dutt with dramaturgical opportunities that had not existed earlier: the availability of a five-act Shakespearean dramatic structure that could override the elements borrowed from Sanskrit drama;

access to the medium of print, which gave drama "literary" weight and an existence independent of the stage; and connection to an emergent but precarious urban performance culture. Since the Bengali public theater did not come into existence until 1872, and Dutt's career as a playwright was concentrated between the years 1858 and 1861, he was dependent on the private patronage of the Rajas of Paikpara, who supported the Belgatchia Villa Theatre in north Calcutta and had commissioned Dutt to translate Shri Harsha's Sanskrit play *Ratnavali* in 1858 so that they could invite English guests, including the governor of Bengal, to the performance.

As authorial events, the writing, performance, and translation of *Sharmishtha* are therefore bound up with Dutt's literary-cultural aspirations, his excitement about giving culturally resonant ancient matter a modern theatrical form, and his enthusiasm for the collaborative/public nature of performance. Using the momentum created by the showcasing of *Ratnavali*, he wrote *Sharmishtha* in a few weeks during the same year because he wanted to revive the lost "genius of the drama" in Indian culture and offer a worthwhile full-length Bengali (rather than English) work for performance at the Belgatchia. In the preface to *Sermista*, he described the original play as "the first attempt in the Bengali language to produce a classical and regular Drama" of the kind that could contribute to "our rising national Theatre."[19] There is no record that the English version was ever performed, and the Bengali *Sharmishtha* was revived only twice in Calcutta (in 1867 and 1873), but despite its light footprint on stage the play brings together classical myth, Western dramatic form, Sanskrit dramaturgy, and the translational medium of English in a definitive colonial model of hybrid modernity. As Dutt's references to the "genius of the drama" and the model of a "classical and regular Drama" also make clear, his goal is nothing less than to restore this genre to the premier status it held in classical Indian culture. The past thus emerges as the highest form of cultural capital in the nationalist project of regeneration that becomes the Bengal, and subsequently the Indian, Renaissance.

In both versions of the play, Dutt follows the story line of the *Mahabharata* myth closely, dramatizing it in a (consciously Shakespearean) structure of five acts and thirteen total scenes. In the English translation, the dialogue borrows in equal measure from the idiom and syntax of Elizabethan blank verse, eighteenth-century poetic diction, and the declamatory style of orientalist versions of Sanskrit drama that had begun with Jones's translation of *Shakuntala* in 1789 and continued in Wilson's *Select Specimens of the Theatre of the Hindus* in 1827. The result is mawkish, as when Sharmishtha asks if she has "not like a bedlamite mixed with worm-wood and gall the honied draught destiny gave me to drink," or when Yayati dismisses an underling's reference to the fable of the Lion and the Mouse with "Nay, my good fool, the strong-corded net that misfortune hath woven round me, would defy the sharpest teeth of such a mouse as thou art!" (*Sermista* 10, 22). As lovers, Yayati and Devayani, and later Yayati and Sharmishtha, are clearly modeled on Dushyanta and Shakuntala in Kalidasa's play, with no attention to emotional plausibility or consistency. The Vidushak is part Sanskrit jester, part Shakespearean court fool; the loyal servants Purnika and Devika are symmetrical types from Sanskrit drama. Dutt is performing here what Sudipto Chatterjee describes as the balancing act of being "Bengali/Indian and English/Western at the same stroke," of connecting to a high-cultural indigenous past while following "the theories and praxis of European theater."[20]

Dutt's decision to gloss over the moral and ethical issues raised by the actions of all the principal characters reflects his ambivalent sense of proximity and distance from the mythic content. The two women are equally ardent in their wooing of Yayati, and equally successful. Yayati discovers Sharmishtha's passion for him at the end of Act 3, and at the beginning of Act 4 we learn that she has borne him three children, including Puru. Dutt rationalizes Yayati's dalliance, which he knows is morally unacceptable to his audience, with the statement that he "wishes to paint the manners of the age in which Yayati is said to have flourished, as he finds them described in the *Mahabharata* and other old works" (*Sermista*, 49). At the end of the play the women reconcile with exaggerated gestures of love and forgiveness. Most important, Dutt's play follows the *Mahabharata* exactly in the handling of Yayati's negotiations with his sons. Devayani's sons refuse the exchange, and are cursed; Puru, a mere child, accepts, and is blessed. The play ends with Shukracharya's benediction and prayer for Sharmishtha's everlasting glory.

Dutt and his pretext set up the sharp contrasts that highlight Karnad's modernist swerve away from colonial modernizations of myth as subject. All of the basic choices involved in *Yayati*—form, content, language, writing conditions, the urge toward publication, expectations regarding reception, and so on—are inadvertent, unexpected, and at least initially directionless from the author's standpoint. Like other members of his generation who "came of age" after independence, Karnad is acutely conscious of India's recently acquired political autonomy and nationhood, but as a trained mathematician heading to Oxford on a Rhodes Scholarship, he has not forged a writerly relationship either with his country or with any community of contemporaries. Unlike Dutt, he has no sense of a national theatrical tradition, no awareness of usable Indian models in drama, and no connection to theater as a form of institutionalized performance. As the play takes shape in 1960–61, before, during, and after the passage to England, even its eclectic synthesis of the Greek tragic playwrights, Jean Anouilh, Jean-Paul Sartre, and Eugene O'Neill draws on abstract textual encounters, not actual experiences in the theater based on the communality of spectatorship.[21] As a process with an unforeseen outcome, the writing of *Yayati* is therefore a galvanizing event for Karnad in three major ways: the psychodrama of authorship reveals that ancient myth carries its own meanings even as it becomes an impersonal means of displacing personal turmoil; every aspect of the play confirms the movement away from orientalist and cultural-nationalist valuations of the past, even though the play "nailed" its author to that very legacy; and the surprisingly positive reception of the play in print and performance creates the authorial identity as playwright that Karnad prioritizes for the rest of his richly varied, multimedia creative life.

The palimpsest of *Yayati* was created over several decades in two languages, but given my unfamiliarity with Kannada, Karnad's translation of 2008 has to serve in my discussion as the "authorized" version he wished to make public. The outstanding feature of *this* play, especially in comparison with Dutt's *Sharmishtha/Sermista* pairing, is the thoroughness with which it reshapes mythical material, redistributes thematic emphases, and invents new characters to structure the story as an ironic drama of discontent, futility, and death. Yayati is a self-centered epicurean whose egotism and coarse sensuality position him as an "antihero" in the modernist tradition of Anouilh: he invites the curse because he cannot overcome his desire for Sharmishtha, even though Devayani has warned him about the destructive consequences of his choice. Pooru (Karnad's variant spelling of the name) is a philosophical but self-hating "outsider" who feels unsettled by the questionable legitimacy of his birth, and oppressed by the weight of dynastic tradition. When the curse is pronounced, Pooru accepts it because he thinks the sacrifice of his youth would counteract his feelings of unworthiness and enable him to fulfill his destiny as a Chandravanshi prince.[22] However, in a deviation from the *Mahabharata* story, Karnad's Pooru has just returned home with a new bride, Chitralekha, who tries to accept his sacrifice but commits suicide in revulsion at the thought that Yayati is now her rightful husband. Too late, Yayati tries to atone for his actions by restoring Pooru's youth and withdrawing into the forest, but Sharmishtha points out to him the foundation of his "glorious future": "a woman dead, another gone mad, and a third in danger of her life" (*Yayati*, 68). The counter-oedipal logic of the traditional Indian family structure leads a self-doubting son to surrender to the will of a self-centered father, even though his decision destroys everyone in his circle. Like the effete figures in T. S. Eliot's "The Dry Salvages," who "had the experience but missed the meaning," Pooru ends the play on a note of stark bewilderment, unable to comprehend the point of what he has endured.

Karnad's portrait of an overbearing patriarch and a weak-willed son is a displaced expression of his resentment against the element of "emotional blackmail" and male generational conflicts in family relations, and this method of indirect reference to the present characterizes all his myth and history plays. But the most memorable feature of *Yayati* and a striking accomplishment for a twenty-two-year-old author is its quartet of sentient, articulate, embittered and yet self-possessed women, all of whom are subject in varying degrees to the whims of men, but succeed in subverting the male world through an assertion of their own rights and privileges. Devayani the brahman queen and Sharmishtha the slave-princess are caught in a fierce rivalry that allegorizes the hierarchical divisions of caste while also visiting upon both women the destructive effects of Yayati's amoral desire. Such a triangulation, between two men and one woman or one man and two women, reappears so consistently in Karnad's myth and folk-based plays as to constitute a basic plot device as well as a central thematic. In *Yayati*, the fictional Chitralekha adds another dimension to gender conflicts because, unlike Pooru, she rejects the king's authority over her and sees no reason to interest herself in Yayati's "unborn future" (65). Before killing herself, she also reminds Yayati that incestuous adultery between them would be the logical implication of his assumption of Pooru's youth. As the play's most complex female character, Sharmishtha is quite unlike her counterpart in the *Mahabharata* or in Dutt: she endures rather than seeks Yayati's attentions, knows that she is doomed by his pursuit of her, and confronts him with the immorality of his quest for a surrogate victim. In dialogue that is transparently contemporary, she also tries to dissuade his son from assuming the curse because "that is utter stupidity! Pooru, the desire for self-sacrifice is a rank perversion" (50). This chorus of unusual female voices, mixed in with the flawed male utterances, humanizes the myth and gives it ethical and dialectical weight, especially because of the fully realized interiority of Karnad's imagined mythic figures.

The structure of the play is another locus for the ironic—and modernist—disruption of norms. In both *Sharmishtha* and *Yayati*, the use of an epic Sanskrit source prompts the inclusion of Sanskrit dramaturgical elements, but Karnad limits his borrowing to the classical/folk convention of the *Sutradhar* (the master of ceremonies who mediates the action for the audience) and uses it only as a detachable, self-reflexive frame at the beginning and end, leaving the intervening action of the play completely undisturbed by metatheatrical "intrusions." In the prologue the Sutradhar rehearses the conventional claim that he is "responsible" for the text to be presented as well as its effective performance, but the real purpose of his set piece is to establish the play's modernist credentials. "We turn to ancient lore," the Sutradhar contends, "not because it offers any blinding revelation or hope of consolation, but because it provides fleeting glimpses of the fears and desires sleepless within us. It is a good way to get introduced to ourselves" (6). By insisting that "a play based on myth" is not a "mythological," he connects *Yayati* to chaotic human experience ("not a well-charted map but a network of paths") rather than to the structures of religious devotion (the desire for "divine grace" and redemption).[23] The Sutradhar also declares that the play contains no gods and deals with death, deliberately invoking Nietzsche and the existentialist philosophy of Sartre and Camus, two authors read widely by Karnad's generation of writers and intellectuals in India. The short epilogue at the end of the play is an exercise in pure irony. The Sutradhar "erases" the existentialist despair of Pooru's final cry, "What does all this mean, O God? What does it mean?," by insisting that the conventions of Sanskrit drama demand a happy ending, and so we must accept the "authority of the epics that Pooru ruled long and wisely and was hailed as a philosopher king" (69–70). Ancient myth yields modernist meaning, but form also subverts content: Karnad continues in the 2008 text of *Yayati* the self-undermining use of traditional conventions he had begun in *Hayavadana* (Horse-head, 1971) and repeated in *Naga-mandala* (Play with a cobra, 1988).

What deepens the irony is that the four-act drama sandwiched between the prologue and epilogue is a showpiece of Western-style construction, observing the *Aristotelian* unities of time, place, and action to maximize the affective impact of unraveling relationships in a structure that deviates substantially from the original story. The action begins early on the evening of Pooru's return to the capital city with his bride Chitralekha, moves through the quarrel between Devayani and Sharmishtha, Yayati's seduction of Sharmishtha, and Shukracharya's curse against Yayati, and concludes with Chitralekha's suicide that same night, after Pooru's assumption of his father's curse has transformed him into a decrepit old man. The unchanging setting for the entire play is the "inner chamber" in Yayati's palace, which is the royal couple's bedchamber, but is also the scene of seduction, Pooru's fond memories of his dead mother, and Chitralekha's final confrontation with Yayati. This continuity in time and space creates an atmosphere of relentless crisis, sustained in turn by the perlocutionary thrust of the dialogue. As characters spar with each other and try to "make things happen" through actions as well as words, details from the past are filled in, and old antagonisms erupt in the present, culminating in the curse pronounced by Shukracharya, the most powerful perlocutionary act of all.

The third distinctive feature of the revised *Yayati* is antithetical to the first two because it highlights the invocation of ancient social hierarchies and tribal identities. It is essential to the play's psychosocial codes that Yayati is a *Chandravanshi* king, Devayani a *brahman* queen in a *kshatriya* palace, Shukracharya a *brahman* sage with the power to curse, Sharmishtha an *Asura* princess who describes herself as a *rakshasi* (demoness), and Chitralekha an *Anga* princess already disappointed in her weak, "mongrel" husband. Sharmishtha's partly subhuman or nonhuman identity accounts for her ungovernable behavior and Yayati's fascination with her, as he explains to Devayani when she wants to know why he desires Sharmishtha (fig. 3.1): "Because I feel bewitched by her. Even now, at this moment, I want her. I have never felt so entranced by a woman. What is it? Is it some spell she has cast? Some secret sorcery? I can feel youth bursting out within me again. Her beauty, her intelligence, her wit, her abandon in love. Not to marry her is to lose her, don't you see? I must have her. I have to keep her with me. Please try to understand" (30).

FIGURE 3.1. Amrish Puri as Yayati and Tarla Mehta as Sharmishtha in *Yayati*, directed by Satyadev Dubey, Indian National Theatre, Bombay, 1967. Photo credit: Rajeev Puri.

What kinds of "contemporary" meanings do these ancient, mythic markers of identity carry? Do they represent the dichotomy of culture and nature, mind and body, high and low birth? Or the destructive effects of desire in a repressed and repressive patriarchal culture? Or the erasure of individual identity in group-speak and group-think, a form of social and cultural determinism—or all of the above? The play invites these interpretations, but it is also worth noting that the social-cultural polarities represented by the two principal women are translated into their sexual natures and are absorbed into the sexual rivalry that becomes the engine of destruction. Similarly, Chitralekha's suicide follows her horrified reaction to the actual sight of Pooru's decrepit body, and her revulsion against the father-in-law who has become the logical stand-in for her husband. The "ancient" identity categories estrange and defamiliarize these characters, whereas the triangulation of the relationships between Devayani-Yayati-Sharmishtha and Pooru-Chitralekha-Yayati refamiliarizes them. Karnad's revised text, designed for efficient staging, stays brilliantly suspended between the ancient and the contemporary.[24] The myth belongs simultaneously to the past and the present, offering opportunities for philosophical reflection without the constraints of realism or the need for a contemporary setting. In comparison, Mohan Rakesh's approach to the past, discussed in the sections that follow, blurs the distinction between myth and history and translates the historic/public into the intensely personal.

In terms of the juxtaposition of Dutt and Karnad, some remarkable coincidences can be noted in conclusion. Across more than a century, two playwrights at the very beginning of their careers are drawn to the same myth from the *Mahabharata* for their first full-length plays, in Bengali and Kannada, respectively. Unlike the premodern poets mentioned in Karnad's 1995 interview, the playwrights' shared challenge is not to "translate" the classic but to mold the mythic material available again for urban literary drama under entirely new conditions into a "play" on a recognizably Western model, embodied by Shakespeare in the case of Dutt, and Anouilh and other modernist myth-makers in the theater in the case of Karnad. This turn toward Western forms is the cosmopolitan choice for bringing the classic into modernity, first under colonial and later under postcolonial cultural-political conditions. The plays are then rendered into English by the authors themselves, very promptly by Dutt (in 1859) and very belatedly by Karnad (in 2008), modeling all that is implied and accomplished when a work in a "regional" Indian language is carried across into the globally accessible medium of English. The playwrights' work of translation has a further dimension: Dutt and Karnad are the two most systematically bilingual modern Indian playwrights, producing original Indian-language as well as Anglophone drama, and functioning as the exclusive translators of their work across both languages. Beyond this, the shared myth from the *Mahabharata* is an index of the distance between modern and modernist authorship, established by the radically different ways in which the Yayati myth shapes the playwrights' historical self-positioning, perceptions of the past, cultural aspirations in the present, literary objectives, and approaches to form, language, and meaning.

MOHAN RAKESH AND THE REMOTE INDIAN PAST: A MODERNIST CALIBRATION

Mohan Rakesh's earlier profile as a self-fashioning modernist needs expansion in the context of this chapter: he is the consummate practitioner of modernist *classicism* in Indian theater, which can also be described as the "delivery" of the classic to readers and viewers via works that bring his distinctive brand of author, form, and language-centered modernism to the matter of the past. Because of his untimely death at the age of forty-seven, most of the shorter works he wrote for performance—one-act plays, radio plays, and plays of "stasis" (*bij natak*)—were published not in his lifetime but posthumously, and the process of systematic retrieval was not completed until Jaidev Taneja's edition of the *Mohan rakesh rachanavali* (The works of Mohan Rakesh, 13 vols., 2011). When the numerous works in which Rakesh engages with past narratives are considered together in this standard compendium, several significant patterns emerge. He produced novels, short stories, plays, and nonfiction on an extensive scale and at a dizzying pace, but drama was the *only* genre in which he traveled backward in time: the rest of his creative output was concerned with the recent ("modern") past or the contemporaneous present. In the plays set in earlier times, he also bypassed myth altogether and focused on iconic figures in ancient history, caught at life-altering moments in their lives: Vardhaman Mahavir, the founder of Jainism (seventh century BCE) in *Vida nisha* (The night of separation, one-act play, 1954); Gautam Siddhartha, the founder of Buddhism, and his half-brother Nanda (sixth century BCE) in *Raat bitane tak* (Until the night ends, radio play, 1957) and *Laharon ke rajhans* (full-length play, 1957–68 in various versions); Emperor Ashoka, the most famous convert to Buddhism (third century BCE), in *Kalinga vijay* (Victory over Kalinga, two-act play, 1945–1958 in three different versions); and Kalidasa, the foremost Sanskrit poet-playwright (fifth century CE) in *Ashadh ka ek din* (full-length play, 1958).[25] The preferential relationship between the remote past as subject and drama as form continued in the sphere of translation: the *only* published Hindi translations by Rakesh in which ancient India is the setting and Sanskrit the source-language are two full-length plays—Shudraka's *Mrichchhakatika* (The little clay cart, 1961) and Kalidasa's *Shakuntala* (1965)—and a one-act adaptation of Bhasa's *Swapna vasavadattam* (The dream of Vasavadatta), based on the Marathi playwright Vasant Sabnis's shortened Sanskrit adaptation of the original.

Given Rakesh's copious output in multiple literary genres, his decision to limit historical subject matter exclusively to *plays* of various kinds reflects the prominence of Indian classical antiquity as well as its drama in his education, which included master's degrees in Sanskrit and Hindi (following a BA in English), the experience of acting in and directing Sanskrit plays in college, and struggles with the translation of Sanskrit drama that were eventually successful in the case of Kalidasa and Shudraka. This multifaceted pedagogic immersion in classical Sanskrit and the postclassical traditions of Hindi poetry, prose, and theater created in Rakesh a much more serious, almost "scholarly" understanding of cultural and literary history, in contrast with Karnad's instinctual gravitation toward myth. But over the same time period, and during the two subsequent decades, he also turned classical pedagogy into a large-scale creative engagement with ancient Indian history, its religious underpinnings, and the literature it produced. Indeed, if the dates for the writing, revision, publication, and performance of Rakesh's original history plays, and of his three translations of classical Sanskrit drama, are taken collectively into consideration, as a *playwright* he appears to be almost continuously involved with historical subject matter and historic ancient works from 1945 until 1968. The process ends only in 1969 with *Adhe adhure*, the one full-length play published and performed in his lifetime that has the contemporary setting of postindependence Delhi.

Rakesh's "classicism" is therefore practiced and refined over a lifetime, and one of its qualities is a decisive modernist rejection of orientalist and cultural-nationalist aggrandizements of the past—"modernism" being defined here as an iconoclastic attitude toward cultural history as well as a set of aesthetic choices. Explaining why he did not send out his first short story about Nanda and Sundari for publication, he notes that "the characters and situations in the story were 'historical' in the general sense of the term, and I've always had a kind of aversion towards literary works with historical contexts" (*MRR*, vol. 3, 92).[26] However, he did put the two-acter *Kalinga vijay* into print in 1945 because "in a play that [historical] context does not seem as unnatural as in a short story" (92). Rakesh clearly prefers the dialogic genre of theater to the diegetic modes of prose fiction and nonfiction to carry on his conversations with history, and his preface to the first edition of *Laharon ke rajhans* (1963), which as an authorial statement appears strategically *between* his two full-length history plays, becomes a condensed manifesto on his approach to history-as-literary-and-theatrical-source.

His first goal in this preface is to rescue history from the "traditionalist attitudes and beliefs" that obsessively "place our civilizational symbols on a superhuman plane [because] any evidence of ordinary humanity in them hurts us" (*POM*, 231). Humanizing his historical characters is especially critical for Rakesh because they are remote as well as world-altering figures, apotheosized altogether beyond the human scale. Second, from the viewpoint of the present, the value of historical icons is symbolic, not literal, especially if very little is known about them with any certainty. "Kalidasa," therefore, may not be a historically verifiable individual, but it was important to imagine him as a protagonist in *Ashadh ka ek din* because Rakesh "could not find a better label, a better signifier, for our cumulative creative energies up to this point in time" (*POM*, 232). The third categorical distinction is between "history" and its literary uses.

> The dependence on history or historical figures does not turn literature into history. History accumulates facts, and presents them in a temporal sequence. This has never been the objective of literature. Filling the empty chambers of history is also not an area of accomplishment for literature. Literature is not bound by the time of history, it articulates history inside time; it does not separate one era from another, but joins many eras together. . . . For this reason, history is not expressed in literature through its incontrovertible events, but through an imagination that links events together and creates a separate, new history of its own kind. This creation is not history in the conventional sense. To look for that kind of history one really should go to the scholarly tomes of historians. (*POM*, 232–33)

Consistent with this separation, Rakesh's full-length history plays have intertextual connections not with written or published *historiographic* sources (that are the norm in Western historical drama) but with the *literary* output of his historical subject (Kalidasa in *Ashadh*) and a Sanskrit verse epic (Ashvaghosha's *Saundarananda* in *Rajhans*). The principle of creative license is especially well-articulated in relation to the second play. Rakesh argues that Ashvaghosha took the story of Nanda and Sundari "much further" than the commentary on them in the *Dhammapada* (the canonical third century BCE collection of the Buddha's sayings), and he is free to develop the same narrative into an "imaginary" representation "because of the reconfiguration of circumstances in the fullness of time" (*POM*, 233). Like the imagined life of Kalidasa in *Ashadh*, Nanda and Sundari's crisis is "merely a launching pad" for a conflict that is "modern" (Rakesh's term). "The people deeply devoted to ancient texts should not be taken aback" by this; instead, they should "find the satisfaction of history based on facts in a different place, and . . . not search for it in this play" (*POM*, 233). The matter of history sustains itself because it speaks to and in the present.

This theoretical and polemical space-clearing by Rakesh creates the appropriate framework for considering what he sees as the modernity latent in specific chronotopic moments in the remote Indian past, some of which appear more than once in his drama. Rakesh's plays about Mahavir and Gautam Buddha reveal his fascination with two transformative historic/al moments when new indigenous religions emerged on the subcontinent to challenge the hegemony of Vedic Hinduism, and did so through theological systems based coincidentally on the principle of Enlightenment through a complete monastic renunciation of the world. In all versions of the plays involving this history, Rakesh's primary emphasis is on the agonizing conflict between an established worldly life of power and self-indulgence and the new prospect of liberation through ascetic discipline, for men as well as women. A revealing dramaturgical move is to keep the male religious actualists Mahavir and the Buddha firmly off the stage, and to focus instead on the women they leave behind—wife Yashoda and daughter Sunanda in *Vida nisha*, and on a much more elaborate scale, the childless Sundari in the pretexts and texts of *Laharon ke rajhans*. The figure of the abandoned wife turns the spiritual conflict into a conjugal one, bringing fully into play the sanctity and mystique associated with the rites and rights of marriage in Hinduism. The departing husbands cannot respond to their wives' grief, only profess their inability to stay. In *Ashadh ka ek din*, the forsaken woman, Mallika, is Kalidas's muse and lover, not his wife, but the persistent motif of the charismatic man who walks away from a desolate mate reappears in this play in the context of literary (rather than religious) greatness. *Kalinga vijay* is the only play in which Rakesh moves away from female abjection to give three women the power to bring about a monumental change of heart in an invincible conqueror. In Emperor Ashoka's court, his wife Asandhimitra takes the lead in converting him from the bloodlust of war to the enlightened pacifism of Buddhism, helped by the grieving mother of one dead soldier and the wife of another, who together bear witness to the ruined lives that are the price of Ashoka's victory over the Kalinga region. Abjection in the other plays, however, does not mean absence or silence, and all the plays about the past separately or together underscore Rakesh's radical regendering of history. Whatever their position in the sociopolitical hierarchy and whatever the limits of their agency, women dominate the plays, as wives, mothers, daughters, courtesans, servants, and victims. Rakesh also often uses fictional license to portray socially subordinate women as articulate and fearless, capable of bending powerful men to their will even as the men's wives capitulate. Against this varied backdrop, Rakesh's well-documented twenty-year struggle with the figure of Sundari positions her as the most poetic, complex, and wayward embodiment of gendered power and abjection in the history plays, making her the active agent in all three versions of the dissolution of her life with Nanda.[27]

RAKESH, ASHVAGHOSHA, AND THE THEATRICALIZATIONS OF HISTORY

In the introduction to her translation of *Saundarananda*, Linda Covill notes that the legend related in the poem "was widely known. . . . Ashvaghosha's 'Handsome Nanda' is the longest, most complex and most convincing formulation of a popular legend that engaged the Buddhist imagination for many centuries," and existed in Pali, Sinhala, Sanskrit, Chinese, and Tibetan versions.[28] The poem's eighteen Cantos construct a "spiritual biography" of Nanda, which begins with descriptions of the city of Kapilavastu, the Buddha's father, King Shudhhodhan, and the Buddha himself as "the realized one" (Cantos 1–3); moves on to the intensely passionate relationship of Nanda and Sundari, Nanda's forced initiation, and the couple's laments (Cantos 4–7); and then settles into the long narrative of Nanda's desperate initial resistance against his monastic conversion, followed gradually by a state not only of acceptance but of triumph and spiritual bliss (Cantos 8–18). The Buddha takes a very active, even coercive role in the liberation of Nanda from the sensory world and the endless cycle of birth and death, whereas Sundari does not appear in the poem after the sixth Canto. In Canto 8, titled "The Attack on Women," Sundari becomes emblematic of her "ruinous" gender, and Nanda is described as a caged bird who has been set free but wants to return to captivity because he is unwilling to recognize that "women's hearts are cunning, utterly duplicitous, pernicious and superficial" (167). The second half of *Saundarananda* is dominated by the presence of the Buddha, his teachings, his personal interventions in the *agon* of Nanda's spiritual makeover, and Nanda's tribute to the Buddha when his knowledge has been perfected. In the final verses of the poem, Ashvaghosha describes its spiritual message as the gold that is hidden in the "ore-born dust" of poetry (365).

Given the multiple intertextual relationships Rakesh established with *Saundarananda* over two decades, a summary of the source-story of Nanda and Sundari is useful in clarifying his modernist reorientations. In the part of the epic focused on this couple, Ashvaghosha follows the convention of creating a dominant *rasa* (flavor or essence) in each Canto: Canto 4 invokes mainly the *shringara rasa*, associated with romantic-erotic love and beauty, and Cantos 5–7 highlight the *karuna rasa*, which evokes pathos, alongside *viraha*, the sorrow of separation. Nanda is introduced briefly in the second Canto as the younger son of King Shuddhodhan, blessed with "superlative looks" that make him seem like "the god of love in human form," but he is also "for ever idl[ing] away his time in pleasures" (59). A perfect match for Nanda, "with her captivating beauty and manner to match, in the world of humankind she, Sundari, was the loveliest of women" (81). In the fourth Canto, the union of Nanda and Sundari is portrayed in terms of unrestrained carnality: "Blind with passion, the couple took their pleasure in each other . . . as though they were a home to joy and rapture, as though they were a vessel for arousal and satiety. . . . [They] gave each other pleasure by exciting passion in each other, while in languid moments they teasingly inebriated each other by way of mutual entertainment" (81–83). Nanda has defied the Buddha's call for renunciation by continuing his hedonistic lifestyle in Kapilavastu, but the erotic mood is soon interrupted in this Canto when Nanda discovers that his brother had arrived at his doorstep to receive alms, and then returned empty-handed because all the servants were attending to their master's pleasure. Nanda decides to go to the Buddha's riverside *vihara* (monastery) to offer his apology, and he promises Sundari that he will return quickly, before the sandalwood *visheshaka* (cosmetic mark) made by him on her cheek has dried. However, the Buddha prevents him from returning home because he wants Nanda to be liberated from the "dirt of the defilements," and Nanda is ordained as a *bhikshuka* (mendicant) against his wishes. Sundari is utterly distraught at the news but unwilling to accept that "her husband, though demonstrably passionate and attuned to her, had taken refuge in the *dharma*" (117); she becomes convinced that he is abandoning her for another woman. Nanda, in turn, bears "the signs ordained by the teacher on his body, but not in his heart" (133), and knows that his renunciation is not complete if his desires persist. However, his resolution to "go home again, and make love legitimately, as I please" (145) is scuttled by the attack on women, and in Canto

10 he forgets Sundari immediately when the Buddha takes him to heaven and tempts him with the *apsarases* (celestial women). The remainder of the poem charts the spiritual journey that gradually empties Nanda of all desire and brings success in the ultimate Buddhist quest: freedom from the sensory world, and an end to the inexorable cycle of birth and death.

Rakesh's multiple dramatizations of this poetic content (as a short radio play and two interconnected full-length plays for the stage) share one dominant goal: to extract the story of Nanda and Sundari from a narrative in which their relationship represents only a subordinate strain, and develop it into a fully gendered confrontation between man/woman, attraction/repulsion, pleasure/pain, self-indulgence/self-denial, and mutuality/singularity, against the backdrop of the monumental sociopolitical and spiritual transformation brought about by Buddhism as a new religion of enlightenment. The Buddha is a galvanizing offstage presence in all three versions, but the plays are not about his unilateral intrusions into Nanda's life, or Nanda's long passage to enlightenment; instead, they trace the effects of his message on the privileged and companionate couple whose sense of self compels them to resist his call on emotional and philosophical grounds, but whose relationship fails due to growing incomprehension and antagonism in the face of the life-altering challenge. These are the "modern" meanings Rakesh reads into the ancient narrative "because of the reconfiguration of circumstances in the fullness of time," bringing the plays incrementally closer to his own troubled marriages and the toxic portrait of conjugal and family life in the last play published before his death, *Adhe adhure* (1969). In the process of reconfiguration, three prominent thematic shifts appear on a limited scale in the radio play, *Raat bitane tak* (hereafter *RBT*), and are fully developed in the two versions of *Laharon ke rajhans* (hereafter *LKR 1* and *LKR 2*).

First, Rakesh places women and their diverse voices at the center so that the misogyny of Ashvaghosha's text can be decisively undone. In *RBT* Sundari and Nanda are given approximately equal time and weight, but in the stage plays Sundari (the name means "beautiful woman") is a willful but elegant and vulnerable presence, and Nanda appears as the pliant and ultimately reactive husband whose crisis never takes precedence in the conjugal drama. In all three plays, Sundari is initially outspoken in her mockery of the Buddha and contempt for his other-worldly preoccupations because she sees her own privilege and sway over Nanda as an affirmation of the power of femininity. The metamorphosis of Prince Gautam Siddhartha into "the

PALIMPSESTS OF THE PAST

FIGURE 3.2. Vinita Rallin as Sundari and Chetana Tiwari as Alka in *Laharon ke rajhans*, directed by Shyamanand Jalan, Anamika, Calcutta, July 1966. Photo credit: Natya Shodh Sansthan.

Buddha," she tells her maid Alka, was a womanly failure on the part of his wife, Yashodhara, who needed to be more like Sundari: "her femininity did not have the allure which would have enabled her to keep Prince Siddhartha bound by her side forever.... You are very innocent right now, Alka! You cannot understand what the attraction of woman can accomplish. Yashodhara could not understand it either" (*MRR*, vol. 4, 207; fig. 3.2).

Interestingly, the resistance to this position also comes from women who are articulate and self-possessed, despite their subservient social positions. In *RBT* Alka tells Sundari that the people's overwhelming response to the Buddha's message is real, not a passing fad, and the courtesan Chandrika stops dancing as the night wanes because at dawn she is going to begin a new life as an ordained *bhikshuni*. In *LKR 1*, Sundari's reaction to Nanda's ordination therefore expresses not only shock but feelings of humiliation and hurt pride because she cannot understand how *her* husband could go away from her and then "let all of this happen. Why did you let it happen?" (*MRR*, vol. 3, 84). In *LKR 2* this emotion hardens into a settled contempt for Nanda, but what she feels and says always supersedes his perplexities.

Second, *RBT* is the only work in which the frank carnality of Nanda and Sundari's relationship (as described by Ashvaghosha) finds even brief expression: they do begin a night of erotic celebration (a *kamotsava*) that is captured in the sounds of music, dancing, and progressive intoxication, but these are drowned out by the resonant Buddhist chant as the Buddha arrives incognito on their doorstep: *Buddham sharanam gachchhami / Dhammam sharanam gachchhami* (I'm going to take refuge in the Buddha / I'm going to take refuge in *dharma* [*MRR*, vol. 4, 219]). In contrast with both *Saundarananda* and *RBT*, Rakesh's portrayal of Nanda and Sundari in *LKR 1* and *2* is conspicuously *de-libidinized*: he replaces carnality (which would be difficult to present on the urban Indian stage, in any case) with a fragile mutuality that is constantly being threatened by the outside world and gives the couple's interactions a kind of repressed, active-passive quality as they move toward inevitable separation. This qualitative change underscores that the Buddha's message has already seeped into the consciousness of all those characters in the play who have not yet responded to his call, sapping them of energy and will, whatever their social standing. For example, in Act 1 of both plays, Sundari's carefully planned *kamotsava* fails to happen because her guests refuse the invitation, and even the servants express distaste about being drawn into the festive preparations the night before Princess Yashodhara's ordination as a *bhikshuni*. In Act 2, after Sundari's night of rage, the couple try to regain their equilibrium through moments of intimacy and devotion, but the conjugal scene is disrupted first by the Buddhist chant, which startles Nanda and causes him to break Sundari's mirror, and then by Nanda's departure for the *vihara*. As the action unfolds, Sundari comes through not as an apotheosis of sensuality but as a peremptory princess, a remorseful and affectionate wife, and a woman wounded by what she sees as her husband's cowardly capitulation to his charismatic brother. Moving along this narrative arc, Nanda is by turns protective, apologetic, uxorious, reflective, or despondent in relation to Sundari, but he is never an aggressively masculine or carnal presence.

Third, Rakesh preserves the "historical/poetic" claim that Nanda's ordination was not voluntary but brought on by a specific sequence of events, and he also retains that sequence as a core plot device in all three works: the Buddha fails to receive alms in Nanda's palace home; Nanda wants to make amends, inscribes the sandalwood mark on Sundari's forehead, and promises to return before it is dry; he then comes back in mendicant's clothes, with a shaved head, precipitating the marital crisis. The circumstantial conversion, however, is not portrayed by Rakesh merely as an act of capitulation because Nanda responds to it in spiritual and philosophical terms that vary from play to play. The elements of mutuality and acceptance are strongest in *RBT*. Sundari does not accuse her husband of infidelity or collapse at the sight of him, but voices her state of confusion and dread as she waits for him to return. Nanda gives clarity to his experience by understanding the end of the night they were trying to prolong desperately as the beginning of a spiritual rebirth: "the night is over, Sundari. I have put the darkness inside myself in Gautam Buddha's alms-dish. You can now put the darkness within yourself into my alms-dish" (*MRR*, vol. 4, 219). At the very end of the play we see (or hear) Sundari beginning to hesitantly voice the words of the chant. This element of resolution disappears entirely in the two full-length plays. In *LKR 1* Nanda tries to repudiate his ritual transformation on the philosophical-spiritual grounds that he has not relinquished any of his attachments and desires, but Sundari accidentally catches a glimpse of his altered appearance and reacts with revulsion, claiming that "the person who has returned is really someone else," not her husband (*MRR*, vol. 3, 84; fig. 3.3).

FIGURE 3.3. Vinita Rallin as Sundari and Shyamanand Jalan as Nanda in *Laharon ke rajhans*, directed by Shyamanand Jalan, Anamika, Calcutta, July 1966. Photo credit: Natya Shodh Sansthan.

Nanda leaves home again, to compel the Buddha to restore his old self because he believes Sundari cannot bear to see his shorn head and beggar's clothes, and Sundari's despair at the end—"That's all these people are able to understand!" (87)—comes from the realization that Nanda has failed to grasp her sense of humiliation and betrayal as a woman, and hence trivialized her crisis. In *LKR 2*, Rakesh brings the couple face-to-face in a third-act confrontation that is a displaced version of gender conflicts in the life of the late-twentieth-century (male/Indian) writer, moving ancient history and poetry firmly to the sidelines.

The discussion of *Saundaranand* and Rakesh's three dramatic versions of it in this section has considered the ways in which he maintains a broad narrative connection to his source while deviating from it in thematically decisive ways. This refashioning is a core feature of the postcolonial modernist fictionalization of history, and Rakesh complicates that paradigm by anchoring his fiction in poetry rather than written history, and by producing multiple versions of the classic. Shaping this intertextual density are the narrative's figural elements, which create through modernist symbolism and dialectic the particular atmosphere, tone, and philosophical texture of the two full-length plays. These features, invented by Rakesh, are my subject in the final section.

"THERE IS SOMETHING THAT SHOULD HAVE BEEN IN THIS PLAY": *LAHARON KE RAJHANS*, 1963-1968

Lampstands and Drifting Swans: 1963

The intensely poetic-symbolic genesis of the story of Nanda and Sundari in Rakesh's dramaturgy is captured by two images that he himself describes as seminal. The first image formed inexplicably in his mind when he first read through Ashvaghosha's poem—of two metal lampstands, one tall, with a male figure at the top, arms outstretched and eyes lifted toward the sky; the other short, with a female figure at the top, arms drawn in and eyes bent toward the ground. In the preface to the 1968 edition of the play, Rakesh notes that over twenty years, "I don't know how many times and in how many different ways I have watched the misty scene between these lampstands change. . . . I have not had this experience with any other work until now. I have made changes in other works as well, but by staying very close to the original—more or less along its margins.... But this is not the case with *Laharon ke rajhans*" (*MRR*, vol. 3, 91).

The second image emerges in a couplet near the end of the fourth Canto in *Saundarananda*:

> *tam gauravam buddhagatam chakarsha bharyanuragah punarachakarsha*
> *so' nischayanna apiyayo na tasthau taranstarangeshviva rajahamsah*

("Reverence for the Buddha drew him on, love for his wife drew him back again. He hesitated, neither going nor staying, like a king-goose pushing forward against the waves")

(COVILL 91)

In the original poem, the lone swan riding against the waves symbolizes Nanda's dilemma, with his older brother and his wife standing for two irreconcilable extremes. Rakesh adapts the image to his play by changing Ashvaghosha's single *rajahamsah* (more accurately translated as "royal swan") into plural swans who belong effortlessly *to* the waves as they drift, swimming neither with nor against the current.

The symbolism of these dissimilar images anchors the portrait of conjugality, and what it implies in relation to home and belonging, in both versions of *Laharon ke rajhans*. The lampstands are described as stage props at the beginning of the stage directions in Act 1, and they play a conspicuous role in the blocking of action in Acts 2 and 3. As material objects, they appear to set up a contrast between the outward-looking, liberated man and the shrinking, self-absorbed woman, the inequality in their statures just one more confirmation of their prescribed gender roles. But in a letter to Shyamanand Jalan dated August 25, 1965, Rakesh explains the symbolism in different terms: "The core conflict in the play is the conflict between earthly and non-earthly values. Sundari, as a symbol of the earth, wants to keep man and his consciousness tied to herself. Man wants to be tied in this way, but also wants to rise above that, wants to find some fulfilment for himself through an other-worldly curiosity" (*SN*, 208).

Sundari is focused on the concrete particulars that make her life possible; Nanda has an interest in engaging with abstractions; and the Buddha is the visionary who tells the entire world to transcend its worldly concerns

FIGURE 3.4. Seema Biswas as Sundari and Jitendra Shastri as Nanda in *Laharon ke rajhans*, directed by Kirti Jain, National School of Drama Repertory Company, New Delhi, 1992. Photo credit: Kirti Jain and NSD Repertory Company.

(figs. 3.4 and 3.5). Hence "Sundari and the Buddha," Rakesh adds in the letter to Jalan, "are not two persons or personalities, they are two visions of life or two *vital forces* under whose influence [Nanda's] mind is in a constant state of revolt" (*SN*, 208). The symbolism of the lampstands conveys not a reductive view of gender but the struggle between competing (though unequal) selfhoods in Sundari and Nanda, which progresses from mutual misunderstanding in *LKR 1* to mutual hostility in *LKR 2*, while retaining the basic differences outlined by Rakesh.

Perspectives on gender are complicated further by the parallels and counterpoints Rakesh creates between Nanda, Sundari, and two socially subordinate characters, the palace attendant Shyamang ("the dark-bodied one") who, like Nanda, "thinks too much," and the maid Alka ("diamond," but also "girl with beautiful hair"), who is deeply attached to Sundari but thinks for herself.[29] Sundari's overt antipathy toward Shyamang, added to her ambivalence toward Nanda, aligns the two men further and emphasizes her impatience with male interiority, in contrast with the affection and empathy she displays toward Alka. At the same time, the simple, mutually nurturing love

FIGURE 3.5. Seema Biswas as Sundari and Jitendra Shastri as Nanda in *Laharon ke rajhans*, directed by Kirti Jain, National School of Drama Repertory Company, New Delhi, 1992. Photo credit: Kirti Jain and NSD Repertory Company.

between Alka and Shyamang becomes the obverse of the fraught relationship between Nanda and Sundari, especially when it becomes apparent that Sundari understands her underlings better than she does her husband. Shyamang's psychic collapse, captured in onstage and offstage ravings throughout both plays, parallels Nanda's loss of self, and his cries for relief from darkness mark the modernist displacement at the end of the play.

Shyamang also gets drawn into the reconfigured symbolism of the royal swans, who in this play signify not indecision or natural indolence (as in *Saundarananda* and *RBT*) but beauty, splendor, and loving companionship. The swans have long inhabited a lotus pond on the grounds of the palace, and Sundari has taken pleasure in their daily calls. However, pushed into uncontrollable panic by a gigantic imaginary shadow, Shyamang hurls stones at the pair of swans, injures them, and causes them to fly away. In Act 3, Sundari is unable to understand how the swans could have abandoned their accustomed habitat so easily:

SUNDARI: . . . Would their wings have had enough strength to let them fly away somewhere of their own accord? And the pond where they had been for so long, its familiarity, its attraction—could it have been given up so easily?

ALKA: It's possible that their being hurt was exactly the reason why they flew away ...

(MRR, VOL. 3, 68)

The swans' disappearance heightens Sundari's anxiety at Nanda's prolonged absence from the home to which *he* is accustomed, and she later makes the symbolic connection between the two explicit: "The desolate lotus-pond there, the desolation of this chamber here ... it seems that today home is no longer my own home" (86). The swans' departure overdetermines the separation of Nanda and Sundari and is also the most powerful image among a range of other symbols that are omens of defeat: the strings of decorative leaves that Shyamang cannot untangle in Act 1, the crushed garlands strewn around Sundari's chamber in Act 2, the mirror that Nanda shatters in this chamber when he is startled by the abrupt end of the *bhikshu* chant, the cosmetic mark that Sundari fails to maintain until Nanda's return, and, finally, the forcibly shorn hair that is a synecdoche for the end of Nanda's privileged life.

In the atmosphere of malaise that is generated by this focus on separation and failure, Rakesh creates some space for dialectic, in the exchanges not only between Nanda and Sundari but between them and the various "outsiders" who question their way of life. In one of the closest citations of *Saundarananda*, the *answers* discovered by Ashvaghosha's Nanda at the end of his quest become the *questions* posed by Rakesh's Nanda to the monk Ananda who has ordained him, introducing an element of the "drama of ideas" into a play dominated by repressed emotion.

> If he [the Buddha] had my head shorn, did I become more true as a person? If he had had my tongue or my arms and legs cut off, would I have become even more true? Can anyone say with certainty who is really under an illusion, him or me? (*Moving away from the mirror*) He said, "I am not me, you are not you, he is not he ... all are images created by a moving finger in the sky—they vanish even as they are being made, and their non-presence is no different from their presence." ... But I ask you, if there is no difference between presence and non-presence, then why were my locks cut off? (*Walking again toward the swing and the lampstand in the rear*) And even if they *were* cut off, what difference does it make? Are they not going to grow back in a few days? (*Stopping near the swing*) It would have made a difference if my heart had actually

changed, if my eyes had changed. In my heart there is still the same love for you, in my eyes there is still the same image of your beauty. (80)

Nanda's profession of his love for Sundari suggests that by the play's end the symbolism of the lampstands has changed again. The uneasy earlier dynamic between the two has morphed into a series of binary oppositions, with Sundari embodying the first term and Nanda the second: assertive/diffident, proud/humble, ambitious/restrained, impatient/understanding, egotistical/self-abnegating, bold/timid, self-centered/other-centered, willful/reflective, spontaneous/cautious, decisive/indecisive, and visceral/cerebral. Indeed, the couple could stand for the mind/body dualism, rescued from dwindling into allegorical abstractions by the singularity of Rakesh's simultaneously historical and modern/ist dramatization. The play ends as Nanda's crisis is beginning, and because in this version the couple do not come face-to-face, Sundari's response remains the shallower one.

Interlude in Calcutta: The "Playwright's Theater" in Practice, 1966

In his commentary on the 1968 version of *Laharon ke rajhans*, titled "This altered form of the play," Rakesh notes that after the publication of *LKR 1* in 1963 he had "an answer to every question posed by someone else" about the play, but "no answer . . . to some questions of my own," which crucially included the following: "Why can't Nanda face Sundari after his return? If he feels that he is weak, what is the reason?" (*MRR*, vol. 3, 98). Authorial dissatisfaction of this kind usually remains tangential to the form of a play fixed by print and performance, but Rakesh was offered an unusual opportunity to revisit his work in April 1966, when the Calcutta-based director Shyamanand Jalan invited him to participate in the rehearsals for a July production, and to rewrite the third act in collaboration with him and his theater group, Anamika. Jalan had just returned from a four-month theater tour of Europe and the United States with the conviction that the playwright, not the director, was the central figure in theater.[30] This accorded well with a desire Rakesh had harbored since the beginning of his career as a playwright, and expressed in the essay, "The Playwright and the Stage" (1966): of "joining the creative process of playwriting with the experimentalism of the theater," so that plays would ideally be published after they had been tested on stage, and the living author would function as an "integral part" of the culture of performance (*POM*, 236, 234). Rakesh was careful to stress that this "playwright's theater" did not marginalize the director, but pursued a form that could be "explored and refined only through collaborative efforts between the playwright, the director, and the actor" (237). The formulation of these ideas in his essay in fact *followed* his experience in Calcutta, which he described as "perhaps the first time that the processes of writing and presentation could be joined together" in Hindi theater, or even urban Indian theater more generally (238).

With the principle of collaboration established, Rakesh's mandate from Jalan and the actors was to remedy the evasions of 1963 and bring Nanda and Sundari face-to-face in a "confrontation," so that the drama of their separation could acquire depth. But for nearly three months, what Rakesh described as "a joint quest for Nanda and Sundari's destiny, [b]ut even beyond that, the ordinary destiny of woman and man," proved to be singularly elusive (*MRR*, vol. 3, 103). He was certain that "Nanda can no longer exist with Sundari on the old terms," and he "[kept] searching for the words with which I could put this anguished man before Sundari" (104). But Sundari had become so unmanageable that the playwright could not be certain she would listen to Nanda, or accept defeat in any form; nor could she be killed off, as in her portrayal as the "Dying Princess" in an Ajanta cave painting: "the playwright and the director were both helpless about being defeated at the hands of this character" (105). The revelation that enabled Rakesh to overcome this impasse was not about communication and mutual empathy but their obverse: an acceptance of the characters' inability to break through their confusion and despair toward some understanding of what had led to the end of their life together.

> Isn't this presence of woman and man before each other the very condition towards which they evolve? For them to be face-to-face and not be able to get their points across to each other, isn't this their very reality? I felt that what was really wrong was the attempt to carry Nanda and Sundari beyond this resolutionless resolution, towards any kind of definite end. That kind of resolution may carry the play towards a conclusion, but that would not be the reality of Nanda and Sundari. (105)

The playscript was completed when Rakesh arrived at this insight two days before opening night in July 1966. The version of Act 3 in this performance also became the ending in light of which Rakesh rewrote the beginning and the middle of the play in 1966–67.

"This Altered Form of the Play": Confrontation and Failure, 1968

The 1968 version of *Laharon ke rajhans* is in many respects a crisper version of the 1963 text because of both the addition and subtraction of material. The dialogue and stage directions are modified or shortened in many places for greater clarity and economy of expression. There is also a great deal of new dialogue, especially in Act 3, to intensify some features of the play, add more substance to the secondary relationships, and most important, to stage the final contest between Nanda and Sundari. The effects of the Buddha's call to renunciation are more pervasive and more palpable, so the play now *begins* with the *bhikshu* chant, which is like a symbolic death knell for the *kamotsava* Sundari has planned as "the biggest celebration ever in this palace" (*MRR*, vol. 3, 109). Sundari's contempt for the Buddha and his wife is more pronounced, and she expresses her resentment against Shyamang more openly because he is among those "who are always trying to figure out when and how they can destroy the joy that prevails" in her palace (118). The identification between Nanda and Shyamang is stronger, and the latter's psychological collapse takes on a more dire aspect as he spends a large part of the action in a state of unconsciousness. Other palace attendants, especially Shwetang and Alka, are more pointedly concerned about the well-being of their master and mistress, and function as a kind of chorus when they comment on the anguish that is about to overtake the latter's lives. Nanda is more openly affectionate and passionate as a husband, and Sundari more vocal about his weaknesses and her power over him, so that, as the *bhikshu* Anand points out, Nanda inhabits an opulent palace but has no real home "where your soul would find some rest" (159). Cumulatively, these changes set the stage for the showdown in the third act.

After this massive preparation, though, the encounter fails to rise to the level of a genuine dialogue because of a fundamental breach between the communicants. Nanda is eager to discuss what he considers the newly discovered "reality" of his life, and to convince Sundari that his ordination was the result of his own inner compulsions, and not choices imposed by anyone else (166). Sundari, however, insists obdurately that she has "always known" Nanda's reality, that the "real meaning" of his life is not profound but "very, very trivial," and that "there is nothing more to know about it than what I've come to know" (165). Sundari's reason for recoiling from Nanda after his initiation is substantially the same as in *LKR 1*, but she also has new dialogue now that belittles Nanda openly for his susceptibility: "I have known that you are just as ordinary as other ordinary people. That they can be influenced easily, and you can be influenced just as easily. The only difference is that people are perhaps influenced once, but you can be influenced again and again—you can be influenced by just anyone at all" (167). The problem is therefore spelt out more fully, but is essentially the same as in *LKR 1*: Sundari-as-woman has no use for male interiority, and she feels compelled to dismiss the forms of interiority in Nanda that imply conflict, doubt, and indecision.

Nanda's rejoinder to Sundari expresses his growing resistance to her trivialization of his misery.

> I know that you can't bear to listen to all this.... because you think you're the only center around which I revolve like a star in orbit. But I find myself to be the kind of broken star that has no orbit, that has no axis.... When I was with him, my heart was yearning to be here. Now that I'm before you, my heart is yearning for some other place. Because whether here or there, in every place I experience myself as equally incomplete. (168–69)

When even this passionate outburst elicits only the belittling comment from Sundari that she expected his "greater meaning" to be something more than the familiar platitudes he has offered, Nanda realizes that he and his inner turmoil add up to nothing in Sundari's eyes: "while I'm here I'm always just as small as your vision wants to make me. And if that very small being wants to look for a point in his life, how far can he go?" (169). Sundari's response to this moment of irrevocable crisis, which is also the last speech in the play, is a question for Nanda: after every quest that he undertakes in search of life's meaning and the words to express it, "Why is it that you remain exactly the same? The same ... the same ... the same!" (170).

In the course of this conversation, the play breaks free of its historical moorings and becomes a clash between a beautiful, self-regarding woman's desire to control and belittle the introspective man in her life and the compulsion the man feels to reject that control. In this respect, *LKR 2* connects not so much to its many pretexts of 1957–1966 but to the slow collapse of a middle-class family in its most significant posttext, *Adhe adhure*. In this play, the middle-aged married couple are named Savitri and Mahendranath, but they are identified in the dialogue as Woman and Man, establishing both the centrality of the gender conflicts and their allegorical dimension.

Furthermore, the idea that from the woman's standpoint all men eventually turn out to be the same disappointing man is literalized through the theatrical device of a single actor playing four different roles in relation to Savitri, the thirty-nine-year-old modern urban counterpart of Sundari: those of husband, current boss, former lover, and concerned family friend.

In *Adhe adhure*, the discussion about the failure of conjugal relationships also takes place not between Savitri and Mahendranath but between her and the longtime family friend Juneja, played by the same actor; throughout the dialogue, they are identified as "Woman" and "Man-4." Man-4 puts his finger on one core problem when he points out to Woman that "if instead of Mahendranath there had been any one of these other men in your life, after a year or two you would have begun to feel exactly the same thing, that you've gotten married to the wrong man" (*MRR*, vol. 3, 247). The second problem according to Man-4 is that one of Woman's preoccupations as wife has been to "prove how in every respect he [Mahendranath] is deficient and small in comparison with this man, or that man, or me, or you, or everyone else . . . Whatever he's not, that's what he should be, and whatever he is . . ." (248). This conversation about the inevitability of discontent (or worse) in marriage culminates in Woman's anguished response, which is a variation on Sundari's, and the rejoinder by Man-4:

WOMAN: I've already told you, enough! All of you . . . all of you! Exactly the same! You are all exactly the same! The masks are different, but the face?—everyone's face is the same.

MAN-4: And even then you have continued to feel that you can actually exercise any choice. But moving from right to left, from front to back, from this corner to that corner . . . have you really seen the possibility of choice anywhere? Tell me, have you seen it anywhere?

(250)

Adhe adhure was published the year following the 1968 version of *LKR 2*, and it is possible to see the gender dynamic in *LKR 2* as a historically situated foreshadowing of the coming allegory in *Adhe adhure* rather than as an "augmentation" of what was left unsaid in *LKR 1*.

The other suggestive subtext of *LKR 2* is the narrative of Rakesh's two failed marriages (1950–61), and a third marriage (1963–) that was more companionate but no less turbulent, and ended with his death in 1972. The intimate connection between Rakesh's personal life and his work, which according to

Taneja made him a "restless, impatient, unstable, disturbed, and dissatisfied" person all his life (*MRR*, vol. 1, 11–12), is most clearly evident in his diaries, which cover the period from 1948 to 1967 and were published posthumously in 1985. The entries reveal that after deciding to marry Sheela Meherwal in 1950, Rakesh tried desperately to get out of the obligation, and the couple had a strained relationship until Sheela left for Agra in 1952 to take up a position as a college lecturer in economics. Rakesh marked the day of his decision to end the marriage (January 26, 1957) as a day when he tried to end six years of suffocating estrangement, despite the birth of a son in May 1956: "If I cannot love a woman, how can I spend my life with her? . . . To compensate for my own deficiencies, I want to take refuge in a person who can draw me to herself, bind me to herself" (*MRR*, vol. 1, 138). The second marriage, to Pushpa Chopra, lasted only a little more than a year (1960–61). In 1963, Rakesh eloped to Bombay with Anita Aulak, the older daughter of Hindi author Chandra Aulak, who was trying to mold herself as a writer and did have a significant literary career, especially after Rakesh's death.

The consistent sentiment expressed in the diaries over more than two decades of marriage to three different women is Rakesh's desire for solitude so that he can have an uninterrupted literary life, an expectation that compromises domestic life and creates a deep ambivalence toward the idea of home. What Rakesh also communicates as a painful revelation is the first two wives' disregard for his life as a writer and their lack of interest in his writing, which surfaces as indifference toward his complicated interiority as an intellectual, emotional, and creative being, the real-life equivalent of the conflict between Nanda and Sundari, particularly in *LKR 2*. Rakesh's third wife, Aulak, was much more invested in literary creativity of her own and Rakesh's, but at least the diaries suggest that she could not garner much respect from him as either a wife or a writer, although she has served as his literary executor since 1972. Taneja captures the poignance of this existence when he describes Rakesh as "a man wandering about in search of a home, carrying around his complicated mentality and the unfortunate tale of woe that was his married life" (*MRR*, vol. 1, 34). Instead of a man thrown into crisis by the loss of his "handsome" looks (as in history), Nanda becomes, in Act 3 of *LKR 2*, a version of the prodigiously creative and troubled man whose struggles are of no interest to the woman who shares his life. The ancient narrative generates a unique modernist arc that moves through history and poetry and ends as a direct gloss on the existential present.

PALIMPSESTS OF THE PAST

The creative evolutions charted in this chapter indicate that the instability marking the textual life of Karnad's *Yayati* and Rakesh's *Laharon ke rajhans* over many decades was ultimately a sign of authorial discontent, but there are also qualitative differences between these powerfully inventive and palimpsestic constructions of myth and history as modernist topoi. Karnad took up a well-known episode from the *Mahabharata* that already had a prominent "modern" literary and iconographic history, and his ironic version of the narrative marked his difference from that prior trajectory even if he was not invoking it consciously in 1961. When the English translation of 2008 appeared in print, he also dismissed the earlier versions as irrelevant because his critique of amoral patriarchy and his investment in self-possessed women had remained thematically constant. Rakesh, on the other hand, used a lesser-known Sanskrit poetic source with Buddhism as its subject, assuming a more specialized knowledge of the classical language and ancient history on the part of his contemporary audience. The emotional and spiritual crises he portrayed in his principal characters arose from the uncompromising centrality of renunciation in Buddhism as a system of religious beliefs and practices. He also processed the source material through three different forms—short story, radio drama, and three-act play—and each new iteration altered the relations, motivations, and outcomes relating to the main characters. Karnad's personal view of the Yayati myth was absorbed into and sublimated by the structure and affect of his play, whereas the crucial nodes in Rakesh's remote history drew ever closer to his personal life, and by the end seemed to be replicating his own failures of intimacy. The final irony here was that even the fully rewritten 1968 version of *Laharon ke rajhans* resolved nothing: the publisher continued to reprint the 1963 text in defiance of the author's instructions, and readers as well as theater directors continued to express their preference for it, provoking Rakesh into a last despairing comment about the modernist absence of closure:

> Even now, it's not as though disagreements and arguments about the play have come to an end. But . . . I now find myself outside of [the play]. Some people ask even now that the earlier version of the play should continue to be published simultaneously. I don't agree with this because. . . . in the next twenty years I could be tempted to write it four more times in four other ways. . . . Is there any creative work whose form a person can ever regard as definite and final in the course of his life? (*MRR*, vol. 3, 107)

Chapter Four

MODERNISM, REALISM, AND THE POSTCOLONIAL URBAN PRESENT

> For the stage has turned into the point of intersection for pairs of worlds distinct in time; the realm of drama is one where 'past' and 'future,' 'no longer' and 'not yet,' come together in a single moment. What we usually call 'the present' in drama is the occasion of self-appraisal; from the past is born the future, which struggles free of the old and of all that stands in opposition.
>
> —GYÖRGY LUKÁCS, "THE SOCIOLOGY OF MODERN DRAMA" (1909)

> A play lives when it is being acted on stage, and at that moment it is absolutely contemporary. It belongs to the moment when it is being watched. The playwright, the artists, the director, the audience—all live and create a meaning in that moment of time.
>
> —GIRISH KARNAD, IN A 1995 INTERVIEW[1]

TIME PAST AND TIME PRESENT

Writing during the first and last decades of the twentieth century, from distinctly different cultural locations, Lukács and Karnad offer two versions of the same intuitive perception: that both the drama form and its enactment on stage create a sense of continuity rather than disjunction in relation to the passage of time. If the object of representation is the past, it is refracted through the present and prefigures a future; if the focus is on the present, it serves, as Lukács suggests, as the meeting ground of past and future. Karnad stresses, further, that the "time" of drama is in a vital way the moment of its live performance, regardless of its narrative setting, so the *reception* of a play on stage always belongs to the present. Other perspectives on the radical contemporaneity of drama and theater appear in Peter Szondi's argument that "because the Drama is always primary, its internal time is always the present," or in Mohan Rakesh's insistence that theater connects with its time not through "the things and events here and now" but through the writer's "contemporary vision"—"a phenomenon of the mind that gives a particular direction to its faculties and makes it see and interpret things in a light that emerges from the events and attributes of the age."[2] This is the principle that enables Rakesh to claim, despite his immersion in the remote Indian past, that he is "not really aware of having written anything that is not contemporary."[3]

The experiential currentness of theater in all its forms, however, does not preclude the claim that in the *writing* of drama a direct engagement with "time present" rather than time past involves a qualitatively different relationship *to* that present on the author's part, and a different set of aesthetic and political choices. In modern Indian theater, engaging with the past and contending with the sociopolitical present are the two most prominent—although not always equally visible—impulses from the very beginning, and the differences between the two are especially evident when they are embodied in the same playwright. If Michael Madhusudan Dutt turns to the *Mahabharata* for his first full-length play in Bengali and its English translation in 1858–59, in 1861 his translation of Dinabandhu Mitra's *Nildarpan* (The indigo mirror, 1860), a play criticizing the colonial government's ongoing agrarian policies in Bengal, precipitates the first major crisis of theater-related censorship in India. The output of Dutt's contemporary, Ramnarayan Tarkaratna, is dominated by myth-based plays and translations from the Sanskrit (Narayana Bhatta's *Venisamhar* in 1856, Shri Harsha's *Ratnavali* in 1858, and Bhavabhuti's *Malatimadhav* in 1867), but his first and best-known play, *Kulinkulsarvasva* (For the well-born, lineage is everything, 1854), attacks the practice of polygamy among upper-caste Hindus. As a playwright, theorist, and translator, Bhartendu Harishchandra balances his engrossing interest in the culture of Sanskrit with original plays allegorizing India's abject state under colonial rule. The colonial state is a predictable target in literary works energized by anticolonial nationalism, but interestingly, drama dealing with contemporary subject matter directs criticism reflexively at the structure of Hindu/Indian society as persistently as at the alien ruling class. The divisiveness of caste, corrupt social customs relating to marriage (polygamy, dowry, child brides, the trauma of widowhood), patriarchal control and the subjugation of women in relation to education and professionalization, male chauvinism and gender discrimination within the family, regionalism, communalism, the false consciousness of colonial subjects, and complicity with the colonial state are among the self-targeting themes that appear in the forms of tragedy, melodrama, social comedy, satire, allegory, farce, musical drama, and reformist drama from the 1850s to the 1940s.[4]

In this chapter, I am concerned with the resolute revamping of some of these earlier forms and conventions through which modernism becomes a vital aesthetic-political force in theatrical representations of the *postcolonial* urban present—offsetting, counterbalancing, and eventually overtaking the narratives of myth, history, legend, and folklore. As the previous chapter indicated, the postindependence modernist reckoning with the past dismantles long-standing orientalist, idealist, and nativist constructions of nation and culture that are no longer satisfying to a cosmopolitan and self-critical postcolonial mindset. A similar reckoning with the present creates a body of drama that captures the day-to-day stresses and strains of a rapidly modernizing, newly independent nation grappling with the effects of colonialism, industrialization, urbanization, uncontrolled development, economic precarity, the splintering of family and community relationships, and the escalation of conflicts over class, gender, sexuality, religion, region, and language. The primary representational mode in this modernist drama of the present is a "selective" and experimentally oriented realism, building on the association between realism and "contemporary reality" that has characterized the mode since its European inception in the mid-nineteenth century. However, the postcolonial iterations posit a new symbiotic relationship between modernism and realism/naturalism that diverges both from the well-known antipathy between these modes in twentieth-century Western discourse and from earlier Indian forays into realism.[5] In my analysis, realism is therefore the enabling mode for engaging with the postcolonial present, and modernist realism emerges as an offshoot of the larger rehabilitation of realist aesthetics after independence. The new composite form focuses on the personal and social spheres, but it also appears in some major works of political theater to intertwine domesticity with ideology, the private with the public.

The next few sections deal with some defining features of Western realism, their eccentric accommodation by Indian playwrights over several decades, and the decisive shifts that produce the modernist-realist synthesis after independence. These comparisons uncover cross-cultural connections between authors and works that are largely ignored in modern Indian theater history and underscore the cosmo-modernist dimension of India/West relations. I then consider three plays, written in three different languages and locations over a twenty-eight-year span, which exemplify the refraction of everyday life through defamiliarizing modernist techniques.

These plays are neither "representative" nor "singular"—rather, they reveal in their individual ways a broadly shared inclination among playwrights to channel mundane urban experience in unexpected directions through specific choices of form, structure, and characterization. Badal Sircar's *Ebong indrajit* (And Indrajit, Bengali), written in 1962–63 and first performed in 1965, is considered the "first fully conscious expression" of the postindependence realization that "a determined effort at looking at one's surroundings" had become an urgent necessity.[6] Mahesh Elkunchwar's *Atmakatha* (Autobiography, Marathi, 1988) is described by the author as a "family play," but it is also a play "about writing, the one thing that has haunted me, the relationship between the artist and his art, the reality and the art, between experience taken at the imaginative level, as a direct experience, and as experience narrated to you."[7] *Tara: A Play in Two Acts* by Mahesh Dattani (English, 1990) is another "family play," a grimly ironic one in which the family's physical and emotional destruction due to corrupt patriarchal choices is recreated in the excruciating memories of one surviving member. A short concluding section reflects on the paradox that the multilingualism of Indian theater has impeded rather than encouraged the kind of close analysis that unlocks the thematic density of these modernist-realist plays as embodiments of individual and social experience in a fraught postcolonial present.

WESTERN CLASSIC REALISM AND MODERN INDIAN THEATER: A LESS PERFECT UNION

Among modern Western developments that have had a demonstrable influence on Indian theater since the late nineteenth century, realism stands out as the mode, style, and form with the most long-drawn-out and complicated relationship to theater theory as well as practice over a 150-year span. Movements such as symbolism, expressionism, existentialism, and the theater of the absurd influence Indian playwrights at the stylistic and philosophical levels to varying degrees, but unlike realism, they are not *consistently and substantively* acknowledged or theorized in theater discourse across the Indian languages. There are, moreover, no parallels in India to the European avant-garde's attacks on realism/naturalism from primitivist, Futurist, Vorticist, Dadaist, and Surrealist positions (roughly 1890–1930), so there is also no concerted reaction *against* realism in colonial theater over the same time period. The relationship to Western models, however, is erratic and discrepant for three main reasons. First, the environments, customs, beliefs, social structures, institutions, and economic-political circumstances of "modern" Indian society do not match their Western correlates, regardless of the phase or aspect of modernity that is under consideration. Second, as a form with a particular set of representational conventions, realism follows a different chronology and line of development in modern Indian theater, shaped by its own distinctive social-cultural-political contexts. Third, the actual practice of realism in colonial-era drama and theater reveals various forms of dissonance between form and content until the transformations of the mid-twentieth century offer new opportunities for reconciliation and invention. Juxtaposing prominent features of Western realism with their Indian approximations therefore clarifies the historical trajectory along which Indian realisms and their modernist variants can be placed.

Western Realism and the Stage-World Continuum

Emerging in the mid- to late-nineteenth century as a "distinct aesthetic and literary phenomenon," European realism is widely considered to be "a response to important social and epistemological developments of the age: the consolidation of modern industrial society and its urban classes, the diffusion of Marx, Darwin and Comtean positivism and a paradigmatic shift towards materialist scientific and sociological explanations in general."[8] In the pioneering "Realist Manifesto" of 1855, the French painter Gustave Courbet rejects "the useless goal of art for art's sake" and makes a commitment "to translate the customs, the ideas, the appearance of my epoch, according to my own estimation; to be not only a painter, but a man as well; in short, to create living art."[9] In drama and theater, realist aesthetics have a revolutionary effect on theory and practice because the intrinsic verisimilitude of these interrelated forms maximizes the potential for likenesses to life. Key figures such as Ibsen and Zola posit two principal obligations for playwrights: to choose the life they observe around them as the subject of drama, and to choose conventions of representation—in terms of narrative structure, setting, character, and language—that recreate this "natural" existence, on the page, and in concrete material terms, on the stage. Ibsen's goal of making a "sense of reality" the quality that "the modern dramatist should above all aim at" is corroborated by Shaw's observation that Shakespeare "put ourselves on the stage but not our situations. . . . [Ibsen] gives us not only ourselves, but ourselves in our own situations."[10] Zola defines "the power of reality" as "the new life of modern art," and his passionate advocacy of naturalism posits a decisive difference between "the naturalistic formula, which makes the stage a study and a picture of real life; and the conventional formula, which makes it purely an amusement for the mind, an intellectual speculation."[11] "The future," he predicts, "will have to do with the human problem studied in the framework of reality. The drama will either die or become modern and realistic."[12] An essential component of this modernizing energy, moreover, is a sense of rupture with both past and present forms: the "classical drama" of the previous two centuries "no longer correspond[s] with a living and actual reality"[13]; and forms closer in time (melodrama, comedy, farce, pantomime, burlesque, highbrow Romantic drama, and even the pseudo-realist well-made play) are rejected because of their contrived and exaggerated "theatricality."[14]

Two other features of major realist drama as practiced by authors such as Ibsen and Chekhov are relevant to my analysis: the focus on the bourgeoisie as a social class, and the use of the bourgeois home as a principal setting. The centrality of bourgeois realism to the very definition of modernity appears in Lukács's claim that "modern drama is the drama of the bourgeoisie; modern drama is bourgeois drama."[15] In literary/theatrical representations of the urban and exurban worlds created by nineteenth-century European industrial capitalism, the bourgeoisie occupies a "settled" position between the plutocrats and the class of industrial and agricultural workers. In English usage the term "middle class" is much more common than "bourgeois," but it signals the same intermediate positioning between the class of rich manufacturers/titled aristocrats and poor workers.[16] Franco Moretti describes the bourgeoisie defined in this way as a possible new European ruling class because it combines the advantages of property, education, professionalization, and culture. Its "recurrent traits" are "energy . . .; self-restraint; intellectual clarity; commercial honesty; [and] a strong sense of goals"; it does not romanticize itself, and accepts an "essentially unheroic" existence.[17] This median class is a dominant subject in "antitheatrical" realist drama, and the choice of the bourgeois home as setting literalizes the notion of *theatrum mundi* in a new way. Una Chaudhuri argues that "the theatrical version of the literalized home is to be found in realism. . . . The fully iconic, single-set, middle-class living room of realism produced so closed and so *complete* a stage world that it supported the new and powerful fantasy of the stage not as a place to pretend in or to perform on but a place to *be*, a fully existential arena."[18] The shift from verse to conversational prose as the medium of serious drama supports this fantasy and makes the space of home the crucial testing ground for familial, conjugal, social, and, occasionally, political relations. The dialectical structure in turn creates the conflicts endemic to realist drama—between home as haven and prison, between individual desires and social norms, between law and morality, and between timid ambition and the certainty of failure.

Realism has maintained a durable and significant presence in Western theater despite avant-garde and modernist attacks for reasons that may also explain its long gestation in India under substantially different generative conditions. From Eric Bentley to Raymond Williams, major twentieth-century theorists of modern drama have endorsed realism and naturalism as rich, versatile modes for representing contemporary life and its environment. Williams in fact describes the arrival of naturalism as "the decisive moment, in all modern drama. . . . It is one of the great revolutions, in human consciousness: to confront the human drama in its immediate setting, without reference to 'outside' sources and powers."[19] Much more recently, Toril Moi has mounted a passionate critique of the "ideology of modernism" that led to "a particular hatred of realism, considered intrinsically reactionary, simply because it attempted to represent reality."[20] In the Indian variant, as I have already indicated, modernism and realism are complementary rather than mutually opposed aesthetic practices. But Moi's reassessment of Ibsen as a foundational figure of modernity because of his commitment to ordinariness and his profound understanding of gender relations brings late-nineteenth-century arguments about the value of realism full circle, and completes the framework in relation to which discrepant Indian realisms can be approached.

Realism and Modern Indian Formations: Proximity and Distance

As a British colony in South Asia with a precolonial political history of empires, kingdoms, and principalities and an economy based heavily on agriculture, nineteenth-century India cannot parallel *any* of the developments that bring about the realist-naturalist turn in nineteenth-century

Europe. Industrialization, urbanization, a clear class structure, the growth of empirical science, gradual secularization, widespread literacy, access to education, the emergence of modern professions, democracy—all the constituents of modernity that shape the Western *zeitgeist* appear either in a nascent form or are absent in colonial India. The same is true of the private sphere, in which entrenched patriarchal norms and idealized conceptions of the extended family produce radically different conjugal and filial relationships, especially those between parents and children. The hierarchies of caste in Hindu society complicate any economically determined conception of class; affinities or differences of religion, region, language, and community are just as important to the construction of social identity as any other philosophical, ontological, or material determinants. Two other interconnected factors are relevant to cultural forms: the development of industrial capital in India follows a direction substantially different from the West; and there is consequently no "bourgeoisie" in the Western sense to serve as a prominent subject of modern Indian writing, especially in fiction and drama. Because the workings of capital and their social ramifications are central to the Western realist aesthetic, the Indian deviations need brief explanation before I trace the evolution of realism as a mode of engagement with the present across the colonial/postcolonial divide.

During the colonial period, the growth of capitalism in India was severely hampered by British disinterest in fostering capitalist production relations. Amiya Kumar Bagchi notes that "[t]he British were themselves capitalists. But they were interested in introducing capitalist relations into India only in so far as they would increase the revenue and profit . . . gathered by the British tributary state and by the British or the European capitalist class in general."[21] Profits from speculation during and after World War I did create many of the large Indian industrial houses, and some of these supported the cause of anticolonial nationalism, especially under Gandhi's leadership after 1920. But Bagchi's profile of the postindependence period is a catalogue of failures on the part of the capitalist class, who have "erected formidable obstacles against the development of industrial capitalism in India" because of their extra-economic motivations, self-interest, and parochialism. "Big Indian capitalists," he argues, "by and large remain casteist, communalist, collaborationist, authoritarian, and thrive by corruptly utilizing governmental machinery."[22] Where labor is concerned, "nonmarket factors" such as religion, caste, and the feudal practice of bondage in the countryside add to the sources of exploitation, and union activity is seriously undercut. Since 1982, the Subaltern Studies collective has based its revisionist historiography on the premise that the Gramscian binary of dominant and subaltern has greater explanatory potential in India than the classic Marxist categories of capitalist/ bourgeois and proletarian.[23]

The socioeconomic structures produced by this history are quite unique to India because *in its totality* the country does not resemble any other colonial or postcolonial space closely. There is a class, or more precisely a demographic, in modern urban India that occupies a position between conspicuous industrial or mercantile wealth and varying degrees of poverty, but even in the neoliberal economy of the early-twenty-first century this collective does not constitute a parallel to the settled, prosperous, and cultivated bourgeoisie of the modern West. Because of gender inequalities in terms of access to literacy, education, and professionalization, women become visible as citizen-subjects only in the later twentieth century, and only on a limited scale. Individualism is a fraught idea, especially when home and family life are shaped by the emphasis on caste, community, and religion, traditional marriage practices, and the institution of the extended family. Since independence, "middle class" *has* become a standard term in urban Indian contexts, but the porous boundaries of this category are indicated by the constant use of the qualifier "upper," which denotes a relatively stable degree of economic prosperity, and "lower," which signals precarity and the real prospect of sliding back into poverty. The lack of inherited wealth, the phenomenon of single-income households, governmentally subsidized lifestyles that provide security and social prestige without commensurate economic returns, an inflationary economy, and high rates of unemployment even among the educated are additional factors that have kept the Indian middle class in a state of crisis. This is the unruly social text underlying urban plays set within the middle-class family home from the 1920s onward, and neither family circumstances nor the qualities of home as intimate personal space can support a definition of modern Indian drama as "the drama of the bourgeoisie."[24] The evolution of realism in urban Indian theater contends with these systemic differences from the West and involves an extended process through which the form of realist theater becomes a viable means of engaging seriously with the sociopolitical present, in both modern and modernist works.

MODERNISM, REALISM, AND THE POSTCOLONIAL URBAN PRESENT

Realism and Urban Indian Theater: The Long Road to Reconciliation

Published in the Bengali magazine *Aryadarshan* in 1875, an essay titled "Acting for the Theatre" appears to contain one of the earliest evocations of the realist aesthetic in an Indian language. The pseudonymous author, very likely the actor-manager-playwright Girish Chandra Ghosh, asserts that "it is necessary to create an illusion in the minds of the spectators, so that it seems to them that everything they have witnessed has actually been happening. . . . [The creation of] theatrical illusion is the ultimate test of dramatic staging" (*POM*, 26). The idea of "illusion" here clearly denotes a selective verisimilitude rather than the replication of mundane reality that Western classic realism demands. Three decades later, Rabindranath Tagore does refer directly to realism/naturalism, but he takes the opposite view by describing the mode as an expression of Europe's obsession with "the truth of material fact," which "must make the imaginary simulate the actual and beguile them as it beguiles children" (*POM*, 72). "Naturalism," he claims in a vivid metaphor, "enters art like a colourful glass-fly but sucks it dry from the inside like a borer beetle" (*POM*, 72, 73). The contrast between the 1875 essay and Tagore's critique opens up a useful third space for understanding the points of divergence between the high period of realism and naturalism in Western theater (1880–1910) and contemporaneous Indian trends.

At the time when Zola's call is for a theater of the present that offers "an exact reproduction of the environment" to satisfy "our obsessive need for reality,"[25] colonial Indian theater, both literary and commercial, is engaged in a complicated negotiation with the *past*. In one direction, following the orientalist recovery of classical Sanskrit literature and the high value placed on Sanskrit drama, playwright-theorists such as Dutt, Harishchandra, and Tagore reflect seriously on the legacy of Sanskrit aesthetics, theater and performance theory, dramatic genres, and staging conventions to determine how this recursive culture can be adjusted to fit the expectations and tastes of a contemporary urban audience because it cannot be revived in its original form. In another direction, commercial theater artists draw on regional presentational styles and the full range of performing arts to devise indigenized and syncretic forms that are "new" and immensely popular, but consistently nonrealist or antirealist when compared to Western works from the same or later periods. Interestingly, the physical spaces, production technologies, and institutional practices of theater in cities such as Calcutta and Bombay are clearly based on Anglo-European models; the texts-for-performance have nothing substantive in common with the Western realist-naturalist revolution.

Mainstream colonial commercial theater from about 1870 to 1930 is in fact wide-ranging in terms of content, which includes myth, history, the lives of religious/spiritual icons, contemporary social issues, political disaffection, adaptations of classic and contemporary stories or novels, and translations from Sanskrit, Shakespeare, and other Indian languages.[26] *All* of these subjects, however, are refracted through presentational styles that highlight music, dance, spectacle, melodrama, and declamatory acting: although the "entertainment-for-profit" model dominates theater activity, the mimetic method is flamboyantly theatrical and multimedial, even when the goal is to engage seriously with past or present subject matter. The cult of the cross-dressed male actor, and the resulting exclusion of actresses until almost the 1930s, add to the elements of artificiality. The three principal theater formations of the colonial period—the Bengali public stage, the Marathi *sangeet natak* (musical drama), and the Parsi theater of spectacle—are therefore fundamentally antithetical to the "likeness to life" and "slice-of-life" approaches. The same is true, albeit for different reasons, of topical or reformist works such as Jyotiba Phule's *Tritiya ratna* (The third gem, 1855), Bhartendu Harishchandra's political allegories (1875–1881), and Gopal Ganesh Agarkar's version of *Hamlet* (1883), which belong to the opposite category of closet drama and do not reach the stage in their own time. Tagore occupies a unique intermediary position in this performance economy because his symbolist-poetic plays (more than sixty in all) are also not intended for the commercial theater, but he has the private means to produce them either at Jorasanko (his residence in Calcutta) or at Santiniketan (the university he founded near Calcutta in 1901).

All these models begin to shift around 1915, however, because a succession of playwrights in active theater languages such as Marathi, Hindi, and Kannada acknowledge the influence of pioneering realists such as Chekhov, Shaw, and above all, Ibsen, followed later by the American trio of O'Neill, Miller, and Williams.[27] If the substantial and well-documented field of Marathi theater is used as an example, the first major plays that register the influence of Ibsen and the "new" idea of realism are Mama Varerkar's *Haach mulacha baap* (He is the groom's father, 1916), Ram

Ganesh Gadkari's *Ekach pyala* (Just one glass, 1917), and Varerkar's *Satteche gulam* (Slaves to entitlement, 1922), dealing respectively with the problem of dowry in marriage, the fatal effects of alcoholism, and the resistance to Gandhian nationalism on the part of an entitled Indian elite. *Ekach pyala* is considered the first "experimental" play in Marathi because it combines a serious family-oriented social message with the immensely popular musical form of the *sangeet natak* that Gadkari had practiced throughout his career. *Satteche gulam* is the first colonial play to address the issues of native political complicity and corruption directly, instead of resorting to allegory through the narratives of myth and history. Varerkar's autobiography, *Majha nataki sansar* (My theater world) records the excitement of what he knew were groundbreaking artistic innovations for his time: "We had decided to do something new for *Satteche gulam*, something that would radically alter the face of the stage. In order to create a realistic stage set.... [w]e decided to think of ... architecture rather than painting. We abolished wings and flies. The solidity of doors and windows was to be shown, not just painted. Similarly the depth, length and width of rooms was to be represented to make them look real."[28]

This movement toward the box set of realism was received enthusiastically and began a trend, but in general the new departures continued alongside the older formal conventions and extravagant staging practices. *Haach mulacha baap* is a highly topical social problem text but is described in the subtitle as "a prose-and-verse domestic play," and includes a *Sutradhar*, the metatheatrical mediator borrowed from Sanskrit drama. *Ekach pyala* becomes a sensationally successful *musical* when it is produced in 1919, shortly after the author's death at the age of thirty four. As a poet-playwright Gadkari is a poignant and progressive figure, but he is also an "unrealistic, unnatural, melodramatic, illogical" author whose text is "heavily laden with figures of speech, hyperbole, overly decorative style, and page after page of unrealistic and extremely sentimental dialogue" (Sathe, vol. 1, 240).

The second phase in the evolution of realism appears in the 1930s and 1940s, in the work of popular playwrights such as Shridhar V. Vartak, P. K. Atre, and M. G. Rangnekar, and in the efforts made by the Natyamanwantar group (cofounded by Vartak in 1933) to "modernize" all aspects of theater. Sathe describes this as a period when "Marathi theater was moving from Shakespeare to Ibsen and Shaw" (vol. 1, 372), and playwrights could acknowledge these influences openly, although the continuing dominance of *sangeet nataks* reflected the tension between popular taste and reformist impulses.[29] Vartak's *Andhalyanchi shala* (School for the blind, 1933), considered the first "Ibsenian" (and hence fully modern) play in Marathi, is in fact adapted from *A Gauntlet* (1883), a play by Ibsen's brother-in-law and Nobel laureate Bjørn Bjørnson. The stage directions even specify that Ibsen's portrait and Shaw's bust must appear among the living room props. Another play by Vartak, titled *Takshashila*, is an adaptation of Ibsen's early historical play *The Vikings at Helgeland* (1857). Atre and Rangnekar are much more prolific than Vartak, and their combined output indicates that the full-length prose play, set in the present and not dependent essentially on music, has become a viable form in multiple dramatic genres.[30]

The problem with the Ibsen-Shaw vogue even in this second phase, however, is the playwrights' inability to move away from melodrama, sentimentality, and eventual conformity with the sociocultural status quo, especially in their treatment of women. *Andhalyanchi shala* was Natyamanwantar's first production in 1933, with minimal music and the inclusion of actresses from "good" families shoring up the claims of progressive dramaturgy. Using a privileged but socially conscious young woman as his protagonist, Vartak does try to create a "drama of ideas" about class, gender inequality, and generational relationships, but critics agree that he poses no real challenge to patriarchal norms, and he resolves conflicts by placing "natural" human love above reason. Shanta Gokhale notes that "as a writer, Vartak is not mature enough for realism," and "*Andhalyanchi shala* is perhaps more interesting as a sociological document than as a play."[31] One of Atre's most successful plays, *Gharabaher* (Out of the house, 1934) takes up the issue of women's freedom, but with a similarly compromised resolution in which an abused wife eventually returns home because her obligations as a mother override all other considerations, and women "have to accept the slavery of the horrible world of men who pay them in return."[32] In *Kulvadhu* (Dynastic bride, 1942), which intentionally echoes *A Doll's House*, Rangnekar goes a step further by portraying a very successful film actress who gives up her career to escape an abusive husband, only to join her parents-in-law in their village home.

This collective failure to take a genuinely bold or progressive stand on social problems despite the Ibsenian veneer clarifies several features of the Indian co-optation of realism. Transitional playwrights active during the two decades preceding independence are constrained by rapidly changing marketplace conditions and a complacent, largely conservative urban audience. In a 1992 memoir, Rangnekar rationalizes the superficiality as a "need of the times": "All theater companies and their plays had folded up by then. The age of cinema had begun.... At such a time, the only way the audience could be pulled back to the theater, was to write small, light, entertaining plays which wouldn't tax the mind. That was the only way to face films."[33]

Sathe describes Vartak's flawed play as a reflection of the confusion resulting from "the interaction between Western and Indian cultures, which are at two different stages of social evolution" (vol. 1, 373). The West orientalizes India and India misreads Western modernity: "often, only superficial or formal elements of modernity are adopted, while the original value systems remain intact, producing devastating anomalies" (vol. 1, 373). Other differences stem from the contrast between the presence of a fully developed bourgeoisie in Europe and its absence in India: "Naturally, the individualistic sensibility as played out in theater is somewhat hollow and related more to form than content" (Sathe, vol. 1, 370). The "form" of realism offers a focus on the urban present that is sociopolitically attractive in the mid-twentieth century and staging conventions that can root out the self-indulgent colonial culture of music and spectacle. Realist "content," on the other hand, brushes up against entrenched social structures and attitudes that cannot yet be radically challenged.[34]

Form and content are reconciled in dramatic/theatrical realism only after the fundamental institutional and aesthetic shifts of the mid-twentieth century (discussed in chapter 2), which end the colonial commercial superstructure and its monopoly on theater as a profit-driven industry. In the active languages of Marathi, Bengali, Gujarati, and Telugu a commercially oriented urban theater continues on a modified scale, but the center of gravity shifts to the decommercialized performance economy that emerges specifically to support the rapid advances in playwriting, production, and multilingual circulation after 1950. The practice of realism is a prominent feature of this new theatrical landscape, and some of the drama appears to be a "conventional" parallel to the "classic" realism practiced by the playwrights Ibsen, Shaw, and Chekhov. But as the preceding discussion indicates, even conventional realism is a major index of modernity and a pretext for modernism in relation to *Indian* theater history, whether individual playwrights acknowledge any conscious Western models or not. In its aesthetically viable form, realism becomes possible only through a systematic detheatricalization or outright rejection of colonial theater forms, and through active resistance to the decolonizing ideology that demands a return to precolonial *antirealist* performance styles as the only authentic bases for the new Indian theater. Furthermore, it becomes meaningful as an image of contemporary life by being carefully accommodated to the socioeconomic, cultural, and political circumstances of a newly independent, rapidly developing nation.

In the larger historical perspective, postindependence realists are therefore positioned strategically between the past and the future. The objects of realism—the urban inhabitants of postindependence India—still do not replicate the Western bourgeoisie, but they are modern individuals of a qualitatively different kind than their colonial counterparts, and their embodiment in drama reflects this difference. The plays are in turn translated into major performance events for a relatively small but receptive audience by a new generation of directors, actors, designers, and technicians who choose the urban proscenium stage as their principal spatial platform. As postindependence theater evolves, all forms of realism depend on these new conjunctures of text, performance, and reception. In the next section I consider key theoretical positions that secure the place of realism in the "new national" canon, and the departures from convention that make realism an important site of modernist experiment in the work of major playwrights, off and on the stage.

MODERNIST REALISM IN THE POSTCOLONY

In its mature postindependence forms, realism creates the postcolonial urban present as material for representation on stage; major modernist playwrights, most of whom also practice other dramatic modes and styles, give that representation a sharply critical, antiromantic, subversive, and often experimental edge. Interestingly, preindependence fiction serves as a precursor for postindependence theater in both these respects because realism emerges as a socially progressive alternative to romance and fantasy in the forms of prose narrative by the late nineteenth century, a couple of decades before it begins to counter the dominance of music, dance, and spectacle in the forms of theater. As a notable innovation, *modernist realism* also comes first to fiction: Vinay Dharwadker uses the term to describe Mulk Raj Anand's novella *Untouchable* (1935), in which the narrative of a single day in the life of a young latrine-cleaner combines Joycean modernist form with highly charged social, political, and ethical content.[35] In comparison with Anand's landmark work, Ibsenian realism in Indian drama of the 1930s is "more modern" than what precedes it, but flawed and confused in terms of its own form and social message. Modernist realism remedies that lack, and the verisimilitude and performativity particular to drama allow qualitatively greater experimental freedom in the representation of postcolonial "reality" on stage.

A smaller subset of modernist-realist plays disrupt the expectations of linearity and predictability in the handling of time, place, character, and dialogue to defamiliarize the dramatic action, without surrendering the qualities of verisimilitude that establish the stage-world continuum. In both kinds of plays (created in a range of languages, including English), home, family, and personal/social relationships take on traits comparable to Western realist drama for the first time, while retaining their "intrinsic" local and regional ambience. The crucial differences between these realist works, moreover, involve the nature of the author-audience relationship more than questions of aesthetic value. In Marathi, for example, playwrights such as V. V. Shirwadkar, Vasant Kanetkar, and P. L. Deshpande are prolific literary realists who achieve success in both commercial and noncommercial venues but provide superior entertainment in both instances without seriously disturbing the audience's self-image. In contrast, an iconoclast such as Vijay Tendulkar dispenses with the naivete and histrionics of earlier drawing room drama and assails middle-class life with a vehemence that recalls Zola more than Ibsen. He is unquestionably the most important practitioner of the form of urban realism that Shanta Gokhale describes as the "preferred mode of writing and presentation" during the first experimental phase of Marathi playwriting after independence—the mode through which "the 'modern' sensibility could best express itself."[36] Sathe goes further in characterizing the realistic, sociopolitically engaged, cosmopolitan, and formally experimental drama of the 1950s as a "quantum leap" not only in Marathi but in Indian theater, noting that after 1955 "theater became 'modern' in the true sense, at least in the 'realistic' sense, through the plays of Tendulkar."[37] Tendulkar serves as the paradigmatic figure of modernist realism in my analysis because his works offer the most sustained and transformative theatrical engagement with postcolonial urban life on the part of any individual author.

Authorship and the process of writing are central to Tendulkar's aesthetic, and his theory of realism appears in a series of statements about his own choices and preferences. In a 1989 interview, responding to speculations about his indebtedness to certain Western playwrights, he states that "I write about the life around me. If it is accepted that I depict human life from my point of view, then I am ready even to accept that I have borrowed when actually I have not."[38] In the lectures titled *The Play Is the Thing*, the terms "real," "reality," and "real life" appear persistently to establish the stage-world connection. Maintaining that "the illusion of reality on stage can be as powerful as on the screen," Tendulkar claims he could not "proceed to write a play unless I saw my characters as real-life people," rendered as "living and real" beings on stage (*PTT*, 27, 15, 24).[39] But however "near to reality" the fiction in the play happened to be, it also had to be "complete in itself" (*PTT*, 11). Tendulkar is emphatic about the autonomy and interiority of the figures who inhabit the astonishing expanse of his fictional world, spanning nearly fifty plays of varying length: "My characters are not cardboard characters; they do not speak my language; rather I do not speak my language through them; they are not my mouthpieces; but each of them has his or her own separate existence and expression" (*PTT*, 5).

Almost always, the lives of these characters unfold against the backdrop of an encroaching industrial metropolis, and within the space of a middle-class home populated by parents and children, husbands and wives, women and men. Tendulkar views these relationships as essentially frictional and exploitative, so the action in even his relatively moderate plays moves toward moments of reckoning that become points of no return for characters bound to each other by ties of family or community.[40] Another recurring pattern is that of nonconformist individuals pushing back against social norms, disrupting conventional expectations of "genteel" behavior within and outside the home. In the controversial plays (including *Shrimant* [The man of means, 1955], *Gidhade* [Vultures, 1970), *Sakharam binder* [Sakharam the book binder, 1972], and *Baby* [1975]), Tendulkar's (admittedly personal) belief that an essential animality lurks beneath the civilized façade of daily life leads to grotesque portraits of psychological brutalization, emotional collapse, and physical violence among his characters, sometimes ending in death. All of the realist plays are set in the present and collectively constitute a rich repository of national experience in which the themes of class, caste, religion, region, gender, sexuality, love, intimacy, friendship, morality, ethics, and community appear as natural concomitants of dramatic action rather than as carefully programmed occasions for ideological debate. As Tendulkar noted at the end of his acceptance speech for the Saraswati Samman, "The writer is not a visionary or a dialectician. He does not consult the stars. He does not derive answers from any mathematical formulae. He feels or he knows. Having known, he feels perturbed."[41]

Tendulkar's example establishes the city, the chronological present, the space of home, factious human relationships, credible dialogue, and proscenium staging as staples of the "new" (modernist) realism, coalescing into a model that is influential even when it is not overtly acknowledged. In different permutations and with varying emphases, these elements appear in the work of his contemporaries and successors on a scale large enough to constitute a major formation in late-twentieth-century theater. No other contemporary author is as prolific or consistent as Tendulkar, but the map of postindependence realism includes select plays by first- and second-tier playwrights such as Badal Sircar, Mohan Rakesh, Girish Karnad, G. P. Deshpande, Mahesh Elkunchwar, Madhu Rye, Indira Parthasarathy, Mahasweta Devi, Satish Alekar, Jaywant Dalvi, Bhisham Sahni, Datta Bhagat, Mahesh Dattani, Manjula Padmanabhan, Asghar Wajahat, Shanta Gokhale, Cyrus Mistry, Partap Sharma, Gurcharan Das, Dina Mehta, and Poile Sengupta. All of these authors have a more or less prominent presence in print and performance, with Bengali, Hindi, Kannada, Marathi, Gujarati, Tamil, Urdu, and English as the original languages of composition; in translation their work circulates transregionally, and much of it has a national profile. In addition, every active theater language includes a substantial body of city-and-family-centered closet drama that is published with little or no expectation of performance.

Moving beyond Tendulkar's emphases, there are other theoretical positions relating to modernist realism that are worth noting because of the energy with which they question competing viewpoints. The commitment to ordinariness, which counteracts personality cults in politics and the propensity for self-aggrandizement in nationalist writing, is a case in point. Mohan Rakesh speaks for the mundane when he argues that "works portraying an unfamiliar and extraordinary existence are never as popular as those which portray ordinary, everyday life. I live an ordinary life, and from every angle I'm a very ordinary person. That is why I find it completely natural to write stories, to mold this atmosphere of ordinariness into stories" (*SAS*, 42). Another recurring argument is a defense of the city and urban Indian experience, offered initially by Rakesh, and later by Mahesh Elkunchwar and Mahesh Dattani, to question the claim that villages are the "authentic" repositories of Indian life and culture. In a statement typical of the nativist position, Habib Tanvir asserts that "the true pattern of Indian culture in all its facets can best be witnessed in the countryside," and villages have preserved "the dramatic tradition of India in all its pristine glory and vitality . . . even to this day."[42] Rakesh's rejoinder is blunt about the competing claims of village and city within the modern Indian nation, in relation to both life and literature:

> Villages are decidedly not at the centre of the political, economic, and communal vortices which create the problems hampering our progression, although village life is certainly being affected by them. Is it right that the artist who believes in the forward movement of life, and wants to help determine the shape of its future, should distance himself from a particular kind of life because it seems so appalling? . . . And is there really nothing healthy and beautiful in middle-class life in the cities? . . . And is life in the villages really only beautiful and brilliant? (*SAS*, 22–23)

In a short essay titled "Three Little Slices of Urban Indian Life" at the beginning of *City Plays* (1994), a collection representing works by Elkunchwar, Manjula Padmanabhan, and Shanta Gokhale, Dattani explains that the term "little" is not belittling but an acknowledgment of the "weight and beauty" of personally meaningful experience: the plays "are representative of the time and place of the authors, true to specifics either in their lives or incidents that affected them deeply."[43] There is no apology, moreover, for the "ugly face of Indian society . . . that has been successfully mirrored through these plays," because "holding a mirror up to our society is necessary in order to understand the source of its ugliness, and the beauty that eludes it."⁴⁴ Dattani's continuing fascination with the city (specifically, Bombay/Mumbai) as a site of conflict and survival reappears in his own play *The Big Fat City* (2014) and the television film of the same title (2017), both directed by him, although the response to these works has been surprisingly negative when compared with the strong reception of his earlier urban-realist plays.

Not all of Elkunchwar's plays are in the realist mode or set in the city, but among postindependence playwrights he offers the most powerful arguments for a present-oriented urban realism because this choice combines the elements of form, content, style, affect, and enactment into a coherent aesthetic that fulfills his needs as a self-styled "'litterateur' in the theater."⁴⁵ He wants the freedom to write about the life around him in his own way and is opposed to ideologically motivated positions that seek to nullify his experience and artistic preferences. But in the polarized postindependence environment, his interventions also have a broader relevance and stand out because of their directness and clarity. In a well-known 1989 interview, Elkunchwar disputes the claims that "indigenous" forms of theater exist only in the village, and folk theater forms mark a "return to one's roots," because for him the legacies of modernity are equally real: "Neither position has ever convinced me—in the first place, why should theatre in the villages alone be considered indigenous, and not theatre in the cities? An Indian who gets a Western education is also part of the Indian reality; an Indian theatre that is influenced by Western theatre—especially after such a long history of exchange—is part of our Indian experience."⁴⁶

Elkunchwar insists, in fact, that the process of post/colonial modernization has created a deep urban-rural divide, and the paradoxical form of "urban folk theatre" is really a kind of "artistic kleptomania" that packages colorful folk content for a city audience deeply alienated from the countryside. He is equally skeptical, although not dismissive, about the body-centered, avant-garde Third Theater of Badal Sircar, because "my play has to have an existence outside of its staging if it is to be of any use to me, if why I write it at all is to have any meaning."⁴⁷ In rejecting these trends, Elkunchwar fashions himself as an "urbanized individual" who prefers to work within proscenium conventions because they have a long history in urban India and are malleable. He also openly professes an affinity for the kind of realism practiced by Ibsen and Chekhov, and hence dismisses the discredited "old school" realism of Vartak and Rangnekar in Marathi as irrelevant. Live theater for Elkunchwar is a form of intimate emotional communication between character/actor and viewer, and it is his ability to create this experience within the parameters of realism that has earned him the title of India's supreme realist.

The overtly experimental end of modernist realism deviates from conventional realism in several ways: by adopting a metatheatrical, self reflexive structure; by disrupting a linear temporal connection between the past and the present; by abandoning the idea of dramatic character as the embodiment of individuality; by manipulating stage space so that it does not replicate any one "real" environment; and by inserting elements of fantasy into daily life that invite the willing suspension of disbelief. The characters' dialogue and behavior remain mainly realistic; the structure and content of the action do not. These features also appear in different combinations along the dramatic spectrum, but they collectively constitute the artistic means by which playwrights circumvent predictable forms of verisimilitude. In Madhu Rye's metatheatrical "rehearsal play," *Koi pan ek phoolnu naam bolo to* (Tell me the name of a flower, Gujarati, 1967), the lead actress in a professional theater company commits a real murder during a performance, and the explanation for her action involves the abusive and exploitative "real-life" relationships between the group of actors and a playwright who functions as a manipulator behind the scenes. Actor-director Om Shivpuri describes Rakesh's *Adhe adhure* as "the first meaningful Hindi play about contemporary life. . . . [in which] characters, situations, and psychological states are realistic and believable," but as noted earlier, all four middle-aged male characters are played here by the same actor.[48] In terms of the organization of stage space, G. P. Deshpande's *Uddhwasta dharmashala* (The ruined sanctuary, Marathi, 1974) alternates between the home of a Marxist professor of Chemistry and the office where an Inquiry Committee, modeled on the House Un-American Activities Committee, has assembled to investigate his subversive activities on campus. Dattani's *Dance Like a Man* (English, 1989) takes up an aging couple who have been classical *Bharatanatyam* dancers, and he traces their frictional relationship to a dark past in which their younger selves are portrayed by the same actors who play their adult daughter and her fiancé in the present. All these plays are set in the postcolonial metropolis, deal with middle- or upper-class characters, contain realistic dialogue, and create or invoke the space of home; in their individual ways, they all utilize, but also exceed, the realist mode.[49]

The last notable feature of postcolonial modernist realism is its prominent stage life, secured by leading directors, actors, and other urban theater artists who work outside the marketplace. This is not the modernist "theater at odds with the value of theatricality," which in Puchner's analysis rejects not only artificially heightened action but the act of performance itself, as embodied in the repulsive figure of the "mimicking" or "impersonating" actor.[50] What I have described earlier as the "proto-modernist antitheatricalism" of Harishchandra, Tagore, and Prasad is a literary-poetic reaction against the commercialism of colonial theater, similar to Brecht's rejection of Western "culinary theater" and Grotowski's critique of "rich theater" as profit-making enterprises driven by popular taste. Modernist theater emerges in India only after these marketplace pressures have come to an end, and its movement from writing/print to performance follows the processes of deferral and actualization discussed previously. What I want to emphasize here are the deeply collaborative and lasting "protheatrical" relationships that develop between modernist playwrights and leading directors who work with a wide range of materials within the proscenium but have a special commitment to new plays. Vijaya Mehta launches the careers of Tendulkar and Elkunchwar in Bombay, and Sombhu Mitra performs the same role for Badal Sircar in Calcutta—and both directors are also accomplished realist actors who perform often in their own productions. The directing work of Satyadev Dubey (Bombay), Shyamanand Jalan (Calcutta), and Rajinder Nath (Delhi) is like a triangulated crusade for modernist realism. Each director undertakes productions of multiple works by Tendulkar, Rakesh, Sircar, Elkunchwar, and G. P. Deshpande; Nath extends the roster to include Mahasweta Devi, Madhu Rye, and Bhisham Sahni. Ebrahim Alkazi, Om Shivpuri, and Alyque Padamsee are other major directors with breakthrough productions of modernist-realist plays. Equally important, the slate of actors with outstanding credentials in realist/modernist drama during its most active theatrical phase includes Shriram Lagoo, Tripti Mitra, Sulabha Deshpande, Arvind Deshpande, Sudha Shivpuri, Manohar Singh, Surekha Sikri, Uttara Baokar, Amol Palekar, and Dinesh Thakur. Modernist realism gives new form to the postcolonial present, and inspired collaborations transform it into lived experience in the theater: as objects of analysis, the plays that follow are products of this reciprocal exchange.

EVAM INDRAJIT (AND INDRAJIT): THE (NEOCOLONIAL) WASTELAND

WRITER: Undramatic. It's all totally undramatic. You can't make a play out of these people. It isn't possible. . . .
AMAL: What sort of play do you want to write? Social?
WRITER: What do you mean—Social?
VIMAL: You don't even know what Social means? Then what are you going to write?
KAMAL: Social means—about this day and age—about our time, you know . . .
WRITER: Yes, of course, I'll write about our times.
AMAL: What's the plot?
WRITER: There isn't one.
VIMAL: I see . . . what about the theme?
WRITER: The theme? Well . . ., us!
KAMAL: Who 'Us'?
WRITER: Well, all of you, Indrajit, me . . .
AMAL: Us? Good luck to you then.
VIMAL: What drama is there in our lives, mate?[51]

Badal Sircar's *Evam indrajit* is described in Satyadev Dubey's introduction to the English translation as "a milestone in the history of modern Indian drama" and a play that "makes its presence felt" in relation to Indian theater history, because of the stylized brilliance with which it captures the featureless existence of a handful of middle-class characters in the postcolonial metropolis of Calcutta (v). Noticed less often is the continuity Sircar establishes between this wasteland and the oppressive legacy of colonialism, not only as a socioeconomic liability but as an epistemological and existential burden that determines the life cycle of the postcolonial subject and empties it of value. In his "Minute on Education" (1835), Thomas Macaulay had described the propagation of English as the only means by which the colonial state could "form a class who may be interpreters between us and the millions whom we govern; a class of persons, Indian in blood and colour, but English in taste, in opinions, in morals, and in intellect."[52] Sircar's play is an ironic update on how that comprador class is doing more than a century later, unmoored from its colonialist origins and inhabiting a world in which English has come to coexist fully with Bengali, Sircar's original medium and one of India's premier literary/theatrical languages. Amal, Kamal, Vimal, and Nirmal (whose real name is Indrajit), picked out randomly from an audience by the Writer, embody the forms of false consciousness that originate in the colonial past and control the postcolonial present, making *Evam Indrajit* a highly condensed, metatheatrical epic of modern Indian urban experience.

The choice of Calcutta/Kolkata as the 1960s setting of the play has historical, sociological, and existential resonance for Sircar. As a locale close to the first British military victory in India (the Battle of Plassey, 1757), the site of the first British fortifications (Fort William, built in 1696 and expanded in 1781), and the capital of British India from 1772 to 1911, Calcutta is the quintessential colonial/ist city, but it also became the seat of the Bengali urban intelligentsia during the nineteenth century and continues to be the powerful center of Bengali culture in India. Sircar's approach to it as a postcolonial abyss stems from his belief that colonial cities "did not emerge as the natural products of the indigenous economic development of the country, but were created to serve the colonial interests of a foreign power," leading to "an unfortunate dichotomy between urban and rural life."[53] As an architect and urban planner by profession, Sircar is uniquely positioned to assess the uncontainable complexity of Calcutta as *mahanagar* (uber-city); as a lifelong inhabitant of the city born late in the colonial period (1925), he is also acutely aware that he has no other viable subject as a playwright.[54] The Writer in *Evam indrajit*, a metatheatrical stand-in for Sircar, confesses at the very beginning to his audience that the choices of a metropolitan location and middle-class milieu are overdetermined by the gaps in his own knowledge and experience.

WRITER: I know nothing about the suffering masses. Nothing about the toiling peasants. Nothing about the sweating coal-miners. Nothing about the snake-charmers, the tribal chieftains or the boatmen. There is no beauty in the people around me, no splendour, no substance. Only the undramatic material—Amal, Vimal, Kamal, and Indrajit. . . . (6)

Ironically, this undramatic quartet is still part of an elite in 1960s Calcutta because it includes the small percentage of inhabitants who have college degrees. The degree reflects neither intellectual ability nor a genuine education, but it does push the recipients into "the middle-income group" and makes them "well aware of their difference from the rest," although within the group "there is enough disparity of income" (6).[55] Satyadev Dubey provides another sociocultural perspective by pointing out that the middle class considers itself the (apolitical) backbone of Indian society, and its ambitious members fill key areas such as the defense and administrative services. "*Evam Indrajit*," then, "is in some ways about the residue . . . those who have failed to adjust, align, and ceased to aspire, and also those who are enmeshed in the day to day struggle for survival" (vi).

Circumscribed in these ways, the play's five male and two female characters are based to different degrees on the absurdist principle of intragender interchangeability (Didi and Gogo, Rosencrantz and Guildenstern, the two Conchitas in Bunuel's *That Obscure Object of Desire*). The Writer has no name, but the fungible quality of the other men is marked, first, by the phonetic and semantic parallelism of their names. "*Mal*," the same Indo-European root that appears in the English words "malfeasance" and "malediction," means dirt, filth, and more specifically, excrement, in Sanskrit and the modern languages derived from it. "*A-*," "*Vi-*," and "*Nir-*" are prefixes that mean "not," "devoid of," or "the opposite of." In their very naming, A-mal, Vi-mal, and Nir-mal are thus pure, uncorrupted, undefiled men. "*Kamal*," the word for the lotus flower, denotes the same quality, because the lotus retains its pristine beauty even though (in India) it often grows in heavily polluted and stagnant bodies of water.[56] Indrajit, in contrast, is one of the names of Meghnad, a major mythical figure in the Sanskrit epic, the *Ramayana*.[57] He acquired the name after defeating Indra, the God of Heaven, in a contest that demonstrated the superiority of his demon lineage over one of the most powerful Hindu deities. In Sircar's play, when the character whose real name is Indrajit chooses to call himself Nirmal Kumar Ray because "one invites unrest by breaking the norm" (5), the incongruity between past epic splendor and an antiheroic present becomes palpable. The symbolism of identical names, moreover, is literalized at the level of the performative: across the play's three acts, Amal, Vimal, and Kamal always appear together, exchange clothes, speak in the same order, play the same array of rapidly changing roles, and utter dialogue that is either verbally or semantically identical, so that without any loss of "drama" they can be gathered together into the acronym "AVK" (fig. 4.1).

After the Writer manages to persuade Indrajit that he must avoid the fate of being "Nirmal," he dreams of doing "something unusual, important, unprecedented" (58), makes unconventional life choices for a time,

MODERNISM, REALISM, AND THE POSTCOLONIAL URBAN PRESENT

FIGURE 4.1. Ram Gopal Bajaj, B. P. Sinha, Dinesh Thakur, and Om Shivpuri in *Evam indrajit*, directed by Mohan Maharishi, Yatrik, New Delhi, 1967.

and disappears for a few years. He is also the only one with a social conscience who reacts to injustice against the helpless, such as a young widow abandoned by her husband's family, or children in abject poverty. But "it's a pointless anger. It's blind. Powerless. It only beats its head against the wall" (23), and at the end there is only an admission of failure:

INDRAJIT: . . . The light never came. The sky didn't burn. I could not leave the solid earth.
MANASI: Why not?
INDRAJIT: I didn't have it in me to do that. Never did. I just dreamt that I could, that's all. So long as I couldn't accept my ordinariness I dreamt. Now I accept it.
MANASI: Indrajit. . . .
INDRAJIT: No Manasi, don't call me Indrajit. I am Nirmal. Amal, Vimal, Kamal, and Nirmal. Amal, Vimal, Kamal, and Nirmal. . . .

(58–59)

As a character, even Indrajit is not truly autonomous because he functions as the Writer's alter ego and shares some of the latter's spaces and relationships. Conversely, the Writer's singularity as the metatheatrical master of ceremonies is limited because he is sometimes indistinguishable from Indrajit, and he breaks character briefly to play other theatrical roles as well. In general, through quick role-switching, the structures of authority and privilege in the play are shown to be completely fluid and reversible: each man is both teacher and student, interviewer and interviewee, boss and subordinate, a besieged husband and father struggling to survive and an upper-class snob savoring his forms of entitlement.

The two women belong to different generations, and the principle of interchangeability also functions differently with them. The older character is called "Auntie," but "only for convenience. She could be 'mother', 'elder sister', anything" (3): her only dialogue in the play is either about feeding "her boy" or denouncing his intellectual and creative pursuits because she finds them pointless (the "boy" is sometimes the Writer and sometimes Indrajit). Auntie may be given other names, but she remains always and only herself, the nurturing but exasperating Indian maternal figure. The younger woman is called "Manasi" by the Writer (from *manas*, mind), but we never learn her real name because "all women are Manasis" (52). Instead of being part of a cluster of identical women, Manasi is one woman who plays all the feminine roles in relation to the five men. She is the Writer's muse, Indrajit's reluctant love-interest, the mercurial object of male desire in the street, an office secretary, the wife of Amal, Vimal, and Kamal, and, eventually, even Nirmal's wife when he ceases to be Indrajit—but this Manasi, we learn, is different from the "other Manasi." As the muse, Manasi is a counterpoint to the anti-intellectual Auntie, but is limited to two stock queries for the Writer and Indrajit: "have you written anything?" and "are you finished?" Her only "realistic" role is that of the sympathetic mate who refuses to marry Indrajit because they are cousins, and chooses to pursue a lonely but independent life as a schoolteacher while she and Indrajit keep up a platonic long-distance friendship. Delibidinizing heterosexual relationships is one of the play's signature moves (fig. 4.2).

In terms of structure, the play consists mainly of a series of stylized tableaus that take these characters "[f]rom home to school. From school to college. From college to the world. They are growing up. They are going

FIGURE 4.2. Vishwa Mohan Badola as Indrajit and Sudha Shivpuri as Manasi in *Evam indrajit*, directed by Mohan Maharishi, Yatrik, New Delhi, 1967.

round. Round and round and round. Amal, Vimal, Kamal. And Indrajit" (19). The movement forward in time is hobbled by a fundamental disconnection—the public life of the characters (school, college, office, business) follows the patterns of education, professionalization, and employment that originated in the previous century to produce the desired class of colonial "interpreters"; their private lives (home, family relationships, marriage, children) continue to follow traditional Indian norms, leading to an existential mishmash. In the college classroom scenes, Sircar satirizes the top-down systems of rote learning (traceable to colonial pedagogy) that reduce each student to a "roll number" and bombard a roomful of passive recipients with random bits of multidisciplinary "knowledge." Ironically, the same process also produces ostensibly cosmopolitan subjects because the students' "gossip" always consists of "Cricket, cinema, physics, politics, literature" in a global frame (10). The sample conversation in Act 1, for instance, touches on the latest cricket Test Match, Yul Brynner, Marlon Brando, Einstein, time as the fourth dimension, the complete plays of Bernard Shaw, local theater activity, and the relation between "beautiful" literature and "dirty" politics (7–9). Even Indrajit's fantasies of escape to faraway places filled with exotic fauna are derived from *The Simple School Geography*, a sixth-grade textbook. The anxiety over anonymous annual exams, the tension of job interviews, the tedium of office life, and the strain of professional one-upmanship are legacies of a colonial-style liberal education that are entrenched in the play's postindependence world. Marriage, children, and a host of other family responsibilities are the burdens imposed by traditional Indian social expectations, made worse by the lack of resources and the fear of old age. The two women predictably embody the worst aspects of "tradition"—motherhood is reduced to an obsession with producing and consuming food, and Manasi's romantic-sexual union with Indrajit is prevented by her reluctance to engage in what she considers a socially transgressive act. Manasi, like almost everyone else, is a follower of rules.

In addition to this historical perspective on the Indian metropolis and its inhabitants, *Evam indrajit* has three thematic concerns that move outward from national to global, and then to what can only be described as cosmic stances. As the sum of its history, politics, society, and culture, the modern Indian nation is an implied referent throughout the play, but its progress since independence from Britain on August 15, 1947, comes in for specific attention at the beginning of Act 3, during a card game between AVK. They agree initially that "Now we have to build a self-sufficient, self-supporting society" (47), but within a dozen lines, moving rapidly through the world's major political systems and ideologies, their stichomythic dialogue arrives at a denunciation of the national government and politics in general, and then devolves into a catalogue of personal complaints. Momentary interest in the nation gives way to the conclusion that you must "Just concern yourself with your own work. / If I am alive, all is well" (47). In a radically different register, the Writer takes the earth itself, and what happens on it over time, as the real measures of human existence: "the earth goes on, the century goes on. Our earth—our century.... We are here, still here, here on earth" (29). The poem that follows this dialogue contains the refrain that "The earth is crushed, but it's still alive / The century's old, but it listens still" (29). In this viewpoint that is both cosmopolitan and universalist, ethical individuals are obliged to grapple with all the acts of injustice and inhumanity, committed anywhere and at any time, that constitute the world's unwritten history. So Sitanath in Sircar's *Baki itihas* (The rest of history, 1965) commits suicide because he can no longer bear the guilt of accumulated atrocities, and in *Tringsha shatabdi* (The thirtieth century, 1966), the atomic holocaust in Hiroshima and Nagasaki prefigures a future genocidal dystopia. Indrajit adds another layer to the world-centered view when he brings up "the insignificance of this minute earth" and its inhabitants in the immensity of cosmic space and time. Inclined to believe in the value of his own life, he forgets "how ephemeral my life is in the total flow of time—a mere second. I forget that my existence is a pointless particle of dust" (41). The trivial lives of AVK become more trivial in comparison with Indrajit's because of their unbroken self-absorption.

Alongside the surface cosmopolitanism of pedagogy and the inclusiveness of intellectual/ethical positions, the cosmopolitan reach of *Evam indrajit* as a literary-theatrical construct appears in the echoes of earlier twentieth-century modernist, existentialist, and absurdist works that Sircar integrates into the texture of everyday Indian life. The metatheatrical structure evokes Pirandello's *Six Characters in Search of an Author* (1921), but with a difference. In the Italian play, fictional characters already locked into an inexorable chain of events are abandoned by their author and interrupt a rehearsal in progress at a professional theater so the company of actors can script their tragedy and enact it on stage. In Sircar's play, it is the author searching for characters whose lives can serve as material for drama, but the quest fails because of the shapeless quality of those lives, and the author's inability to devise a plausible structure for them. The play, then, is structured around the Writer's failure to create a play. The interchangeable nature of Sircar's characters can also be traced back to Brecht's concept of alienation or estrangement, which rejects the Aristotelian definition of character as a stable ethical essence (*ethos*) and opposes a primarily affective connection between character/actor and audience. Some of Sircar's characters have distinct selves some of the time, and others do not, but they are all equally alienated and alienating in that they do not invite a primarily emotional response. The other Brechtian device in *Evam indrajit* is the use of diegetic prose and verse for choric comment. Brecht often uses diegetic statements at the beginning of an act or scene to prefigure and comment on the action so the audience can reflect on what is going to happen, instead of merely being caught up in a chain of events. Sircar gives the diegetic/ choric functions to the Writer so all of the action in its different settings is filtered through his critical, skeptical sensibility.[58] All three acts also end with poems, the first two recited only by the Writer, and the third by the Writer, Indrajit, and Manasi. Although the verses are not set to music, they perform the same gestic function as the songs in Brecht.

Other important influences emerge in Sircar's evocation of major existentialist and absurdist voices. The metaphors of the closed circle and the Ferris wheel, signaling that there is "no escape" from repetitive but meaningless action, recall Sartre's *No Exit*. The Writer's description of himself, Indrajit, and Manasi as the "cursed spirits of Sisyphus" recalls Camus (59). The Beckettian absurd is invoked in mimed action, nonsensical speech, and childish rhymes. In the office, letters are written but not posted, files are switched pointlessly between the "In" and "Out" trays, and the dictation of business memos consists only of stock phrases, with no substantive content. Indianizing Kafka, Sircar clearly views the modern office, where men are addressed as "Sahib" (the sycophantic colonial equivalent of "Sir") and "babu" (smug official) as the ultimate site of mind-numbing routine: "After the files, tea. Then files. Then snacks. Then files. Then tea. Then files. Then tram-bus-train. There are bigger offices where even more important business is transacted. There, files—then tea—then files—then lunch—then files—then coffee—then files and then office transport, taxi, car" (32).

Toward the end, the Writer's conclusion that he, Indrajit, and Manasi will have to go on writing, talking, and living even when there is nothing to express, communicate, or live for is a more verbose formulation of the last line in Beckett's *The Unnamable* (1953): "I can't go on, I'll go on." Beckett's *Waiting for Godot* is also clearly a referent when the metaphor of a closed circle shifts to that of an open road, which must be taken even when there is nowhere to go: "Forget the questions / Forget the grief, / And have faith / In the road. / No shrine for us / No God for us / But the road, / The endless road" (59).

My description of *Evam indrajit* as the portrait of a "neocolonial wasteland" acknowledges the power of T. S. Eliot's poem to capture the quality of unregenerate modernity in other places, but the closest verbal allusions in the play are also to Eliot's early and late verse. Multiple repetitions of the phrase "That's all" by the Writer and AVK in the office (33) are intentional echoes of Sweeney's summing up of life to a bored Doris in *Sweeney Agonistes: Fragments of an Agon* (1926).

SWEENEY: Birth, and copulation, and death.
    That's all, that's all, that's all, that's all,
    Birth, and copulation, and death.
DORIS: I'd be bored. . . .
SWEENEY: You'd be bored.
    Birth, and copulation, and death.
    That's all the facts when you come to brass tacks:
    Birth, and copulation, and death.[59]

Sweeney's phrase is picked up a few pages later and rendered by the Writer as "Birth, marriage and death! Birth, then marriage and then death" (36), to give the Indian audience a sanitized version of Eliot's dialogue, but also to mock the centrality of marriage in the Indian sociocultural imaginary. Late in the play the opening lines of "Burnt Norton" ("Time present and time past / Are both perhaps present in time future, / And time future contained in time past")[60] are paraphrased in a reflection on temporality. "What is behind is ahead," Indrajit says; "There is no distance between the past and the future. What's there in the past is in the future as well" (55). The Writer gives the same perception a nihilistic turn when he declares: "We have no hope because we know the future. Our past is one with our future. We know what's behind us will also be ahead of us" (59). In Eliot's *Four Quartets* the eternally oppressive presence of time is redeemed through religious faith; in Sircar's godless absurdist world the only choice is despair, and the only liberation comes with death. Finally, the opening line from "East Coker"—"In my beginning is my end"[61]—becomes Indrajit's justification for the Writer's unfinished play because "Its end is its beginning" (59).

In this densely allusive, stylized, and poetic evocation of a postcolonial present, where does realism fit in? It plays a prominent role, in fact, because much of the dialogue between the seven characters, in domestic, social, and professional settings, is "realistic." The speech captures college gossip, life at home, conversations between (unacknowledged) lovers, a householder's complaints about the impossibility of making ends meet, and disheartened admissions of professional failure, among other familiar moments. Everything and everyone in *Evam indrajit* belongs recognizably to the Calcutta of the early 1960s, but every component is also estranged through stylization. This interruption of the urban realist narrative by a host of other devices suggests that even in his early proscenium plays Sircar saw realism as both necessary and inadequate for dealing with urban life, which in *Evam indrajit* registered India's failure to reinvent itself after the colonial interlude. As noted previously, after 1973 Sircar abandoned the proscenium for the Third Theatre—the mobile, body-centered "theatre of urban-rural synthesis" which became thereafter his signature method for engaging politically with the life of the nation.

ATMAKATHA (AUTOBIOGRAPHY): REALITY, FICTION, FALSEHOOD

Mahesh Elkunchwar's *Atmakatha* is in almost every respect the antithesis of *Evam indrajit*—it is set in the privacy of home rather than in proliferating public spaces; deals with intimate relationships between mature characters who are portrayed in the style of classic realism rather than Brechtian alienation; places the fictional version of a highly successful author of realist fiction rather than a failed playwright at its center; and consistently employs the medium of realistic prose dialogue rather than undifferentiated speech, stylized stichomythia, and verse. Bombay is implied but never explicitly mentioned as the characters' urban environment. Unlike Sircar's entanglement with colonial burdens, postcolonial anomy, twentieth-century literary forebears, and the like, in Elkunchwar's play the city, the nation, and the world remain firmly offstage. The experimental dimension of *Atmakatha* as a work of modernist realism lies, instead, in its handling of time and space.

The temporal structure of the play creates unpredictable alternations between the present, which involves four characters, and some events in the past that occurred at different times between three of these characters, but are not recreated in chronological order. In one sequence of scenes set in the present, Anantrao Rajadhyaksha (Raja for short), a celebrated seventy-eight-year-old Marathi novelist, is recording material for a prospective autobiography in his own home with the help of a young research student, Prajnya. In the second sequence, which also unfolds in the present, Raja's former wife Uttara and her much younger sister Vasanti, with whom Raja had fallen in love thirty years earlier, reflect on what led to the affair, the destruction of their relationships, and the lives they have led since then. The event in the very recent past that has led Raja and Uttara to resume contact after nearly three decades is her decision to publish the letters he wrote to her after the break-up, but their accounts of what led to her decision, and when, are not compatible. Similar discrepancies exist between Raja's flashbacks (recounted to Prajnya) about how Uttara discovered and reacted to the affair, and more mature, less melodramatic accounts of the same day by Uttara and Vasanti. The Rashomon effect created by these competing narratives, which are not just recalled but actually enacted as self-contained dramatic scenes with shifting points of view, is complicated further by the appearance of the fictional versions of the sisters, named Urmila and Vasudha, whom Raja had created for a transparently autobiographical and very successful novel published soon after his relationships with both women ended. In a face-to-face confrontation with Raja-as-author, the fictional selves protest against the simplistic and sentimental portraits of them that have been fixed forever in the work of fiction, and their consequent loss of agency.

Back in the present, Vasanti reveals to Uttara in their final scene that Raja is the real father of her grown-up son Dilip, although she was married at that time to Devadatta, a struggling writer who was ill and died early. The "truth" of this confession, which could potentially transform Raja's life because he had always wanted children and Uttara was barren, is also left indeterminate, because it contradicts both Raja's and Vasanti's earlier accounts of their relationship before and after the split. However, in Raja's *novel*, romantically titled The Misty Path, Vasudha *is* pregnant when she leaves, and Anand (the character based on Raja) is indeed the father of her son Pradeep. *Atmakatha* therefore juxtaposes conflicting accounts of "reality" with its novelistic representation, triangulating unstable male and female versions of events with the fixity of fiction. The renewed contact with both women over the phone, the confrontation with their fictional selves, and ethical doubts about his own authorial motives make Raja increasingly uncertain about his planned autobiography, and he abandons the idea altogether in his final scene with Prajnya when she confesses that she has fallen in love with him.

The spatial arrangement that makes these temporally disjunct scenes performable is the division of the stage into three areas designated as A, B, and C, which respectively represent Raja's home (stage left), Uttara's home (stage right), and an empty space that is occupied by Urmila and Vasudha, the fictional versions of Uttara and Vasanti (stage center). The stage directions specify that "A shows the study of a highbrow, affluent, and acclaimed writer.... B is designed to suggest a luxurious living room. C is totally empty."[62] The materially differentiated spaces signify a physical and symbolic separation between the characters, and their handling in performance is structurally crucial because *Atmakatha* has no act and scene divisions, only fluid shifts from one space to another. Sometimes the action takes place only between characters in one brightly lit area while the other two remain dark. At other times, Raja in A speaks on the phone to Uttara or Vasanti in B, and vice versa. In a more complicated variation, a phone conversation between Uttara in B and Raja in A takes place within a longer scene between Uttara and Vasanti in B, or Raja walks into C for a conversation with Uttara in the middle of a scene with Prajnya in A. In both cases, the past is embedded within the present. The most provocative use of this device happens late in the play, when Raja walks into C inadvertently and is confronted by the fictional pair of sisters from his novel (fig. 4.3).

FIGURE 4.3. Shriram Lagoo as Rajadhyaksha, Jyoti Subhash as Uttara/Urmila, and Suhas Joshi as Vasanti/Vasudha in *Atmakatha*, directed by Pratima Kulkarni, Roopvedh, Bombay, 1988. Photo credit: Mahesh Elkunchwar.

The manipulations of space-time create an experimental vehicle for the play's principal themes, which include a new kind of power balance between men and women, the culture of a vibrant literary language like Marathi, and the correlations between reality, fiction, and falsehood. The first theme deals with the personal and takes a progressive approach to gender relations; the other two involve a chaotic public world and reinforce the secondary status of women in literary culture and fiction. In terms of its handling of complex intimacies, *Atmakatha* is an unusual quasi-realist play about socially well-positioned adults who knowingly violate sexual norms and accept the long-term consequences of their actions. For Elkunchwar, the triangulated relationship between Raja, Uttara, and Vasanti is "what is most interesting about *Atmakatha*," and neither their transgressive acts nor their subsequent behavior are subjected to any trite social or moral judgments.[63] Raja explains his affair with twenty-year-old Vasanti partly as an act of compassion because Uttara was treating her harshly in their home, but he also admits that he is "just as unable to understand" the event, and sometimes, "things just happen" and have to be accepted (29, 34); Vasanti explains it as an act of revenge against her sister's "haughty self-assurance," made easier because "from the very first day that's all I could see in his eyes" (37, 38). Raja is not just a predatory male, and Vasanti is not just his abject victim. Uttara's reaction when she "discovers" the affair does not consist of hysterical threats (as Raja claims), but of despair at the destruction of three lives, without the redeeming presence of children (28). Similarly, in a remarkably even-toned scene, Vasanti voluntarily confesses the affair to Uttara because it would mean that she's "free of it" (36). Both sisters leave home that same night to build independent lives elsewhere: Uttara has lived alone but with her "dignity intact" (50), and Vasanti has settled into a pattern of serial monogamy after Devadatta's death; she maintains very little contact with her adult son. As she tells Raja with deliberate nonchalance in their first phone conversation in the present, she is now living with her much younger Muslim lover, Salim, "in a righteous town like Pune" (13).[64] Vasanti's second (alleged) liaison with Raja is even more deliberately transgressive: she claims to have seduced him during Devadatta's terminal illness because she was nettled by his indifference toward her—but the stage direction notes here that "It's not clear whether she's lying or telling the truth" (50). The reason for keeping the truth about Dilip from Raja for decades, she says, was that she "didn't want to have the reins of my life trapped in his hands" (51).

These declarations of independence in the intersecting narratives of *Atmakatha* evoke an emergent urban culture in which educated, accomplished, mature women exercise an unusual degree of freedom in relation to "traditional" Indian social norms and find it possible to lead unconventional lives. After Uttara discovers the affair, she does not make sanctimonious appeals to marital fidelity or the ideal of home; instead, she offers to get out of Vasanti's way, only to be refused. Like twin Noras, both women slam the door in a decisive act of departure, although Raja feels that Uttara threw away her career as a dancer and Vasanti left him for "a down-and-out writer without looks, talent, or brains" (27). Because Vasanti values her freedom, Dilip does not get to grow up as the son of a famous writer. Uttara, in turn, tells Vasanti that she decided to publish Raja's letters so that "people could get to know the truth. There are such horrible misconceptions about you and me in society" (14). These are all urban, and urbane, structures of support for women who have stepped off the beaten path while remaining within the relatively secure parameters of middle-class city life. The young research student, Prajnya, embodies the continuation of these freedoms in her generation. She is working toward a doctoral degree and dealing on terms of blunt equality with a major writer—like Vasanti a generation earlier, she also develops an emotional attachment to him that is compelling for her, although her confession brings Raja to a standstill. That all three women in the play are bound in different ways to the same man seems masculinist, but Uttara recognizes that the ultimate loser is Raja. After a long period of estrangement, in their "declining years" the two sisters have "come together again. We visit each other all the time, you and me. He has absolutely no one with him" (38). Elkunchwar's only concession to sentimentality may be the figure of the lost son, which appears at the end to hold an uncertain promise of redemption for Raja.

In an essay on Lillian Hellman, Judith Barlow notes that "realism has come under perhaps its greatest assault in recent years from materialist feminist critics who, following a variety of postmodern theories, question the nature and value of both representation and narrative."[65] Sue-Ellen Case, who wants realism to be cast aside because its "consequences for women are deadly," presents a compelling argument about the implications of realism's dependence on the space of home: "Realism, in its focus on the domestic sphere and the family unit, reifies the male as sexual subject and the female as the sexual 'Other.' The portrayal of female characters within the family unit—with their confinement to the domestic setting, their dependence on the husband, their often defeatist, determinist view of the opportunities for change—make realism a 'prisonhouse of art' for women."[66]

This analysis extends transculturally to Indian modernist-realist plays, in which home is predominantly a place of victimage for women as wives, mothers, sisters, daughters, and lovers (the two women in *Evam indrajit* are no exception). In *Theatres of Independence*, I had described the experience of women characters in realist contemporary drama as "overwhelmingly that of oppression, marginalization, exploitation, violence, and even death.... Qualitatively different attitudes to gender ... emerge ... [only] when male authors move out of the urban social-realist mode into the anti-modern, anti-realistic, charismatic realm of folk culture."[67] Elkunchwar stays within this general paradigm in his best-known realist play, *Wada chirebandi* (Old stone mansion, 1985), but dismantles it three years later in *Atmakatha*, bringing some of the liberatory qualities of folk culture into an urban narrative. Women now exercise as much control over the space of home as men—they stay, or leave, as they choose, and make their homes elsewhere when they need to. The roles of wife and lover are fluid, not fixed, and motherhood is not central to them. Female will and desire shape events of many different kinds. The agency that the three female characters in *Atmakatha* possess at least in relation to their personal lives stands out with refreshing clarity against the dominant narratives of patriarchal control.

The caveats lie, as I have suggested, in the public world generated by a language and its literature. Elkunchwar's description of *Atmakatha* as a play "about writing, about creativity," and "the relationship between the artist and his art" does not take the next step and mention the vital role that the *literary culture* of a major language like Marathi plays in the career of an individual writer, and the extent to which leading writers are public figures, often with distinct political profiles. In these respects, the play reflexively demonstrates why modern Indian languages do not function as "vernacular" media in modern India. As a major Indo-Aryan language with about eighty-three million speakers recorded in the 2011 census, Marathi connects authors to a tradition of modern writing that has been continuous since the mid-nineteenth century; a vibrant print and performance culture covering the full range of literary, theatrical, critical, and paraliterary genres; a large community of nationally recognized authors in the present;

and a sizable audience of devoted readers and viewers. To write in Marathi is to inhabit a language-world with its own metropolitan centers, a strong regional base, and sufficient national visibility to ensure effective transregional circulation.[68]

The figure of Rajadhyaksha in *Atmakatha* indicates that writers *matter* in Marathi literary culture, in good and bad ways: their works are read, their careers get close attention, and as they gain celebrity status, their private lives become objects of public consumption. "At one time," Raja tells Prajnya self-mockingly, "I made myself famous all over Maharashtra with my love affair. Even now people tell each other that juicy and amazing story" (21). The success of the thinly disguised autobiographical novel following this notoriety made him a household name and created the audience's voyeuristic appetite for personal testimonials or nonfictional accounts of that same life (such as letters and an autobiography). In the present Raja oscillates between feelings of contentment with his fame (all those "committees, seminars, conferences," foreign trips, and awards by which he measures success) and resentment against readers for not respecting his "great restraint" as a writer, which Prajnya describes as concealment (21). As he and Uttara argue about their respective rights to a privacy they know they do not have, the metaphors evoke crass consumption. "She finally published the letters," Raja notes; "people gorged on our lives. What did she get out of it?" (11). Vasanti's view is that the letters gave people "tasty fodder to chew on. Now as soon as his autobiography comes all of it will start all over again" (14). These exchanges imply a robust, print-centered literary sphere in which new writing is consumed rapidly and on a large scale, very much like the products of popular and mass culture.

Vasanti is vengefully indifferent to Raja as a writer, but as a young acolyte who is working on a thesis on him and finds the daily contact exciting, Prajnya provides the "outsider's" standpoint and creates yet another perspective on the literary culture of Marathi. Her relationship with Raja is disarmingly informal and affectionate, but also intellectually combative. She prefers his lyric poetry to all the other "boring" work, questions his lack of interest in major contemporaries like the modernist poet B. S. Mardhekar, finds it strange that he supported Devadatta financially but ignored him as a writer, and expresses her disappointment that he did not oppose Indira Gandhi openly during the Emergency or return his Padma Bhushan (a high civilian honor), like other prominent writers.[69] The scenes between

Raja and Prajnya bring to life the writer's role as a politically engaged public intellectual—the play in fact begins in the middle of a sentence as Raja is recalling the relationship between Tilak and Gandhi, the leading anticolonial nationalist figures in their respective generations, and the qualities of "idealism and commitment" that effectively informed all writing during the nationalist movement (2). Raja earned his political credentials by going to prison for the nationalist cause, which makes his inaction during the Emergency all the more noticeable. Lying beyond the conscious or unconscious literary community that exists within a given period is therefore the public sphere, in which writers participate simply by virtue of their visibility and authority.

The portraits of Raja as a private and public individual that I have discussed so far are ambivalent but not damning; a harsher picture emerges when Elkunchwar deals reflexively with the ethics of realism (the life-art relationship) and the problem of male authorship. Both issues are central to the long scene in which Raja inadvertently walks into the empty space (C), reserved for the fictional versions of Uttara (Urmila) and Vasanti (Vasudha), and initially mistakes them for the real-life originals (42–47). The first problem is the Pirandellian one of ontological fixity—once captured within a fictional narrative, characters can neither change nor escape their story. As Vasudha says of Uttara and Vasanti, "they will be free in five or twenty-five years. We are immortal. Whether anyone reads his book or not" (44). A single reader, she continues, can force them to "live" again simply by opening the book. The problem is compounded by the stark gender imbalance in the ranks of authorship: men far outnumber women in all of the modern Indian literary genres, and in the extreme case of theater (which has the fewest "conventional" women authors), "the women that men created" is actually a recognized critical subject.[70] As the object of male representation (rather than self-representation), Vasudha feels that "these people take possession of our entire lives" (42), and an unscrupulous author of realist "autobiographical" fiction can manipulate the narrative very much to his own advantage.

This, in fact, is Vasudha/Vasanti's main charge against Raja's "autobiographical" novel—that he uses it to exercise in fiction the power he did not and could not have in real life. In both life and fiction, he fails to understand the sisters and demeans them. Uttara is stereotyped as the hysterical and vengeful wife, and Vasanti as the helpless victim forced to find a surrogate father for her son while the idealistic real father is in prison for his political beliefs. The discovery of the affair in the novel is handled in the melodramatic and sentimental style that leads to a "terrible scene" between the sisters, but Raja admits to Prajnya that it was "all colored by the imagination" (31). Urmila/Uttara is resigned to this misrepresentation, but still tells Raja that if he had "let us grow, let us behave according to our own ways, then your own novel would have been so much better. It's not good to make your characters dance according to your whims in this way" (45). As a female reader, Prajnya arrives independently at the same judgments when she notes that Raja created a sanitized, self-privileging version of events, casting himself as the "pitiable" hero who is caught between a shrewish wife and a seductive twenty-year-old, and then abandoned by the younger woman for another (second-rate) writer who dies prematurely of alcoholism. In the magic-realist, metatheatrical dimension of *Atmakatha*, two women created by a man, and their "real-life" counterparts, get to protest and complain about their treatment, becoming metonymic voices in the debate over gender and authorship.

Raja's response to the women's critique is defensive and contradictory. On the one hand, he claims that he decided to keep "the real people . . . constantly in view," and took great care to do so; indeed, he feels in retrospect that his mistake was to "describe all the events as they had happened in real life" (26). On the other hand, he admits to being unfair and subjective, and describes the process of writing as a personal quest for clarity: "Urmila and Vasudha are Uttara and Vasanti—I am able to say this but also not able to say this. It's an attempt to understand both of them" (26). The most interesting exchange about the aesthetics and ethics of realism takes place between him and Prajnya.

PRAJNYA: When you say you don't understand human relationships, do you mean the relationships in your private life, or do you mean the relationships between characters in your literary works?

RAJA: Both. Or rather, the relationships between characters in my literary works are an attempt to understand the relationships whose shape I cannot grasp in my private life.

PRAJNYA: There must also be a huge play of the imagination in efforts of this kind?

RAJA: Yes, the two very often get thoroughly mixed up.

MODERNISM, REALISM, AND THE POSTCOLONIAL URBAN PRESENT

PRAJNYA: Then actuality . . . authenticity . . . what remains of that? . . . .
RAJA: The authenticity of these relationships has to be sought only in the autonomous world of art, not in the outside world. (24)

Prajnya's rejoinder, which echoes Raja' own admissions, brings home the contradiction and circularity of the life-art relation.

PRAJNYA: Then in novels of this kind, how much is true, how much is imaginary, how much is a mixture of the two, and how much is blatantly false? And if we are not supposed to look for connections in the outside world, then how is that novel autobiographical? And if we are not supposed to call it that, then why is event after event picked off from the life that has already happened? (24–25)

It is clear that Prajnya has seen through Raja in their pointed conversations, and Vasudha/Vasanti and Urmila/Uttara have categorically rejected his claims of empathy. And yet the play ends with Prajnya's confession of love, which according to Elkunchwar is explained by "something of a pure core about this man" (viii). *Atmakatha* portrays male authorship as privileged, exploitative, self-serving—but ultimately irresistible.

TARA: DISABLED SELVES AND THE LONG REACH OF PATRIARCHY

Mahesh Dattani's play, like *Evam indrajit*, also has a failed writer at the center—twenty-two-year-old Chandan Patel, now known as Dan, who tries every day in his London bed-sitter to give dramatic form to memories of his family in Bombay so he can atone for the death of his twin sister Tara (a name that means "star"). As in *Atmakatha*, the past alternates with the present in a nonlinear pattern, but here the acts of recall belong exclusively to Dan, and they appear as a sequence of "scenes" he presents metatheatrically as a play-in-progress within the play. The earliest event retrieved from the past is the surgery that made medical history when a team of surgeons headed by Dr. Thakkar successfully separated Chandan and Tara—fraternal twins conjoined in utero in uniquely complex ways—at the age of three months. The second block of time covers a twelve-month period beginning with the Patel family's arrival in Bombay from the southern city of

Bangalore, when the twins are fifteen, and ending with Tara's death the following year due to complications following a kidney transplant. The diasporic present in London is one of bitter reclusiveness for Dan: his attempts at fiction have failed because they do not exoticize India sufficiently for a Western audience, and "back home, of course, Indo-Anglian literature isn't worth toilet paper."[71] The attempts to sublimate his grief and guilt through the act of playwriting have also failed so far because drama, unlike poetry, is not emotion recollected in tranquility, and he has to "relive that charge over and over again" (1). On the particular day enacted in the outer play, Dan does succeed in scripting selective parts of his past, but he tears up the typescript near the end because instead of making amends to Tara he has merely added to the number of people who betrayed her by appropriating her tragedy.

The multilevel set in *Tara* also parallels the principle of three distinct spaces in *Atmakatha*. Dan's sparsely furnished London flat is "the only realistic level" (1). A chair on a higher plane is occupied by Dr. Thakkar, who maintains a "godlike presence" throughout the play. The Patel family's Bombay home appears at the lowest level and covers most of the stage, but "it is seen only in memory and may be kept as stark as possible" (1). The street outside the home is "suggested by cross lighting," and the suburban neighborhood beyond it is only inferred (1). Like *Evam indrajit* and *Atmakatha*, *Tara* again indicates that postindependence modernist-realist playwrights have little interest in recreating the space of the "bourgeois home," or in maintaining a linear temporal progression, in the style of Western conventional realism. In the first two plays, even the conception of dramatic character is destabilized by the idea of interchangeability and the juxtaposition of real and fictional selves, respectively; Dattani's characters are more "realistic" in comparison, but they are mediated through Chandan/Dan's sensibility and subject to his manipulations. In all three plays, the realist core consists, then, in the characters' *dialogue*, which catches the rhythms of ordinary speech and positions them in time and place.

Dattani brings two new dimensions to the discussion of modernist realism—he writes originally in English, and due in part to his own privileged background as the son of a successful Gujarati businessman in Bangalore, much of his drama deals with "a better class of person," to borrow with ironic intent the ironic title of John Osborne's 1981 autobiography. Both these choices have sociocultural ramifications because the link between English and social privilege in India is seen as creating stark inequalities in the spheres of education, employment, professionalization, and social mobility, widening the gap between different sections of the urban population, and worsening the disconnect between urban and rural areas.[72] In Dattani's case, because the multilingual field of postindependence theater continues to be predominantly non-Anglophone, the choice of English was controversial and attracted a great deal of attention in the early phases of his career. He dealt with the challenge by claiming that English was the natural language of expression for him as an English-educated, postcolonial urban playwright, and by naturalizing the medium so that it captured the qualities of spontaneous dialogue effectively, without awkwardness or unintentional self-parody.[73] Taken together, Dattani's plays offer in English the most sustained portrayal of the urban upper class in contemporary Indian drama, similar to what Tendulkar accomplishes in Marathi, although the latter's milieu is much more mixed in terms of class.

Although filtered through Dan's consciousness and presented discontinuously, the Patel family comes through vividly in the action of *Tara*, outwardly displaying the signs of affluence, cosmopolitanism, and liberalism associated with its status. The conventions of "family drama," however, are keyed not to the mundane but the extraordinary in this play. The family is atypical although not exceptional in 1980s India because the parents, Patel and Bharati, married across the boundaries of region and language—they are both Hindu, but he is of Gujarati origin, and she belongs to the Kannada-speaking region of Karnataka. More unusual is Patel's estrangement from his own relatives and his decision to live in the home of his wealthy father-in-law in Bangalore, but he is also a high-ranking business executive who has moved his nuclear family to Bombay following the old man's death. Chandan and Tara have been exceptional since before their birth because conjoined twins are usually identical, not fraternal like them, and following the medical miracle of their separation, at the age of sixteen they are the oldest such surviving twins in the world. Each of them has a prosthetic leg and follows a relentless routine of hospital visits, but Tara also needs a kidney transplant for which her mother wants to be the live donor. As Tara's health deteriorates, Bharati's high-strung behavior slides into hysteria, and it is clear that Patel's harshness toward her is fed by some long-held resentments. When Tara returns home from her transplant, Bharati is already institutionalized in a mental health facility, and the children are

FIGURE 4.4. Asif Ali Beg as Chandan, Tarini Bedi as Tara, and Aadya Bedi as Roopa in *Tara*, directed by Alyque Padamsee, Theatre Group, Bombay, 1991. Photo credit: Raell Padamsee.

prevented from seeing her because Patel does not want his wife to have the satisfaction of confessing her past guilt.

The revelation of the "family secret," a familiar structural device in Dattani's drama, destroys the façade of modernity and liberality that the Patels have tried to maintain in their English-speaking, affluent household. Without consulting Patel, Bharati and her wealthy father had bribed Dr. Thakkar to manipulate the twins' operation so that two of the three existing legs were given to the boy rather than the girl, even though her circulatory system provided most of the blood to the limb. The boy's body rejected the leg immediately, but the gratuitous interference with scientific procedure has done long-term damage to Tara, leading to the renal failure and transplant that end her life. The twin disabled bodies of Chandan and Tara, mirroring each other in every respect except that of sex/gender, become cautionary symbols of debased patriarchal authority, made more poignant by the siblings' fierce love and loyalty toward each other (fig. 4.4). The absent grand/father's hubris, in fact, works like a family curse to bring about a scaled-down dynastic tragedy. When Dan receives the news of his mother's death from Patel near the end of the play, he refuses to return to Bombay because "I don't think I can face life there anymore," and having torn up his play because his progress has been "zero," he anticipates his own death (52, 60). It is only in fantasy that Tara can be restored to health and wholeness, when at the very end Dan holds her in a tight embrace and asks for forgiveness.

Dattani's critique of deep-rooted misogyny and gender inequity taps into sociocultural fault lines that are remote as well as proximate, traditional as well as modern. The traditional attitudes can be traced back to a text like the *Manusmriti*, composed in Sanskrit around the beginning of the common era, which claims repeatedly that women cannot have independence at any stage in their life: "in childhood a woman should be under her father's control, in youth under her husband's, and when her husband is dead, under her sons."[74] In the patriarchal structure of Hindu/Indian society, women face erasure on multiple fronts—biologically, because they do not continue the paternal line; juridically, because they do not inherit parental property; and existentially, because their primary function is to be united with suitable mates who accept them as ritual "gifts," and secure the next generation through them. The centrality of marriage in a woman's life leads to the conception of female children (widespread even in contemporary India) as *paraya dhan* (wealth that belongs to someone else), and consequently to the perception that female children are, first and foremost, major material liabilities whose real destiny lies in their marital home. Joined with the traditional practice of dowry, which involves payments in cash and kind to the groom's family, these associations harden the cultural attitude that a girl child is a lifelong drain on the family's resources whose birth is to be regretted, not celebrated.

Tara transposes these long-standing attitudes to the postcolonial present in a brutally honest way. The cumulative advantages of education, wealth, professional standing, and urban privilege, and even the prospect of a medical breakthrough, could not prevent the corrupt patriarchal intervention that destroyed the girl child in a futile effort to benefit the male. Furthermore, neither the dead man nor the "godlike" doctor paid any price for their collusion—the family was left to deal with the aftermath until it fell apart. This is the spectacle of a failed modernity, made more ironic by the claims of modernization, progress, and scientific brilliance that underlie Dr. Thakkar's chorus-like commentary on what he and his team accomplished. Dattani twists the knife deeper by creating a parallel to the injustice against Tara in a horrific practice attributed to Patel's community in Gujarat, which bears the same name. Roopa, the malicious fifteen-year-old neighbor who is the only outsider in the play, tells Tara that the Patels used to drown their female children in milk because their death could then be attributed to choking. The subject comes up again in a conversation between Roopa and Chandan about the 1982 film *Sophie's Choice*, in which a mother at Auschwitz is told that one of her two young children must go to the gas chamber, and she "chooses" her son Jan over her daughter Eva. In complete ignorance of the horrors of the holocaust and with breathtaking moral vacuity, Roopa declares that drowning in milk is a "more civilized" practice than condemning a little girl to the gas chamber.[75] There is an element of vicious regional prejudice against Gujaratis in general, and the Patel community in particular, in Roopa's allegation, but the possibility of its being true is a devastating judgment on Tara's fate. Despite the care and expense that her immediate family has undertaken since her birth, what happens to her is no different from the practice of female infanticide.

This message is coded in *Tara* at the literal and symbolic levels, but Dattani's demystification of the crude instincts that lie underneath the veneer of affluent modernity connects the play to the many forms of gender discrimination that persist in contemporary India despite continual efforts at ideological, political, and social change. The Indian Parliament had to enact the "Pre-Conception and Prenatal Diagnostic Techniques Act" of 1994 "to stop female foeticides and arrest the declining sex ratio in India," because parents were using Amniocentesis, a prenatal procedure for detecting genetic disorders, to identify the baby's sex and abort female fetuses.[76] Despite much greater access to education and professional training since independence, women constitute a relatively low percentage of the Indian workforce, declining from 32 percent in 2005 to 21 percent in 2021. The idea that male children are preferable because they offer future security to parents remains firmly entrenched, despite a decline in the extended family structure and the resilient ways in which parents with only female children are managing to negotiate old age, at least in urban areas. The grotesque term "dowry death" refers to the death by murder or suicide of a new bride who did not bring in enough material incentives at the time of her marriage. According to the Pioneer News Service dated December 15, 2022, twenty women are killed every day for dowry-related reasons in India, and the official figure for the 2017–2021 period stands at 35,493 deaths. The gang rape and murder of a twenty-three-year-old student on a Delhi bus in December 2012, named the Nirbhaya (Fearless) case by national and international media, has become a brutal symbol of the lack of safety for Indian women in public spaces. Dattani's Tara is like an embodiment of the cumulative burden of these injustices, summed up in her last line in the play, after she has discovered her mother's betrayal: "And she called me her star!" (59).

CODA: COSMO-MODERNISM, MULTILINGUALISM, AND THE HERMENEUTIC GAP

Tracing the evolution of realism as a mode, and its connections to modernism, in twentieth-century Indian theater has offered the most comprehensive glimpse so far into how cross-cultural "influences" work across Europhone and non-Europhone fields of theory and practice. Unlike the modernist narratives of history and myth, which in India diverge sharply from Western trends and do not imply any intrinsic formal or structural qualities, realism has indisputably Western origins, and its accommodation over an extended period represents an active and acknowledged desire on the part of Indian playwrights to engage with their own time and place through specific formal-structural constructs that they find meaningful. In this enterprise, they are joined by directors, actors, and other professionals committed to theater outside the entertainment-for-profit model, and by a relatively small but loyal audience. My analysis of the plays by Sircar, Elkunchwar, and Dattani indicates that there is nothing "derivative" about mature forms of realism in Indian theater, and the modernist strain of realism produces works that have no precursors in the modern Indian field.

The formal sophistication and thematic density of these plays, regardless of the original language of composition, also bring up a series of questions. Why have modern Indian theater studies produced so little systematic theater history that can provide a coherent account of movements, forms, styles, and genres? Why is there so little interpretive criticism that can deal adequately with the depth and resonance of individual plays—the meanings they possess when they first appear, in print and performance, and the changes in meaning over time? Why are there no clearly defined "schools" of criticism in modern Indian theater studies? The critical effort invested in this field has lagged well behind the creative effort from the beginning, and this gap can be filled only gradually as Indian theater studies consolidates itself as a scholarly discipline within and outside India. But paradoxically, one prominent reason for the critical deficiencies is precisely the factor that contributes to the singularity of modern Indian theater as a colonial and postcolonial field—its rich multilingualism. The culture of each theatrically active language is extensive and dynamic, and all the components of this culture—playwrights, plays, directors, actors, theater groups, theater spaces, audiences, and so on—receive much greater attention from scholars and critics in that language than they do in transregional and national perspectives. By the same token, critics and audiences in a given Indian language have only limited interest in the artifacts of other languages, and only a small proportion of what is written and produced becomes nationally visible. Realism and modernism are only a couple of topics among numerous others that underscore the need for two large-scale corrective moves in modern Indian theater studies—the development of hermeneutic strategies that can bridge the gap between a play and its interpretations, and the reconciliation of a rich multilingualism with nonprescriptive, nonpropagandist national perspectives.

Chapter Five

MODERNISM AND TRADITION

INDIAN PERFORMANCE TRADITIONS AND MODERNISM

India has an exceptionally large and diverse repertoire of precolonial indigenous performance forms that have passed through the stages of colonial and postcolonial reconfiguration over two centuries and constitute a synchronic storehouse of "tradition" in the present. The oldest body of culturally transmitted works consists of classical Sanskrit drama, which maintained its canonical status as an urban, secular, and written form for more than a millennium (c. 400–1700 CE). During the nineteenth century this drama became a new kind of cultural touchstone when orientalist scholars (European and Indian) evaluated it as the premier Sanskrit genre and placed it in the canons of world literature. As a measure of high culture, Sanskrit retains its historical priority in contemporary India, and Sanskrit plays continue to be published and staged, in original, translated, and adapted versions. However, the vast majority of indigenous postclassical forms that emerged after the decline of Sanskrit (1200 CE–) are oral or unscripted, belong to the countryside rather than the city, and employ major or minor dialectal forms rather than the standard urban locutions of a given regional language. Two sets of key terms encapsulate the otherwise uncontainable transregional diversity of such forms and performative practices: *paramparagat* or *paramparasheel* (i.e., "traditional," from *parampara*, tradition), and *lok-kala/loknatya* (the crafts and performing arts of the *lok*, which means both "folk" and "the people"). The perviousness of these definitions is evident in descriptive labels such as "traditional classical theater" and "traditional folk theater," but it is possible to use some broad principles of classification to separate the types into meaningfully distinct categories. Thus major examples of extant precolonial forms include those that are derived from classical Sanskrit (Kutiyattam and, more recently, Kathakali); have connections to folk (village) culture and seasonal rituals (Bayalata, Bhand Pather, Chhau, Bhavai, Ojhapali); celebrate specific deities in accordance with a religious calendar (Ramlila and Raslila); perform devotion through various forms of narration, music, and dance (Dashavatar, Harikatha, Nata-Sankeertana); and offer secular entertainment to mixed urban-rural (intermediary) audiences (Jatra, Yakshagana, Nautanki, Tamasha). The processes of modernization, industrialization, and urbanization have naturally affected many aspects of traditional communal performance, but the traditions continue to be visible components of regional, especially rural, culture around the nation.[1]

Beginning in the 1950s, the assimilation of these precolonial legacies into a body of postcolonial drama by a heterogeneous group of playwrights initiates a strain of "modernist traditionalism" (or "traditionalist modernism") that is another new postindependence aesthetic, like "modernist realism," but counterpoints realism in every respect and carries a much higher experimental charge in performance. The first major figure in the movement is Habib Tanvir (1923–2009), an active early member of the Indian People's Theater Association (IPTA) whose training at London's Royal Academy of Dramatic Art and Old Vic Theater School (1955–56) paradoxically cemented his commitment to indigenous Indian performance traditions, especially those associated with the large rural and tribal populations in the Chhattisgarh region of Madhya Pradesh, his native state. In 1959, Tanvir's decision to form Naya Theater, a professional company that brought together folk performers and city-trained actors, made regional forms of music and dance (especially Nacha), as well as the "provincial" Chhattisgarhi dialect of Hindi, intrinsic to his work as a playwright and a director. The portrayals of regional history and folklore in Naya Theater plays therefore acquired a performative "authenticity" that was both dramaturgically radical and a significant step toward bridging the urban-rural divide in theater. At the opposite cultural pole, K. N. Panikkar (1928–2016), founder of the Sopanam group in the coastal Kerala city of Trivandrum (now Thiruvananthapuram), emerged as the leading director of Sanskrit plays in revival (1978–), especially the *Mahabharata*-based plays of Bhasa, the earliest extant Sanskrit playwright (second century CE). The performance of these plays in their original language gave Panikkar the opportunity to recuperate the highly stylized, elite representational conventions of classical Sanskrit drama, but it also enabled him to integrate them with regional traditions of ritual, dance, recitation, song, percussive sound, and martial arts, such as Theyyam, Mudiyettu, Kutiyattam, Padayani, Sopana Sangeetam, and Kalaripayettu. Throughout his career, Panikkar also interspersed the Sanskrit repertoire with original Malayalam plays of his own in which folk narratives were rendered through a variety of regional presentational styles.

Chandrashekhar Kambar (1937–), born and raised in a north Karnataka village, brings other distinctive qualities to his brand of traditionalist modernism. Despite a long theatrical career anchored in the metropolis of Bangalore, he describes himself as a "folk person," considers the experience of a village upbringing decisive for his playwriting, and has drawn most extensively on the regional Bayalata folk form in his best known plays. In the remote and politically volatile northeastern state of Manipur, the playwright-director Ratan Thiyam (1948–) has managed the Chorus Repertory Theater since 1976, and like Panikkar, he has brought an immersive commitment to regional forms—Thang-ta, Wari-Leeba, Nata-Sankeertana, and Pena, among others—to original plays based on the *Mahabharata*, as well as Manipuri translations of Mahabharata plays by Bhasa and others. Thiyam's preoccupation with the problems of political oppression and violence has also drawn him to figures such as Antigone, and the ancient Indian emperor Ashoka, who converted to Buddhism after confronting the brutality of his wars of territorial conquest. The last two playwrights in this group are atypical, but for different reasons. After trendsetting modernist incursions into myth and history in the early 1960s, Girish Karnad (1938–2019) began his experiments with traditional forms and narratives in 1971 by combining a twelfth-century folktale with the conventions of Yakshagana, the most prominent regional form in his state of Karnataka. In later plays, however, he used folklore and myth as occasions to create philosophically complex, metatheatrical stage vehicles rather than to highlight traditional performative elements. Finally, Vijay Tendulkar (1928–2008), already familiar as a paradigmatic authorial figure and exemplar of modernist realism, took a singular "detour" into tradition in a collaborative 1972 play in which he used the dance-and-music conventions of Dashavatar, Kirtan, and Tamasha for a highly stylized and corrosive representation of late-eighteenth-century Maratha history.

The signature works produced by these playwrights' tradition-infused modernism embody some of the highest forms of cultural capital and transregional mobility in postindependence theater: Tanvir's *Agra bazaar* (Urdu, 1954) and *Charandas chor* (Charan Das the thief, Chhattisgrahi, 1974); Karnad's *Hayavadana* (Horse-head, Kannada, 1971); Kambar's *Jokumaraswami* (Kannada, 1972); Tendulkar's *Ghashiram kotwal* (Constable Ghashiram, Marathi, 1972); Panikkar's *Madhyam vyayog* (The middle one, Sanskrit, 1978), *Karimkutty* (Malayalam, 1983), *Karnabharam* (Karna's burden, Sanskrit, 1984), and *Urubhangam* (The shattered thighs, Sanskrit, 1987); and Ratan Thiyam's *Chakravyuha* (Battle formation, Manipuri, 1984), and *Uttar priyadarshi* (The final beatitude, Manipuri, 1999). Recognizing these works and their authors as "modernist" is important because in aesthetic as well as political terms they contrast and challenge two other influential postindependence discourses on the uses of tradition: the left-populist approach taken by the IPTA at its founding in 1943, and the cultural-nationalist positions adopted by prominent cultural critics, policy makers, and scholar-administrators, especially after 1960. In the following sections I delineate the constitutive features of modernist traditionalism (which is an admixture of creative principles rather than a "genre") in contradistinction with populist and nationalist approaches, using two iconic works—Tendulkar's *Ghashiram kotwal* and Tanvir's *Hirma ki amar kahani* (The immortal tale of Hirma, Hindi/Chhattisgrahi, 1985)—to explore how the principles are embodied in practice. I frame that discussion, however, with a brief overview of the commonalities of location, circumstance, context, technique, and content that undergird my claims about a *modernist* revamping of tradition.

The playwrights engaged in this practice are city-centered professionals, but with the possible exception of Tendulkar they have strong emotional connections to the village or small town culture of their origin and are more or less deeply versed in regional styles of music, dance, folk performance, and martial arts. Each play in this category takes up one or more specific traditional/folk forms, but the playwrights consistently interweave the performative and presentational elements with a recognizably "modern" dramatic structure, so that the verbal and nonverbal dimensions of the work emerge as equally important. As in other forms of postcolonial Indian modernism, the figure of the author and the effects of proprietary authorship remain central: unlike the remoteness and anonymity of their traditional source narratives and styles, the plays as finished artifacts are firmly situated within the established contemporary oeuvres of their respective authors. Similarly, unlike the culture of orality to which the source materials belong, the modernist works connect to print culture on the same scale and in the same manner as other modernist drama, or even modern drama in general. Publication also stabilizes the text of the plays and turns them into mobile commodities for readers in various places, including the classroom.

Because regional elements are more prominent and sometimes ineffable in traditional narratives, translation and multilingual circulation happen on a comparatively smaller scale in this variety of modernism, but most major works have appeared in at least the two national link languages: English and Hindi. Both in the original and in translation, the nonverbal, "purely" performative dimension also gets diegetically inscribed within the published text, so that the text-performance relation in these plays exemplifies in a particularly heightened way the commonplace assertion that drama is fully realized only in performance. In terms of reception, the plays are hybrid constructs aimed primarily at urban audiences: they draw on, but do not replicate, the narrative content and environment of the source materials, and they are not available with any consistency to semi-urban or rural spectators. Most important, modernist plays making use of premodern tradition are thematically and politically entangled in their own time, and the older world they portray is another defamiliarized image of the present, although the dramaturgical methods are radically different from those of realism. Collectively, these features separate the modernist plays from their traditional source material, and from the two other prominent discourses about tradition.

INSTRUMENTALIZING TRADITION: LEFT-POPULIST AND CULTURAL-NATIONALIST PLATFORMS

The IPTA offered the first "modern" perspectives on tradition in the 1940s when it launched a nationwide movement of protest and resistance against fascism, imperialism, and the brand of bourgeois-nationalist anticolonialism associated with the dominant Congress Party under Gandhi and Jawaharlal Nehru's leadership. As the cultural front (at least initially) of the Communist Party of India, the IPTA modeled itself on a number of international antifascist organizations, while in India it paralleled the Progressive Writers Association, a national organization of novelists and poets launched in 1936. Translating these influences into forms of domestic cultural activism that were focused on theater and dance, the IPTA rejected colonial theater forms in their entirety and based its program for a "cultural awakening of the masses of India" on a revitalization of the country's "traditional arts" and "rich cultural heritage," repurposed now to support "our people's struggles for freedom, economic justice and a democratic culture" (Pradhan, vol. 1, 129).

The organization's interest in traditional arts was the result of a fascinating combination of anticolonial, cultural-materialist, and left-populist perspectives. Its "First Bulletin and Draft Resolution" of July 1943 began with the claim that India's "great cultural heritage" had equaled "the best of the cultural achievements of any other peoples at a corresponding stage of civilisation," but its "life and vigour" had been ravaged by colonialism (Pradhan, vol. 1, 124). Colonial commercial theater became the prime example of this decline, especially because under Anglo-European influences it rejected precolonial Indian performance forms as vulgar and corrupt. Placing expressive culture within the grim mid-twentieth-century contexts of war, famine, brutal political repression, and economic precarity, the IPTA manifesto placed peasants and urban industrial workers at the center of its definition of "the people" and gave "a revival of the folk arts" a key role in the emancipation of this new Indian collectivity (Pradhan, vol. 1, 131). The "recovery of tradition" thus had a corrective historical function, but from a populist standpoint it also had many self-evident advantages in the present. Indigenous performance forms were already familiar to the people and closer to the circumstances of their lives than the overblown spectacles of commercial theater, so they could be powerful mediums for delivering the IPTA's political message. As open air, mobile, and spontaneous nonproscenium forms that could be performed for mass audiences in a variety of locations, they also offered a solution to the problem of strapped production budgets and the urban-rural divide. As Sudhi Pradhan argues, all the major political parties in the 1940s were interested in populist cultural forms, "but mere anti-communism could not lead them further. It was left to the Marxists to disclose the potency of the art forms that are close to the people, their immense possibilities, their untapped source of strength, and thereby 'the opening of the magic door to mass mobilisation'" (Pradhan, vol. 1, xiv).²

In practice, however, the IPTA's use of traditional forms was limited by a number of factors. Since most of its theater workers were city-trained activists, they gravitated toward the social realism of plays such as Bijon Bhattacharya's *Nabanna* (New harvest, Bengali, 1944), Khwaja Ahmad Abbas's *Zubeida* (Urdu, 1944), and Prithviraj Kapoor's *Pathhan* (The frontiersman, Hindi, 1947), or the antifascist/pro-communist propaganda of plays such as Sergei Tretyakov's *Roar China* (performed by the IPTA in 1942), and Thoppil Bhasi's *Ningalenne communistaki* (You made me a communist, Malayalam, 1952). Tamasha and Powada in Maharashtra, Jatra in Bengal, and Burrakatha in Andhra Pradesh were then among the few intermediary/folk genres to be performed successfully before large urban and rural audiences, representing one distinctive part of the IPTA's activist program. After independence, and especially after China's communist revolution in 1949, the organization's adversarial relationship with Nehruvian democratic socialism also reached a point of crisis, and its activities as a national organization effectively ended around 1957. However, the movement's historical role in defining the *culture of the people* as the basis of theater in the new nation has had a lasting impact on all forms of activist political theater; and the connection it forged between tradition and a progressive (although not necessarily factional) politics resonates in the work of modernist playwrights across a wide range of aesthetic and ideological positions.

The second major discourse concerned with precolonial tradition also has a decolonizing thrust, but it is otherwise the exact antithesis of IPTA populism because it makes the emergent nation-state and its bureaucracy the primary custodians of the nation's cultural heritage. Beginning in the decade of independence, the arguments come mainly from influential individuals who are not theater practitioners; they are formulated in short tracts that view the government as a key patron of the arts, or during collective events that are organized by government institutions and lead to published proceedings. The most important institutional initiatives in this process have belonged to the Sangeet Natak Akademi (SNA), created in January 1953 "for the preservation and promotion of the vast intangible heritage of India's diverse culture." In his opening address at the Akademi's inauguration, the education minister Abul Kalam Azad set out the official position by defining the state's role in relation to national culture, democracy, and "the people":

> India's precious heritage of music, drama and dance is one which we must cherish and develop. . . . not only for our own sake but also as our contribution to the cultural heritage of mankind. . . . It will be the aim of this Akademi to preserve our traditions by offering them an institutional form. . . . In a democratic regime, the arts can derive their sustenance only from the people, and the state, as the organized manifestation of the people's will, must, therefore, undertake . . . maintenance and development [of the arts] as one of [its] first responsibilities.[3]

As an "autonomous organization" under the Ministry of Education (from 1953 to 1999) and the Ministry of Culture (since 1999), the Akademi (as noted previously) manages programs at the national and regional levels that include production subsidies, festivals, conferences/seminars, fellowships, awards, conservation projects, research, and publication. In a resource-poor performance economy, this comprehensive roster of activities makes the state-supported cultural bureaucracy a prime source of patronage and enables it to wield disproportionate power as a custodian of "tradition."

The gradual shift from aspirational and relatively inclusive arguments about tradition-as-resource to prescriptive, polemical, and exclusive positions is evident in the activities and events that sequentially define important phases in the cultural-nationalist discourse about tradition from the 1940s to the 1980s.[4] In an argument first presented in 1945 and summarized in an essay in 1956, the influential policy maker Kamaladevi Chattopadhyay stressed the importance of reviving and preserving "the rich heritage on which to build the new theater of today and the structure of tomorrow," but she also recognized that "however marvellous and perfect this traditional theater might be, it can no more serve as a spontaneous and natural medium through which the mind of the people is to manifest itself."[5] In 1956, the formal recommendations of the Drama Seminar echoed the IPTA manifesto in acknowledging that "the regeneration of the Indian theater can only be possible by revitalising the traditional folk forms" and urged the renewal and preservation of these forms around the country through "careful scientific study," but the Seminar offered no categorical assertions about their value to *new* urban drama.[6] That connection appeared five years later, at the Seminar on Contemporary Playwriting and Play Production, which was designed to focus mainly on the playwright-director relationship and the obstacles these professionals faced in their collaborative efforts to create theater without institutional structures of support. As an important subsidiary issue, the organizers noted that "Western dramatic literature and theatrical traditions" had strongly influenced all Indian-language drama, and this strain had "not been fully assimilated in the Indian theatrical tradition."[7] In their respective papers, Sombhu Mitra, V. Raghavan, and Suresh Awasthi therefore speculated on the relative value of three discrete models—Western production styles, Sanskrit plays in revival, and the forms and techniques of folk drama—for "contemporary theater."

A decade later, the 1971 "Roundtable" brought together twenty-one front-rank playwrights, directors, scholars, and critics to focus exclusively on the topic that had been peripheral in 1961: precolonial performance traditions as artistic resources for theater in the postcolonial present. In his introduction to the proceedings published in *Sangeet Natak* (the journal of the Sangeet Natak Akademi), Awasthi expressed his view that "no creative artiste can afford to ignore the situation that we have a vast, rich continuous tradition in these fields of performing arts." He explained that attitudes had changed rapidly during the previous decade because of changes in "our socio-cultural life," which included a new "quest for identity, leading to the exploration and creative utilisation of tradition."[8] Approaching the subject of inherited cultural resources from a variety of viewpoints, other participants at the Roundtable agreed in principle that traditional forms offered theater professionals unprecedented opportunities for creative growth and innovation. But they also stressed the integral relation of these forms to their original environment, their precarious situation in a rapidly modernizing nation, the dilemmas they posed for urban theater workers, the necessity of refashioning them so they could speak to urban audiences around the country, and the concomitant dangers of mere cultural appropriation or empty formalism. In addition, there was substantial agreement among the participants that the choice of traditionalist aesthetics had to be voluntary, not forced. J. C. Mathur cautioned against "any compulsion upon a writer" (40), and Mohan Rakesh stated bluntly: "[the] sort of decision that 'I am going to use such-and-such form for my next play' or 'I am going to experiment with folk tradition because folk tradition should be used'—this sort of thing I totally reject" (39). As SNA secretary, Awasthi felt obliged to clarify in turn that "bodies like the Akademi do not dictate the survival or the creative utilisation of any form," and the choice of traditional forms was "not a question of the Akademi or its grants and finances" (33). More important, he agreed with Ebrahim Alkazi that there was no question "of limiting, or rejecting or discarding the prose theater," but only of recognizing that "here is a great opportunity, a vast store house living side by side inevitably as part of our destiny" (42). The powerful premise underlying the various exchanges, however, was summed up in the Roundtable's recommendations, which asserted that "modern dramatic expression whether in writing or acting or production cannot escape the environment of the traditional theater" (45).

Fourteen years after the Roundtable, the special double issue of *Sangeet Natak* (77–78, 1985), titled "The Traditional Idiom in Contemporary Theatre" and guest edited by Nemichandra Jain, registered a markedly different discursive and ideological moment. The differences did not lie either in the overall identity of the participants or in the range of their opinions, but in what appeared to be a stark disconnect between theater practitioners on the one hand and bureaucratized scholar-critics on the other. Among the contributors, Shanta Gandhi and G. Shankara Pillai had participated in earlier sponsored events, but the thirteen other playwrights and directors represented a new generation of successful theater professionals whose essays reflected a healthy diversity of viewpoints. G. P. Deshpande, Rajinder Nath, Lokendra Arambam, and Rudraprasad Sengupta were strongly critical of the traditionalist wave; Gandhi, Pillai, Manoj Mitra, Bansi Kaul, M. K. Raina, and Vijaya Mehta were ambivalent or cautiously optimistic; and K. N. Panikkar, Chandrashekhar Kambar, and Naa Muthuswami wrote as playwright-directors whose theater had been anchored from the beginning in the traditional forms of their respective regions. The turn toward prescription and exclusion appeared, instead, in the essays by Jain and Awasthi, which defined the basic features of what Awasthi now labeled the "theatre of roots."

In comparison with the institutional discourse that had preceded it, Awasthi and Jain's collaborative manifesto for the newly named theater contained two radical moves: it connected the use of traditional forms directly to a program of cultural decolonization, and it dismissed all theater that did not conform to these goals as derivative, effete, and un-Indian.

The theatrical forms, performance spaces, and staging conventions that colonial urban theater borrowed from the West had been criticized since the 1940s, but they were now recast as colonialist impositions that did not and could not succeed in a postcolonial, "authentically" Indian cultural environment. "After more than a century of almost barren attempts at playwriting and staging after Western models," Jain wrote, "our theatre seems at last ready to reject this imitative pursuit and to venture into its own distinctive, indigenous territory." Among the "many factors... responsible for this development," he included "the impact of the widespread quest for an Indian identity in all aspects of life in our country, including the arts, particularly the theatre; a growing awareness of and dissatisfaction with the imitative nature of our past dramatic efforts and the desire to go to our own roots; increasing exposure to our own traditional theatre forms and their amazing vitality, aesthetic freshness and popularity with people; [and] worldwide disillusionment with realistic theatre and the search for alternatives."[9]

Similarly, Awasthi argued that "the models and conventions of the borrowed realistic theatre always remained alien to our theatrical tradition, and the inherent conflict between the two could never be resolved." Using stronger language, he characterized colonialism as a "violent dislocation" of the unity, continuity, and integrity of Indian cultural traditions, which could now be restored through a quest for origins that was by definition incompatible with urban modernity.[10] Artists B. V. Karanth, Panikkar, and Thiyam had thus "reversed the colonial course of contemporary theatre and put it back on the track of the great *Natyashastra* tradition," restoring "unity in essential theatrical values" (85). Elsewhere in his essay Jain did caution against "a display of formal virtuosity without any serious content, experience of life, or even concern for the text of a play" (12), and Awasthi analyzed the aesthetics of the theatre of roots, but central to both of their arguments about tradition was a totalizing view of national culture.[11]

The *modernist* reshaping of traditional forms I highlight in this chapter is detached both from the IPTA's left-wing populism and the nation-state's bureaucratic co-optation of tradition. Habib Tanvir is a partial exception to the first claim, because the idea of a people's theater that he absorbed during his early association with the IPTA became fundamental to all his work, and he maintained a lifelong relationship with India's leading street theater group, Jana Natya Manch (The people's stage), which is based in

Delhi and affiliated with the Communist Party-Marxist (CPM). However, Tanvir's deep immersion in village culture and the irreducible variety of his theater make it difficult for critics to contain him within any single or simple political mold. The other modernist playwrights/directors who draw on classical, folk, devotional, and intermediary forms do not have overt political affiliations. Their politics consist, instead, in a broadly humanist critique of the inequalities of gender, class, caste, and ownership, and the corrupt forms of (mostly male) power that are exercised in the Indian political and public spheres. When modernists assimilate tradition into their craft, they also do not invoke the nation as a legitimizing entity, or claim to restore the unity and continuity of precolonial culture, or cast their work as a form of cultural restitution, or dismiss other forms of theater. Beyond this dissociation from left-populist and nationalist ideologies, the theory and practice of modernist traditionalism (hereafter MT) reveal some broad areas of agreement among the authors, embedded in highly individualized artistic trajectories.

MODERNISM AND TRADITION: IDEAS AND PRACTICES

The Aesthetics and Politics of Modernist Traditionalism

Modernist engagements with traditional forms of theater and performance have not been given a name or systematically theorized so far, but they *are* namable and theorizable because of the extensive body of self-reflexive commentary, discussion, and debate that leading playwrights, directors, playwright-directors, and other theater professionals have developed around this subject since the 1950s. The modernist turn toward the resources of tradition is eventually motivated by the same impulse that undergirds other modernist genres—they offer another set of opportunities for creating "really new" forms of urban drama in the postindependence period. In particular, the antirealist, environmental aesthetic of indigenous forms strikes a liberatory note for those who are disinterested in, or bored with, "Ibsenism" and its intrinsic medium, prose, even though the mode of realism in Indian theater has the idiosyncrasies noted in chapter 4. Taking up the classical Sanskrit definition of drama as *drishya kavya* (poetry meant to be seen rather than merely heard or read), playwrights Kambar and Panikkar put forward the generally accepted view in MT that drama is an essentially poetic form, and they include modernists such as Lorca, Yeats, Eliot, and Tagore among the important influences on their craft. Poetic dialogue joins with premodern/nonmodern narratives, fluid performance texts, stylized movement, specialized actor training, and regional styles of music, dance, and song to produce integrated forms of "total theater" whose affect is qualitatively—and often stunningly—different from that of other urban forms.

Among modernists, the pursuit of novelty through traditional narratives and presentational styles draws on two basic principles: the plays do not try to reproduce any "authentic" native environments but evolve a radical urban aesthetic; and the *meanings* they communicate possess "contemporary relevance," to adapt a phrase from the 1971 SNA Roundtable. As the Delhi-based director M. K. Raina asserts, "we are not going back to tradition, as some of us claim. We are in the process of creating new thinking, new sensibilities, and therefore new forms."[12] Panikkar echoes this when he explains that his interest in classical and folk traditions is "not a going back, but to go forward there must be support from behind, from our own traditions."[13] Using a different terminology, Naa Muthuswami, a leading playwright-director in the city of Chennai, notes that all the efforts of his group are "aimed at discovering a modern theatrical idiom from traditional theatre forms," and the metaphor he uses—suggesting that traditional aesthetics can yield a new kind of "performance language"—is in fact the one most frequently repeated by all those who are engaged in the task of definition.[14] The related quality of "contemporaneity" is a product of both aesthetic and political factors because the "modernization" of "traditional" matter demands complex coding at the formal, structural, and thematic levels. I return to this issue later in this section, but it is worth noting here that it represents perhaps the starkest difference between modernists and those institutionally positioned theorists who appear to view aestheticized performance primarily as a means of rehabilitating the past and neutralizing colonialism.[15]

Criticizing the "fetish of folk and classic" in his essay for the 1985 special double issue of *Sangeet Natak*, the playwright G. P. Deshpande had concluded that "why [we are] doing what we are doing" with tradition "is the question to ask. It seems to ordinary theatregoers like me that this question is never asked, let alone answered."[16] In fact, proponents of the theatre of roots *have* asked and answered that question in essentialist terms that are not acceptable to Deshpande, but leading modernists have also "explained" the pull of tradition, implicitly or explicitly, by invoking different kinds of relationships with their material. One grouping represents a natal connection with village culture and regional traditions of performance (theater, dance, music, religious worship, martial arts), and includes the playwrights Habib Tanvir, Chandrashekhar Kambar, K. N. Panikkar, and Ratan Thiyam, who have a deep understanding of their respective non urban cultures in emotional, aesthetic, and political terms. Tanvir was born in the district town of Raipur and had a fully urban education in Nagpur, Aligarh, and London, but he chose to spend his career transporting the rural culture of Chhattisgarh to the urban stage. Kambar belongs to the village of Ghodageri in North Karnataka and has described the experience of a rural upbringing as definitive for his work as a playwright, poet, folklorist, theorist, and critic. "I am . . . a 'folk' person simply because I honestly cannot be anything else," he notes while commenting on his relationship with "what is vaguely known as folk theatre."[17] Born in the remote Kerala village of Kavalam, Panikkar grew up in close proximity to the life-rhythms, rituals, and poetry of folk culture, but he added Sanskrit drama and popular regional forms to his complex theatrical repertoire when he moved to the city. Thiyam's elaborate performative aesthetic interweaves Sanskrit elements with ethnic Meitei performance traditions, and this synthesis provides an indirect means of engaging with the volatile politics of insurgency and military repression that has defined Manipur's relationship with the Indian nation-state since the 1960s.

The second grouping consists of "ultramodernist" figures such as Vijay Tendulkar and Girish Karnad, whose birth, upbringing, education, and professional profiles are urban/metropolitan, with no direct connection to folk culture and no deep roots in regional performance traditions. For these playwrights, the turn toward traditional forms is a contingent and self-conscious move, designed to break new creative ground or to take on specific dramaturgical challenges. Tendulkar commented during the 1971 Roundtable that he "would like to indulge in some folk form that would suit my needs—I want to find my way out" (39). He found the Tamasha form deeply liberating at a time when he was "tired" of realism, and he used it in the play *Sari ga sari* (Rain, o, rain, 1964) to mount a new kind of critique of the "white-collar-class" because he thought "the theme would suit the form" (40). The experiment failed at that time but was remarkably successful eight years later in *Ghashiram kotwal*, the only other play in which he drew on regional Marathi performance traditions. During the same discussion Karnad noted with reference to *Hayavadana* that he was "attracted by the *Yakshagana* form. I write a play, in Dharwar, using the *Yakshagana* form, because I feel, in one particular play it helps me to give a form to what I want to say" (24–25). Tanvir, whose relationship to folk forms was qualitatively different from Karnad's, endorsed Karnad's principle of "selfishness" because "that is of the very essence of all creative work.... It is a very subjective process and you really take whatever suits you so that you can project it most effectively" (30). The experimental drive is therefore strongest in the MT plays of Karnad and Tendulkar.

The degrees of ontological proximity to traditional content among playwrights also appear to shape their intuitive relationship with the "forms" they adopt. "I was searching for a form of drama which would adequately express the sensibility to which I was born," Kambar notes. "Bayalata not only gave me the necessary format but also the language."[18] Panikkar recalls that when he began writing *Karimkutty*, his play about the liberation of farm workers, "the rhythm, the music of the village, of the agricultural labourers, the movements, the visual patterns, all came to me as a comprehensive, well-knit thing."[19] G. Shankara Pillai describes this as the ideal state in which a contemporary artist is "spiritually and aesthetically in the ambience of a traditional form.... [G]radually transformed, [it] ultimately provides him with an idiom that successfully conveys his message and meaning which, naturally, are contemporary."[20] Karnad describes a different process when, a quarter century after the appearance of *Hayavadana*, he notes in the author's introduction to *Three Plays* (1996) that the source tale about two men with accidentally transposed heads initially interested him because of the possibilities it offered for the use of masks and music on stage. After two successful plays based respectively on myth and history, he had turned to traditional forms in order to "begin again," and "the attempt ... was not to find and reuse forms that had worked successfully in some other cultural context, [but] to discover whether there was a structure of expectations—and conventions—about entertainment underlying these forms from which one could learn."[21] *Hayavadana* is in fact chronologically the first in a series of major plays—among them *Ghashiram kotwal*, Kambar's *Jokumaraswami*, and Panikkar's *Koyma* (The right to rule, 1986)—in which invented metatheatrical frames subject the methods and conventions of traditional theater to self-reflexive commentary, interrogation, and irony even as they are being employed.

The aesthetics of modernist traditionalism also support a fully political art. Modernists take up the relations of power inscribed in traditional forms and devise new theatrical means for addressing the politics of caste, class, gender, sexuality, region, ethnicity, and structures of governance. This actualization of latent political meaning, which enhances the plays' contemporaneity, is most prominent in the plays of Tanvir and Kambar, and also in Panikkar's *Karimkutty* and *Ottayan* (The lone tusker, 1985) and Thiyam's *Chakravyuha*. When Pillai poses the same question as G. P. Deshpande—"why do we want to turn towards the traditional forms?"—his counterquestions capture the interpenetration of aesthetic and thematic imperatives in MT especially well: "Has the chosen form an immediate and demanding connection with the theme we have to communicate to an audience of modern sensibilities? Are we creating a new myth for twentieth-century society, claiming it demands a ritualistic form of expression, a new pattern of theatre? My emphasis here is on the spontaneous urgency of the whole thing, the natural demand of the subject matter on the playwright and director. If treated otherwise, tradition becomes an ornament to gladden the eyes of the spectator. The goal then is totally defeated."[22]

Two quick examples from the "low" and "high" ends of the MT spectrum can pinpoint how the "new pattern of theatre," with its political investment in the current moment, takes shape within the contours of a prior narrative derived from folklore or epic myth. Kambar's *Jokumaraswami* is based on the annual north Karnataka fertility rite in which low-caste women make clay phalluses to celebrate the eponymous god, and married women feed their husbands a ritual meal that is meant to be instrumental in fulfilling their desire for motherhood. In the play, Gowdathi, wife of the impotent village headman Gowda, mistakenly serves the meal to Basanna, a peasant who is engaged in an ongoing struggle with Gowda over land rights, and becomes pregnant with his child. Basanna pays with his life for the transgression, but the community at large knows Gowdathi is carrying his child, and Gowda has no choice but to accept the outcome. Cast in the Bayalata form, a fertility ritual becomes a fable about the rightful claims of femininity, the regenerative masculinity of the oppressed class, and the symbolic identity between desiring women and fertile land, both of which flourish because of the peasant's labor. Thiyam's *Chakravyuha* is based on an episode in book 7 of the *Mahabharata*, where Pandava elders use flattery to persuade Abhimanyu, the recently married son of Arjun (the supreme archer), to penetrate an impassable wheel-shaped enemy formation while his father is away. Abhimanyu enters the maze but cannot recall the cosmic formula for exiting it, and he is killed by not one but seven principal Kaurava warriors: on both sides of the conflict, the old sacrifice the young for the sake of dynastic ambitions they cannot fulfill themselves. In *Chakravyuha*, elements from Sanskrit dramaturgy and ritual combine with multiple Meitei performance traditions to constitute a singularly complex performance text, but the play self-consciously superposes the epic war on the traumatic history of insurgency and counterinsurgency in the state of Manipur. Abhimanyu's sacrifice becomes the occasion for attacking "the cult of heroism which is only too often held up to the Manipuri youth . . . to drive them to senseless acts of virtual suicide."[23]

The "contemporization" of tradition that *Jokumaraswami* and *Chakravyuha* bring about is a widely shared feature within the MT corpus, with each play connecting in its own way to a prevailing sociopolitical narrative. This modernist bent prefigures in interesting ways the shifts in sociological, anthropological, and cultural approaches to traditional and (especially) folk culture over the past few decades, in both scholarly and general criticism. In the seminal 1991 collection that announced "the study of folk expression and performance in South Asia has come of age," the emphasis was on deromanticizing folklore and decoding the politicality of its "texts."[24] The editors argued in their introduction that the readerly pleasures of folklore must coexist with the awareness that "folkloric production is inevitably political. This politics is not the politics of blood and glory, but it is no less political for being about selves, about narrative strategies, and about the fictional realities and the realities engendered by fiction."[25] Modernist drama, then, is one more fictional form for embodying the politicality of tradition.

In a similar way, the predilection for subversion and transgression in MT communicates in new ways what is already being expressed in the traditional forms. In a study of women's speech genres in rural Rajasthan, Raheja and Gold urge the recognition "that tradition and resistance are seldom antithetical, that each culture harbors within itself critiques of its most authoritative pronouncements; and . . . while such critiques frequently take the form of such ostensibly 'traditional' forms of speech as proverbs, songs, and folktales, they enter at the same time into the realm of the political, as they are deployed in the construction and reconstruction of identities and social worlds in which relations of power are deeply implicated."[26] The idea of folklore and other oral traditions as sites of gendered resistance by women is now established as a prominent strain in anthropological and sociological studies of these topics in relation to South Asia.[27]

The scholarly arguments have been echoed, often in advance, by modernists who practice or write about traditional theater. The playwrights Balwant Gargi and Adya Rangacharya describe the folk stage as rude, spontaneous, boisterous, and brilliantly vulgar, and Karnad ascribes "the energy of folk theater . . . [to] the fact that although it seems to uphold traditional values, it also has the means of questioning these values, of making them literally stand on their head."[28] C. N. Ramachandran puts forward the interesting thesis that the "rigid formalism" of sophisticated literature "analogously reflects the acceptance and endorsement of a rigidly structured society on the basis of caste/class in which every member's rights and duties are fixed," whereas the structures of "folk literature oppose and reject—symbolically at least—existing social structures."[29] He points out that the purpose of the outer frame in folk drama is to deglamorize and humanize the gods and heroes in the inner play—a feature that is rarely mentioned in propagandist views of tradition. Commenting on Kannada folk theater, H. K. Ranganath mentions several popular forms (such as Mukkunda Govinda and Sangya Balya) in which "social themes" coalesce around conjugal relationships that are disrupted by extramarital liaisons, giving the upper hand to women, or to men from the lower castes and classes. If gender has emerged as the "central focus" in South Asian folklore studies, it has been an intrinsic feature of the folklore itself and has appeared as a central thematic in folk-based modernist plays since the 1970s.[30]

The Ethics of Appropriation

The foregoing discussion of modernist aesthetics and politics in relation to tradition is implicitly based on "best practices"—a coming together of authorial identity, form, and content in ways that have aesthetic unity and ethical integrity. The strength of modernist reflections on tradition is that they also identify and address areas of potential failure, including some persistent aesthetic and ethical issues—the problem of the rural-urban divide that affects all aspects of theater, the problem of dissonance between form and content in drama, and the precarious sociology of folk culture in modernity. The majority of playwrights and directors associated with MT acknowledge that they have an inescapably urban mindset, whereas folk theater is intimately connected with the life cycles, rituals, and communal relationships of village life. Amitav Roy describes this theater as "both congregational and participative, a sacred rite or ritual that makes the community whole, purifies it and purges it of its sins, and puts it into a creative rhythm with both seasonal-natural and supranatural forces."[31] With industrialization and dystopic urbanization steadily widening the economic and cultural gulf between city and village, the issue of how urban theater workers can make effective and ethical use of traditional forms becomes a persistent modernist concern. Raina cautions against the kind of cultural theft—what Mahesh Elkunchwar memorably calls artistic kleptomania—in which the urban theater worker picks up and markets a "product" for profit, without understanding "its history, its anthropology, its religion and, therefore, its link with the past."[32] Bansi Kaul maintains that urban artists like him absorb influences and "ultimately search for our own theatre, a product of our way of life. . . . Traditional and folk forms inspire and support us to create newer idioms for communication."[33] Tanvir presents a more complex dynamic in which urban and rural cultures merge in such a way that "your urban culture emerges transformed, having absorbed and assimilated all these forms. And then it [the village form] may not remain the same. Yet its vitality should flow into the veins of the urban culture with the inevitable death of the folk form. Now this is the thesis on which most of us, even unconsciously, work" ("Roundtable," 31). The entire debate becomes more poignant because MT is the only nonactivist form of urban theater that has confronted the inequality of urban-rural relations without romanticizing or sentimentalizing the village.

Closely related to the problem of urban alienation from rural expressive culture is the separation of form from content in actual theater practice—a rupture explained by several factors. First, the elements of music, dance, movement, and stagecraft that characterize the "production style" of a particular traditional form *are* in fact detachable from the original narrative elements and performative circumstances, even though such a separation arguably leads the "theater" component to "lose its life force immediately, like a flower plucked off a tree."[34] The *possibility* of such detachment is precisely what produces the "Kathakali *King Lear*," the "Yakshagana *Macbeth*," the "Nautanki *Inspector General*," and so on, and since the 1970s these hybrid (and iconic) works have been foundational to the "soft interculturalism" of major Indian and Western directors, including B. V. Karanth, Sadanam Balakrishnan, Bansi Kaul, Neelam Mansingh Chowdhry, Egil Kipste, Richard Schechner, and especially Fritz Bennewitz. Second, tradition "sells"—as a spectacle for the entertainment of urban Indian audiences, but, more seductively, at international festivals and other venues outside India, especially when the national government follows a policy of representing "Indian theater" abroad through works that assimilate traditional forms. Ideally, the "myth of the community" that undergirds traditional forms in their native environment would generate a corresponding myth that expresses a "collective urban consciousness" for its citified producers and consumers.[35] As the earlier discussion of the playwrights' relationship to their material indicates, many modernist plays succeed in making that leap. But proclaiming the use of traditional forms as a decolonizing cultural obligation, or providing monetary assistance to theater workers interested in "experimenting" with traditional forms, are moves that are likely to promote precisely the kind of tokenism that detaches style from substance. As Deshpande complains, a facile approach reduces nonurban forms to "bedtime stories ... [that] put you to sleep with the complacent belief that you have done your duty by Indian culture and towards the 'other' Indian people."[36]

There is one other important respect in which modernist perspectives on traditional forms differ from cultural-nationalist and revivalist positions: modernists approach the forms not as immutable essences but as contingent constructs that are subject to changing historical-material circumstances, and prone to attrition. Among the playwrights closest to folk and regional cultures, Tanvir and Kambar candidly acknowledge the feudal roots of folk culture, and Tanvir is outspoken about the disparity between the seductive power of folk forms and the plight of the subjects they represent: "[F]olk forms must die inevitably and without lament.... What I'm trying to say is that whatever folk form exists in primitive economy it is very sentimental to say: 'let us keep poor because our folklore otherwise will die'. Our folklore must die because we cannot afford to remain poor. We must make progress. As we make progress and industries encroach upon our rural economy into these areas where these forms exist and flourish, these forms suddenly change and also die" ("Roundtable," 30–31).

Tanvir therefore finds arbitrary bureaucratic attempts at cultural "preservation" not only pointless but harmful. Significantly, as a playwright who is also "from the village" but disinterested in the theatrical use of folk forms, Elkunchwar echoes Tanvir's positions because he witnessed the same quick erosion of folk practices when agricultural activities began to be mechanized in his native Vidarbha region, and the "social need" that had created folk theater ceased to exist. Elkunchwar sees these changes as inevitable, and sentimental efforts at preservation as unnecessary, because "forms" in themselves do not confer identity: "It's only because my roots are strong that I can easily accept the fact that an art form which was alive for two thousand years has come to an end within twenty-five years due to changing circumstances" (*POM*, 379). Tanvir and Elkunchwar's shared understanding of village life cuts across their fundamental artistic differences as playwrights.

In the preceding discussion, I have defined certain uses of traditional forms in postindependence theater as "modernist" in part because they deconstruct politically doctrinaire and nationalistic appropriations of the same resources. Instead of offering direct protest in the style of left-populism, or prioritizing issues of essential cultural identity, authenticity, and aesthetic recursiveness in the cultural-nationalist manner, modernist playwrights use tradition as the volatile ground on which power relations of various kinds are renegotiated, in plays that are aesthetically inventive and sociopolitically discerning. The recourse to tradition also connects playwrights more intimately to *particular* regions, narratives, aesthetic forms, and languages than other contemporary forms of theater practice. Most important, in a subcontinental perspective the storehouse of traditional narratives and representational conventions is so vast that the *precise* ways in which these elements combine to create the overall affect of a particular modernist work can be gauged only through individual analysis. In realist drama there are broad structural and thematic overlaps between works because of recurring elements such as the space of home, intergenerational conflicts, and conditions of victimage, but no notable play produced by the intersection of modernism and tradition shares either its narrative (text) or its presentational style/s (performance) with any other play. My modernist readings of Tendulkar's *Ghashiram kotwal* and Habib Tanvir's *Hirma ki amar kahani* in the remainder of this chapter keep this singularity in view and attend to the local/regional roots of these plays as attributes that can potentially become part of the transnational mosaic of modernism.

MODERNISM, TRADITION, AND HISTORY IN THE POSTCOLONY: TWO PLAYS

Placing *Ghashiram kotwal*

Ghashiram kotwal is set during the late-eighteenth-century reign of the Peshwa rulers in Pune, the city in present-day Maharashtra that symbolized Maratha political power and brahman dominance before British territorial conquest absorbed the entire region into the expansive Bombay Presidency. The key historical figure in the play is Nana Phadnavis (1742–1800), the Chitpavan brahman minister known as the "Maratha Machiavelli" who exercised virtually complete control over administration, finance, and diplomacy under the Peshwas. During a crucial phase in the colonial wars, Nana's decision not to support Tipu Sultan, the defiant Muslim ruler of Mysore, against the British led to Tipu's death in 1799, and the Second Anglo-Maratha War followed shortly after that (1803–1805), ending the Maratha empire as well. Tendulkar, however, keeps the colonial thematic firmly offstage (except for a few British soldiers in two crowd scenes) so that he can focus on Nana's public manipulations and private appetites, and offer a portrait of power that remains exclusively "Marathi/Indian." The play's narrative content is simple, and the action follows a predictable tragic arc. The (fictional) title character, a brahman from the northern city of Kannauj, arrives in Pune with great expectations but is spurned as an outsider despite his high caste status. When he fails in his initial attempts to gain favor with Nana Phadnavis, he offers his daughter, Lalita Gauri, to Nana in return for the position of chief constable. Ghashiram then unleashes a reign of terror in the city to avenge his earlier humiliation, but his obsession with punishment eventually leads to the death of a group of brahman travelers from southern India, and he is swiftly deposed and stoned to death.

The play began its initial run in December 1972 under the auspices of Pune's Progressive Dramatic Association (PDA), but was canceled after nineteen performances because of widespread public protests, especially by the Chitpavan brahman community in Pune and elsewhere. A new group (Theatre Academy) was formed quickly so that performances could continue in Bombay and other cities around the country. In the decades since then *Ghashiram kotwal* has emerged as the most-performed contemporary Indian play, with more than five thousand shows in India and abroad. But it remains as much of an anomaly in Tendulkar's urban realist oeuvre as *The Threepenny Opera* would be if it had been authored by Ibsen or Chekhov rather than Brecht. In one direction, Tendulkar's ability to create a full-fledged "musical" from an eclectic synthesis of folk, religious, and intermediary theatrical and musical forms depends on his immersion in the culture of Marathi (especially in the Pune region), and his collaborations with a brilliant music composer (Bhaskar Chandavarkar), an outstanding choreographer (Krishnadev Mulgund), and an inspired director (Jabbar Patel). In another direction, he merges an aurally and visually sublime performance aesthetic with corrosive satire and grotesque action to produce a theatrical masterwork that is distinctly his own.

These contradictory qualities raise a number of interpretive issues. Although *Ghashiram kotwal* is a deeply subversive work, it has been regarded since its inception as a foundational contribution to the (predominantly nationalistic) theatre of roots, along with Karnad's *Hayavadana* (1971) and Kambar's *Jokumaraswami* (1972); and although it uses Maratha history to excoriate brahman culture, Tendulkar has persistently described it as ahistorical in intention and nonreligious in its politics. The "roots" designation is dubious because it considers Tendulkar's *use* of a "traditional idiom" but not the *effects* it creates, and the playwright's disclaimers about his own intentions have a contextual rather than a textual explanation. Given the exceptional place of *Ghashiram* in Tendulkar's playwriting career, some clarifications are therefore necessary for placing the work in perspective. Tendulkar stands clearly apart from those contemporaries who devoted much or all of their creative life to exploring antirealist traditional performance modes—among them Kambar, Tanvir, Panikkar, and Thiyam. Unlike some of these playwrights, Tendulkar did not produce a body of theoretical or polemical writing critiquing Westernized modernity and advocating a return to indigenous representational modes. He did not make public statements that attempted to devalue realist theater or to erase the achievements of playwrights who were disinterested in premodern Indian aesthetics and performance genres. He also never issued any dicta on "national culture" or a "national theater," and he was either barely present at or entirely absent from the principal state-sponsored forums on the theatre of roots, such as the 1971 Roundtable or the special double issue of *Sangeet Natak* on the "Traditional Idiom in Contemporary Theatre."

So how *should* we understand Tendulkar's use of what is clearly a "traditional idiom in contemporary theatre"? The strong thesis would be that *Ghashiram kotwal* is a modernist deconstruction of religious and historical "tradition" through the figural resources of repetition, incongruity, and irony. Form in the play is at war with content, and content is at war with the cultural postures that valorize Indian/Hindu concepts of purity and piety and enforce heroic rather than satiric or ironic views of society and nation. This sensory-moral affect recalls works like *The Threepenny Opera* (1928) and Wole Soyinka's *Opera Wonyosi* (1976), which use music to strew the action with more, not less, poison. Tendulkar's play is a signal example, then, of using the master's tools to dismantle the master's house, and subverting the rhetoric of cultural nationalism on its own grounds. My discussion of *Ghashiram kotwal* in the following sections focuses on two instrumental facets of modernist theater making: the simultaneous representation and dehistoricization of history, and the experimental shaping of traditional matter to maximize irony at the levels of staged action, characterization, musical codes, and the aesthetics of movement. Tendulkar's singular turn toward tradition, I argue, brings the latter unexpectedly, and transformatively, into the fold of the postcolonial modern.

Theatricalizing History

Since the first turbulent production of 1972–73, *Ghashiram kotwal* has come to be surrounded by a host of arguments, explanations, and clarifications about intention and affect, some of which have consciously or unconsciously misrepresented its meanings and undercut its impact. In March 1973, when the group Theatre Academy was formed in Pune specifically to deal with public protests against the play and to continue performances, the entire episode was rightly construed as a defense of artistic freedom. The play was not a historical or social treatise but a vividly imagined work for the theater, and the various artists associated with it had the right to continue its public staging despite the alleged offense to particular social and political groups. Over the next decade *Ghashiram kotwal* consolidated its reputation as an extraordinary artistic vehicle, but because of the persistent cultural controversy there was also a systematic effort to negate the "historicity" of the play and to downplay the historical narrative as "incidental" to its real meaning. This approach achieved its reductio ad absurdum in 1980, when the play was invited to the Berlin International Theater Festival, and the Shiv Sena, with the support of Union Information and Broadcasting Minister Vasant Sathe, secured a stay order from the Bombay High Court to prevent Theatre Academy from honoring the invitation.[37]

Theater and film personalities such as Satyajit Ray, Sombhu Mitra, Utpal Dutt, and Mrinal Sen expressed public support for the play, and eventually Prime Minister Indira Gandhi herself intervened personally so that the group could travel abroad. However, "the staging of the play came with a rider. The Court issued an order that before each performance, a statement, which was approved by it should be read out. This statement publicly praised the achievements of Nana Phadnavis and stated that the play was not based on history. Theatre Academy followed the court order."[38] The play's director, Jabbar Patel, adds that "everywhere we went, the Indian ambassador came to check if we were following the court order. Of course, we followed it like honest Indians."[39]

There are two fallacies inherent in the court-ordered disclaimer: that in order to be legitimate, a playwright's vision of history has to conform to official history or an objective "reality"; and that an extraneous "announcement" can override an audience's actual experience of a performance. In his response to the controversy, Tendulkar questions the first fallacy by separating "history proper" from its artistic representations. "*Ghashiram kotwal* is not a historical play," he argues in the author's statement prefacing the published Marathi text; "It is a play, just a play. . . . To say with reference to a literary work of art that it is historical, or mythic, or social, is meaningless. Time very quickly turns the social into the historical, and the historical into the mythic."[40] In relation to the historical characters, "to investigate whether their actions were proper or improper, and whether their existence was fundamentally meaningful or not, may be the business of the scholar of history, but it is not the playwright's business. It is for this reason that I consider *Ghashiram kotwal* an ahistorical play."[41] In fact, he sees no essential difference between *Ghashiram* and his "social" plays because "this raw material has been taken from history exactly as it is taken also from contemporary life-situations."[42]

Tendulkar's second strategy is to claim a "transhistorical" meaning for his work. In the foreword, he asserts that in his view "*Ghashiram kotwal* points towards a distinctive social condition. That condition is neither old nor new. It is bound neither by some geographical boundary nor by time. It transcends place and time, and therefore 'Ghashiram' and 'Nana Phadnavis' also transcend place and time."[43] His response to Samik Bandyopadhyay's question—whether the play was conceived as "an exposé of brahmin corruption and pretensions, or as a study of the power game in more general terms"—also redefines the issue to argue for a broader perspective and focus on a familiar political process. "Broadly speaking, I had in mind the emergence, the growth and the inevitable end of the Ghashirams. Also those who create, and help Ghashirams to grow and the irony of stoning to death a person pretending that it is the end of Ghashirams. The rest just happened . . . or happened at a subconscious level. The decadence of the class in power (the brahmins, incidentally, during the period which I had to depict) also was incidental, though not accidental."[44] Critics of Tendulkar's work routinely reiterate these positions, as in Manoj Bhise's comment that the play is "a metaphor or an allegory of power-hungry people in all walks of life—social, political, and even educational. There are Ghashirams and Nanas everywhere."[45]

These are valid arguments insofar as they posit that *Ghashiram kotwal* is not obliged to be a faithful dramatic rendering of any recorded history, and that its meaning transcends the specific temporal setting. Mohan Rakesh defends his portrayal of Kalidasa as a self-centered aesthete in *Ashadh ka ek din* on similar grounds—by asserting that "history is not expressed in literature through its incontrovertible events, but through an imagination that links events together and creates a separate, new history of its own kind" (*POM*, 233). Unlike Girish Karnad's *Tughlaq* (1964), *Ghashiram kotwal* is also not the kind of "history play" that draws intertextually on precolonial and colonial historiographic sources, and pointedly questions institutionalized history as a form of knowledge. Tendulkar is therefore on firm ground when he claims the freedom to deviate from sanctioned versions of history and the written record. In the antirealistic, richly musical form that he adopted in the play, historical "accuracy" and "realism" appear to be even more superfluous concerns. But he overstates the case, and contradicts the performative affect of his own work, by describing the play as "ahistorical" and the cast of brahmans as "incidental," because such a position artificially separates the medium from the message and content from meaning. The complex response to history in postcolonial Indian modernisms (discussed in chapter 3) gives special urgency to the relation between a historical fiction and "history proper," especially in the performative genre of theater, and no serious play that engages with history can detach itself casually from the effects of that textual or epistemological intervention. Regardless of the license Tendulkar may have taken with official history, *Ghashiram kotwal* has now entered the social imaginary as another form of mediated knowledge of the Peshwa rulers, Nana Phadnavis, and the Chitpavan brahmans of Pune. The many levels at which the play manipulates its audience's knowledge of, and attitudes toward, that particular history also create its multiple resonances in the present.

A historically situated brahman identity is what *Ghashiram kotwal* enacts from beginning to end, at the level of both text and performance. The second line of the play establishes the "godlike brahmans of Pune" (*punyache baman hari*) as a primary collective presence, embodied in the dancing, singing, swaying "human curtain" of twelve hyperbolically marked, identically clad adult brahman men.[46] The history of Pune as a stronghold of brahman culture, which earned it the title of *punya nagari* (pure or sanctified city), makes this spectacle both possible and plausible. Except for the dancer Gulabi, there are also no major nonbrahman characters in the play, and except for Nana, Ghashiram, and his daughter Lalita Gauri, the remaining characters are identified only by their caste, as "brahman," "bamman," or "baman" (fig. 5.1).

This focus on a specific identity continues in the play's major structural topoi: the brahman community in Pune; the rituals and accompaniments of Hindu worship, both Shaivite and Vaishnavite; the hedonistic figure of Nana Phadnavis, representing the apex of social as well as political power; and the contrapuntal figure of Ghashiram Savaldas, the brahman outsider whose ascent and swift decline shape the action. The places and rituals of Hindu worship, with their associations of essential purity, dominate the first half of the play, and the traditions of Marathi (Hindu) devotional music dominate the musical content. Nana's concupiscence and cunning appear as the grotesque obverse of his status as the purest of the pure—the brahman chancellor of a powerful brahman confederacy based in Pune. What Ghashiram perceives as the loss of caste in his humiliation by the Pune brahmans also becomes the motive for his terrible revenge on the

FIGURE 5.1. Mohan Agashe as Nana Phadnavis, Rajani Chavan as Gulabi, Sujal Watwe as Lalita Gauri, and Chandrakant Kale as the Sutradhar, *Ghashiram Kotwal*, directed by Jabbar Patel, Theatre Academy, Pune, 1973. Two of the brahmans are onlookers, while two others have their backs turned towards the audience. Photo credit: Mohan Agashe and Theatre Academy.

city, and the excesses of his reign as chief constable are directly linked to a fanatical obsession with restoring and preserving the purity of thought and conduct that is appropriate to the *punya nagari*. Far from being incidental or accidental, the ontological condition of brahmanism holds the play together, and the consequent claims of purity, ascendancy, and privilege are subjected to relentless attack.

If the Hindu/brahman matrix offers the principal sociocultural perspective on Pune, the insider/outsider dichotomy introduces the main political perspectives. The territoriality and parochialism of the Pune brahmans neutralize the commonality of caste and set up the intersection of caste and religion with regional culture and language, offering a symbolic parallel to a very prominent strain in Shiv Sena politics from the 1960s to the present. As a Hindi-speaking native of the north Indian city of Kannauj, Ghashiram has no *locus standi* in Pune despite his brahman lineage, and he first appears in the humiliating guise of a servant in a brothel. His attempts to claim a common heritage with the Pune natives set up his tragedy, and Tendulkar underscores the sense of cultural difference by writing most of the following dialogue in Hindi, not Marathi:

1 SOLDIER: Hey, who are you?
GHASHIRAM: I'm Ghashiram Savaldas from Kannauj.
2 SOLDIER: Come on, get lost. Why have you come here?
GHASHIRAM: Brahmans are being honored here. They're being feasted.
1 SOLDIER: So what business do *you* have here?
GHASHIRAM: I'm a brahman too.
2 SOLDIER: You, a brahman? Where's your tunic, the holy thread around your neck, the marks of ash on your forehead, the perfumed tablets?
1 SOLDIER: Where are your Vedas? And now tell me the secrets of the four Varnas—
2 SOLDIER: Looks like a crook—
1 SOLDIER: Looks like a thief—
GHASHIRAM: No, I'm a brahman—from Kannauj—I'm new in Pune. (18)

Not surprisingly, Ghashiram feels that he has been turned from a pristine brahman into "a shudra, a criminal, a useless animal. . . . A devil on the inside and a pig on the outside," and he threatens to "make everyone a pig like me" (21). This episode has its perfect antithesis toward the end of the play, when Ghashiram arrests a group of hungry brahmans from southern India for stealing fruit from the constabulary and causes twenty-two of them to die of suffocation in a jail cell. Ghashiram is just as alienated from this southern contingent of brahmans as the Pune brahmans were from his northern traits, although the high caste identity of the dead men is ironically the key reason for the public outcry that leads to Ghashiram's swift demise.

The primacy of brahman selfhood in *Ghashiram kotwal*, undercut ironically by regional identity, connects up with two cruxes in the twentieth-century history of the Maharashtra region. The first is the significance of Pune as a cradle of Hindu nationalist thought during the period of anticolonial nationalism, embodied variously in such figures as Gopal Krishna Gokhale, Bal Gangadhar Tilak, and Vinayak Damodar Savarkar.[47] The second is the city's continued association with Hindu nationalism after independence (Gandhi's assassin, Nathuram Godse was a native, for instance), and somewhat more tenuously in the 1960s, with the forms of regional and linguistic chauvinism that were a central part of the Shiv Sena's platform (captured in the party's slogan, "Maharashtra for the Maharashtrians"). Tendulkar noted that he was motivated to write the play after observing firsthand the reign of terror the Shiv Sena had unleashed in Bombay during the 1960s in its attempt to contain the communist influence. The reign of terror in Ghashiram's historical Pune is an evocation—symbolic, not literal—of that destabilizing postcolonial experience. In historical as well as contemporary contexts, the play grapples with casteism, regional chauvinism, patriarchy, and a corrupt and coercive nation-state, and it would be impossible to argue that these are not critical issues for either the past or the present it represents. And precisely because *Ghashiram* confronts these issues, it is among the most unforgiving postindependence attacks on cultural and political ideologies that attempt to aggrandize the structure of traditional Hindu society and revive it in the present.[48]

Performing Tradition: Repetition, Incongruity, Irony

In the performance of *Ghashiram kotwal*, history and tradition are embodied in a powerful semiotics of sight and sound that gathers meaning through patterns of repetition and incongruity. The dominant visual experience is that of the moving "human curtain" of twelve interchangeable actors in traditional brahman attire (henceforth referred to as the "brahman line"), functioning as a ubiquitous collective presence but also breaking up into smaller units as necessary. Correspondingly, the main aural experiences come from four well-known regional traditions—the *kirtan* (collective devotional singing), *abhang* (popular poems by major saint poets set to music), the *lavani* (erotic songs associated with the intermediary *Tamasha* form), and *natya sangeet* (the stage music specific to musical theater in Marathi).[49] Overtly religious framing continues in the stylized movements derived from the regional *dashavatar* form, which is named for the ten incarnations of Lord Vishnu. The professional "low caste" dancer Gulabi interrupts these dominant religious/Hindu/brahman codes by bringing in the secular-popular *Tamasha* style, and the *mujra*, a north Indian Muslim courtly form practiced by trained courtesans. The singular quality of *Ghashiram kotwal* as a modernist experiment in the "traditional idiom" is that in affective terms this rich intertexture of music and dance is intrinsically contradictory: it creates pleasure at one level but unease at another, because it incrementally heightens the incongruity between the impurity of the pure and the vulgarity or profanity of the sacred.

The brahman line is Tendulkar's innovation on the choric function in drama. Like the Greek chorus, it is never absent from the otherwise bare stage, and it has the power to observe and comment but not intervene directly in the action. Unlike the Greek chorus, the brahman line assumes a variety of dramatic functions, collectively and individually, by dissolving and reconstituting itself as required by the action. In the first scene, for example, the line breaks up into individual members who profess different occupations and claim to be from different parts of India, but whose urgent desire is to head to Gulabi's brothel, the *Bavan-nakhani* (a pleasure dome with fifty-two chambers), for their daily diet of erotic play. In the brothel the men are an undifferentiated mass of concupiscent drunks. In Ganesha's temple they listen to a religious discourse as Nana attempts to seduce Lalita Gauri. And in scenes of humiliation, injustice, or grotesque violence, they turn their backs on the audience to signify a deliberate moral aporia. The shifting roles and unstable ethos of the brahman line are alienating in the Brechtian sense, and also allow Tendulkar to limit the individualization of character in his play. Nana and Ghashiram among the men, and Gulabi and Lalita Gauri among the women, are polarized but variously active dramatic figures who are given some conventional prose dialogue alongside stylized movement and delivery; the remaining characters are nameless beings who appear in crowd scenes, speak minimal dialogue, or mime their action. The uninterrupted presence of the brahman line also allows the play to be structured as a succession of dramatic vignettes interspersed with musical "interludes," except that in *Ghashiram* music is also a mode of action, and song a mode of participation.

The fundamentally religious identity of the brahman line, expressed through appearance, dialogue, and song, highlights the incongruity between the sacred and the profane in the play. Two images from Vaishnava mythology concentrate this anomaly: the descent of Mathura into the

Bavan-nakhani; and the morphing of Nana Phadnavis, the aging polygamous roué, into Lord Krishna, dallying with the cowgirls (*gopis*) or joined in a perfect union with his consort Radha. Mathura is the birthplace of Krishna, the city considered more wondrous than the three worlds of the cosmos (*Mathura teen lok se nyari*). Its descent into the brothel simultaneously marks the ironic degradation of the holy city and the equally ironic "purification" of the carnal place. Similarly, Nana's apotheosis into Lord Krishna at the time of his seventh marriage elevates him to the status of the divine lover, and transforms the gardens of Pune into the gardens of Mathura, sublimating lust into religious ecstasy.

The juxtaposition of religious symbolism and debased action is most intense in the scene of Gauri's seduction in Ganapati's temple. At the beginning of the scene, the *Sutradhar* (master of ceremonies) metamorphoses into a *kirtankar* (lead devotional singer) and begins an *akhyan* (religious discourse) before a miscellaneous audience. The stage directions state that "Nana ogles the women while smelling the flower in his hand; he pays no attention to the *kirtan*. . . . The sounds from the *kirtan* cannot be heard for some time; it is only a visual tableau" (18). Registering the confusion between piety and lust, the Sutradhar's *abhang* turns suddenly into a *lavani*, then back again into an *abhang*, and the alternation continues as Nana propositions the "tender, beautiful, sinless" girl.

NANA: (in a lustful voice) Child, what do you want? Hm?
(Startled, the girl looks back)
This Nana will fulfill all of your desires.
(He puts a hand on her shoulder. She shrinks and moves farther away)
Oh, don't be shy. This is my wada [home], and this is a private hall. No one will see. No one in Pune today has the audacity to spy on the great Nana Phadnavis.
GIRL: He'll see.
NANA: He'll see? Who?
GIRL: (pointing to the Ganapati idol): He.
NANA: That idol of holiness? The lord of all blessed events? The creator of bliss? Look, he has two wives. One sits on this thigh, the other on that thigh. If you sit on this thigh of mine, he will have nothing to say about that. (18–19)

Ganapati, or Ganesha—in Hinduism, the son of Lord Shiva—is the most powerful deity in Maharashtra, embraced especially by the Shiv Sena, and worshiped by Hindus everywhere as the "remover of obstacles." Nana's co-optation of Ganesha into his schemes of seduction is a stunning moment in the play, replete with meaning for the world outside.

The music created for the brahman line makes the simultaneous presence and irrelevance of religious sentiment even more pervasive. The chants are anchored not only in fulsome praise of Ganesha, a Shaivite deity, but in invocations of the principal incarnations of Vishnu—the gods Rama and Krishna. The main refrains are *Radhe Krishna Hari, Govind Murali* and *Rama Shiva Hari, Mukund Murari*, with *Radhe Krishna Hari, Mukund Murari* as a recurring variation. "Govind," "Mukund," and "Murari" are all names for Krishna; Radha is his consort, and the "murali" is his flute. "Hari" is a name for Vishnu, Rama is his incarnation, and Shiva is the god of destruction in the Hindu trinity, complementing Vishnu's status as the god of preservation. The brahmans' chants therefore keep all the major Hindu gods and key elements of Hindu worship in circulation as the action moves through its grim arc of oppression, violence, and death. The lyrics underscore a double disconnection: the religious emotion is unvarying and mechanical, detached from particular circumstances; and the particular circumstances, however dire, remain untouched by the religious sentiment. When Ghashiram begins his reign of terror as the constable of Pune, the brahmans talk about how "Pune lost heart," but their only remedy is to keep up the chant of *Rama Shiva Hari, Mukunda Murari*. Throughout the "ordeal scene," in which a brahman accused of stealing is forced to hold a heated iron ball in his hands to prove his innocence, the brahman line has its back to the audience. But after the ordeal ends, as the tortured brahman is hurling curses at Ghashiram, the *Sutradhar* and the others in the line immediately start chanting *Radhe Krishna Hari / Mukund Murari* with instrumental accompaniment, as if to purposely drown out his expression of rage. Then they line up to conceal the scene of the action. The action behind them first ceases to be visible and then ceases to be audible (40). The stage directions articulate the dramatic function of the religious lyrics, which is to neutralize the drama. At the very end of the play, therefore, the chant is exactly what it was at the beginning, the interlude of Ghashiram's life and death already erased from the collective consciousness of the singers (fig. 5.2).

FIGURE 5.2. The brahman line in the final scene of the play, with Nana Phadnavis and Gulabi. The corpse of Ghashiram (Ramesh Tiledar) lies on the stage floor. Photo credit: Mohan Agashe and Theatre Academy.

Tanvir, *Adivasi* Politics, and Tradition as Reflexive Subject

Habib Tanvir's critical reputation as "one of the most significant cultural figures of modern India" rests on the extraordinary range and boldness of his theater work, which involved the roles of playwright, director, actor-manager, translator, adapter, set designer, lyricist, composer, singer, choreographer, theorist, and critic.[50] His membership of the IPTA and the Progressive Writers Association in the 1940s fostered a progressive politics that understood society in materialist but also humanist terms, and this instilled a special sense of solidarity with the urban working class and the rural poor in India. Training at the Royal Academy of Dramatic Art and the Old Vic Theatre School, followed by extensive travels in Europe (1955–1957), paradoxically convinced Tanvir that he belonged culturally to India and would be most creative in that environment; India, in turn, needed to "fall back upon its traditions in theatre in order to evolve a new type of theatre that will be both authentic and contemporary."[51] But the same institutional and artistic experiences, especially during an eight-month stint at the Berliner Ensemble in Germany, also strengthened a cosmopolitan engagement with early modern and modern European theater, leading him to translate, adapt, and direct works by a dozen European playwrights over the next fifty years, with Chhattisgarhi, Hindi, Urdu, and English as his languages. Immediately after his return to India, Tanvir's decision to include six folk actors from Chhattisgarh in his "plebeian" version of Shudraka's classical Sanskrit play, *Mrichchhakatika* (titled *Mitti ki gadi* [The clay cart], 1958), was the breakthrough event that led to the formation of Naya Theatre as a professional company of rural-urban actors in 1959, followed by decades of radical experiments with the resources of "tradition."

Tanvir's distinctive modernist traits are that he makes a strikingly unconventional break with proscenium realism; anchors postcolonial urban theater in the rural culture of orality; does not merely use folk narratives but brings folk performers onto the stage to enact their stories in their own language, with music and dance as integral elements; and over a long career, makes the body of the folk/tribal actor a transformative medium for the performance of a wide array of ancient, modern, and contemporary Indian as well as European works. In addition, the progressive yet utopian politics Tanvir brings to his "rustic" material focuses on issues of social inequity, patriarchal oppression, political corruption, and religious bigotry primarily through comic-satiric action, leading critics to note that he has "re-invented the idea of the 'political' in theatre," and "revealed . . . a strong and vibrant protest tradition lying underneath" the traditional theater forms.[52] Anuradha Kapur in fact views Tanvir's multifaceted engagement with traditional materials as a complex but quintessential expression of the "modern" in Indian theater, because he goes beyond the "traditional modern binary" to focus on "the most 'up-to-date' constituents of the present" and on "*contemporary* forms of the folk and the popular." Hence Tanvir "both assembles and takes apart traditional devices and conventions in the *process* of play-making, causing a rupture in the modernist sense and yet sustaining a course through the traditional *by* use and handling."[53] In the modernist postindependence reshaping of tradition, Tanvir's practice most fully embraces the carnivalesque.

As a relatively late play, *Hirma ki amar kahani* (The immortal tale of Hirma, 1985) continues this complex interweaving of aesthetic and political strands in Tanvir's dramaturgy, but it also has several unusual features. It is his only full-length play based on actual mid-twentieth-century political events in the Chhattisgarh region, and unlike Tendulkar, who described *Ghashiram kotwal* as ahistorical and apolitical, Tanvir identifies Pravir Chandra Bhanj Deo (1929–1966), the last king of the predominantly adivasi[54] princely state of Bastar, as the real-life model for Hirma, and acknowledges that "all the events in the play are more or less true to his life."[55] Bastar was established in 1324 CE by a branch of the regionally powerful Kakatiya dynasty, and like numerous other princely states scattered throughout the subcontinent, it continued to have traditional rulers during the colonial period, although it was an administrative unit within the large British territory of Central Provinces and Berar. In December 1947, Pravir Chandra signed the instrument of accession through which Bastar joined the Indian Union as part of the state of Madhya Pradesh, but he maintained his politico-economic and ceremonial roles as large-scale landowner, de facto leader and spokesman for the adivasi population (although he was a high-caste Hindu, not an adivasi), and the *raj purohit* (royal priest) who officiated at all the religious rituals foundational to community life. The conceptually "irrational" but existentially real aspect of Pravir Chandra's charisma—which he encouraged actively—was that the adivasis at large regarded him not only as their *Maharaj* (great king) but as an invincible *Mahaprabhu* (great god) whose tantric powers could turn bullets into water (fig. 5.3).[56]

In an effort to resolve ongoing conflicts with the state government over his property rights and what he perceived as an assault on adivasi ways of life, Pravir Chandra sought election to the state's Legislative Assembly as a member of the ruling Congress Party in 1957, but he had resigned in frustration by 1960. As his relationship with the government deteriorated steadily during the 1960s, he fomented a state of civil unrest by calling on his supporters to stage large protests, and eventually barricaded himself in the ancestral palace at Jagdalpur with thousands of adivasis armed with bows and arrows. On March 25, 1966, Pravir Chandra was shot dead, along with an unspecified number of supporters, during a police raid on the palace, and the Judicial Inquiry Commission appointed by the government in response to widespread outrage concluded later that his death was "accidental."[57]

Tanvir's investment in these political events and their sociocultural ramifications is overdetermined by the centrality of Chhattisgarh's culture,

FIGURE 5.3. Poster for the film "I Pravir, the Adivasi God" (2022) directed by Vivek Kumar, based on Pravir Chandra Bhanj Deo's autobiography of the same title. https://www.opindia.com/2022/09/watch-exclusive-film-on-pravir-chandra-bhanj-deo-the-adivasi-god/

language, and people to his craft, but a play about unrest and violence in a majority adivasi region is inevitably a microcosm of the very large problem of tribal life in Indian modernity. There are historic adivasi settlements all around India (the total current population is 104 million, with nine million living in Chhattisgarh), and the sources of conflict with modern institutional structures have remained essentially the same from colonial to postcolonial times.[58] Invoking the need for development and progress, governments want to assert control over the remote but resource-rich areas (forests, rivers, hills, mountains) that form the natural habitat of adivasi communities, but for the latter this infiltration represents a loss of freedom, material resources, livelihood, and culture. The government presence is widely regarded as a screen for illegal and corrupt incursions that endanger the environment and often expose adivasi men and women to extreme forms of economic/sexual exploitation. During the colonial period, the Santhal, Munda, and Bastar rebellions (1855–56, 1899–1900, and 1910) were notable expressions of what was a more or less continuous history of adivasi resistance against the British regime. Recognizing the scale of the problem, Article 342 of the Indian Constitution adopted in 1950 listed 730 "Scheduled Tribes" that would be eligible for special protections from the government, and a Ministry of Tribal Affairs was created in 1999 "with the objective of providing a more focused approach towards the integrated socio-economic development of the Scheduled Tribes (the most underprivileged section of the Indian Society) in a coordinated and planned manner."[59] Falling randomly between these postindependence initiatives, the events of 1966 in Bastar continue older patterns, prefigure later crises, and point to the adivasi predicament as the sign of another "unfinished project of modernity" in India.[60]

Tanvir's political objectives in *Hirma* involve both the aesthetics of representation and what he describes as "the process of assimilation of a primitive people—a terrible process which has precedents all over the world" (*LTH*, 4). Without naming any proponents of the theatre of roots, he separates himself from their goals by stating his (modernist) intention to let them know "through this production . . . that I do not look at things the way they do, that there are two distinct camps and I'm certainly not in the rightist camp" (*LTH*, 66). He also refers to "the theatre of debate and agit-prop that I did during the IPTA days," which resurfaces in the dialectic between Hirma, his brother Bira, and various government agents throughout the play (*LTH*, 66). Political issues specific to the play are addressed in Tanvir's preface to the English translation of *Hirma*, titled "A Dilemma of Democracy," which traces one major part of the problem to the inherently contradictory nature of erstwhile feudal states like Bastar—they are culturally rich but deeply unjust societies, and the seeming benevolence and patronage of rulers like Pravir Chandra are marred by self-interest and cruelty. For Tanvir, the inception of a modern democratic nation-state in 1947 made it clear that "the feudal system had to go," but the upheaval in Bastar also raised the second problem of "whether we are giving the tribal a better alternative for governance" (*LTH*, 3). Writing *Hirma* in the mid-1980s, two decades after Pravir Chandra's assassination, he felt that the harrowing nature of the crisis made it "more or less imperative for me to confront it politically," without the exoticization of tribal life practiced by "most people today," because he said he did not want to "turn my back on it" (*LTH*, 66). Tanvir knows that "the play does not, cannot offer a solution," but feels that "it does present the dilemma in its naked form. . . . the conflict between democracy and socialism, democracy and fascism" (*LTH*, 4).

Pravir Chandra/Hirma is caught between his desire to retain ancestral forms of power (reflected especially in his autocratic will to govern) and the all-powerful but already corrupt machinery of the nation-state, which uses the rhetoric of modernization and development to rationalize its aggression. The adivasi population is caught in the middle of this unresolvable conflict, manipulated by its deified leader and utterly disregarded by the government.

Complementing the political thematic, Tanvir's staging of Chhattisgarh's recent history in *Hirma* gives the play's performative dimension a unique metatheatrical slant. Instead of serving mainly as an aesthetic and political resource *for* theater, as it does in every other play by Tanvir and his MT cohort, "tradition" is also the reflexive subject *of* the play: *Hirma* portrays the endangered, trauma-ridden state of the way of life that has sustained those very traditional cultural practices (language, dance, music, ritual, religion, performance) that are vital to the composition and reception of Tanvir's theater. In a similarly metatheatrical orchestration, at one level the adivasi actors are playing roles, as they have done from time to time in Tanvir's plays after 1959, and especially after 1973. But at another level, the roles are real, not fictional, and they are playing themselves—adivasi men and women, collectively enacting on stage the history that has profoundly impacted their region and their lives.[61] They cease to be performers and become participants in the real life drama of political intrigue, popular revolt, and eventual subjection that ended in the death of their god/king.

This erasure of the subject/object distinction in *Hirma ki amar kahani* opens up another perspective on Tanvir's modernist repurposing of tradition that is worth noting, although it is implicit rather than explicit in the play. Tanvir is in many respects a poster child for cosmo-modernism, the compendium of cosmopolitan qualities invoked in the title of this book because it is central to so many modernist careers in Indian literature and theater. He was the first leading postindependence playwright and director to make a lifelong commitment to traditional Indian materials, but as mentioned previously, he also developed a remarkable trans/national reach by absorbing the works of a large number of other Indian and foreign playwrights into his repertoire. Through translation, adaptation, the dramatization of prose narratives, and directing work, Tanvir engaged with Shudraka, Bhasa, Bhavabhuti, Vishakhadutt, Mahendra Vikram Varman, and Krishna Bhatta from the classical Sanskit period; Shakespeare, Molière,

Goldoni, Gogol, Gorky, Dostoevsky, Chekhov, Wilde, Lorca, Brecht, and Zweig from early modern and modern Europe; and Tagore, Premchand, Agha Hashr Kashmiri, Vijaydan Detha, Manoj Mitra, Shankar Shesh, Safdar Hashmi, Asghar Wajahat, Sisir Das, and Rahul Varma from modern and contemporary India.[62] In Naya Theatre productions after 1959, most of these "borrowed" source-texts were rendered into the folk/adivasi performative aesthetic, bringing a great deal of world theater onto urban Indian stages in a radically estranged idiom. When the native practitioners of that aesthetic play *themselves* in *Hirma*, the cumulative memories of their acts of cultural ventriloquism hover just beneath the surface. What makes these evocations more poignant is that in its long theatrical history, Naya Theatre performed only four original plays that were based on narratives of different kinds *from* Chhattisgarh: *Gaon ke naon sasurar, mor naon damad* (The name of the village is Sasural, my name is Damad, 1973); *Charandas chor* (1974); *Bahadur kalarin* (Brave Kalarin, 1978); and *Hirma ki amar kahani* (1985).[63] *Hirma* is therefore Tanvir's last original play involving Chhattisgarh as narrative source, although his last production for Naya Theatre premiered a full twenty-one years later, in 2006.

Modernist Form and Affect in the Play of Hirma

Hirma is understandably regarded as Tanvir's most overtly political play, but after *Shajapur ki shantibai* (1978), his adaptation of *The Good Person of Szechwan*, it is also his most Brechtian play. The eight months Tanvir spent at the Berliner Ensemble in 1956–57 had confirmed Brecht's powerful influence on him at a formative stage in his career, and an essay titled "Brecht for One Producer," published in the theater journal *Enact*, explains why: "Above all, Brecht teaches you to be yourself.... [I]f the Indian playwrights evolve a truly indigenous theatre, it will be a truly Brechtian theatre as well."[64] His particular focus on *Good Person* began with an English production for the College Drama Teachers' Workshop in Pachmarhi (Madhya Pradesh, 1961), and the fully indigenized Chhattisgarhi version with Naya Theatre actors followed in 1978. Describing Brechtian theater in India as *pharmakonik*—not a "faithful" replication of epic theater methods but an imaginative offshoot suited to local objectives—Prateek argues that Tanvir "appropriated not only the European model of Brechtian theatre but also the urban Indian variant by creating a regional version of Brechtian theatre."[65] The "regionalization" was necessary to express the periphery's resistance to urban centers, and the rural Chhattisgarhi content was necessary to resist the Indian government's efforts to homogenize and nationalize folk theater. Although the processes of indigenization and regionalization were at the core of the *Shajapur* experiment, the play also crystallized the two Brechtian techniques most compelling for Tanvir—alienation or estrangement, and *gestic* realism.

Twenty minutes into a 2007 documentary on his work, Tanvir mentions Madan Lal, one of the principal Naya Theatre folk actors, and comments: "I noticed that alienation was part of the genius of the Chhattisgarhi actor.... I gave a lecture at the National School of Drama with Madan Lal... and I said, 'this man has not known the name of Shakespeare, does not know Brecht, but he knows his "alienation" theory, and epic theatre, and all that. Because it's in his blood. And *this* is the explanation for "alienation." The way *he* is doing it.'"[66]

The actors' estrangement from their roles, and the emphasis on critical reflection rather than emotional identification on the audience's part, are goals well suited to the three principal constituencies portrayed in the play: Hirma and his associates, the state-level politicians and bureaucrats, and the adivasis. Caught in a historic power conflict, the first two groups are ethically compromised to a degree that disallows identification and empathy. Tanvir's dialectical presentation of their opposing viewpoints in the scene set in the state legislature produces the only moments in the play that approach recognizable political discourse.[67] Member 1 (played by Tanvir in 1985!) voices the complaint that adivasis are being deprived of the habitat they have lived off of for hundreds of years, and the dispossession is destroying their art and culture. Member 2 and the Minister, voicing the government's position, talk about the emancipation of adivasis through education, not song and dance, and stress the need for equitable government policies, dismissing the first member's demands as the sign of a "feudal conspiracy." By the time of its contentious ending, however, this scene has abandoned dialectic and given in to the escalating crisis driven by irrational excess on one side and duplicity on the other. Hirma is benevolent and paternalistic in some scenes, but cruel, wasteful, and egomaniacal in others; the adivasis' unquestioning devotion is both a political tool and fuel for his fantasies of godhood. Contrasting the constant frenzy in Hirma's camp, every member of the machinery of government displays the cavalier confidence that comes with the knowledge of absolute control without accountability—as the judicial finding of "accidental death" in Hirma's case demonstrates. For its own place-time, *Hirma* creates a narrative arc of unresolvable conflict and inevitable doom that also appears in postcolonial classics such as Chinua Achebe's novella *Things Fall Apart* (1959) and Wole Soyinka's play *Death and the King's Horseman* (1985), except that the antagonisms portrayed by Tanvir are postindependence, intracultural, and intranational. Alternatively, *Hirma* can be placed beside classics of *postcolonial* corruption such as Soyinka's *Opera Wonyosi* (1977) and Achebe's *Anthills of the Savannah* (1985). The play's basis in fact rather than fiction suggests a third analogy—with the deromanticized approach to history that Brecht takes in plays like *Edward II* (1924) and *Galileo* (1943).

Tanvir's portrayal of the third group is even more ambivalent, although the survival and welfare of the adivasis are the ostensible reasons for Hirma's revolutionary zeal and the government's violent imposition of "order." With the exception of a few abject individuals with limited stage time, the adivasis appear mainly as a voiceless collective that materializes anywhere and everywhere—in the fields, in the streets, in Hirma's palace—to oppose guns with arrows, and perish in large numbers (fig. 5.4).

FIGURE 5.4. Hirma (Bhulwa Ram) addressing his adivasi followers in *Hirma ki amar kahani*, directed by Habib Tanvir, Naya Theatre, New Delhi, 1985. Photo credit: Nageen Tanvir.

Member 2 had criticized the reduction of adivasis to song-and-dance exotics, but most of their appearances in the play are in fact as ritual dancers (typical stage directions: "On the occasion of the sprouting of seeds, a Madia adivasi dance is in progress" [7]; or "Adivasis enter singing and dancing. Hirma is sitting on his chariot and distributing money" [36]; even on the day of his death, "Adivasis are dancing. Hirma is also with them" [67;]). The community's political agency as Hirma's supporters, which the government finds threatening, is also not the sign of a developing political consciousness in an independent nation because what rouses them to action most effectively is their devotion to the local goddess (Danteshwari Devi), and her surrogate, their god Hirma. Even the radical organization of an all-female "party wing" of red-sari-clad women by Baigin Bai, Hirma's adivasi common-law wife, does not introduce any element of individual will or agency because the women turn into just one more faceless crowd. The play reenacts a momentous crisis, but Tanvir's ideological opposition to feudalism makes Brechtian alienation and moral ambivalence the appropriate affective devices for staging the system's demise.

Tanvir's second Brechtian move is to interrupt the linear narrative (consisting of three acts and a total of twelve scenes) with choric elements of two kinds—regularly spaced songs, and a running commentary on events by the Collector, Kalhan, who is the district's highest administrative officer, as well as Hirma's hunting partner, friend, and confidante for a time. In his three earlier Chhattisgarh plays, Tanvir had written and composed some original songs but also used existing numbers that were predominantly or exclusively in dialect, to match the plays' dialogue. In contrast, the eight songs in *Hirma* are original pieces written and composed specifically for the play, use mainly standard Hindi rather than Chhattisgarhi, and are *gestic* in intention, in that they invite reflection on particular events or comment on general social issues. The song that opens the play is a good example of the Brechtian function of music. It claims through an intricate structure of repetitions, and without mentioning any characters, that a throne, a country, a life, and many other things were "snatched away" merely because an unnamed person was deprived of a valuable ring. The reference is to Hirma's decision to pull off a diamond ring from the finger of Kalhan's wife Renuka because she had decided on a whim to take it from his jewelry box and claim it as a gift. The song begins as soon as Kalhan enters the first scene and connects with a cryptic exchange several scenes later, when Kalhan arrives to tell Hirma he must leave the region of Titur Basna (the fictional name for Bastar):

HIRMA: Kalhan, is this your answer because you didn't get a diamond ring?
KALHAN: Hirma, you and I are both caught in the web of politics. What does a diamond ring have to do with it? I have to follow my orders. I haven't come to give any answer. I'm waiting for your answer. (35)

The opening song subtly prefigures what becomes explicit in this scene—the bureaucrat's envy of the aristocrat, the changing power equation, the high price of a woman's greed, and Hirma's helplessness before the dictates of a government he does not consider legitimate. Other songs echo Brechtian positions when they describe adivasis as servants as well as masters of the land (40), or divide the world into the haves and the have-nots (48), although the second song acknowledges (Indian/adivasi) forms of false consciousness when it claims god as the only refuge of the poor.

Kalhan is the play's Brechtian narrator: like Wang the Water Seller and Shen Te in *The Good Person of Szechwan*, who address the audience in regular metadramatic "Interludes" between scenes, he comments on the action in diegetic set pieces throughout the play, including the prologue and epilogue; as an amoral or immoral presence (unlike Wang), he takes advantage of Hirma's generosity, exploits him for professional advancement, and causes his death by refusing to issue stand-down orders to the police even after the reason for their siege of Hirma's palace has ceased to exist. (See fig. 5.5.)

Alternatively, Kalhan can be regarded as an updated version of the *Sutradhar* of Sanskrit theater, a mediating presence who holds the various strands of the action together. His principal dramatic function is to reinforce the continuity between colonial styles of governance and the machinery of the new Indian nation-state—he is a career administrator, an "old ICS man" who "knows all the shenanigans of politics," and regards his role in the history of Titur Basna as one "of great importance" (8).[68] Although Kalhan claims to be interested in bringing democracy to the region, he actually becomes the government's proxy for figuring out how to weaken the power of the palace so that the intended "development" (a euphemism for illegal land-grabs and deforestation) can take place. His supposedly complex feelings toward Hirma are nowhere in evidence when he introduces the day

MODERNISM AND TRADITION

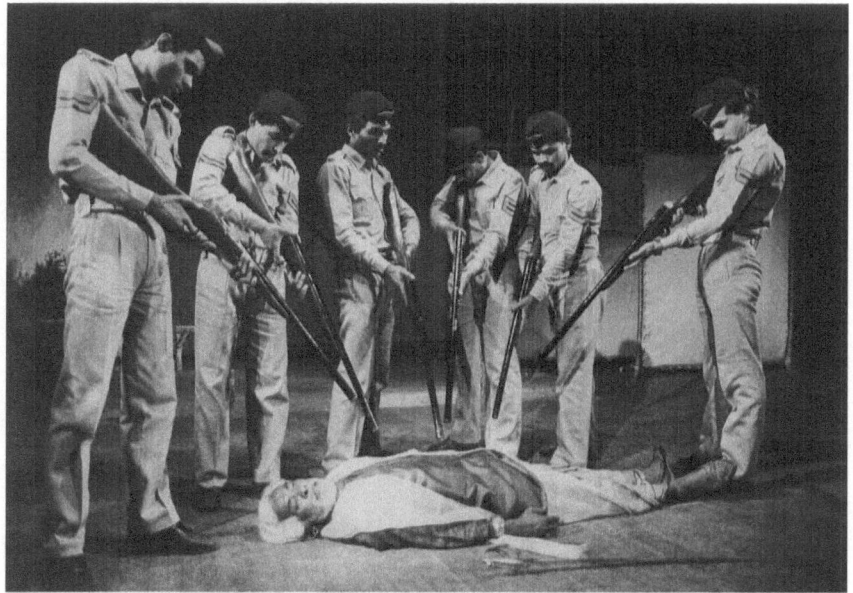

FIGURE 5.5. Hirma shot dead by the police in his palace at Jagdalpur. Scene from *Hirma ki amar kahani*, directed by Habib Tanvir, Naya Theatre, New Delhi, 1985. Photo credit: Nageen Tanvir.

of Hirma's death with clinical detachment and engineers the assassination. He ends the play on a despairing note, however: an impostor has begun to claim that Hirma did not die and will make a miraculous return, and the adivasis are no further along the path of development. Kalhan admits lamely in his penultimate speech that "there is either something flawed about the way in which we think about development, or there is something fundamentally wrong about the adivasis' habits of thinking and understanding" (71). The last image in the play is a "timeless" one, of adivasis singing and dancing as they refuse to accept that Hirma has died (fig. 5.6).

Finally, the three worlds in *Hirma* generate a brilliant three-tier use of language for coding region, ethnicity, class, circumstance, and hierarchy, in ways that are fixed in some instances and fluid in others. The main index of difference is the relationship between Chhattisgarhi and standard Hindi—the first belongs mainly to Hirma's camp and the second to the government agents, but there are also many overlaps. Some adivasi characters speak only in dialect (Baigin Bai, Hirma's supporters Lorma and Saheba); most of the

FIGURE 5.6. Adivasis dancing in celebration. Scene from *Hirma ki amar kahani*, directed by Habib Tanvir, Naya Theatre, New Delhi, 1985. Photo credit: Nageen Tanvir.

bureaucrats, politicians, and policemen use Hindi; and other characters move between the two as needed (Hirma, Bira, and Hirma's former ward Dumraj, who sometimes switches from one language to another within a single piece of dialogue). Conversely, because Kalhan prides himself on local knowledge, he occasionally speaks to Hirma in dialect. Chhattisgarhi is therefore the "people's tongue," the language of those who belong to the land, and Hindi is the language of officialdom, of callous outsiders who have come to interfere in people's lives without real knowledge or empathy. But whether they speak it or not, all of the characters *understand* both languages because that is a precondition for negotiating their complex world. In the equation between language and power, the most interesting use is reserved for English, which provides (through transcription into the Hindi script) the full vocabulary of government control. English articulates political structures and processes (Chief Minister, Chief Secretary, Council of Wards, Development Authority, Committees, party ticket, election, party politics, party wing, floor-crossing, constitution, etc.); the forms of administrative control and the resistance to them (Collector, ADM, forest rights, shifting cultivation, protest, levy, truck, market, tax, delegation, clerk, policy, etc.); and the deadly machinery of "law and order" (Superintendent of Police, constable, inspector, sub-inspector, circle inspector, order, police action, action till the end, duty, etc.) As the inherited language of power in the play, English indicates that the postcolonial state has fully internalized repressive colonial systems, leaving little room for the accommodation of local contexts. Once "orders" are "confirmed," the storming of Hirma's palace is "no problem" for the "police." This complex interplay of languages and hierarchies is fundamental to *Hirma*, but it appears on the page and in performance only in the original trilingual text—there is no hint of it in the existing English translation.

I have argued in this chapter that the older world portrayed in modernist constructions of tradition is a defamiliarized and inherently political image of the present. Connecting the content of *Ghashiram kotwal* and *Hirma ki amar kahani* with twenty-first-century conditions can be one measure of that relatedness. The Shiv Sena's antipathy to left politics, and its emphasis on regional identity in terms of language and social structure in the Maharashtra of Tendulkar's time, has expanded since the 1990s into a full-scale decolonizing revisionism. The city of Bombay became Mumbai in 1995 so that it could invoke the local goddess Mumbadevi rather than the sixteenth-century Portuguese Basilica of Bom Jesus in Goa; the Victoria Terminus, the Prince of Wales Museum, and the Santa Cruz International Airport were all renamed after Chhatrapati Shivaji, the Sena's patron figure, in 1996, 1998, and 1999, respectively. Vinayak Damodar Savarkar (1883–1966), the Pune-educated Chitpavan brahman revolutionary who coined the term "Hindutva" ("Hinduness"), and put out the call to "Hinduize all Politics and Militarize Hindudom," is a key ideologue for the Hindu fundamentalist Bharatiya Janata Party (BJP) that has held national power since 2014. Savarkar's acolyte Narendra Modi—whom Tendulkar attacked for his complicity in Gujarat's anti-Muslim violence of 2002—has been India's Prime Minister since 2014, and won reelection in 2024, although with significantly fewer seats in Parliament. The figural brahman ascendancy in *Ghashiram* has evolved into a literal majoritarian Hindu-supremacist ascendancy positioned against minorities of all kinds, including the historically underprivileged sections of Hindu society.

In relation to the crisis addressed in *Hirma ki amar kahani*, the killing of Pravir Chandra is considered one important reason for the beginning of an antigovernment Maoist insurgency in the late 1960s that has gradually placed large parts of Chhattisgarh beyond state control, especially with the escalation in violence following the formation of the Communist Party of India-Maoist in September 2004.[69] Bastar is in fact a prime example of the momentum that Naxalite movements, named after the first Maoist uprising in Naxalbari village (West Bengal) in May 1967, have gained in tribal areas all around the country because the historical patterns of forcible government control over natural resources and exploitation of tribal labor are continuing under an increasingly authoritarian state, while the problems of poverty, illiteracy, and isolation remain unresolved. Sumanta Banerji places Naxalbari and Chhattisgarh at the two ends of Maoism's fifty-year "journey in India": armed groups reportedly have a presence in more than a hundred districts in thirteen Indian states, but Chhattisgarh, Jharkhand, Odisha, and Andhra Pradesh are the four geographically contiguous states that dominate the "Red Corridor," with more or less continuous violence between insurgents and security personnel. Even government reports acknowledge that the rural poor gravitate toward Maoists because they offer "parallel structures of decentralized administration as an alternative to the police-politician-contractor dominated hierarchical power structure."[70] To deepen the irony, the district of Dantewada in Bastar, named after the patron goddess of Pravir Chandra and his followers, has become "the rebel stronghold" in Chhattisgarh, appearing persistently since 2007 as the site of gruesome encounters. In April 2010, "the deadliest attack by the Maoists on *Indian security forces*" happened in the dense Mukrana forests of this district, when members of the Central Reserve Police Force were ambushed by hundreds of insurgents, and seventy-six policemen died.[71] In May of the same year, the first attack on a civilian bus killed more than forty passengers and a blast in April 2023 killed eleven. Violence occurs with unabated regularity in Dantewada, and it has been in the news most recently for a clash in October 2024 which claimed the lives of at least thirty-one "suspected" Maoist rebels.

In the spring and summer of 2023, government provocation, ethnic differences, and tribal identities combined to give the long-standing issues of tribal rights and belonging a grotesque new twist in the already volatile northeastern state of Manipur. Ethnic identities are fundamental to the entire population and demographic distribution of the state: the majority "native" group, the Meitei (53 percent), are predominantly Hindu and inhabit the urbanized Imphal valley; the Kuki-Zo tribes (16 percent) live in the surrounding hills, are Burmese in origin, and mainly Christian. Because of Myanmar's political instability, an influx of Chin refugees has added to the Kuki population, and the ongoing insider/outsider debate has been exacerbated by the charges of illegal poppy cultivation and unauthorized occupation of forest land against the Kukis. In February 2023, the BJP government in the state began evictions in Kuki settlements, and in April it recommended that the Meitei community be added to the list of Scheduled Tribes in the national constitution, with its accompanying protections and privileges. Both were seen as deliberate antitribal moves, and the resulting violence had already claimed nearly two hundred lives by the end of July (with many more wounded), led to the destruction of seventeen churches, and displaced 55,000 residents. On May 4, as riots broke out between the Meitei and Kuki communities, two Kuki women (twenty-one and forty-two years old) were mobbed, stripped naked, and paraded to an open field, where the younger woman was gang-raped. When the video surfaced on July 19 after an internet shutdown in the state, the national and international outrage led to an ultimatum from the Supreme Court to the central (BJP) government (which had been silent), a statement from the UN Human Rights Commission, and a debate in the EU Parliament (which the Indian government opposed). Intermittent violence over the next twenty months led to the resignation of the Chief Minister, Biren Singh, in February 2025. As these events have unfolded, a recurring question in journalistic media has been: Will Manipur ever trust India again? This query makes explicit the secessionist alienation that the remotest northeastern state feels in relation to the Indian Union. The fault lines that the plays by Tendulkar and Tanvir exposed decades ago in an evolving Indian polity are creating deep fissures in present-day civic and political life, and a "national" solution is not in sight.

CONCLUSION

Cosmo-Modernism and Theater in Retrospect

Early in the introductory chapter of this book, I claimed that "the mid-century revolution in urban cultural forms accompanying the end of British colonialism in India created the largest clustering of 'modernist' as well as 'postcolonial' writing outside the circuits of Europhone textuality and performance." I also used the neologism "cosmo-modernism" to suggest that leading Indian modernists bring a "full consciousness of the world"—an immersive grasp of modern literature and a philosophical understanding of the global crisis of modernity—to their craft, while remaining rooted in the regional languages and literary-cultural histories that position them within the national mosaic. The reasons why this substantial geomodernist formation remains on the margins of the new modernist studies bear reiteration here: Anglophone Indian and Indian diasporic writing have found some representation in discussions of global modernism, but the non-Europhone modern languages employed as original media for writing and performance are more or less inaccessible outside India; and Indian-language modernisms have not so far been theorized or interpreted *systematically* in ways that would offer generative methodological models to the field of Indian modernist studies.

CONCLUSION

My reconstructive goals in this book are to create literary-historical, theoretical, aesthetic, and political perspectives that can demarcate Indian modernisms as a distinctive phase in the evolution of Indian modernity, to connect these developments with the larger terrain of global modernisms, and to use the new frameworks for conceptualizing a significant proportion of later-twentieth-century Indian drama and performance as sites of modernist practice. This approach also supports the related aims of positioning Indian modernisms clearly in relation to transnational modernist studies, placing greater emphasis on the performative in modernist studies, and giving Indian theater a new visibility in modernist theater studies. A synoptic view of my arguments over five chapters reconfirms that the pivotal critical move in relation to Indian modernities and modernisms is to understand how the historically ingrained culture of multilingual literacy responds to the transformative effects of colonialism and its aftermath because in India the axis of language operates in ways that have no parallel in the colonial or postcolonial world. As the imperial language, English became a modernizing force during the nineteenth century, but from the beginning it neither diminished nor displaced the literary-theatrical cultures of the Indian languages. On the contrary, the interpenetration of Indian and Euro-Western aesthetic systems led to the explosive literary growth that has been described as "the Indian Renaissance" for many decades. Novels, short stories, secular epic poems, the personal lyric, theoretical authorial reflections, occasional manifestoes, speculative essays, workshop criticism, autobiographies, memoirs, diaries, and letters were among the literary forms that entered the creative economy of Indian languages for the first time in the nineteenth century. In the realm of performance, Anglo-European influences led to the emergence of urban theater as a secular commercial institution around 1860, also for the first time in history; and although the performance spaces, production technologies, and material practices of the new system followed English models, its forms, narratives, and presentational styles were overwhelmingly Indian, as were its languages. The uncontainable expansion of print culture after 1800 was another measure of the consolidation of Indian-language networks: although forms of orality continued in urban as well as rural locations, the forms of writing and performance were absorbed more or less efficiently into the culture of print.

Multilingual literacy thus both precedes and succeeds colonialism: in fact, the mid-twentieth-century rupture from colonial practices that energizes modernism, especially in drama and theater, is compelling precisely because of the power Indian-language expressive forms had gathered over the previous century. Since the "modern period" almost always extends from the early-nineteenth century to the present in Indian periodizing schemes, a heuristic distinction between "colonial modernity" and "postcolonial modernism" is useful for marking important differences. Colonial drama and theater were modern forms engaged variously in reflexive social critique, reconstructions of the past, celebration of religious icons, anticolonial politics, and pure entertainment, but every one of their constituent features was unacceptable to the modernists who began their careers in the 1950s, following the most intense phase of anticolonial nationalism, famine in Bengal, another global war, and the holocaust of Partition.[1] The comparison between Michael Madhusudan Dutt's *Sharmishtha* (1858) and Girish Karnad's *Yayati* (1961) in chapter 3, for example, highlights the differences between modern (colonial) and modernist (postcolonial) responses to the same well-known myth from the *Mahabharata*, and the movement from a flawed Ibsenism in the 1930s to the storied career of Vijay Tendulkar in Marathi (dealt with in chapter 4) charts a similar qualitative progression in relation to the mode of urban realism. However, in neither the modern nor the modernist context are the playwrights involved in "vernacular" cultural production, and in neither temporal frame do they represent a cultural periphery compelled to respond to a present or absent imperial center.

The key concept relating to theory as well as practice in my analysis, therefore, is not "vernacular cosmopolitanism" or "rooted cosmopolitanism" (theorized respectively by Homi Bhabha and Anthony Appiah two decades ago[2]) but "cosmo-modernism," with the first term denoting the sense of membership in a world community, and the second symbolizing the production of significant and substantial modernist oeuvres. "Vernacular" and "rooted" forms of cosmopolitanism have been central to debates on this subject since their introduction by Bhabha and Appiah, but considered from the standpoint of the Indian modernist formation I have mapped in this book, both theories reflect the preoccupations of a privileged, mobile, and diasporic postcolonial intelligentsia. My focus, instead, is on the cosmopolitanism of the stay-at-home Indian-language writer, shaped by simultaneous access to the cross-cultural inflows made available by colonialism and the intrinsic continuities of Indian culture. Exploring the fertile connotations of "cosmo-modernism" in relation to such careers is a more productive conclusionary choice than debating the ir/relevance of diasporic models to my material.

As self-fashioning modernists, Dharamvir Bharati and Mohan Rakesh offer the two most ambitiously cosmopolitan profiles among their contemporaries; through theory, polemic, criticism, and literary journalism they connect transnationally with the literary, cultural, and political spheres of their time. Bharati theorizes the crisis of modernity on a world-historical scale, but in a decolonizing pan-Asian perspective also focuses on the philosophical, ethical, and creative challenges confronting Asian and Indian writers. Rakesh's lifelong critical engagement with Euro-Western literature and theater is what feeds his conviction that Indian/Hindi writers must devise their own forms of expression to contend with the life around them. Yet both of these playwrights also engage in conscious or unconscious citations of precisely those high modernist works that carry singular prestige in mid-twentieth-century India. Bharati's *Andha yug* (Blind epoch, 1954) is a condensed modernist epic like *The Waste Land*, gathering its fragmented evocation of a doomed civilization into poetic drama that is set in the immediate aftermath of the eighteen-day Mahabharata war. Rakesh's *Ashadh ka ek din* (One day in the season of rain, 1958) is a quasi-Joycean portrait of the artist as a young and middle-aged man who chooses exile in the metropolis to become (offstage) the exquisite symbol of his race, but eventually returns in despair to the provincial sources of his inspiration, trying unsuccessfully (onstage) to reconnect with the muse he had abandoned. The filtering of immensely consequential theological history through epic poetry and the lives of one married couple in *Laharon ke rajhans* (The royal swans on the waves, 1963–1968) has no evident parallels in modernist drama, but the charismatic offstage presence of the Buddha in this play is unsettling in ways similar to the evocations of Christ and religious experience in some of Eliot's major poems, from "Gerontion" and *The Waste Land* to "Journey of the Magi" and *Four Quartets*.

Other playwrights forge transnational connections in less comprehensive but no less generative ways. Girish Karnad's reading of Anouilh, Sartre, O'Neill, and Greek tragedy gives him a form for *Yayati*. *Tughlaq* gets written because as a Rhodes Scholar at Oxford he discovers historians of India in the Bodleian Library, pores over every available modern history play, and has access to classics of historical cinema such as Eisenstein's *Battleship Potemkin* (1925). An early proscenium play by Badal Sircar, like

CONCLUSION

Evam indrajit, carries echoes of Eliot, Kafka, and Beckett, while his move to a "Third Theater" of urban-rural synthesis draws on Jerzy Grotowski's Poor Theater, Richard Schechner's Performance Group, and the Living Theater of Julian Beck and Judith Malina. In his rejection of war and atrocity in plays such as *Baki itihas* (The remaining history, 1965) and *Tringsha shatabdi* (The thirtieth century, 1966), Sircar invokes the unbearable history not of any one country or region but of the world as a whole, and the cosmopolitan Kantian principle of universal hospitality clearly augments the Gandhian creed of nonviolence in the playwright's ethical-humanist stand. Vijay Tendulkar's first national-level success, *Shantata! court chalu ahe* (Silence! the court is in session, 1967), follows the central plot device of a spontaneous but deadly "mock trial" that appears in Friedrich Dürenmatt's novel *A Dangerous Game* (1956), which was written initially as a radio play. Mahesh Elkunchwar's favorite playwright is Chekhov. Habib Tanvir considers his Indianness completely compatible with Brechtian epic theater, and Chandrashekhar Kambar discusses the quality of alienation as central to folk theater, but in ways different from Brecht. As these modernists position themselves in relation to their world, they think habitually and consistently beyond the nation.

The second vital site of cosmo-modernist contact is translation in its interlingual, intercultural, and transcultural forms because the urban culture of performance in India is saturated with European, American, and more selectively, world drama in multiple languages. Karnad's epiphany during Alkazi's 1956 English production of Strindberg's *Miss Julie*, mentioned in chapter 2, is a representative early moment in a continuous process that brings together a major foreign playwright in translation, a leading director, and unusually receptive viewers. In fact, it is possible to argue that the translation, publication, and production of plays from around the world are activities that often carry higher cultural capital in the postindependence performance economy than original Indian plays, old or new. For example, late-twentieth-century versions of Shakespeare involve leading modernist poets such as Harivansha Rai Bachchan and Raghuvir Sahay (Hindi), Vinda Karandikar and V. V. Shirwadkar (Marathi), Masti Venkatesha Iyengar (Kannada), and Firaq Gorakhpuri (Urdu); the translations are arguably modernist works in their own right, and some of them have led to landmark productions. Among modern/ist playwrights, Chekhov, Lorca, Gorky, Gogol, Maeterlinck, Tolstoy, and Tennessee Williams have been translated by major novelists, poets, and playwrights such as Rajendra Yadav (Hindi), Sahay (Hindi), Safdar Hashmi (Urdu), and P. L. Deshpande, Vyankatesh Madgulkar, Vijay Tendulkar, and V. V. Shirwadkar (Marathi). Brecht is the European playwright with the strongest list of Indian translators, including Kamleshwar in Hindi, C. T. Khanolkar, Madgulkar, and Deshpande in Marathi, Badal Sircar in Bengali, Habib Tanvir in Chhattisgarhi, and K. V. Subbanna in Kannada. In addition, the widespread practice of Indianizing foreign playwrights (through adaptation or transculturation) intensifies the cross-cultural synergy of these works well beyond what simple interlingual translations would accomplish. When such versions also add a prominent indigenous performance form or presentational style to the Indianized content, the performance text becomes an experimental vehicle at the radical end of the spectrum because it transforms the original work on so many unexpected levels.

In inter- or transcultural theater translations of this kind, the director is often a more prominent figure than the original playwright or translator because the auxiliary performance elements they introduce are mainly nonverbal and extratextual. The Yakshagana version of *Macbeth*, for example, is orchestrated primarily by the director, B. V. Karanth, as he works through Sahay's translation of Shakespeare, just as Tanvir-as-director recreates *The Good Person of Szechwan* in the performance idiom of Chhattisgarhi. However, leading directors create extensive translational/transnational relationships even when they work within more conventional parameters. If we take Shyamanand Jalan in Calcutta, Satyadev Dubey in Bombay, and Ebrahin Alkazi in Delhi as members of a metropolitan modernist directorial trifecta, the modern/ist playwrights they brought to the postindependence Indian stage would include Büchner, Ibsen, Strindberg, Chekhov, Shaw, Pirandello, Brecht, Lorca, Sartre, Camus, Anouilh, Eliot, Osborne, Bond, and Beckett. This pattern was substantiated by a significant number of Euro-American counterparts who visited India to direct specific productions, or committed themselves to more sustained contact. The East German director Fritz Bennewitz spent a total of twenty-two years in India, collaborating with Alkazi, Vijaya Mehta, B. V. Karanth, K. V. Subbanna, Kumar Roy, and Amal Allana, among others, on productions of Volker Braun, Brecht, and Shakespeare. Carl Weber, the West German director, further consolidated Brecht's presence in the Indian repertory. Richard Schechner directed Brecht and Chekhov, and the younger Australian Egil

CONCLUSION

Kipste directed Rostand.[3] Grotowski's extended stay in India during his "Theater of Sources" phase, Peter Brook's epic *Mahabharata* (1985), and Eugenio Barba's *Dictionary of Theatre Anthropology* (1991) kept the major European interculturalists prominently in view during the 1970s and 1980s. India may not be very visible on the world's stages, but the world has been present on Indian stages on a large scale since independence.

Turning now to the other connotation of "cosmo-modernism"—the vigor of modernist careers in the theater—a plausible point of departure is the multidimensional complexity of such careers. As noted previously, for authors like Bharati, Rakesh, Tendulkar, and Kambar, drama and theater represent only one strain in a composite literary profile that includes fiction, nonfiction, poetry, theory, criticism, and literary journalism. At the theater-and-practice-oriented end are figures such as Sircar, Tanvir, Panikkar, Thiyam, and Dattani, who combine playwriting with the additional roles of actor, director, theater manager, and mentor. Tanvir and Panikkar are also composers, choreographers, and set designers, among other artistic pursuits relating to production. As authors, Elkunchwar and Karnad are primarily playwrights and commentators on theater, and along with Rakesh, they are the exceptions who did not have any regular connection with specific theater groups or theatrical activities. But even Elkunchwar's career involved more or less intensive work with directors such as Vijaya Mehta, Satyadev Dubey, and Shriram Lagoo in Bombay, and Karnad had a full-fledged career as an actor, director, and screenwriter for film and television in Kannada, Hindi, and English. One of the most important collaborations in the parallel cinema movement during the 1970s was between Karnad as lead actor, Tendulkar as screenwriter, and Shyam Benegal as director of the acclaimed films *Nishant* (Evening's end, 1975), and *Manthan* (The churning, 1976). Although the details vary individually, each of the playwrights mentioned here is a powerful contributor to the modernist project, and each has had a career spanning four to six decades.

The substantive nature of modernism as textual/performative practice is also evident in the enormous range of narratives and experiences it encompasses in postindependence drama and theater. In chapters 3 through 5, "modernist" serves as the qualifying term in a succession of speculative genre descriptors that invoke myth, history, urban life in the present, and traditional forms of performance as material for drama. It is therefore possible to speak of "modernist classicism," "palimpsestic modernism," "modernist realism," and "modernist traditionalism" for the first time in Indian theater studies, and with some qualifications, in modernist theater studies more broadly. In each case, the specific Indian content shapes the genre or set of generative principles, whether playwrights are engaging with the ubiquitous cultural presence of mythology, the debates over history and historiography, the idiosyncrasies of realism as a mode, or the contested legacies of tradition in performance. In modernist drama, myth signals not regeneration but ambivalence and sometimes overt evil; a historical narrative underscores the need to break free of institutionally legitimized history; metatheater disturbs the linearity and authority of realism; and tradition takes on avant-garde aesthetic qualities as well as contemporary political meanings to counter the regressive cultural politics of certain decolonizing programs. Major plays emerging from this ferment connect with what has preceded them in their own language and in other Indian languages, but as suggested previously, they also have family resemblances to similar conjunctures of form and content in Euro-American modernisms. My claim that Indian languages have produced the largest clustering of modernist and postcolonial writing outside the Europhone domain is borne out in the case of drama and theater by the breadth, variety, and complexity that these forms of postcolonial modernism display at multiple levels, and the credible definitions to which they lend themselves.

A retrospective view also brings into focus a tentative chronology for *this* modernist formation, which is specific to its place-time. With the exception of younger playwrights such as Thiyam and Dattani, and an exceptionally resilient playwright like Karnad, whose last play was published a few months after his death in 2019 at the age of eighty-one, the vital phases of the other major careers considered here belong mainly to the period between 1950 and 1990. Tendulkar, Elkunchwar, Panikkar, Kambar, and Tanvir are occasionally active beyond the latter date, but their best work appears in the decades during which authors born roughly between 1925 and 1945 hit their stride. The completion of this key phase in modernist theater in the 1990s coincides with a fundamental post–cold war transformation of India-as-polity. The Alkazi Theatre Archives' series on "Staging Transitions" associates the 1990s with "major economic and political policy changes and structural adjustments that altered the socio-political and cultural landscape of the nation.... This decade was consequential to culture, and especially theatre, as the shifting policies had a direct bearing

CONCLUSION

on the functioning of this space."[4] The interrelated processes of liberalization, privatization, and globalization, culminating in full-scale neoliberalism, ended the government monopoly that had protected India's mixed economy from free market forces for half a century. This paradigm shift has progressively worsened the struggles over social justice and equity that independent India has faced from the beginning as a postcolonial nation with dire problems of poverty, illiteracy, and overpopulation. In addition to the widening class rifts, issues of gender, sexuality, caste, religion, ethnicity, region, and language keep up more or less continual conditions of crisis in different parts of the country. Even the relatively limited historical perspective offered by seventy-five years of independence suggests that the constitutional principles of secularism, social equality, and cultural plurality that had defined India as an imagined community in the mid-twentieth century have eroded under the pressures of majoritarianism, crony capitalism, and most of all, religious fundamentalism. Violence against women, homophobia, continued oppression of the lower Hindu castes, communalism, chauvinism of region and language, and ethnic conflict in volatile regions such as Kashmir, Assam, and Manipur have come to dominate the homogeneous time of the nation.[5]

The ebbing of mainstream modernism in theater around the time India began its slide into "the ranks of 'flawed democracies'" (Jasanoff) has had the effect of bringing identity politics into the foreground and strengthening theater forms that have a resistant and oppositional edge. As mentioned previously, "women's theater" in all its manifestations has undergone the most dramatic transformation: as authors, auteurs, directors, actors, devisers, managers, and performance artists, women have acquired a prominence that has no precedent in Indian theater or cultural history. The street theater movement, growing in visibility since its beginnings in the 1940s, entered a qualitatively different phase of nationwide action after the murder of Safdar Hashmi, the founder of Jana Natya Manch, by Congress Party operatives on January 1, 1989, during a performance of his play *Halla bol* (Raise a clamor). Other important loci of activism include feminist forms of "acting up," the critique of caste oppression in plays by members of the formerly untouchable Dalit communities, and the deconstruction of heteronormativity in queer theater (addressing gay, lesbian, and transgender themes). Community-based theater has acquired an outstanding model in Jana Sanskriti, the organization founded by Sanjoy Ganguly in 1985 to bring Boalian Forum Theater techniques to rural Bengal. Boal considered it the largest and most important establishment disseminating his methodology outside Brazil; approaching theater as "a politics and an ethics," the movement is now national in scope, and one of its key goals is to stop "the insane, inhuman behaviour of capital in the name of globalization."[6]

Occupying a different kind of artistic niche and gaining new prominence in the post-1990 landscape were artists such as Heisnam Kanhailal (1941–2016) of Kalakshetra, Manipur, and Veenapani Chawla (1947–2014) of Adishakti Theater Arts, Auroville. Kanhailal's "predominantly non-verbal and gestural" theater dispensed decisively with the traditional playscript in favor of a fluid performance text that communicated meaning "through the body, through silence, through sounds, through rhythm, through symbolic gestures—in short, through the totality of the performance."[7] Combining the influence of her spiritual mentor Sri Aurobindo with the Grotowskian ideal of lifelong training for the performer, the distinction between *natyadharmi* (performance-specific) and *lokdharmi* (quotidian) behavior, and the rigorous somatic discipline of traditional forms such as Kutiyattam, Chawla evolved an acclaimed experimental style that Elkunchwar describes as "a true fusion between the modern and the traditional."[8] If the past three decades of theater and performance are considered collectively, the dispersal of modernism's already centrifugal energies into an ever-expanding, heterogeneous cultural sphere becomes abundantly clear.[9]

These developments do not take away from the vitality and accomplishment of four decades of modernist practices, and it is possible to argue that the modernist synergy between authorship, print, and performance has continued, albeit in an attenuated form. Plays by Makarand Sathe, Manjula Padmanabhan, Ramu Ramanathan, Poile Sengupta, Manav Kaul, Abhishek Majumdar, and Anupama Chandrasekhar, for example, maintain a notable presence in print as they gather differential performance histories. Padmanabhan, a professional cartoonist and children's book author, was the first winner of the International Onassis Award for Theater (1997). Sathe is an architect who has been closely associated with the Marathi theater group Asakta in Pune, and he has had several plays published in English translation; he is also both author and translator of an encyclopedic three-volume history of Marathi theater. Ramanathan is a director, journalist, and print-media specialist as well as a prolific playwright in English. Kaul writes plays in Hindi and English, and is also a well-known actor, director, novelist, and filmmaker. Majumdar is trilingual in English, Hindi, and Bengali, and his plays have been produced at the Royal Court Theatre and the National Theatre in London, in addition to prominent venues in India. Chandrasekhar's appearances at the Royal Court and National have made her a runner-up for the Evening Standard Theatre Award's Charles Wintour Prize for Most Promising Playwright (2008), and a shortlisted nominee for the John Whiting Award and the Susan Smith Blackburn Prize. These details resemble the patterns of multigenre, multilingual, and multimedial creative production that had appeared among the two previous generations of modernists. In addition, some of the younger playwrights have established connections with the postcolonial Indian diaspora in the West that were not available to their precursors, and their modes of cosmopolitan connection to the world at large are therefore closer to those theorized by Bhabha and Appiah. However, these playwrights do live mostly in India, and their profiles bear out the generational difference: the high-octane quality of earlier modernist careers in the theater, and the processes that bound together playwrights, directors, actors, translators, and audiences in contingent but intensely productive relationships are no longer in view.

The preceding discussion of post-1990 trends makes it clear that what follows the high period of modernism in India is not any version of Euro-American postmodernism; it is a multifaceted movement that questions hegemonic structures of various kinds in an effort to connect theater closely to real-life struggles. Indian expressive forms remain largely outside the Western dynamics of modernism-postmodernism because the country's political economy, society, and culture do not conform in any recognizable way to the generative conditions of postmodernism, including those defined by influential theorists such as Fredric Jameson, Jean-François Lyotard, and Linda Hutcheon.[10] The challenge or antithesis to modernism comes, instead, from traditionalist, nativist, and cultural-nationalist positions that appear in their most powerful versions in relation to drama, theater, and performance—since these cultural forms have a very long precolonial history, rejecting all aspects of the "alien" modernity that was institutionalized in colonial urban theater and taken forward after independence becomes a major decolonizing project. This critique of "Westernized modernity," and the corresponding claims of representational authenticity, involve a number of fallacies that I have addressed elsewhere in my discussion of orientalist and cultural-nationalist negations of the modern present in India.[11] Here it is worth noting that the culture-specific *historicity* of the modernity-modernism relation in India invoked in various contexts throughout this book becomes entangled in a *dehistoricized* ideological rejection of that entire colonial and postcolonial trajectory. As modernism continues to adapt to changing conditions in India, its obverse is not a post- but an antimodernism—a specifically Indian form of traditionalism in theater that is antimodernist because it is opposed to cosmopolitan forms of modernity in their totality. What unfolds over a century, therefore, is a new variation on the tension between modernist antitheatricalism and theatrical antimodernism, recasting modernism as the anti-anti-modernity aesthetic.

The final issue that needs reconsideration is the perceived "canonicity" of modernist drama and theater. As a transitional period, the 1990s brought out with new clarity the predominantly male, upper-caste, and middle-class identities of the formative figures in postindependence theater, which included not only modernists but major left-wing political playwrights such as Utpal Dutt and G. P. Deshpande, and the absurdists C. T. Khanolkar and Satish Alekar. Some recent critical arguments suggest that this gendered profile implies the playwrights' complicity with ingrained systems of domination and oppression, or that focusing on them implies a dismissal of women theater artists and activists.[12] A large number of the authors and works discussed in this book—effectively constituting the modernist field—belong to the male "canon" and could therefore be seen as merely perpetuating the older hierarchies of class, caste, gender, region, and language. In the Indian theatrical context, however, ideological dismissals of this kind need careful analysis and a nuanced response.

First, the postcolonial "canon" came into existence despite the virtual absence of usable theater traditions or institutional structures of support because of a spontaneous nationwide movement among playwrights, directors, performers, technical professionals, and translators who were determined to overcome their circumstances and engage with drama and theater in all their modes of existence—writing, print, multilingual performance, and nationwide circulation. Second, modernism was the *principal* driving force behind the movement, and its place in Indian theater cannot be recovered without systematic attention to its major practitioners, whose "canonicity" was also not an a priori condition but an *effect* of their art, achieved under conditions of precarity. Third, as chapters 3 through 5 make clear, the

CONCLUSION

use of modernist theater forms and practices in no way precludes the politics of gender, caste, class, ideology, region, or language: rather, modernists approach these categories in highly individualized ways, in their texts and collaborative performances. Their political positions do not cancel but complement the feminist politics of gender. Fourth, the authorship of modernist drama is predominantly male over several decades, but the *representations* of women and femininity—initiated by male authors and realized by leading actresses under the tutelage of male and female directors—have the effect of revolutionizing the portrayal and understanding of gender in comparison with preindependence models. The forms of woman-centered performance that have gained prominence since the 1990s "make women visible" in new roles, but they also build on a visibility enhanced by decades of provocative representation enabled by the resources of myth, history, realism, and antirealism.

Finally, whatever the "canonical" status of postindependence Indian theater practitioners is within national boundaries, in a transnational frame they continue to inhabit the margins of contemporary theater studies, even when compared with their African and Caribbean counterparts, regardless of the kind of theater under scrutiny. The major methods and approaches evident in recent scholarship on transnational modernisms are not extendable to Indian theater for the same reasons that explain the near-invisibility of Indian-language modernisms in global frameworks. In Western scholarship "transnationalism" most often implies a focus on Anglophone or Europhone materials across national boundaries, or a connection with the experiences of immigration and exile, or attention to forms such as music, dance, cinema, and architecture, which do not rely primarily or exclusively on language; literary scholarship that takes up comparisons *outside* the global Europhone domain still constitutes the rare exception rather than the norm.[13] Consequently, after the cosmopolitan and transnational reach of modernist Indian theater has been considered at length, as in this book, taking that critical discourse *further* would once again involve the same problems of linguistic-cultural access and disciplinary limitations that I set out to overcome. These critical handicaps cannot be overlooked or dismissed on the grounds of intranational cultural politics, especially when the cultural critique rests on totalizing assertions about structures of hegemony and dominance in what is in fact a very diverse sociocultural field. The challenge modern

CONCLUSION

Indian-language theaters of all kinds have posed since their inception is for scholarship and criticism to "step up" and deal adequately with works created by generations of mostly unprivileged but determined artists. Along that continuum, Indian theatrical modernisms represent a particular conjuncture of theory, history, language, form, content, textuality, performance, and reception, and this book can claim to mark a new departure in modernist theater studies only by making these features visible on their own terms.

NOTES

INTRODUCTION: INDIAN MODERNISMS IN A GLOBAL FRAME

1. In fact, the ability of scholars trained in English literary studies to make a serious transition to materials in other South Asian languages has been one of the transformative disciplinary shifts in my generation, both in India and abroad. It has brought the critical orientations and methods of mainstream literary studies, especially postcolonial studies, to the study of South Asia. The importance of this shift for modernist studies in particular is discussed in chapter 2.
2. Aparna Bhargava Dharwadker, *Theatres of Independence: Drama, Theory, and Urban Performance in India Since 1947* (University of Iowa Press, 2005).
3. Aparna Bhargava Dharwadker, ed., *A Poetics of Modernity: Indian Theatre Theory, 1850 to the Present* (Oxford University Press, 2019).
4. Vassiliki Kolocotroni et al., eds., *Modernism: An Anthology of Sources and Documents* (University of Chicago Press, 1998).
5. Laura Doyle and Laura Winkiel, eds., *Geomodernisms: Race, Modernism, Modernity* (Indiana University Press, 2005), was chronologically the first collection to assemble a "global set of texts in relation to modernism" and to "collapse the margin and center assumptions embedded in the term" (4, 6). In this volume English, French, Spanish, and Portuguese were the European languages of settler and imperial colonialism that enabled discussions of transatlantic, African, Latin American, Caribbean, and Indian modernisms; the two non-European languages represented were Arabic and Chinese. In Peter Brooker et al., eds., *The Oxford Handbook of Modernisms* (Oxford University Press, 2011), the domain of Euro-American modernisms expanded to include Scottish, Irish, Welsh, Nordic, central European, and Anglophone Canadian writing; Hispanic America, Australia, and New Zealand connected Spanish and English to settler colonialism; Africa, the Caribbean, and India placed English and French in colonial/postcolonial contexts; and as

noncolonized East Asian cultures, China and Japan exemplified the development of modernism outside Europhone circuits. Mark Wollaeger and Matt Eatough, eds., *The Oxford Handbook of Global Modernisms* (Oxford University Press, 2012), added the Balkan languages (Albanian, Romanian, Bulgarian, Turkish, Greek, Serbian, and Croatian) as well as Vietnamese, Afrikaans, Hebrew, and Yiddish, but the "Arab world" remained on the sidelines. Stephen Ross and Allana C. Lindgren, eds., *The Modernist World* (Routledge, 2015), included "Middle East and the Arab World" as one of its eight regions, added Korean among the East Asian languages, and brought more Southeast Asian languages into the discussion (Laotian, Cambodian, Thai, Malay, Bahasa, Filipino, and Tagalog). By omitting Europe and North America from its purview, the most recent collection by Alys Moody and Stephen J. Ross, eds., *Global Modernists on Modernism: An Anthology* (Bloomsbury Academic, 2020), offers the most substantial discussions so far of European languages in the settler and imperial colonies of Latin America, the Caribbean, and sub-Saharan Africa, as well as major languages in the non-Western world (Arabic, Farsi, Turkish, Bengali, Hindi, Malay, etc.) in addition to Chinese and Japanese. Additional comments on the representation of Indian languages in these collections appear later in this section.

6. Wollaeger, introduction to *Oxford Handbook of Global Modernisms*, 11.
7. The questioning of Anglo-American hegemony by scholars of modernism during the 1980s was the first sign of an overt critique directed against a particular language as well as some specific locations associated with it, and for many reasons English has been singled out more frequently than other world languages for its conspicuous power as a global medium. For instance, a key point in Jonathan Arac's critique of Franco Moretti's method of "distant reading" is that it perpetuates "the unavowed imperialism of English; the diminishment of language-based criticism in favour of a monolingual master scheme." Arac, "Anglo-Globalism?," *New Left Review* 16 (July–August 2002): 44. In the introduction to *Geomodernisms*, Doyle and Winkiel note that "the globalization of criticism, like that of trade, inevitably sends forth the specter of appropriation, and this collection walks under its shadow. After all, this collection is in English" (6). In the introduction to *Global Modernists on Modernism*, Moody and Ross express wariness about "the colonial overtones of attempting canon formation in a field with global scope, especially from within the Anglophone academy and in the English language" (19). These self-reflexive positions are placed in perspective by Arac's trenchant "summary" of the "relation of English, as the global language of exchange and information, to the hundreds of languages and cultures that globalization brings into interaction with each other. Globalization pluralizes: it opens up every local, national or regional culture to others and thereby produces 'many worlds'. Yet these many worlds can only be known through a single medium: just as the dollar is the medium of global commerce, so is English the medium of global culture, producing 'one world'" (35). In contrast to these forms of critical awareness about English, Lawrence Rainey's substantial collection of modernist writing, *Modernism: An Anthology* (Wiley-Blackwell, 2005), demonstrates the continuation of an older linguistic imperialism by defining "modernism" overwhelmingly as Anglo-American writing in English by twenty-two authors, from Ezra Pound to Samuel Beckett, with even the rest of Europe relegated to four "continental interludes."

INTRODUCTION

8. For examples of an exclusively Anglophone focus in critical discussions of Indian modernism, postcolonialism, cosmopolitanism, etc., see Fawzia Afzal-Khan, *Cultural Imperialism and the Indo-English Novel* (Penn State University Press, 1993); Rosemary Marangoly George, *The Politics of Home: Postcolonial Relocations and Twentieth-Century Fiction* (Cambridge University Press, 1996); Ariela Freedman, "On the Ganges Side of Modernism: Raghubir Singh, Amitav Ghosh, and the Postcolonial Modern," in Doyle and Winkiel, *Geomodernisms*, 114–29; Susan Stanford Friedman, "Paranoia, Pollution, and Sexuality: Affiliations Between E. M. Forster's *A Passage to India* and Arundhati Roy's *The God of Small Things*," in Doyle and Winkiel, *Geomodernisms*, 245–61; Rebecca L. Walkowitz, *Cosmopolitan Style: Modernisn Beyond the Nation* (Columbia University Press, 2006); Teresa Heffernan, *Post-Apocalyptic Culture: Modernism, Postmodernism, and the Twentieth-Century Novel* (University of Toronto Press, 2008); Stephen Morton, *Salman Rushdie: Fictions of Postcolonial Modernity* (Palgrave Macmillan, 2008); Jon Hegglund, *World Views: Metageographies of Modernist Fiction* (Oxford University Press, 2012); Jessica Berman, "Neither Mirror nor Mimic: Transnational Reading and Indian Narratives in English," in Wollaeger and Eatough, *Oxford Handbook of Global Modernisms*, 205–27; Geetha Ramanathan, *Locating Gender in Modernism: The Outsider Female* (Routledge, 2012); Robert Michael Kirschen, *James Joyce and Post-Imperial Bildung: Salman Rushdie, Tayeb Salih, and Tsitsi Dangarembga* (Digital Scholarship@UNLV 2013-05-01T07:00:00Z, 2013); Brian May, *Extravagant Postcolonialism: Modernism and Modernity in Anglophone Fiction, 1958–1988* (University of South Carolina Press, 2014); Jens Elze, *Postcolonial Modernism and the Picaresque Novel: Literatures of Precarity* (Palgrave Macmillan, 2017); Steve Pinkerton, *Blasphemous Modernism: The 20th-Century Word Made Flesh* (Oxford University Press, 2017); Richard Begam and Michael Valdez Moses, eds., *Modernism, Postcolonialism, and Globalism: Anglophone Literature, 1950 to the Present* (Oxford University Press, 2019); Sourit Bhattacharya, *Postcolonial Modernity and the Indian Novel: On Catastrophic Realism* (Palgrave Macmillan, 2020); and Carey Mickalites, *Contemporary Fiction, Celebrity Culture, and the Market for Modernism: Fictions of Celebrity* (Bloomsbury Academic, 2022). The exclusive focus on Anglophone *fiction* in these works adds the problem of marginalized genres to the problem of marginalized languages in contemporary criticism that is ostensibly transcultural in scope.
9. Anand, Rao, and Narayan were recognized from the beginning as modernist innovators in Indian English fiction, with varying connections to the Anglophone West. The work of their major successors is entangled in the late-twentieth-century contexts of postcolonialism, diasporic displacement, postmodernism, and the resurgent interest in world literature. The sources cited in note 8 also coincidentally encapsulate these new thematics in the writing of Desai, Rushdie, and their younger contemporaries.
10. The role of translation in the intranational as well as international circulation and reception of modernist theater in Indian languages comes in for fuller discussion in chapters 2 and 3.
11. The two essays on India in Doyle and Winkiel's *Geomodernisms* focus on the Anglophone novelists Amitav Ghosh and Arundhati Roy and the photographer Raghubir Singh. In the *Oxford Handbook of Modernisms*, the discussion of Indian literary/theatrical modernisms is limited to four pages and is overshadowed by the attention

given to visual art and architecture. The two essays on India in the *Oxford Handbook of Global Modernisms* deal with Anglophone fiction of the 1930s and representations of urban women in silent and talking cinema of the 1920s and 1930s. In *The Modernist World*, sustained attention to literature is possible because there are six other essays dealing with Indian modernisms in various media. Even in this volume, however, South Asia is the only world region not to have a separate essay on drama and theater because unlike its "Arabic" or "Chinese" correlates "Indian theater" simultaneously involves about sixteen active modern Indian languages. In Douglas Mao, ed., *The New Modernist Studies Reader* (Cambridge University Press, 2021), the arrangement of essays is thematic rather than geographic, and the only Indian authors mentioned briefly are Rabindranath Tagore and G. V. Desani. Published during the same year, Sean Latham and Gayle Rogers, eds., *The New Modernist Studies Reader: An Anthology of Essential Criticism* (Bloomsbury Academic, 2021), eschews India altogether.

12. See Vinay Dharwadker, "Modernism and Its Four Phases: Literature in South Asia," in Ross and Lindgren, *Modernist World*, 127–35; Vinay Dharwadker, "The Modernist Novel in India: Paradigms and Practices," in *A History of the Indian Novel in English*, ed. Ulka Anjaria (Cambridge University Press, 2015), 103–18; and Vinay Dharwadker, "Mumbai's Marathi Modernists: A Memoir from the Margins," *Journal of Postcolonial Writing* 53, nos. 1–2 (2017): 88–107. Alys Moody and Stephen J. Ross, eds., *Global Modernists on Modernism* (Bloomsbury, 2020), take the radical step of excluding Euro-American materials altogether from their definition of the global, divide the rest of the world into fifteen regions, and present a selection of theoretically significant source texts to understand "how global modernists conceptualized themselves as modernist, and, in doing so, to advance a new understanding of global modernism itself" (1). In this anthology, see also Rudrani Gangopadhyay, "Modernism in South Asia," 241–44.

13. Dharwadker, "Modernism and Its Four Phases," 128, 129. Oddly, Dharwadker's carefully historicized and contextualized discussion of significant modernist formations across the Indian languages in this essay is at variance with comments by the editors of the volume in which it appears. In their introduction, Ross and Lindgren describe South Asia as "maybe the most linguistically diverse region on earth" but add immediately that it "has been constructed as a region by centuries of imperialist administration. The massive number of languages and dialects jostling on the cultural landscape of South Asia means that modernism of necessity abandoned any pretense to universality: it had either to adapt or to perish" (11–12). They also describe "literary production in South Asia" as a signal example of how "local conditions force modernism to abandon its tendencies towards decontextualization and dehistoricization in favor of adapting to local pressures and demands" (11). Every assertion in these comments is questionable and contradicted by Dharwadker's argument. The identity of South Asia/India as a cultural region is not merely a product of "imperial administration" but a singularly complex geocultural phenomenon unfolding over the *longue durée* (as demonstrated brilliantly in Sheldon Pollock, ed., *Literary Cultures in History: Reconstructions from South Asia* [University of California Press, 2003]). Indian literary modernisms are not limited to the merely local, nor do they abandon universality. As this book demonstrates in multiple contexts, situating themselves deliberately within a global literary culture is a defining trait

INTRODUCTION

of twentieth-century Indian modernists. India's modernist classics would take their rightful place in the postcolonial corpus if they could be made accessible to readers outside India. In their comments, Ross and Lindgren appear to dismiss unfamiliar forms of cultural complexity as confusion or simplification—a reductive move that would not be made in the case of modernist works in the West.

14. Moody and Ross, *Global Modernists*, 15. In terms of the languages represented, the contents of the volume also yield the following interesting patterns: (1) Regions involving multiple languages—Latin America (Spanish, Portuguese), the Caribbean (English, French), and sub-Saharan Africa (English, Afrikaans); (2) regions identified with one dominant language—"the Arab world" (Arabic), the Caucasus (Russian), and the South Pacific (English); (3) nations identified with one dominant language—Turkey, Iran, China, Korea, Malaysia, and Japan; (4) an ethnoreligious diaspora (Ashkenazi Jews) unified by one language (Yiddish); and (5) a region (South Asia) represented asymmetrically here by two countries (India and Pakistan) and by six languages that are all spoken and written mediums in India, although one of them (Urdu) is also the national language of Pakistan. India thus emerges even in this non-Western perspective as the most polylingual nation and as a unique amalgam of national and regional identity.

15. Gangopadhyay, "Modernism in South Asia," 241.
16. Tim Armstrong, *Modernism: A Cultural History* (Polity Press, 2005), 5.
17. Susan Stanford Friedman, *Planetary Modernisms: Provocations on Modernity Across Time* (Columbia University Press, 2015), 52.
18. Michael Wood, "Modernism and Film," in *The Cambridge Companion to Modernism*, 2nd ed., ed. Michael Levenson (Cambridge University Press, 2011), 217.
19. Dipesh Chakraborty, *Provincializing Europe: Postcolonial Thought and Historical Difference* (Princeton University Press, 2000), 148.
20. Ross and Lindgren, *Modernist World*, 2–3.
21. In the online catalogue of the Library of Congress (accessed September 14, 2024), the keyword *adhunika* yields a total of 7,242 records, including 6,109 books in multiple languages; *adhunikata* yields 405 records, including 357 book-length works; *adhunikatavad* produces 0 records.
22. That this distinction is made necessary by the specific context of literature and art is clear from the *Oxford English Dictionary* entry on "modernism," in which the term is defined as "a usage, mode of expression, peculiarity of style, etc., characteristic of modern times" and describes "the methods, style, or attitude of modern artists, writers, architects, composers, etc." A "modernist" is, rather tautologically, "a supporter or follower of modern ways or methods; an adherent of modernism."
23. In actual practice, colonial cultural forms did not jettison tradition but became eclectic fusions of the old and the new. As Sudipta Kaviraj notes, "Modernity presented writers with two different literary worlds, one drawn from Indian traditions, the other from the West. Authors improvised by using elements from both aesthetic alphabets and produced new forms that were irreducible to either." Sudipta Kaviraj, "The Two Histories of Literary Culture in Bengal," in Pollock, *Literary Cultures in History*, 558. Hence a "distinctively Indian . . . species of the literary modern" emerged from the colonial encounter, one that distanced itself from but also assimilated tradition (558).
24. Amit Chaudhuri, ed., *The Picador Book of Modern Indian Literature* (Picador, 2001).

25. Govind Chatak, *Adhunik natak ka masiha mohan rakesh* (Mohan Rakesh, the messiah of modern theater), (Indraprastha Prakashan, 1975); and Trilokchand Tulsi, *Bharatendu aur adhunikata: bharat mein adhunikata ka sutrapat* (Bharatendu and modernity: the inception of modernity in India), (Vishveshvarananda Vaidik Shodh Sansthan, 1988).
26. Urmila Mishra, *Adhunikata aur Mohan Rakesh* (Modernity and Mohan Rakesh) (Vishvavidyalaya Prakashan, 1977); Prabhakar Machwe, *Modernity and Contemporary Indian Literature* (Chetana, 1978); Nalini Natarajan, *Woman and Indian Modernity: Readings of Colonial and Postcolonial Novels* (University Press of the South, 2002); and Sukrita Paul Kumar, *Conversations on Modernism, with Reference to English, Hindi, and Urdu Fiction* (Indian Institute of Advanced Study, Shimla, in Association with Allied, 1990).
27. Abu Sayid Ayub, *Adhunikata o rabindranath* (Modernism and Rabindranath [Tagore]), trans. Amitava Ray (Sahitya Akademi, 1995).
28. According to 2024 figures in WorldCat, 7,050 of the 7,242 records in the first category and 397 of 405 records in the second belong to the post-1940 period.
29. Kaviraj, "Two Histories," 558.
30. U. R. Anantha Murthy, introduction to *Vibhava: Modernism in Indian Writing*, ed. U. R. Anantha Murthy et al. (Panther, 1992), 1.
31. Dharwadker, "Modernism and Its Four Phases," 130–34.
32. In her discussion of emergent reading practices, Priya Joshi refers to "the virtually ceaseless circulation and consumption of print and textuality" in India from the mid-nineteenth century onward, noted by Indians and British colonial officials alike. Priya Joshi, *In Another Country: Colonialism, Culture, and the English Novel in India* (Columbia University Press, 2002), 35. The numbers are admittedly small—the 1881 census records full male literacy at 6.6 percent and female literacy at 0.3 percent—and "the 'reading public' . . . is not in any reasonable way 'middle class,' nor collectively even of a single class" (45), but literature becomes a distinct strain within the totality of print. Samarpita Mitra, *Periodicals, Readers, and the Making of a Modern Literary Culture* (Brill, 2020), describes colonial Bengal as an "under-capitalized society" marked by widespread impoverishment and nonliteracy, but one that allows the construction, at least figuratively, of a "society of readers" (*pathak samaj*) (23–24). "Literary sense and the cultivation of it thereof was commonly held to be a key indication of a mature and articulate public culture" in this society (140), and "reading modern literature . . . [was] a way towards enhancement of life" (211). Joshi's case study for colonial reading habits is in the public circulating library; Mitra's is in the monthly Bengali literary magazine.
33. Christopher Innes, "Modernism in Drama," in Levenson, *Cambridge Companion to Modernism*, 128; and Christopher Innes, "Shifting the Frame: Modernism in the Theatre," in Thormählen, *Rethinking Modernism* (Palgrave Macmillan, 2003), 204.
34. Stephen Watt's brief essay on "Drama" in *A Companion to Modernist Literature and Culture*, ed. David Bradshaw and Kevin J. H. Dettmar (Blackwell, 2006), 237–44, elides the issue of modern*ist* form altogether by using "modern drama" as its defining subject. The even shorter section on "Modernist Drama" in *Modernism: A Sourcebook*, ed. Steven Matthews (Palgrave Macmillan, 2008), 10–13, uses Yeats, Pound, and Eliot as exemplars whose work for the theater was defined by "extremely stylized action," "resolutely anti-realistic" staging, and an "alarming sense that it may

INTRODUCTION

be understood only by the elect few" (11). The two recent collections representing "the new modernist studies" indicate a decisive movement away from drama/theater /performance as objects of analysis. *The New Modernist Studies Reader: An Anthology of Essential Criticism*, ed. Sean Latham and Gayle Rogers (Bloomsbury Academic, 2021) ignores the forms altogether. Steven S. Lee's essay, "Revolution's Demands: Modernism, Socialist Realism, and the Manifesto," in Mao, *The New Modernist Studies*, pivots from theater to "theatricality," the quality that Martin Puchner assigns to Marx's *Communist Manifesto*—and the manifesto genre in general—in his *Poetry of the Revolution: Marx, Manifestos, and the Avant-Gardes* (Princeton University Press, 2005). Tellingly, in Puchner's analysis as interpreted here by Lee, a manifesto "gains authority" only when it "ceases to be theatrical," and "once . . . the performative purges the theatrical" through the act of revolution (political or aesthetic), "the manifesto loses relevance and perhaps even ceases to be a manifesto" (Lee, 229).

35. See Ric Knowles et al., eds., *Modern Drama: Defining the Field* (University of Toronto Press, 2003); and Christopher Innes and F. J. Marker, eds., *Modernism in European Drama: Ibsen, Strindberg, Pirandello, Beckett* (University of Toronto Press, 1998).

36. See Thormahlen, *Rethinking Modernism*; Levenson, *Cambridge Companion to Modernism*; Innes and Marker, *Modernism in European Drama*; Alan L. Ackerman and Martin Puchner, eds., *Against Theatre: Creative Destructions on the Modernist Stage* (Palgrave Macmillan, 2006); Elin Diamond, "Modern Drama/Modernity's Drama," in Knowled et al., *Modern Drama*, 3–14; Penny Farfan, *Performing Queer Modernism* (Oxford University Press, 2017); James F. Knapp, "Primitivism and Empire: John Synge and Paul Gauguin," *Comparative Literature* 41, no. 1 (Winter 1989): 53–68; Kurt Eisen, "Theatrical Ethnography and Modernist Primitivism in Eugene O'Neill and Zora Neale Hurston," *South Central Review* 25, no. 1 (Spring 2008): 56–73; Katherine E. Kelly and Penny Farfan, "Staging Modernism: Introduction," *South Central Review* 25, no. 1 (2008): 1–11; Katherine E. Kelly, "Pandemic and Performance: Ibsen and the Outbreak of Modernism," *South Central Review* 25, no. 1 (Spring 2008): 12–35; and Penny Farfan, "Editorial Comment: 'Modernism,'" *Theatre Journal* 65, no. 4 (December 2013): i–iv.

37. Martin Puchner, *Stage Fright: Modernism, Anti-Theatricality, and Drama* (Johns Hopkins Press, 2002), passim; Olga Taxidou, *Modernism and Performance: Jarry to Brecht* (Palgrave Macmillan, 2007), xiv.

38. Interestingly, many professional meetings in the United States have played a prominent role in emphasizing the staging and performance of modernist works, and some of these have led to special issues of theater journals or collections of essays. A symposium titled "Staging Modernism," organized at Texas A&M University in March 2006 by Katherine E. Kelly and Penny Farfan, became the basis of a special issue of *South Central Review* 25, no. 1 (Spring 2008), which was guest-edited by the symposium organizers. At the 2009 annual meeting of the Modern Language Association in Philadelphia, December 27–30, a sequence of three panels arranged by the Drama Division were titled "Modernist Topoi in a Transhistorical Key." Kelly and Farfan were also among the organizers of a Working Group titled "Performing Modernism" at the 2010 annual meeting of the American Society for Theatre Research in Seattle, November 17–20, which contributed in part to the December 2013 *Theatre Journal* special issue on modernism, edited by Farfan. Most recently, an essay titled "Comparative Modernist Performance Studies: A Not So Modest

Proposal," coauthored by Julia A. Walker and Glenn Odom, appeared in the *Journal of Dramatic Theory and Criticism* 31, no.1 (Fall 2016): 129–53.
39. Tutun Mukherjee, ed., *Staging Resistance: Plays by Women in Translation* (Oxford University Press, 2005).
40. For a discussion of this revolution in relation to modern Indian theater history, see A. Dharwadker, general introduction to *A Poetics of Modernity*, xcii–xcvi.
41. The overt and covert politicality of modernist realism as well as modernist traditionalism in postindependence theater is discussed in chapters 4 and 5, respectively.

1. MODERNISM, INDIA, AND THE AXIS OF LANGUAGE

1. Chris Baldick, *The Concise Oxford Dictionary of Literary Terms* (Oxford University Press, 2001), 255.
2. Baldick, *Concise Oxford Dictionary of Literary Terms*, 182–83.
3. For a full list of titles that maintain an exclusively Anglophone focus in discussing Indian modernism, postcolonialism, and cosmopolitanism, see Note 8 in the introduction to this book.
4. See, for example, Sukrita Paul Kumar, *Conversations on Modernism, with Reference to English, Hindi, and Urdu Fiction* (Indian Institute of Advanced Study, Shimla, in Association with Allied, 1990); Anantha Murthy et al., ed., *Vibhava: Modernism in Indian Writing* (Panther, 1992); Vasudha Dalmia, "Neither Half nor Whole: Mohan Rakesh and the Modernist Quest," in *Poetics, Plays, and Performances: The Politics of Modern Indian Theatre* (Oxford University Press, 2006), 117–49; Alpana Sharma Knippling, guest ed., special issue on "South Asian Modernisms" in *South Asian Review* 33, no. 1 (2012); Anjali Nerlekar, *Bombay Modern: Arun Kolatkar and Bilingual Literary Culture* (Northwestern University Press, 2016); Amal Allana, *The Theatre of E. Alkazi: A Modernist Approach to Indian Theatre* (Theatre and Television Associates, 2016); Vinay Dharwadker, "Mumbai's Marathi Modernists: A Memoir from the Margins," *Journal of Postcolonial Writing* 53, nos. 1–2 (2017): 88–107; Jennifer Dubrow, *Cosmopolitan Dreams: The Making of Modern Urdu Literary Culture in Colonial South Asia* (Permanent Black, 2018); the section on South Asia in Alys Moody and Stephen J. Ross, ed., *Global Modernists on Modernism: An Anthology* (Bloomsbury Academic, 2020), 241–79; and discussions of cosmo-modernism and postcolonial modernism in Aparna Bhargava Dharwadker, *Theatres of Independence: Drama, Theory, and Urban Performance in India Since 1947* (University of Iowa Press, 2005), 186–203 (on Dharamvir Bharati); Aparna Dharwadker, "Mohan Rakesh, Modernism, and the Postcolonial Present," *South Central Review* 25, no. 1 (Spring 2008): 136–62; and Aparna Dharwadker, "Modernism, 'Tradition,' and History in the Postcolony: Vijay Tendulkar's *Ghashiram kotwal* (1972)," *Theatre Journal* 65 (December 2013): 467–87.
5. The career of Mulk Raj Anand (1905–2004) can serve as a paradigmatic example of the difference between Anglophone and non-Anglophone Indian writers in terms of their recognition as "modernists" and their international visibility. Anand was enabled both by the colonial connection and the medium of English to leave Punjab at the age of twenty and begin an unprecedented twenty-year stint in England in 1925. As an undergraduate at the University of London and a doctoral candidate

1. MODERNISM, INDIA, AND THE AXIS OF LANGUAGE

in philosophy at Cambridge, Anand struck up literary friendships with members of the Bloomsbury Group who are recalled in his memoir. See Mulk Raj Anand, *Conversations in Bloomsbury* (Arnold Heinemann, 1981). He met E. M. Forster while working on Eliot's magazine, *The Criterion*, became a friend of Picasso, covered the Spanish Civil War as a journalist, and worked with George Orwell on the BBC's Eastern Service during World War II. Anand's debut novel, *Untouchable* (1935), now considered a modernist classic, was inspired by Joyce's intermingling of the aesthetic and the political in *A Portrait of the Artist as a Young Man* (1916). Eleven more works of fiction and nonfiction appeared from both British and Indian publishers during the next decade as Anand divided his time between the two countries, becoming increasingly involved with the Indian nationalist and progressive movements. He returned permanently to India in 1946, and the notable diasporic careers of writers Bharati Mukherjee, Salman Rushdie, Amitav Ghosh, and Rohinton Mistry are in some ways variations on his groundbreaking initiatives, however different the content of their writing. Regardless of genre, no major non-Anglophone Indian author can claim either a similar biography or a comparable critical reception.

6. Geeta Kapur, *When Was Modernism? Essays on Contemporary Cultural Practice in India* (Tulika, 2000), 297–98.
7. Partha Mitter, *The Triumph of Modernism: Indian Artists and the Avant-Garde, 1922–1947* (Reaktion, 2007), 11.
8. Mitter, *Triumph of Modernism*, 7.
9. Quoted in Romi Khosla, "The New Metropolis: Nehru and the Aftermath," *Social Scientist* 43, nos. 3–4 (March-April 2015): 11.
10. Source untraceable.
11. Marion von Osten, introduction to *Transcultural Modernisms*, ed. Model House Research Group (Sternberg, 2013), 13.
12. Michael W. Meister, *Traditional and Vernacular Architecture: Proceedings of the Seminar* (Madras Craft Foundation, 2003), 9, 14.
13. "Eighth Schedule to the Constitution of India," *The Constitution of India* (Ministry of Law and Justice, 2007), 30.
14. The well-known "three-language formula" in India's education policy has undergone several modifications since its first appearance in the 1968 "National Policy Resolution," but the adherence to some combination of three languages as an intrinsic part of the school curriculum has continued. Most urban Indians learn the majority language of their particular region, Hindi (or another Indian language), and English. In addition to native speakers, those who acquire any given language as a second or third language are therefore a crucial part of the total statistical picture.
15. Sheldon Pollock, introduction to *Literary Cultures in History: Reconstructions from South Asia*, ed. Sheldon Pollock (University of California Press, 2003), 30–31.
16. Douglas Mao and Rebecca L. Walkowitz, "The New Modernist Studies," *PMLA* 123, no. 3 (2008): 740.
17. Amiya Dev, "A Note on Modern Bengali Writing," in Anantha Murthy et al., *Vibhava*, 12.
18. In India, the dominant/subaltern binary has much greater relevance in historiographic and sociopolitical contexts (especially in relation to the politics of race, gender, and class) than in literary-cultural contexts because the power of the modern Indian languages as literary media both precedes and succeeds colonialism. As

1. MODERNISM, INDIA, AND THE AXIS OF LANGUAGE

Pollock argues, the literatures of South Asia are "unmatched in world literary history and unrivaled in the resources they offer for understanding the development of expressive language and imagination over time and in relation to larger orders of culture, society, and polity" (in Pollock, introduction to *Literary Cultures in History*, 2). Outside the disciplines of area studies and philology, however, these literatures have not received much scholarly attention, and they are objects of criticism primarily in their own languages. For a discussion of the "ironic" centrality of modernism to postcolonial writing, see Simon Gikandi, "Preface: Modernism in the World," *Modernism/Modernity* 13, no. 3 (2006): 419–24. For discussions of the "autonomy" of Indian literary-theatrical modernisms, see A. Dharwadker, "Mohan Rakesh, Modernism, and the Postcolonial Present," and "Modernism, 'Tradition,' and History in the Postcolony"; V. Dharwadker, "Nations, Modernisms, Anti-Nations: Five Theses on South Asian Arts and Cultures," keynote address, conference on "Nationhood and Nation-Building in South Asia" (Stanford University, April 29, 2010); and Alpana Sharma Knippling, "Decolonizing the Modernist Mind," *South Asian Review*, 33, no. 1 (2012): 13–29.
19. Dev, "Note on Modern Bengali," 7.
20. Anantha Murthy et al., *Vibhava*, 2.
21. Dalmia, "Neither Half nor Whole," 117–49; and Dubrow, *Cosmopolitan Dreams*.
22. Anantha Murthy et al., *Vibhava*, 1, 3.
23. Vinay Dharwadker, "Modernism and Its Four Phases: Literature in South Asia," in *The Modernist World*, ed. Stephen Ross and Allana C. Lindgren (Routledge, 2015), 127–35; and Nerlekar, *Bombay Modern*.
24. Ariela Freedman, "On the Ganges Side of Modernism: Raghubir Singh, Amitav Ghosh, and the Postcolonial Modern," in *Geomodernisms: Race, Modernism, Modernity*, ed. Laura Doyle and Laura Winkiel (Indiana University Press, 2005), 117, 126.
25. Manishita Dass, "Visions of Modernity in Colonial India: Cinema, Women, and the City," in *The Oxford Handbook of Global Modernisms*, ed. Mark Wollaeger and Matt Eatough (Oxford University Press, 2012), 631.
26. Rudrani Gangopadhyay, "Modernism in South Asia," in Moody and Ross, *Global Modernists*, 241.
27. For comments on Homi Bhabha's influential concept of "vernacular cosmopolitanism," see the conclusion in this book.
28. Susan Stanford Friedman, "Periodizing Modernism: Postcolonial Modernities and the Space/Time Borders of Modernist Studies," *Modernism/Modernity* 13, no. 3 (2006): 429; and Doyle and Winkiel, *Geomodernisms*, 6.
29. Gikandi, "Preface," 422; and Rebecca L. Walkowitz, *Cosmopolitan Style: Modernism Beyond the Nation* (Columbia University Press, 2006), 10.
30. Mark Wollaeger, Introduction to *The Oxford Handbook of Global Modernisms*, ed. Mark Wollaeger and Matt Eatough (Oxford University Press, 2012), 6–7, emphasis added.
31. Moody and Ross, *Global Modernists*, 13.
32. Immanuel Wallerstein, *World Systems Analysis: An Introduction* (Duke University Press, 2004), 23, emphasis in original.
33. Wallerstein, *World Systems Analysis*, 23.
34. A remarkable aspect of the literary-humanist turn toward world-systems theory is the tacit acceptance of a starkly amoral materialist framework. Volume 1

1. MODERNISM, INDIA, AND THE AXIS OF LANGUAGE

of Immanuel Wallerstein's four volume *The Modern World System* (Academic, 1974–1989) "explains" that India remained an external arena while Amerindia became integral to the world-system in the sixteenth century precisely because Europe could not conquer India at this time, while the New World became subject to genocidal conquest and rapacious exploitation. In volume 3, systematic colonization is described as "the renewed economic expansion (and monetary inflation) of the period 1733–1817 (more or less)," when "the European world-economy broke the bounds it had created in the long sixteenth century and began to incorporate vast new zones into the effective division of labor it encompassed" (vol. 3, 125). In India, the basis of "incorporation" was a systematic destruction of existing industries: with cotton as the crucial commodity, the East India Company "succeeded in converting India from a manufacturing country into a country exporting raw produce" (vol. 3, 138), with finished luxury products occasionally valued at five thousand times the cost of the raw material. The upheavals of neoliberalism and globalization in the early twenty-first century are presented as "competition" between semi-peripheral states that are struggling to maintain a trade balance between exports and imports, using "protectionist" policies that interfere with the world market, and trying to forestall competition as they attempt to improve their own efficiency (Wallerstein, *World Systems Analysis*, 30). This is a strange discourse to choose as an entry into the world's "aesthetic cultures": its single-minded analytical vocabulary pragmatically excludes ethical and moral valuations.

35. Pollock, *Literary Cultures in History*, 22.
36. Interestingly, with *Shantata* the plurality of original and translated versions extends beyond theater to the medium of film as well. The first film based on the play was in Marathi (1971), with the acclaimed trifecta of Satyadev Dubey as director, Tendulkar as screenwriter, and Govind Nihalani as cinematographer; it was credited with launching the New Cinema movement in Marathi. In 2008 another noted director, Chandrakant Kulkarni, produced a second version in Marathi. Ritesh Menon directed an English script in 2009 with Nandita Das in the lead, and a Hindi version in 2017.
37. Sulabha Deshpande mentions thirteen translations of *Shantata* in a December 2013 interview titled "The Rest Is History" (https://thebigindianpicture.com/2013/12/the-rest-is-history/). The Wikipedia article on the play reports that it has "been translated into 16 languages in India and abroad" (https://en.wikipedia.org/wiki/Shantata!_Court_Chalu_Aahe#:~:text=Court%20Chalu%20Aahe%20(Silence!,Deshpande%20as%20the%20main%20olead).
38. For a discussion of orientalist constructions of "Indian theater" during the colonial period, and the neo-Orientalism of postwar Western scholarship on the subject, see A. Dharwadker, *Theatres of Independence*, 128–32 and 147–61.
39. Employing chronological frameworks suitable for their particular subjects, contributors to this volume discuss the literary cultures of three pan-Indian languages—Sanskrit, Persian, and English—and more than ten modern languages, from the time of their emergence to an appropriate terminal date, usually sometime in the "modern" period. The evolution of a language and its cultural forms over time and the modernizing effects of colonialism and its aftermath are also topics that come up for discussion in numerous essays. But because each essay reconstructs the literary culture of an individual language, the many discussions of modernity do not converge

1. MODERNISM, INDIA, AND THE AXIS OF LANGUAGE

to produce interlingual, interregional, or national perspectives, and there is no specific recognition in any essay of *modernism* as a dimension of modernity. Indeed, the index to the volume as a whole includes only two references each to modernism and modernization, and three references to modernity. These gaps in a collection described as "the first comprehensive history of the rich literary traditions of South Asia" highlight the need for critical methods that can recover the intersecting trajectories of modernity and modernism and position Indian modernisms systematically and self-consciously within the larger arc of Indian and global modernities.

40. Doyle and Winkiel, *Geomodernisms*, 4.
41. Wollaeger, Introduction to *Oxford Handbook of Global Modernisms*, 12; Ross and Lindgren, *Modernist World*, 3.
42. Susan Stanford Friedman, *Planetary Modernisms: Provocations on Modernity Across Time* (Columbia University Press, 2015), 7–8.
43. Gikandi, "Preface," 420, 421.
44. Gikandi, "Preface," 420.

2. MODERNITY, MODERNISM, AND INDIAN THEATER

1. Aparna Bhargava Dharwadker, ed., *A Poetics of Modernity: Indian Theatre Theory, 1850 to the Present* (Oxford University Press, 2019), xxxv. This anthology of primary sources in modern Indian theater theory includes many of the essays cited in this chapter and throughout the book; they were either written originally in English or have been made available in English translation. The volume is cited hereafter in the text as *POM*.
2. For a discussion of the pervasive presence of the past in nineteenth-century Indian theater as a form of "cultural recursiveness," see A. Dharwadker, *A Poetics of Modernity*, xlvi–li.
3. All three of these authors represent crucial phases in colonial modernity, and as noted in chapter 1, Tagore has been claimed as an early modernist as well. I use the phrase "proto-modernist" to define their theoretical positions vis-à-vis theater because these positions are uncannily close to Martin Puchner's argument about the constitutive role of a constructive antitheatricalism in twentieth-century *Euromodernist* theater. "The negation and rejection inherent in the term *anti-theatricalism*," Puchner suggests, is "not to be understood as a doing away with the theatre, but as a process that is dependent on that which it negates, and to which it therefore remains calibrated. Even the most adamant forms of modernist anti-theatricalism feed off the theatre and keep it close at hand." See Martin Puchner, *Stage Fright: Modernism, Anti-Theatricality, and Drama* (Johns Hopkins Press, 2002), 2.
4. Sudhi Pradhan, ed., *Marxist Cultural Movement in India: Chronicles and Documents*, 3 vols. (National Book Agency, 1979–1985), vol. 1: 127, 125. All further references to this collection appear in the text.
5. See Jayant Kastuar, introduction to *Indian Drama in Retrospect* (Hope India, 2007), 281–338.
6. Fredric Jameson, *A Singular Modernity: Essays on the Ontology of the Present* (Verso, 2002), 197.
7. See Rebecca L. Walkowitz, *Cosmopolitan Style: Modernism Beyond the Nation* (Columbia University Press, 2006); Jessica Berman, *Modernist Commitments: Ethics,*

2. MODERNITY, MODERNISM, AND INDIAN THEATER

Politics, and Transnational Modernism (Columbia University Press, 2012); and Jean-Michel Rabaté, "Editor's Introduction: Cosmopolitan Modernism, Polylingual Strategies and Cultural Hybridity," *Journal of Modern Literature* 37, no. 1 (2013): v–vi.

8. Susan Stanford Friedman, *Planetary Modernisms: Provocations on Modernity Across Time* (Columbia University Press, 2015), 213 and passim. In this imaginative and meticulously theorized study, premodern Chinese, Iraqi, and Indian authors/artists appear alongside familiar early-twentieth-century high modernists (Joyce, Woolf, and Pound) and key figures in the more recent "circulating" and "diasporic" modernisms of the late twentieth century (Tyeb Salih, Arundhati Roy, and Aime Cesaire).
9. Bharati's collected works were published in 1998: *Dharamvir bharati granthavali*, 9 vols., ed. Chandrakant Bandavidekar (Vani Prakashan, 1998]), cited hereafter in the text as *DBG*. In ascending numerical order, the volumes contain novels and long short stories; short stories and one act plays; poems and verse drama; essays; literary criticism; memoirs; travel writing; translations; and research writing. Mohan Rakesh's collected works appeared in 2011: *Mohan rakesh rachanavali*, 13 vols., ed. Jaidev Taneja (Rajkamal), cited hereafter in the text as *MRR*. In ascending numerical order, volumes contain memoirs; early works; full-length plays; one act plays; short stories; novels (2 volumes); essays and criticism; miscellaneous writings; letters; plays in translation; and fiction in translation (2 volumes). Vijay Tendulkar's collected works have not yet appeared (and are unlikely to), but just in the original Marathi, his plays, screenplays, novels, short stories, essays, and nonfiction works total about seventy individually published volumes.
10. Bharati, "Modernity, or a sense of crisis," *DBG*, vol. 4, 476–78.
11. Bharati, "Cactus," *DBG*, vol. 4, 70–71.
12. See Douglas Mao and Rebecca L. Walkowitz, eds., *Bad Modernisms* (Duke University Press, 2006), 3.
13. A substantial discussion of Bharati appears in Aparna Bhargava Dharwadker, *Theatres of Independence: Drama, Theory, and Urban Performance in India Since 1947* (University of Iowa Press, 2005), especially 186–203.
14. Eugenio Barba, "The Steps on the River Bank," in *Rasa: The Indian Performing Arts in the Last 25 Years*, vol. 2, ed. Ananda Lal and Chidananda Dasgupta (Anamika Kala Sangam, 1995), 20.
15. Mohan Rakesh, *Bakalam khud* (With his own pen) (Rajpal, 1974), 93–94; cited hereafter in the text as *BK*.
16. Partha Chatterjee, "Talking About Our Modernity in Two Languages," in *A Possible India: Essays in Political Criticism* (Oxford University Press, 1997), 263, 269.
17. Chatterjee, "Talking About Our Modernity," 270.
18. Mohan Rakesh, *Sahitya aur sanskriti* (Literature and culture) (Radhakrishna Prakashan, 1990), 109. Cited hereafter in the text as *SAS*.
19. Mohan Rakesh, *Natya vimarsh* (Reflections on theater), ed. Jaidev Taneja (New Delhi: National School of Drama, 2003), 37; cited hereafter in the text as *NV*.
20. Mohan Rakesh, "Looking Around as a Playwright," *Sangeet Natak*, no. 3 (October 1966): 18.
21. Rakesh, "Looking Around," 19.
22. T. S. Eliot, *The Poems of T. S. Eliot*, vol. 1, ed. Christopher Ricks and Jim McCue (Farrar, Strauss, and Giroux, 2015), 183–84.

23. Mohan Rakesh, "Theatre Without Walls," *Sangeet Natak*, no. 6 (October–December 1967), 67.
24. The one major exception to this thematic in Tendulkar's drama is the play *Ghashiram kotwal* (Constable Ghashiram, 1972), a full-fledged "musical" that is set in the late eighteenth century and draws on several antirealistic regional presentational styles and religious traditions to excoriate brahman culture in Pune (a historic city in Maharashtra). In chapter 5 I use this play as a major example of the relation between modernism and its ostensible opposite, "tradition."
25. Vijay Tendulkar, *The Play Is the Thing*, Shri Ram Memorial Lecture no. 10 (Shri Ram Centre for Art and Culture, 1997), 1; cited hereafter in the text as *PTT*.
26. Vijay Tendulkar, "*Majhe lekhan kashasatthi?*" (What is my writing for?), in *Sahityatun satyakade* (Through literature towards the truth), ed. Shirish Pai and Priya Tendulkar (Dimple, 1988), 527.
27. Tendulkar, "*Majhe lekhan*," 526.
28. Tendulkar, "*Majhe lekhan*," 528.
29. Shanta Gokhale, "Tendulkar on His Own Terms," in *Vijay Tendulkar* (Katha, 2001), 80, 104.
30. Gokhale, "Tendulkar," 37. Tendulkar's statement is almost identical to the one by Rakesh in the essay "Looking Around as a Playwright."
31. Vijay Tendulkar, "*Majhe natyashikshan*" (My theater education), in *Natak ani mi* (The theater and I) (Dimple, 1997), 84.
32. All theatrical productions ultimately depend on resources, and by referring to the continuity of Western theater institutions I do not mean to suggest that they are immune to fiscal and artistic crises of the kind that can seriously impede or end their activities. Various economic recessions and the global pandemic that began in 2020 have made the vulnerability of all the arts abundantly clear. But as I argue here, there is a qualitative difference between periodic interruptions within a very large, historically continuous, and multilayered system designed for regular production cycles (in, say, Britain and the United States) and the kind of irregularity, contingency, and precarity that characterize almost all urban theater activity in contemporary India, adding up to a "really poor" performance economy. For a discussion of this poverty as a widespread postcolonial condition, see Aparna Dharwadker, "The Really Poor Theatre: Postcolonial Economies of Performance," *Journal of Dramatic Theory and Criticism* 31, no. 2 (Spring 2017): 99–124.
33. Mohan Rakesh, *One Day in the Season of Rain*, trans. Aparna Dharwadker and Vinay Dharwadker (Penguin Classics, 2015), 220; cited hereafter in the text as *ODSR*.
34. What is unusual about these two prefaces is not the disconnection Rakesh describes but his desire to articulate problems that many equally prominent playwrights of his generation accept without resistance.
35. Rakesh, "Theatre Without Walls," 67.
36. Girish Karnad, "Theatre in India," *Daedalus* 118, no. 4 (1989): 344–45.
37. Girish Karnad, "In Search of a New Theatre," in *Contemporary India: Essays on the Use of Tradition*, ed. Carla Borden (Oxford University Press, 1985), 334.
38. Karnad, "In Search," 340.
39. Karnad, "In Search," 335.
40. Girish Karnad, "An Interview by Kirtinath Kurtkoti," in *Contemporary Indian Theatre: Interviews with Playwrights and Directors*, ed. Paul Jacob (Sangeet Natak Akademi, 1989), 79.

2. MODERNITY, MODERNISM, AND INDIAN THEATER

41. Mulk Raj Anand, "Indian Theatre in the Context of World Theatre," in Kastuar, *Indian Drama in Retrospect*, 294.
42. Sombhu Mitra, "Amateur Theatre in India," in Kastuar, *Indian Drama in Retrospect*, 319.
43. Ebrahim Alkazi, "The Training of the Actor," in Kastuar, *Indian Drama in Retrospect*, 362–63.
44. The primacy of this "group theater" model in postindependence theater activity can be gauged from the large number of successful examples it includes: Shyamanand Jalan's Padatik, Rudraprasad Sengupta's Nandikar, Usha Ganguli's Rangakarmee, and Koushik Sen's Swapnasandhani in Calcutta/Kolkata; Vijaya Mehta's Rangayan, Satyadev Dubey's Theatre Unit, Alyque Padamsee's Theatre Group, Amol Palekar's Aniket, and Lillette Dubey's Prime Time in Bombay/Mumbai; Joy Michael's Ruchika, Om and Sudha Shivpuri's Dishantar, Rajinder Nath's Abhiyan, Barry John's Theatre Action Group, and Arvind Gaur's Asmita in Delhi; P. C. Ramakrishna and the Madras Players, and Gowri Ramnarayan's JustUs Repertory in Madras/Chennai; Neelam Mansingh Chowdhry's The Company in Chandigarh; Bansi Kaul's Rang Vidushak in Bhopal; and Mahesh Dattani's Playpen and Jagdish and Arundhati Raja's Artists Repertory Theatre in Bangalore/Bengaluru. The prominent presence of women in this list (Ganguli, Mehta, Lillette Dubey, Michael, Sudha Shivpuri, Chowdhry, Ramnarayan, and Arundhati Raja) is another confirmation of the much greater success they have had as directors and managers than as playwrights—a gender-driven asymmetry noted in my introductory chapter. In addition, two organizations spearheaded by directors need special mention here because of the radical ways in which they have extended the scope of their activities: the Nilakanteshwara Natya Seva Sangh (Ninasam) founded in the village of Heggodu (Karnataka) by K. V. Subbanna in 1949, and the Dramatic Art and Design Academy, cofounded in New Delhi by Amal Allana and Nissar Allana in 2000 (as an offshoot of their older organization, Theatre and TV Associates). In addition to producing plays, both initiatives are involved in a comprehensive program of theater training, education, outreach, and publication, and therefore follow a different material and institutional structure.
45. Mitra, "Amateur Theatre in India," 319.
46. The work of leading directors (many of them also playwrights and actors) who have secured a modernist repertory on the postindependence stage is documented in A. Dharwadker, *Theatres of Independence*, 397–437. There are many other important directors who do not have an ongoing association with specific groups but who work eclectically for different entities and develop a significant body of work over a period of time. They include Chetan Datar, Jayadev Hattangady, Waman Kendre, Rajiv Naik, and Sunil Shanbag in Bombay/Mumbai; Rustom Bharucha, Suman Mukherjee, and Sohag Sen in Calcutta/Kolkata; and Mohan Maharishi, M. K. Raina, Ranjit Kapoor, and Feisal Alkazi in Delhi. Jabbar Patel (Pune), Prasanna (Bangalore), B. M. Shah (Lucknow), Bhanu Bharati (Jaipur/Ajmer), and C. R. Jambe (Bangalore) are directors based outside the metropole who have significant regional or national profiles. Some of these professionals have a close connection with the media of film and television; others are attached to educational institutions and conduct freelance workshops widely. The quality they share with directors in other categories is that they too are at the center of the creative and artistic processes underlying their

2. MODERNITY, MODERNISM, AND INDIAN THEATER

productions. For a discussion of "Multilingualism, Translation, and Circulation" as a dimension of the performance of new Indian plays, and the role of major directors in bringing world drama to urban Indian stages, see A. Dharwadker, *Theatres of Independence*, 72–84 and 94–96. For a discussion of translation as a constitutive feature of Indian theatrical modernity, see A. Dharwadker, *Poetics of Modernity*, lxv–lxxvii.

47. To date, the Diamond Membership has included Sombhu Mitra, Ebrahim Alkazi, Adya Rangacharya, P. L. Deshpande, Utpal Dutt, Girish Karnad, Habib Tanvir, Badal Sircar, Vijay Tendulkar, B. V. Karanth, K. N. Panikkar, Shriram Lagoo, Chandrashekhar Kambar, Heisnam Kanhailal, Ratan Thiyam, Mahesh Elkunchwar, and M. S. Sathyu. Eleven of these playwrights and directors were featured in the 1989 Nehru Festival. For a list of directors whose careers benefited significantly from the Akademi's seven-year Scheme for Assistance to Young Theatre Workers (1984–91), see chapter 5, note 4.
48. For a substantial discussion of the precarious economics of theater production, not just in India but in other postcolonial locations, see A. Dharwadker, "The Really Poor Theatre."
49. Girish Karnad, "Performance, Meaning, and the Materials of Modern Indian Theatre," *New Theatre Quarterly* 44 (1995): 362, 364.
50. Ebrahim Alkazi, "Journal of South Asian Literature Interviews Ebrahim Alkazi," *Journal of South Asian Literature* 10, nos. 2–4 (1975), 293, 295.
51. Alkazi, "Journal Interview," 294.
52. Alkazi, "Journal Interview," 295.
53. Alkazi's modernist credentials have been consolidated most notably by his daughter, Amal Allana, a leading woman director in her own right, in *The Theatre of E. Alkazi: A Modernist Approach to Indian Theatre* (Art Heritage, 2016) and in her encyclopedic biography, *Ebrahim Alkazi: Holding Time Captive* (Vintage, 2024).
54. "The Ninasam Ensemble" (Pragati, 1996), 1.
55. See A. Dharwadker, *Theatres of Independence*, 414–15, for a list of Ninasam productions and directors from circa 1950 to 2000.
56. Rustom Bharucha, "We Need a House of Our Own: The Impasse of Indian Theatre After Independence," in *2000: Reflections on the Arts in India*, ed. Pratapaditya Paul (Mumbai: Marg, 2000), 43.
57. "Ninasam Ensemble," 1.
58. Nemichandra Jain, ed., *Mohan rakesh ke sampurna natak* (The complete plays of Mohan Rakesh), (Rajpal, 1993).
59. See my introduction to this translation of *Ashadh* (Rakesh, *One Day in the Season of Rain*, 1–46) for a discussion of the historical contexts and the formal, thematic, and affective qualities that have made this play "a foundational work of postindependence urban Indian theatre" (1).

3. PALIMPSESTS OF THE PAST

1. See Simon Williams, "John Millington Synge: Transforming Myths of Ireland," in *Facets of European Modernism: Essays in Honour of James McFarlane*, ed. Janet Garton (University of East Anglia, 1985), 79–98; and John Fordham, "The Revolution of the Scots Word: Modernism, Myth, and Nationhood in Gibbon and MacDiarmid,"

3. PALIMPSESTS OF THE PAST

in *And in Our Time: Vision, Revision, and British Writing of the 1930s*, ed. Anthony Shuttleworth (Bucknell University Press, 2003), 181–203.
2. See Bruce Gaston, "Brecht's Pastiche History Play: Renaissance Drama and Modernist Theatre in *Leben Eduards des Zweiten von England*," *German Life and Letters* 56, no. 4 (October 2003), 345–62; Damon Marcel Decoste, "Modernism's Shell-Shocked History: Amnesia, Repetition, and the War in Graham Greene's *The Ministry of Fear*," *Twentieth Century Literature* 45, no. 4 (Winter 1999): 428–51; and Paul L. Jay, "American Modernism and the Uses of History: The Case of William Carlos Williams," *New Orleans Review* 9, no. 3 (1982): 16–25. Jay's essay also discusses Hart Crane's poem, *The Bridge*, on pp. 16–17.
3. In terms of scholarly criticism, Aparna Dharwadker, "Historical Fictions and Postcolonial Representation: Reading Girish Karnad's *Tughlaq*," *PMLA* 110, no.1 (1995): 43–58, offered the first substantial discussion of the "history play" as a distinct postcolonial/modernist genre in Indian theater. Nandi Bhatia takes up Utpal Dutt's revisionist play about the 1857 Mutiny in "Staging the 1857 Mutiny as 'The Great Rebellion': Colonial History and Post-Colonial Interventions in Utpal Dutt's *Mahavidroha*," *Theatre Journal* 51, no. 2 (1999): 167–84, but her discussion does not use modernism as a specific frame of reference. As noted earlier, chapter 5 in A. Dharwadker, *Theatres of Independence* (165–217), titled "Myth, Ambivalence, and Evil," analyzes revisionary modernist approaches to myth after 1950 and includes a discussion of Bharati's *Andha yug* (1954) as a "cosmo-modernist history of mankind" (186–203). Chapter 6, "The Ironic History of the Nation," offers a revised analysis of *Tughlaq*, along with a discussion of Mohan Rakesh as a postcolonial modernist who uses the "historic" Sanskrit poet Kalidasa for his "portrait of the artist" in *Ashadh ka ek din* (218–67). Vasudha Dalmia's chapter, "Neither Half nor Whole," in *Poetics, Plays, and Performances*, 117–49, focuses on realism more than modernism. Although she comments briefly on the two plays by Rakesh that have historical protagonists, there is no specific commentary on the modernist uses of history, and much of the chapter deals with Rakesh's last play, *Adhe adhure* (Incomplete, unfinished, 1969), which is set in contemporary Delhi. Modernism is connected to history as well as tradition in A. Dharwadker, "Modernism, 'Tradition,' and History in the Postcolony," passim.
4. Shanyn Fiske argues that "The archaic world was formulated and made available for modernist usage by the unique conditions that grafted the development of science, particularly the fields of anthropology, sociology, and psychology onto the well-established roots of classical scholarship, which, until the last decades of the nineteenth century, was dominated by literary/linguistic and textual study. . . . [W]hat we might call the modernist mythopoeic imagination evolves from a nineteenth-century scientific discourse in which abundant empirical uncertainty was seamlessly compensated with literary invention" (Shanyn Fiske, "From Ritual to the Archaic in Modernism: Fraser, Harrison, Freud, and the Persistence of Myth," in *A Handbook of Modernism Studies*, ed. Jean-Michel Rabaté [John Wiley, 2013], 174).
5. In Gerhard Hoffmann, "Myth, Ideology, Symbol and Faulkner's Modernism/Postmodernism in *Go Down, Moses*," *American Studies* 42, no. 4 (1997): 661–78, the author outlines four Western approaches to myth: as a mode of experience (explored in philosophy), a cultural construct (studied in structuralism), an ideological component of culture (critiqued in Marxism), and a part of the inventory of Western

thought (considered in the history of ideas). He then adds a fifth perspective on myth as the possession of "primitive/primal cultures": "In 'primitive,' or rather, primal cultures, mythical experience had social and ethical functions as well as psychological and religious meaning and determined the entire way of life, from ritual to everyday activities" (665). In India, however, myth performs these social and ethical functions not as part of a "primitive/primal" culture but as an omnipresent "classical" legacy. Myth is not a refuge from individual isolation but a continuous presence in everyday life that can be commended or critiqued. In particular, the Indian modernists' approach to myth is not romantic-heroic but skeptical and questioning.

6. In a 1995 interview with A. Dharwadker ("Performance, Meaning, and the Materials of Modern Indian Theatre," *New Theatre Quarterly* 44 [1995], 355–70), Girish Karnad pointed out, in response to a question about contemporary theater's relation to film, video, and other mechanical media, that theater has always been a "parasitical" genre.

> It has always drawn on other forms: on epics in ancient India or Greece, for instance, or on folk tales and novels. . . . Indian theatre has fed almost exclusively on the three epics: the *Ramayana*, the *Mahabharata*, and the *Bhagavata purana*. Poets like Kamban or Lakshmish, who wrote the epics in Tamil or Kannada, thought of themselves as 'translating' the Sanskrit originals, though they also felt free to move away from the original material. The poet himself decided how far he could stray.
>
> When Peter Brook and Jean-Claude Carrière were in India planning their *Mahabharata*, they wanted me to collaborate with them, and that's the first point I made: in India you never reproduce the original epic, you are not supposed to. But Peter had a valid problem: as an outsider, he would not know how far he could stray without destroying the original. He therefore preferred to stick closely to the text of the *Mahabharata*. (364)

In Indian literature and performance, authors therefore draw on the epics but limit themselves to a self-contained segment or episode they can revive and reshape in the image of the present. This broad structural principle of selective elaboration is constant across the differences of period, region, language, and genre, making Brook's nine-hour condensed stage version of the *Mahabharata* intrinsically alien to Indian practice. Tellingly, Brooks's original production did not tour in India, although a sequel titled *Battlefield* premiered in Mumbai in 2016.

7. During the Hindu festival of Dushehra in October, oversized effigies of Ravana are burnt to signify his defeat in battle by Rama. Twenty days later, Diwali, the "festival of lights," commemorates Rama's victorious return from Lanka to his kingdom in Ayodhya. In the annual Hindu calendar, these observances have the same religious centrality as Christmas and Easter in Christianity.

8. See Rakesh Solomon, *Globalization, Nationalism, and the Text of* Kichaka vadha (Anthem, 2014), for a scholarly translation of the play and a critical discussion of its explosive initial reception.

9. Aparna Dharwadker, "Representing India's Pasts: Time, Culture, and the Problems of Performance Historiography," in *Representing the Past: Essays in Performance*

Historiography, ed. Thomas Postlewait and Charlotte Canning (University of Iowa Press, 2010), 168.

10. Prasad's plays were published during the 1920s and 1930s as closet drama, but they have had a few government-funded productions after independence. The "Hindu" mainstream that he, Ghosh, and Roy represent in the colonial period is offset in a limited way by celebratory plays about such famous Mughal emperors as Jahangir (the son of Akbar) and Shahjahan (builder of the Taj Mahal), which remind the audience of another major trajectory in postclassical Indian history, and often reflect the tensions between Islam and Hinduism on the subcontinent. The prominence of Islamic narratives and the Urdu language in Bombay's nationally visible Parsi theater, especially from 1870 to 1910, is a stronger counterpoint to Hindu content in theater.
11. S. L. Bhyrappa, "Mahabharata: My Attempt at a Recreation," in *The Mahabharata Revisited*, ed. R. N. Dandekar (Sahitya Akademi, 1990), 264.
12. Indira Parthasarathy, *Ramanujar: The Life and Ideas of Ramanuja*, trans. T. Sriraman (Oxford University Press, 1997), 6.
13. Adina Ciuguraneau, "History and Myth in Pound's *Cantos*," *British and American Studies* 1 (1996): 100–101.
14. Girish Karnad, *Yayati*, trans. Girish Karnad (Oxford University Press, 2008), vii. All further references to this play appear in the text.
15. Girish Karnad, *Collected Plays* (Oxford University Press, 2017), vol. 3, 3.
16. Mohan Rakesh, *Mohan rakesh rachanavali* (The works of Mohan Rakesh), ed. Jaidev Taneja (Rajkamal, 2011), vol. 3, 91.
17. *The Mahabharata*, trans. and ed. J. A. B. van Buitenen (University of Chicago Press, 1973), vol. 1, 191.
18. *Mahabharata*, 194.
19. Michael Madhusudan Dutt, *Sermista: A Drama in Five Acts* (1859; rpt. A. Pine Educational and Commercial, 1968), ix. All further references to this play appear in the text.
20. Sudipto Chatterjee, *The Colonial Staged: Theatre in Colonial Calcutta* (Seagull, 2007), 107.
21. Karnad's preface to the 2008 translation of *Yayati* describes the one transformative "break" that came his way in 1961: the interest the play generated in G. B. Joshi, the visionary publisher who founded Manohar Granth Mala in the city of Dharwad, and in Kirtinath Kurtkoti, Joshi's principal literary advisor and a leading Kannada critic. Kurtkoti asked Karnad to mail him the script from England, and he "worked on the language . . . which was inevitably wobbly since I had spent my youth preparing to step into the shoes of Eliot and Yeats" (ix). Karnad describes Joshi's decision to publish the play as "an act of immense courage, since there was an even smaller market for drama than for fiction" (ix).
22. "Chandravanshi" means "descended from the moon." The Kauravas, one of the two main branches of the dynastic family in the *Mahabharata*, trace their lineage to the moon as a celestial body, and both Yayati and Pooru belong to this lunar line.
23. After the arrival of talking cinema in India (1931), the use of myth in cultural forms reached an altogether new scale with the development of "mythologicals": full-length feature films in Hindi and many regional languages that were able to deliver fantastic myth-based narratives from Hindu mythology to a mass audience. The synonymy of myth and religion also meant that these films were forms of entertainment as well

as religious experience for the devout. The denial of the "mythological" by Karnad's *Sutradhar* is part of the secularization of myth in *Yayati*.
24. The theatrical strengths of the new version have been tested in a number of productions. Arundhati Raja of Bangalore's Artistes Repertory Theatre directed the draft English translation at the Ravindra Kalakshetra in October 2006, and at Ranga Shankara Theatre in February 2007. The Manipuri adaptation of November 2007 by leading playwright-director Ratan Thiyam was described as a "masterpiece of painting" because of the visual elegance of a large open set with eye-catching wooden surfaces lit with brass lamps. In October 2009 I organized a fully costumed and blocked staged reading as the final event of the 38th Annual Conference on South Asia in Madison (Wisconsin), codirected by Joan Brooks and Barbara Clayton. Enacted by faculty members and graduate students of the Department of Theatre and Drama at the University of Wisconsin, the performance was attended by the playwright himself, who was a keynote speaker at the conference. Two other recent productions of *Yayati* are by Jagriti (Bengaluru, 2017) and Theatre Nisha (Chennai, 2021).
25. In the original Hindi, these plays with historical protagonists appear in the *Mohan rakesh rachanavali* as follows: *Kalinga vijay* 1 (Victory over Kalinga, first version), 2:33–51; *Ashadh ka ek din* (One Day in the Season of Rain, 1958), 2: 389–470; *Laharon ke rajhans* (The royal swans on the waves, 1963), 3: 17–88; *Laharon ke rajhans* (The royal swans on the waves, 1968), 3: 89–170; *Vida nisha* (The night of separation), 4: 119–27; *Kalinga vijay* 2 (Victory over Kalinga, second version), 4: 128–42; and *Raat bitane tak* (Until the night ends), 4: 205–19.
26. In Hindi, the main sources of this "aversion" are the idealized history plays of Jaishankar Prasad, but Rakesh also has in mind here the larger post/colonial nostalgia for India's golden age, in literature, culture, and politics.
27. Rakesh's choice of foundational religious figures as offstage provocateurs is unusual because few prominent *theatrical* works from the past century have taken up this thematic. Western plays that have historical protagonists connected to religion, such as Eliot's *Murder in the Cathedral* (1936), Robert Bolt's *A Man for All Seasons* (1960), and Arthur Miller's *The Crucible* (1953), center on martyrdom, chosen by men whose religious faith finds itself on a collision course with medieval or early modern national politics (embodied in the figure of the king or in a theocracy). All three Anglo-American plays foreground faith and spirituality but address the politics of religion in a fully worldly society. In contrast, Rakesh's "Mahavir" and "Buddha" plays are about the sociology and psychology of religious turmoil in which the political ruler himself is the agent of change, and the change he preaches is a form of total other-worldliness achieved through renunciation. Rakesh also portrays the effects of spiritual turmoil on "real" people who were either contemporaries or later followers of the iconoclastic founders. With its secularized approach to Buddhism, Yukio Mishima's "modern Noh play" *Sotoba Komachi*, included in his 1956 collection of *Five Modern Noh Plays*, could potentially be a suggestive parallel to Rakesh's dramatization of an ancient Sanskrit poem about the Buddha and his circle, but the two works have little in common. Although Mishima takes up the Buddhist concept of *ichinyokan* (sameness and difference in the phenomenal world), the stronger influences on him are those of Nietzschean dualism (the Apollonian versus the Dionysian) and the poetic drama of T. S. Eliot, all refracted through the ravaged environment of postwar Japan. The secularized, reconceptualized, generically varied,

4. MODERNISM, REALISM, AND THE POSTCOLONIAL URBAN PRESENT

and symbolist-modernist theatricalization that Rakesh offers by fleshing out the story of Nanda and Sundari in his Buddha plays appears not to have a close parallel in contemporary theater. In terms of high-profile fictionalizations, the direct representation of figures such as Jesus, Mohammad, and the Buddha has in fact belonged not to drama but to the genres of prose fiction (Salman Rushdie's *The Satanic Verses* [1988]); film (Conrad Rooks's *Siddhartha* [1972], Martin Scorsese's *The Last Temptation of Christ* [1988], Mel Gibson's *The Passion of the Christ* [2004]); and musical theater (Andrew Lloyd Weber's rock-opera *Jesus Christ Superstar* [1970], and Jingoo Lee and Julie Song's *Under the Bodhi Tree* [2017]).

28. Linda Covill, trans., *Handsome Nanda*, by Ashvaghosha (New York University Press and JJC Foundation, 2007), 15–16. All further references to this translation appear in the text.
29. Rakesh notes in his 1968 preface that Shyamang troubled him for a long time, like an unmanageable piece in a board game. But eventually, in the process of writing, he ceased to be "a person . . . [and] turned into an impression" (Rakesh, *Mohan rakesh rachanavali*, vol. 3, 95).
30. No precise information is available about the theater Jalan experienced during his trip, but it is reasonable to speculate that his conclusion was based on the dominant presence of postwar absurdist playwrights in Europe (Beckett, Pinter, Genet, Ionesco) and figures such as Miller, Williams, and Albee in the United States.

4. MODERNISM, REALISM, AND THE POSTCOLONIAL URBAN PRESENT

1. Girish Karnad, "Performance, Meaning, and the Materials of Modern Indian Theatre," *New Theatre Quarterly* 44 (1995): 369.
2. Peter Szondi, "Theory of the Modern Drama, Parts I–II," in *Modern Drama: Critical Concepts in Literary and Cultural Studies*, ed. Martin Puchner (Routledge, 2008), vol. 2, 222; and Mohan Rakesh, "Looking Around as a Playwright," *Sangeet Natak*, no. 3 (October 1966), 18.
3. Rakesh, "Looking Around," 18.
4. *Tritiya ratna* (The third gem, 1855), by the Marathi reformer Jyotiba Phule, is celebrated as the first major play to critique caste-based oppression and to offer education as the means of emancipation for women and "untouchable" communities. Dutt's two Bengali farces of 1860, *Ekei ki bale sabhyata?* (Is this what you call civilization?) and *Budo saliker ghare ron* (The old fool's fads), respectively, satirize young Bengali men for their Westernized boorishness and upper-caste landowners for their immorality and corruption. Harishchandra's best-known anticolonial political allegories in Hindi are *Bharat durdasha* (India's plight, 1875) and *Andher nagari* (Nightmare city, 1881). Gurajada Apparao's *Kanyasulkam* (Girls for sale, 1897, rev. ed. 1909) is a seriocomic approach to the problem of upper-caste older men desiring to marry very young women. Pioneering "social problem" plays in Marathi by Ram Ganesh Gadkari, Bhargavram Vitthal Varerkar, Shridhar V. Vartak, P. K. Atre, and M. G. Rangnekar (1916–1942) are discussed in the section on "Realism and Urban Indian Theater."
5. The avant-garde hostility to nineteenth-century theater is summed up in F. T. Marinetti's blanket condemnation in "The Variety Theatre": "We are deeply disgusted

with the contemporary theatre (verse, prose, and musical) because it vacillates stupidly between historical reconstruction (pastiche or plagiarism) and photographic reproduction of our daily life; a finicking, slow, analytic, and diluted theatre worthy, all in all, of the age of the oil lamp" (in Puchner, *Modern Drama*, vol. 1, 173). Modernism's opposition to the theatricality and strict verisimilitude of realism/naturalism is a well-established critical view, but some recent arguments have proposed realism and naturalism as important precursors to modernism, and even as coeval modes with their own significant history. Claire Warden describes naturalism as an influential force because "it represents a sharp turn in theatre making, a revolutionary reappraisal of the stage" (Claire Warden, "Modernism in European Drama/Theatre," in *The Modernist World*, ed. Stephen Ross and Allana C. Lindgren [Routledge, 2015], 357). Addressing "New Oceanic" locations, David O'Donnell notes that modernism was associated with the "anti-realist European avant-garde" in Australia, New Zealand, and the South Pacific, but it also gained recognition as the first groundbreaking "modern" movement in Pacific theater (David O'Donnell, "Staging Modernity in the 'New Oceania': Modernism in Australian, New Zealand and Pacific Islands Theatre," in Ross and Lindgren, *Modernist World*, 282). The strongest form of the argument for inclusiveness appears in Taxidou's comparison of the Stanislavsky-Meyerhold experiment with Brecht's attacks on naturalism and his quest for a "new realism": "Both the Naturalist and the anti-illusionist traditions form part of the 'new movement' in the theatre. Sometimes for the sake of methodological clarity, and in conjunction with the manifesto fervour of their theoretical works, these schools are defined against each other. They all converge, however, in the figure of the modernist director." (Olga Taxidou, *Modernism and Performance: Jarry to Brecht* [Palgrave Macmillan, 2007], 68.)

Indian theater history adds a new twist to this debate because the opposition to realism comes not from modernists but mainly from those who, like Rabindranath Tagore or the proponents of the "theatre of roots," prefer traditional Indian nonrealist or antirealist conventions of representation.

6. Satyadev Dubey, introduction to Badal Sircar, *Evam Indrajit*, trans. Girish Karnad (Oxford University Press, 1974), v. Sircar's Bengali title was translated as *Evam Indrajit* in every other Indian language, including English, and that translation became so inseparable from the play that I have used it in my discussion as well. *Evam* means "and" in Sanskrit and Hindi and is equivalent to the Bengali *"ebong."*
7. Mahesh Elkunchwar, *Autobiography*, trans. Pratima Kulkarni (Seagull, 1989), vii.
8. Vassili Kolocotroni and Olga Taxidou, eds., *The Edinburgh Dictionary of Modernism* (Edinburgh University Press, 2018), 315.
9. Gustave Courbet, *The Realist Manifesto*, accessed March 10, 2023. https://www.scribd.com/document/370902364/Realist-Manifesto#, 1.
10. William Archer, "*A Doll's House* and the Ibsen Revolution," in Puchner, *Modern Drama*, vol. 1, 95; and Bernard Shaw, "The Technical Novelty in Ibsen's Plays," in Bernard F. Dukore, ed., *Dramatic Theory and Criticism: Greeks to Grotowski* (Holt, Rinehart, and Winston, 1974), 182.
11. Emile Zola, quoted in Eric Bentley, "The Two Traditions of Modern Drama," in Puchner, *Modern Drama*, vol. 2, 82; and Emile Zola, "Naturalism on the Stage," in Puchner, *Modern Drama*, vol. 1, 63.
12. Zola, quoted in Bentley, "Two Traditions," 83.

4. MODERNISM, REALISM, AND THE POSTCOLONIAL URBAN PRESENT

13. Maurice Maeterlinck, "The Modern Drama," in Puchner, *Modern Drama*, vol. 1, 118.
14. As John Gassner, the influential postwar theorist-scholar of modern drama notes, "significant in this concentration on painstakingly represented reality is the veritable passion for *detheatricalizing* dramatic art that seized the theater. The realistic drama is the least theatrical form of drama developed in the Western theatre" (John Gassner, "Forms of Modern Drama," in Puchner, *Modern Drama*, vol. 2, 119).
15. Geörgy Lukács, "The Sociology of Modern Drama," in Puchner, *Modern Drama*, vol. 2, 42.
16. This definition differs from Marx's conception of capitalist and bourgeois as members of a single class that exploits the proletariat, but it encapsulates more accurately the class most frequently portrayed in realist theater, especially in the "classic" realism of Ibsen and Chekhov.
17. Franco Moretti, *The Bourgeois: Between History and Literature* (Verso, 2013), 16.
18. Una Chaudhuri, *Staging Place: The Geography of Modern Drama* (University of Michigan Press, 1995), 8, 10.
19. Raymond Williams, "Excerpts from *Drama from Ibsen to Brecht*," in Puchner, *Modern Drama*, vol. 2, 203, 205.
20. Toril Moi, "Ibsen, Theatre, and the Ideology of Modernism," in Puchner, *Modern Drama*, vol. 2, 309.
21. Amiya Kumar Bagchi, "Reflections on the Nature of the Indian Bourgeoisie," *Social Scientist* 19, nos. 3-4 (March-April 1991): 8.
22. Bagchi, "Reflections," 17.
23. See Ranajit Guha, *Dominance Without Hegemony: History and Power in Colonial India* (Harvard University Press, 1998).
24. Two important essays indicate that late-twentieth-century Indian social scientists closely follow Marx's conflation of capitalist and bourgeois. Suniti Kumar Ghosh's "Indian Bourgeoisie and Imperialism" defines the Indian "big bourgeoisie" as synonymous with Indian "big capital." The capitalists were complicit with the colonial state to some extent, but were transformed into a "national bourgeoisie" by the call of anticolonial nationalism (Suniti Kumar Ghosh, "Indian Bourgeoisie and Imperialism," *Economic and Political Weekly* 23, nos. 45/47 [November 1988]: 2445-46). In "Reflections on the Nature of the Indian Bourgeoisie," Bagchi also focuses on the class of industrial capitalists and their conflicts with labor—the term "bourgeois" appears only once in his essay, on page 4. This conception of the bourgeoisie is even less appropriate for the social texture of Indian realist drama than for its Western equivalents.
25. Emile Zola, "Naturalism in the Theatre," in *Theatre/Theory/Theatre: The Major Critical Texts from Aristotle and Zeami to Soyinka and Havel*, ed. Daniel Gerould (Applause, 2000), 361, 360.
26. In Makarand Sathe's *Socio-Political History of Marathi Theatre: Thirty Nights*, 3 vols. (Oxford University Press, 2015), the typology of colonial plays in Marathi from 1855 to 1920, for instance, includes "musicals," "farces," "cultural nationalist plays" (using either prose or the musical form), "reformist social plays," "political plays," "sociopolitical plays and historical plays," and "experimental theatre" (1: passim). All further references to this multivolume edition appear in the text.
27. The case of Bertolt Brecht belongs to a special category in this context. In one perspective, Brecht's enormous influence in India as the theorist of anti-Aristotelian

4. MODERNISM, REALISM, AND THE POSTCOLONIAL URBAN PRESENT

epic theater and as the leading twentieth-century practitioner of political theater overshadows every other figure from modern Western drama, including Ibsen. But in another perspective, Brecht's influence produces mainly translations and adaptations of his work in various Indian languages, rather than original "Brechtian" plays. In contrast, plays in the realist mode of Ibsen now constitute the largest body of original work in the Indian languages. Brecht is iconic, but the realist models have proved to be more generative.

28. Bhargavram Vitthal Varerkar, *Majha nataki sansar* (My theater world), (Swastik, 1941–1952), vol. 1, 464. Quoted in English translation in Shanta Gokhale, *Playwright at the Centre: Marathi Drama from 1843 to the Present* (Seagull, 2000), 68.
29. The move from Shakespeare to Ibsen is vital for the "modernization" of Marathi theater in the 1930s and 1940s, but the playwrights encounter Ibsen mainly on the page at this time; there is virtually no opportunity for staging his plays in translation. Beginning in 1952, this situation changes radically, with landmark productions of *A Doll's House*, *An Enemy of the People*, *The Wild Duck*, and *Ghosts* by directors such as Sombhu Mitra, Shyamanand Jalan, Satyadev Dubey, B. V. Karanth, and Jabbar Patel in Bengali, Hindi, and Marathi. Ibsen is also a staple in university, community, and amateur group productions, and since 2008 the Norwegian Embassy in New Delhi has sponsored an annual Ibsen Festival.
30. Atre's subtitles, for example, identify specific works as "three-act play," "three-act social play," "social play," "comic play," and so on. He is also the author of several history plays, five *sangeet nataks*, and adaptations of Shudraka's *Mrichchhakatika* and Molière's *The Miser*. Such an eclectic array of genres and sources is a new phenomenon in urban theater, again allowing old and new models to coexist.
31. Gokhale, *Playwright at the Centre*, 74, 77.
32. Quoted in Sathe, *Socio-Political History*, vol. 1, 436.
33. Quoted in Gokhale, *Playwright at the Centre*, 87.
34. The irony of this half-hearted approach is that in several modern Indian languages Ibsen is second only to Shakespeare as a Western influence on "serious" playwrights. Karnad provides a canny account of the impasse by pointing out that individualism was the mainstay of Western realist drama after Ibsen, but

> in India, despite the large urban population, there really has never been a bourgeoisie with its faith in individualism as the ultimate value. [Moreover], From Ibsen to Albee, the living room has symbolized all that is valuable to the Western bourgeoisie.... But nothing of consequence ever happens or is supposed to happen in an Indian living room! It is the no-man's land, the empty, almost defensive front the family presents to the world outside.... The living room as the location of dramatic action made nonsense of the very social problems the playwright set out to analyze.

> In Karnad's view, the playwrights misunderstood the geography of their own homes because "the conceptual tools they were using to analyze India's problems were as secondhand and unrealistic as the European parlor.... The refusal to go beyond the living room exactly mirrored the reluctance of these Westernized, upper-caste writers to go to the heart of the issues they were representing" (Girish Karnad, "In Search of a New Theatre," in *Contemporary India: Essays on the Use of Tradition*, ed. Carla Borden [Oxford University Press, 1985], 100–101).

4. MODERNISM, REALISM, AND THE POSTCOLONIAL URBAN PRESENT

35. Toward the end of his essay, Dharwadker also describes *Untouchable* as "the most typical novel of idealistic realism in modernist literature," one that brings to English the "idealist realism" of Munshi Premchand, India's preeminent twentieth-century author of Hindi and Urdu fiction (Vinay Dharwadker, "The Modernist Novel in India: Paradigms and Practices," in *A History of the Indian Novel in English*, ed. Ulka Anjaria [Cambridge University Press, 2015], 117–18.). In postindependence *theater*, however, modernist realism is very much the opposite of idealism.
36. Gokhale, *Playwright at the Centre*, 102.
37. Makarand Sathe, "Editorial," in *The Vijay Tendulkar Omnibus*, ed. Makarand Sathe (Arvind Kumar, 2007), 11; and Sathe, *Socio-Political History*, vol. 2, 556.
38. Pushpa Bhave, "Vijay Tendulkar: A Study," in *Contemporary Indian Theatre: Interviews with Playwrights and Directors*, ed. Paul Jacob (Sangeet Natak Akademi, 1989), 145.
39. Tendulkar's interest in the verisimilitude possible only in theater is reflected in his comment that "A playwright has to be conscious of the strength of his medium in totality which includes the visual aspect, and [so he] must not rely only on words" (*PTT*, 27).
40. Among Tendulkar's major plays, the following deal with the agonizing dissolution of long-standing relationships: *Shantata! Court chalu ahe* (Silence! the court is in session, 1967), *Mitrachi goshta* (A friend's story, 1981), *Kamala* (1981), and *Kanyadaan* (The gift of a daughter, 1983).
41. Vijay Tendulkar, *Kanyadaan*, trans. Gowri Ramnarayan (Oxford University Press, 1996), 12.
42. Habib Tanvir, "The Indian Experiment," in *Theatre India* (Kerala Sangeet Natak Akademi, 1977), 6.
43. Mahesh Dattani, "Three Little Slices of Indian Urban Life," in *City Plays* (Seagull, 2004), v.
44. Dattani, "Three Little Slices," xii.
45. Mahesh Elkunchwar, "An Interview by Ashish Rajadhyaksha," in *Contemporary Indian Theatre*, 165.
46. Elkunchwar, "Interview," 175.
47. Elkunchwar, "Interview," 165.
48. Mohan Rakesh, *Mohan Rakesh ke sampurna natak*, ed. Nemichandra Jain (Rajpal, 1993), 332.
49. There are other equally prominent plays in which both the evocation and disruption of realism are core objectives. In Sircar's *Baki itihas* (The rest of history, Bengali, 1965), a middle-class couple in Calcutta hears about the suicide of a distant acquaintance and constructs two complete, alternative scenarios to explain that act of self-destruction. Rye's *Kumar ni agashi* (Kumar's terrace, Gujarati, 1975) alternates in time between a social gathering in the present and events in the past to construct contradictory accounts of the events leading up to the protagonist's suicide while he was a college student. In Elkunchwar's *Pratibimba* (Reflection, Marathi, 1987), a nameless paying guest in an unnamed city, the Woman who attends to him and a Girl who visits them discover in succession that they cannot see their reflection in the mirror. In Dattani's first play, *Where There's a Will* (English, 1988), the ghost of a dead patriarch refuses to relinquish his tyrannical hold on his son's family, discovering only near the end that his daughter-in-law engineered his death by withholding critical heart medication. This is still a

selective list: even this overtly experimental strain of modernist realism represents a capacious genre in late-twentieth-century theater.
50. Martin Puchner, *Stage Fright: Modernism, Anti-Theatricality, and Drama* (Johns Hopkins Press, 2002) 7, 143.
51. Badal Sircar, *Evam Indrajit*, trans. Girish Karnad (Oxford University Press, 1974), 12–13. All further references to this play appear in the text.
52. Thomas Macaulay, "Minute on Indian Education," in *Selected Writings*, ed. John Clive and Thomas Pinney (University of Chicago Press, 1972), 249.
53. Badal Sircar, *On Theatre: Selected Essays* (Seagull, 2009), 1.
54. Since the late-nineteenth century, the city of Calcutta has been a continuous subject of realist representation in long and short fiction, poetry, and cinema. However, the atmosphere of entrapment, despair, and irony that Sircar creates in *Evam indrajit* is most closely matched in Ritwik Ghatak's film *Meghe dhaka tara* (The cloud-capped star, 1960), and Satyajit Ray's *Pratidwandi* (The adversary, 1970), both classics of Indian art cinema.
55. The Hindu caste system adds another dimension of privilege. The last names of all four male characters—Ghosh, Bose, Sen, and Ray—belong to the higher castes, like the playwright's own last name, which is usually spelled "Sarkar." Only the Writer remains nameless in the play.
56. "*Keechad mein kamal*," or "the lotus blossom in the middle of muck," is a proverbial compliment to those who remain untouched by the corruption surrounding them.
57. Meghnad was the oldest son of Ravana, the demon king of Lanka who became embroiled in a war with Lord Rama (the hero of the *Ramayana*) after abducting Rama's wife, Sita, and keeping her captive in a garden in his city. In the context of modern Bengali literature, Indrajit is an especially charged name because Michael Madhusudan Dutt's *Meghnad badha* (1861), regarded as the finest epic in modern Bengali, is based on the slaying of Meghnad on the battlefield by Lakshman, Rama's younger brother.
58. For example, commenting on the pairing of "Indrajit and Manasi" in Act 1, the Writer notes that "Hordes of Indrajits and Manasis have appeared from all levels of society, in all forms, with all possible names . . . and it's difficult to say what joys and sorrows, what meetings and partings, what pride and hatred, what mental blows and reactions have shaped their plays. The love of Indrajit and Manasi. An immortal dramatic theme . . ." (5–16). At the beginning of Act 2, he notes that "The world is an office. Like this one. A lot of business is transacted here—very important business. A lot of people work here—Amal, Vimal, Kamal, and Indrajit."
59. T. S. Eliot, *The Poems of T. S. Eliot*, vol. 1, ed. Christopher Ricks and Jim McCue (Farrar, Strauss, and Giroux, 2015), 122.
60. Eliot, *Poems*, 179.
61. Eliot, *Poems*, 185.
62. Mahesh Elkunchwar, *Atmakatha ani pratibimba* (Autobiography and reflection) (Mauj Prakashan, 1989), 1. Unless specified otherwise, all further references to *Atmakatha* are to this Marathi edition and appear in the text.
63. Elkunchwar, *Autobiography*, trans. Pratima Kulkarni (Seagull, 1989), vii.
64. The name of this culturally prominent city in Maharashtra means "pure" or "righteous." In chapter 5, the irony of the name is a prominent part of my discussion of Tendulkar's play *Ghashiram kotwal* (Constable Ghashiram, 1972), which is set in Pune.

4. MODERNISM, REALISM, AND THE POSTCOLONIAL URBAN PRESENT

65. Judith E. Barlow, "Into the Foxhole: Feminism, Realism, and Lillian Hellman," in *Realism and the American Dramatic Tradition*, ed. William W. Demastes (University of Alabama Press, 1996), 156.
66. Sue-Ellen Case, *Feminism and Theatre* (Methuen, 1988), 124.
67. Aparna Bhargava Dharwadker, *Theatres of Independence: Drama, Theory, and Urban Performance in India Since 1947* (University of Iowa Press, 2005), 329.
68. Other relevant facts about Marathi are that it is the third most commonly spoken language in India and the eleventh most commonly spoken language in the world. In the modern period, Marathi has been a fully developed, autonomous medium with the same status as a modern European language, in addition to being part of the complex interactive system of twenty-two official languages now recognized in the Indian constitution.
69. On June 12, 1975, the Allahabad High Court, with jurisdiction in the northern state of Uttar Pradesh, disqualified Prime Minister Indira Gandhi's election to the national Parliament on the grounds of electoral malpractice. Instead of resigning, she declared a state of Internal Emergency on the midnight of June 24/25, suspended the national constitution, jailed opposition leaders, and turned India into a police state. For the next nineteen months (the Emergency ended on March 21, 1977), courageous opposition to her actions was a moral test for writers, artists, and intellectuals, among other groups. In *Atmakatha*, the socialist Uttara goes to prison during the Emergency, whereas Raja, the former "freedom fighter," does not.
70. In 2000, the second number of *Theatre India*, the National School of Drama's English journal, was a special issue on the topic "Women That Men Created," containing essays by Paramita Banerjee, Dilip Basu, A. Mangai, Maya Pandit, Catherine Thankamma, and Kinnari Vohra. For a discussion of the issue of "female authorship" in modern Indian theater, see Aparna Bhargava Dharwadker, *A Poetics of Modernity: Indian Theatre Theory, 1850 to the Present* (Oxford University Press, 2019), xcii–xcvi, and the essays by Amal Allana, Kirti Jain, and Anuradha Kapur included in this volume.
71. Mahesh Dattani, *Tara: A Play in Two Acts* (Ravi Dayal, 1990), 2. All further references to this play appear in the text.
72. In the introduction and chapter 1, I addressed fully the cultural politics of English as a literary and theatrical medium in India and the Indian diaspora, and its deterministic effects on the study of Indian modernisms.
73. At a 1994 seminar, when Dattani was asked why he does not write in his "own language," he responded, "I do" (Nandi Bhatia, "'Provincializing English,' Globalizing Indian English Drama," *Postcolonial Text* 10, nos. 3–4 [2015], 4). In a talk titled "Contemporary Indian Theatre and Its Relevance" (2001), he states: "I would like to make it clear that I am not speaking here today as a representation of the English language theatre in our country. I am here to move beyond this very limited definition of the theatre that I see myself involved with. . . . The conventional way of defining by linguistic and regional divides does not work for creating artistic identities any more" (*POM*, 440, 442). Bhatia's "'Provincializing English'" contains a lucid discussion of the social, political, and aesthetic issues involved in the use of English as a medium in Indian writing, especially in drama. Critics who accept Dattani's choices tend to agree that his Anglophone plays represent a genuine breakthrough in connecting language to experience and have rendered theoretical speculations about the "appropriateness" of English as a theater language in India more or less moot.

4. MODERNISM, REALISM, AND THE POSTCOLONIAL URBAN PRESENT

74. *The Laws of Manu*, trans. Wendy Doniger, with Brian K. Smith (Penguin Classics, 1992), 115.
75. The stylized space of home and its environment in *Tara* indicates that the representation of Bombay-as-setting is also slanted by the extraordinary nature of the narrative. Dattani's plays usually present a layered social milieu in a metropolitan location (Bangalore or Bombay), and the city itself functions as an active agent in the characters' lives. In *Tara* the presence of adult neighbors and two girls named Nalini and Prema is referred to, but only Roopa actually appears. Her morbid curiosity about Tara and Chandan's prosthetic legs, resentment against their precocity, fake friendliness, and callow gossip come to symbolize the stigmatization of disability, more disturbing because it is being mouthed by a child. Later, when she attacks them viciously as "freaks," her character takes on allegorical, witchlike qualities. Beyond this coarsening of childhood, the disfigurement of Chandan and Tara disfigures the city and makes it a dystopian postcolonial site of illness, family dysfunction, and antipathy—a technologically advanced but pitiless machine which destroys the siblings. The antithesis to Bombay is diasporic London, the refuge where Chandan can dissolve his family bonds. But even if his flight is made possible by privilege, it is clear by the end that the burden of the past has destroyed him as a human being.
76. The male Indian population is currently 51.61 percent of the total number, and the problem of unwanted girl children is shared with China, where female feticide and infanticide during the years of the "one child policy" took on especially draconian forms. According to 2021 figures, 51.06 percent of the Chinese population is male. The documentary film, "It's a Girl: The Three Deadliest Words in the World" (2012), directed by Evan Grae Davis, focuses mainly on female feticide/infanticide in India and China.

5. MODERNISM AND TRADITION

1. To avoid unnecessarily cumbersome wording, I have used "tradition" and "traditional" as umbrella terms throughout this chapter when my reference is to the full range of precolonial nonurban forms. However, one or more forms are named specifically when that is necessary for clarity.
2. Habib Tanvir provides the playwright's perspective on this process of discovery when he notes that "The IPTA provided my first schooling in theatre, especially in the folk forms of performing arts," and "made the first big organised effort to align the theatre with the peasantry and the new Indian working class whose cultural base once again was rural and agrarian" (quoted in Anjum Katyal, *Habib Tanvir: Towards an Inclusive Theatre* [Sage, 2012], 23).
3. Maulana Abul Kalam Azad, "Opening Address," Sangeet Natak Akademi Inauguration, 1953, https://sangeetnatak.gov.in/sections/drama.
4. These include two early tracts: Baldoon Dhingra's *A National Theatre for India* (Padma, 1944) and Kamaladevi Chattopadhyay's *Towards a National Theatre* (All India Women's Conference, 1945); the proceedings of the "Drama Seminar" organized by the SNA (April 1956); the Report of the "Seminar on Contemporary Playwriting and Play Production" organized by the Bharatiya Natya Sangh (Indian Theatre Guild, March-April 1961); a ten-year program of traditional performances,

5. MODERNISM AND TRADITION

festivals, and exhibitions in and around Delhi sponsored by the SNA (1965–1975); SNA's "Roundtable on the Contemporary Relevance of Traditional Theatre," reproduced in its journal *Sangeet Natak*, no. 21 (July–September 1971): 5–74; and the special double issue of *Sangeet Natak* titled "The Traditional Idiom in Contemporary Theatre," nos. 77–78 (1985). Through its multiyear "Scheme of Assistance to Young Theatre Workers" (1984–1991), the SNA also sponsored four regional festivals and one national festival every year for artists "engaged with exploring and developing a theatre idiom indigenous in character, inspired by the folk/traditional theatre of the country" (*Annual Report for 1986–87* [Sangeet Natak Akademi, 1987], 39), and in the process galvanized several major careers in the theater. In alphabetical order, directors supported by this scheme who went on to prominent and active careers include Devendra Raj Ankur, Bhanu Bharati, Neelam Mansingh Chowdhry, Probir Guha, Jayadev Hattangadi, C. R. Jambe, B. Jayashree, Bansi Kaul, Waman Kendre, A. Mangai, Prasanna, K. S. Rajendran, and Ratan Thiyam.

5. Kamaladevi, "National Theatre," *Natya* 1, no. 1 (1956): 8–9.
6. *Sangeet Natak Akademi Report, 1953–1958* (Sangeet Natak Akademi, 1958), 31.
7. *Contemporary Playwriting and Play Production: Report of a Seminar, March 31–April 2, 1961* (Bharatiya Natya Sangh, 1961), 2.
8. *Sangeet Natak*, "Roundtable on Contemporary Relevance," 5, 6. All further references to this special issue of the journal appear in the text, and when necessary, the proceedings are referred to under the title "Roundtable."
9. Nemichandra Jain, "Some Notes on the Use of Tradition in Theatre," *Sangeet Natak*, nos. 77–78 (July–December 1985): 9. This special double issue contained an editorial and opening essay by Jain, and sixteen essays by other contributors, many of which are referenced here.
10. Suresh Awasthi, "In Defence of the Theatre of Roots," *Sangeet Natak*, nos. 77–78 (1985): 85.
11. This is an appropriate moment to comment briefly on the fundamental difference between T. S. Eliot's still influential view of the cultural past in "Tradition and the Individual Talent" (1919) and the approach to tradition that emerges in cultural-nationalist discourses in India, especially those that focus on the vast legacy of traditional performance forms. For Eliot, tradition is the cumulative poetic legacy that enables the individual poet to connect idiosyncratically with a usable past, and to appear most original when "the dead poets, his ancestors," speak through him. The poetic faculty mediating tradition is the historical sense, which involves "a perception, not only of the pastness of the past, but of its presence. . . . a sense of the timeless as well as of the temporal and of the timeless and of the temporal together." Such an approach connects the past inalienably to the present, and vice versa: "what makes a writer traditional. . . . is at the same time what makes a writer most acutely conscious of his place in time, of his contemporaneity." Eliot cautions against the reduction of tradition to a "blind or timid adherence" to the successes of the past, because its function in the present is to be an energizing force that allows the poet to circumvent the mere expression of personality and personal emotion in art ("Tradition and the Individual Talent," accessed May 17, 2021, http://www.bartleby.com/200/sw4.html). In contrast, proponents of the theatre of roots posit "tradition" as the counterpoint of "modernity" in a dialectic that sets up *oppositions* between the past and the present, realism and antirealism, individuality and communality,

and the city and the village: tradition appears as immutable and sacrosanct, and the responsibility of artists in the present is to embrace it. The remainder of this chapter demonstrates that modernist playwrights neither view nor use tradition according to these prescriptions.

12. M. K. Raina, "Two Approaches to Tradition," *Sangeet Natak*, nos. 77–78 (July–December 1985): 31.
13. K. N. Panikkar, "An Interview by K. S. Narayana Pillai," in *Contemporary Indian Theatre: Interviews with Playwrights and Directors*, ed. Paul Jacob (Sangeet Natak Akademi, 1989), 62.
14. Naa Muthuswami, "The Challenge of Tradition," *Sangeet Natak*, nos. 77–78 (July–December 1985): 80.
15. For instance, it is very important to Jain that "for the first time after almost a thousand years, an Indian theatrical form seems to be emerging," and his focus is on the historic national-cultural import, not the possible topical resonance, of that form. In fact, he is concerned about the forms being diluted and distorted whenever there is "any attempt to draw upon them for contemporary experience" ("Some Notes," 12). Jain's ideal conception is that of strong plays with mythic or ritualistic subject matter, skilled directors and performers, and "playwrights with a serious social vision who have understanding and insight into the *aesthetics* and *methods* of our traditional theatres" (13; emphasis added). In defining key features of the "theatre of roots" in his essay, Awasthi notes its emphasis on nonproscenium staging, rigorous stylization, the "urge to use the actor's body," and the theatrical transformation of written scripts into performance texts ("In Defence," 86–89, 90–92). It is difficult not to conclude from these discussions that the theater being theorized is significant primarily for aesthetic and ideological effects: its leading proponents do not explain what the theater is *about* in narrative and thematic terms, or how it connects to life in the present.
16. G. P. Deshpande, "The Fetish of Folk and Classic," *Sangeet Natak*, nos. 77–78 (July–December 1985): 50.
17. Chandrashekhar Kambar, "Folk Theatre as I See It," *Sangeet Natak*, nos. 77–78 (July–December, 1985): 39.
18. Chandrashekhar Kambar, "An Interview by Kirtinath Kurtkoti," in *Contemporary Indian Theatre*, 22.
19. Panikkar, "Interview," 59.
20. G. Shankara Pillai, "Traditional Idiom and Modern Theatre," *Sangeet Natak*, nos. 77–78 (July–December, 1985): 46.
21. Girish Karnad, Introduction, *Three Plays*, trans. Girish Karnad (Oxford University Press, 1994), 11.
22. Pillai, "Traditional Idiom," 45.
23. Samik Bandyopadhyay, "The New Karnas of Manipur," *Seagull Theatre Quarterly*, nos. 14–15 (June-September 1997): 74.
24. Arjun Appadurai, afterword to *Gender, Genre, and Power in South Asian Expressive Traditions*, ed. Arjun Appadurai, Frank J. Korom, and Maragaret A. Mills (University of Pennsylvania Press, 1991), 467.
25. Appadurai et al., introduction to *Gender, Genre and Power*, 23.
26. Gloria Goodwin Raheja and Ann Grodzins Gold, *Listen to the Heron's Words: Reimagining Gender and Kinship in North India* (University of California Press, 1994), 193.
27. See Anjali Bagwe, *Of Woman Caste: The Experience of Gender in Rural India* (London: Zed Books, 1995); Gloria Goodwin Raheja, ed., *Songs, Stories, Lives: Gendered*

5. MODERNISM AND TRADITION

Dialogues and Cultural Critique (Kali for Women, 2003); and P. Mary Vidya Porselvi, *Nature, Culture, Gender: Rereading the Folktale* (Routledge, 2016).
28. Girish Karnad, "In Search of a New Theatre," in *Contemporary India: Essays on the Use of Tradition*, ed. Carla Borden (Oxford University Press, 1985), 14.
29. C. N. Ramachandran, "Folk Theatre and Social Structures: Tentative Comments," in *Drama as Form of Art and Theatre*, ed. C. D. Narasimhaiah and C. N. Srinath (Dhvanyaloka, 1993), 21.
30. Appadurai et al., *Gender, Genre, and Power*, 8. For a discussion of "urban folk plays" that place women at the center as subjects and objects of desire, see Aparna Bhargava Dharwadker, *Theatres of Independence: Drama, Theory, and Urban Performance in India Since 1947* (University of Iowa Press, 2005), 327–51.
31. Amitav Roy, "Folk Is What Sells Well," in *Rasa: The Indian Performing Arts in the Last Twenty-Five Years*, ed. Ananda Lal and Chidananda Dasgupta (Anamika Kala Sangam, 1995), 11.
32. Raina, "Two Approaches," 29.
33. Bansi Kaul, "Tradition All Around Us," *Sangeet Natak*, nos. 77–78 (July–December, 1985): 22.
34. Pillai, "Traditional Idiom," 43.
35. Kaul, "Tradition," 23.
36. Deshpande, "Fetish," 49.
37. The Shiv Sena (literally, the army of Shiva) is a Maharashtra-based Hindu fundamentalist party that was founded by Bal Thackeray in 1966 and has been very influential in the politics of the cities of Pune and Bombay. "Shiv" refers both to Lord Shiva, the god of destruction in the Hindu trinity, and to Shivaji, the late-seventeenth-century Maratha king who challenged the power of the Mughals and had his most important fort near Pune. Opposition to communism and to religions other than Hinduism is an important part of the Sena's platform.
38. "Vijay Tendulkar: The Man Who Wanted to Shoot Narendra Modi," *Daily News & Analysis*, May 19, 2008, https://www.dnaindia.com/india/report-vijay-tendulkar-the-man-who-wanted-to-shoot-narendra-modi-1165289.
39. Subuhi Jiwani, "Vijay Tendulkar Is a Scathing Interpreter of Maladies," Daily News Analysis, *The Times of India*, October 7, 2005, https://www.dnaindia.com/analysis/report-vijay-tendulkar-is-a-scathing-interpreter-of-maladies-4810.
40. Vijay Tendulkar, "*Lekhak ka vaktavya*" (author's statement) in *Vijay Tendulkar* (Katha, 2001), 132. The statement appears in this volume in Hindi translation, and I have translated the excerpts used here.
41. Tendulkar, "*Lekhak*," 132–33.
42. Tendulkar, "*Lekhak*," 132.
43. Tendulkar, "*Lekhak*," 133.
44. Samik Bandyopadhyay, Introduction to *Ghashiram Kotwal* by Vijay Tendulkar, trans. Jayant Karve and Eleanor Zelliott (Seagull, 1986), v.
45. Manoj Bhise, "A Dialogue on *Ghashiram kotwal*," in *Vijay Tendulkar's Plays: An Anthology of Recent Criticism*, ed. V. M. Madge (Pencraft International, 2007), 146.
46. Vijay Tendulkar, *Ghashiram kotwal*, 5th ed. (Popular Prakashan, 1995), 1. All further references to the play are to this Marathi edition and appear in the text.
47. These leaders were not born in Pune, but they spent a substantial part of their adult lives there and were deeply influenced by its culture. They also pursued very different styles of leadership, but their common association with Pune creates a political

5. MODERNISM AND TRADITION

significance for the city that makes the comparison valid in the particular context of my argument.

48. Tendulkar's public spat with Gujarat Chief Minister Narendra Modi after the communal carnage in the town of Godhra (February 2002) is perhaps the clearest example of his opposition to militant Hindu nationalism. He later placed his comments about wanting to shoot Modi in perspective by saying that they were an expression of "spontaneous anger, which I never see as a solution to anything. Anger doesn't solve problems." Even Tendulkar's admirers will concede that a play like *Ghashiram kotwal* is a far more effective and enduring cultural statement than the ill-conceived political controversy.

49. In a published interview with Shirish Pai and Priya Tendulkar, the playwright clarified that his intention in *Ghashiram kotwal* was not to make an intervention in the "elite Marathi sangeet natak" tradition, but to draw from "various forms of folk theatre which have historical legends as their subject. This is the reason why the musical element in Ghashiram is closer to folk theatre" than to the *sangeet natak*. Tendulkar mentions the "Indian and foreign musical plays" he had seen earlier as additional influences, but emphasizes that the form of *Ghashiram* owes most to folk theater traditions in Maharashtra that he had experienced first hand ("Samvad Tendulkaranshi" [A dialogue with Tendulkar], in *Sahityatun satyakade: vijay tendulkar yanchya nivadaka sahityacha sangraha* [Through literature towards the truth: selected literary writings of Vijay Tendulkar] [Dimple, 1988], 511). The musical experience of the play is therefore scrupulously regional.

50. Neeraj Malik and Javed Malick, eds., *Habib Tanvir: Reflections and Reminiscences* (SAHMAT, 2010), 5.

51. Habib Tanvir, "Journey Into Theatre," *Nukkad Janam Samvad* 7, nos. 23–26 (April 2004–March 2005): 103.

52. Sadanand Menon, "Reinventing the Political in Theatre," in Malik and Malick, *Habib Tanvir*, 45; and Prasanna, "The True Significance of Habib Tanvir," in Malik and Malick, *Habib Tanvir*, 28.

53. Anuradha Kapur, Foreword to Anjum Katyal, *Habib Tanvir*, x, ix.

54. *Adivasi* ("first" or "original" inhabitant) is the Hindi word for "tribal," and I have used it throughout this chapter as interchangeable with the English word because it is the standard term of reference for tribal populations across India's major Indo-European languages.

55. Habib Tanvir, *The Living Tale of Hirma*, trans. Anjum Katyal and Prabha Katyal (Seagull, 2005), 2. This translation carries a preface by Tanvir titled "A Dilemma of Democracy" (1–4), and a review of the play by Safdar Hashmi titled "Habib Tanvir's Latest Play: *Hirma ki amar kahani*" (66–69). It is cited hereafter in the text as *LTH*.

56. Pravir Chandra published under his own imprint a book in English titled *I Pravir, the Adivasi God* (ASIN: B00FG6GYWG), which served as the basis of a twenty-four-minute documentary with the same title, directed by Vivek Kumar and released in 2022. Tanvir notes in the preface to the English translation of his play that this assumption of godhood was not uncommon: "tribal chiefs frequently believed themselves to be messiahs" (*LTH*, 2).

57. See Nandini Sundar, *Subalterns and Sovereigns: An Anthropological History of Bastar, 1854–1996* (Oxford University Press, 1997), 191–233, for a detailed scholarly account of Pravir Chandra's life and death.

5. MODERNISM AND TRADITION

58. Geographically, this population is so widely distributed across India that Punjab and Haryana are the only states in the country (out of a total of twenty-eight) that do not have a measurable adivasi presence.
59. "Ministry of Tribal Affairs, Government of India," accessed July 10, 2023, https://tribal.nic.in/. In *India's Scheduled Areas: Untangling Governance, Law and Politics*, ed. Varsha Bhagat-Ganguly and Sujit Kumar (Routledge, 2020), the editors acknowledge that "Scheduled Areas are often identified by their geographical isolation, primitive economies, and relatively egalitarian and closely knit society. Irrespective of the constitutional provision for governance and a mandate of devolution of power in terms of funds, functions, and functionaries, the backwardness of these areas has remained a challenge" (i).
60. The continuation of the fraught relationship between adivasi populations and the machinery of the nation-state is evident in studies such as *Social Exclusion and Adverse Inclusion: Development and Deprivation of Adivasis in India*, ed. Dev Nathan and Virginius Xaxa (Oxford University Press, 2012); *Exclusion, Discrimination, and Stratification: Tribes in Contemporary India*, ed. N. K. Das (Rawat, 2013); *Development and Discontent in Tribal India*, ed. Yatindra Singh Sisodia and Tapas Kumar Dalapati (Rawat, 2015); *India's Scheduled Areas: Untangling Governance, Law and Politics*, ed. Bhagat-Ganguly and Kumar (Routledge, 2020); and *Disadvantaged Tribes of India: Regional Concerns*, ed. V. Srinivasa Rao (Rawat, 2021).
61. Thirty percent of the population of Chhattisgarh, which became an independent state in November 2000, is adivasi (about nine million), and about one third of this number live in the large district of Bastar, which is 70 percent adivasi.
62. For a comprehensive chronological listing of Tanvir's works for the theater in all categories, see Katyal, *Habib Tanvir*, 158–65.
63. In Hindi and its variants, "*sasural*" means the home of one's parents-in-law ("*sasurar*" is Tanvir's dialectal variant), and "*damad*" means son-in-law. As a postindependence classic, *Charandas chor*, which won the Fringe First Award at Edinburgh in 1982, has had the same extraordinary reception as Tendulkar's *Ghashiram kotwal*.
64. Habib Tanvir, "Brecht for One Producer," *Enact* 15 (1968).
65. Prateek, *Brecht in India: The Poetics and Politics of Transcultural Theatre* (Routledge, 2021), 111.
66. "Tanvir ka safarnama" (Tanvir's travelogue), directed by Ranjan Kamath (Natakvalas Performance Arts, 2007), 00:20.
67. Habib Tanvir, *Hirma ki amar kahani* (Pustakayan, 1990), 40–47. Cited hereafter in the text as *Hirma*.
68. In 1855, the British colonial government instituted the Indian Civil Service as an elite cadre of administrators, recruited through competitive exams that were held only in London until the 1920s. Indians first entered the service after World War I and represented the native administrative elite until independence. In 1951 the ICS became the Indian Administrative Service, which retains the older associations of entrenched bureaucratic power.
69. Although the first Maoist uprising in India had taken place in 1967, the Communist Party of India-Maoist was formed only in 2004, with the merger of the Communist Party of India-Marxist-Leninist (CP-ML), the People's War Group, and the Maoist Communist Centre of India (MCCI). In 2009, the party was designated a terrorist organization in India under the Unlawful Activities Prevention Act.

5. MODERNISM AND TRADITION

70. Sumanta Banerjee, "From Naxalbari to Chhattisgarh: Half-a-Century of Maoist Journey in India," *Southern Social Movements Newswire*, June 15, 2017, https://www.cetri.be/From-Naxalbari-to-Chhattisgarh?lang=fr. Banerjee expresses a widely held view when he notes that "the Indian state—whether ruled by the Congress or the present Bharatiya Janata Party (BJP)—has been consistently following a policy of belligerent militarist repression against the Naxalite movement, despite repeated warnings by its own agencies that what needed to be done was to redress the economic and social inequities."
71. Wikipedia, "April 2010 Maoist Attack in Dantewada," accessed August 15, 2023, https://en.wikipedia.org/wiki/April_2010_Maoist_attack_in_Dantewada.

CONCLUSION: COSMO-MODERNISM AND THEATER IN RETROSPECT

1. In the larger domain of twentieth-century Indian writing, especially in poetry and fiction, modern/ist critical attitudes toward self-glorifying national narratives emerged during the 1920s. The strident anticolonialism of late-colonial commercial theater, however, continued to highlight cultural-nationalist narratives. In drama and theater, disenchantment and alienation set in closer to the event of independence and the experience of new nationhood in the 1940s, and modernist portrayals of India's past and present moved decisively from the heroic to the ironic register during the following decade.
2. Homi K. Bhabha, "The Vernacular Cosmopolitan," in *Voices of the Crossing: The Impact of Britain on Writers from Asia, the Caribbean, and Africa*, ed. Ferdinand Dennis and Naseem Khan (Serpent's Tail, 2000), 133–42; and Kwame Anthony Appiah, "Rooted Cosmopolitanism," in *The Ethics of Identity* (Princeton University Press, 2005), 213–72.
3. Prominent Indian productions of foreign plays in translation during the 1950 to 2000 period are documented in Aparna Bhargava Dharwadker, *Theatres of Independence: Drama, Theory, and Urban Performance in India Since 1947* (University of Iowa Press, 2005), 420–33.
4. "Staging Transitions: Theatre of the 90s in India," Alkazi Theatre Archives: Notes from the Archive 2021–22 (Alkazi Foundation for the Arts, 2022), 2, 1.
5. There is widespread agreement now among those committed to democracy and secularism that all of these problems have worsened under the repressive and discriminatory policies of Prime Minister Narendra Modi's Hindu nationalist BJP government, which has been in power since 2014. The historian Maya Jasanaoff's opinion piece in the *New York Times* on the occasion of Modi's controversial state visit to the United States in June 2023, titled "Narendra Modi Is Not Who America Thinks He Is," offers a sobering overview directed not only at "Western commentators enthusing about the 'new India'" but at concerned general readers.

> Armed with a sharp-edged doctrine of Hindu nationalism, Mr. Modi has presided over the nation's broadest assault on democracy, civil society and minority rights in at least 40 years. He has delivered prosperity and national pride to some, and authoritarianism and repression of many others that

CONCLUSION

should disturb us all.... Muslim history has been torn from national textbooks, cities with Islamic eponyms renamed and India's only Muslim-majority state, Jammu and Kashmir, stripped of its autonomy.... The share of women in the formal work force stands at around a paltry 20 percent and has shrunk during Mr. Modi's tenure. The share of wealth held by the top 1 percent has grown since he took office and is now 40.5 percent, thanks to crony capitalism resembling the Russian oligarchy's. Unemployment is rising, the cost of basic food is surging, and government investment in health care is stagnating. (Maya Jasanoff, "Narendra Modi Is Not Who America Thinks He Is," *New York Times* June 22, 2023, https://www.nytimes.com/2023/06/22/opinion/narendra-modi-india-democracy.html?searchResultPosition=1.)

6. Sanjoy Ganguly, *Jana Sanskriti: Forum Theatre and Democracy in India* (Routledge, 2010), 127.
7. Rustom Bharucha, *The Theatre of Kanhailal*: Pebet *and* Memoirs of Africa (Seagull, 1998), 1, iv.
8. Shanta Gokhale, ed., *The Theatre of Veenapani Chawla: Theory, Practice, Performance* (Oxford University Press, 2014), xiii.
9. In addition to the sources already mentioned, key works of theory and criticism that map the post-1990 terrain include Rustom Bharucha, *In the Name of the Secular: Contemporary Cultural Activism in India* (Oxford University Press, 1998); C. S. Lakshmi, ed., *Body Blows: Women, Violence, and Survival: Three Plays* (Seagull, 2000); Lakshmi Subramanyam, ed., *Muffled Voices: Women in Modern Indian Theatre* (2002; repr. Har-Anand, 2013); Tutun Mukherji, ed., *Staging Resistance: Plays by Women in Translation* (Oxford University Press, 2005); Sudhanva Deshpande, ed., *Theatre of the Streets: The Jana Natya Manch Experience* (Jana Natya Manch, 2007); Lakshmi Subramanyam, ed., *Modern Indian Drama: Issues and Interventions* (Srishti, 2008); Nandi Bhatia, *Performing Women, Performing Womanhood: Theatre, Politics, and Dissent in North India* (Oxford University Press, 2010); Arjun Ghosh, *A History of the Jana Natya Manch* (Sage, 2012); Amal Allana, ed., *The Act of Becoming: Actors Talk* (National School of Drama and Niyogi, 2013); Ashis Sengupta, ed., *Mapping South Asia Through Contemporary Theatre* (Palgrave Macmillan, 2014); A. Mangai, *Acting Up: Gender and Theatre in India, 1979 Onwards* (LeftWord, 2015); Dia Da Costa, *Politicizing Creative Economy: Activism and a Hunger Called Theatre* (University of Illinois Press, 2016); Gururao V. Bapat and Lata Singh, eds., *Performing Arts in India: Performances of/and Violence* (Indian Institute of Advanced Study, 2016); Ashis Sengupta, ed., *Islam in Performance: Contemporary Plays from South Asia* (Bloomsbury Methuen, 2017); Dorothy M. Figueira, *Art and Resistance: Studies in Modern Indian Theatres* (Peter Lang, 2019); and Ashis Sengupta, *Postdramatic Theatre and India: Theatre-Making Since the 1990s* (Methuen, 2022).
10. For example, capitalism's most fertile affiliation in India is with twenty-first-century neoliberalism, so the model of postwar transformations that Fredric Jameson presents in *Postmodernism, or the Cultural Logic of Late Capitalism* (Duke University Press, 1991) does not fit. The skepticism about metanarratives that Jean-François Lyotard ascribes to postmodernism in *The Postmodern Condition: A Report on Knowledge* (trans. Geoff Bennington and Brian Massumi [University of Minnesota Press, 1984]) is a principal feature of Indian *modernist* writing, especially as it negotiates utopian

constructions of the country's precolonial past. Choosing experimental forms that enter into a dialogue with the literary cultures of their respective languages, Indian-language writers do not adopt on any appreciable scale the postmodern poetics of fragmentation, parody, irony, pastiche, and metafiction analyzed by Linda Hutcheon (*A Poetics of Postmodernism: History, Theory, Fiction* [Routledge, 1988]). Tellingly, in the revised chronology of modernism that scholars of the new modernist studies have developed, modernism both precedes and succeeds postmodernism in the West, although the latter retains its historical place and significance for the later twentieth century. Indian literature and theater simply bypass that intervening stage.

11. See A. Dharwadker, *Theatres of Independence*, 132–46.
12. See, for example, Shayoni Mitra, "Dispatches from the Margins: Theatre in India Since the 1990s," in Sengupta, *Mapping South Asia*, 66, 87; and Mangai, *Acting Up*, 18–21.
13. In fact, *all* "drama" and "theater" in the conventional sense, regardless of their location, are virtually absent from the discussions of transnational modernism that have steadily gathered momentum in the past two decades. The more versatile category of "performance" aligns transnational modernisms with topics such as media studies, cultural studies, the performance of migration, Afromodernisms, foreign modernism, Indian modern dance, and Italian opera. Given the marginality of drama per se, the dismissal of modernist Indian theater as a comprador canon becomes even more questionable. Turning from form to language, it is notable that since the appearance of *Geomodernisms: Race, Modernism, Modernity* (Indiana University Press, 2005), the collection coedited by Laura Doyle and Laura Winkiel, only two recent volumes (also collections of essays) appear to contain transnational comparisons that actively involve non-Europhone literary materials: Pier Paolo Frassinelli et al., eds., *Traversing Transnationalism: The Horizons of Literary and Cultural Studies* (Rodopi, 2011), and Laura Winkiel, ed., *Transnational Exchange* (Special issue of *English Language Notes* 49, no. 1 [Spring-Summer 2011]).

BIBLIOGRAPHY

Ackerman, Alan L., and Martin Puchner, eds. *Against Theatre: Creative Destructions on the Modernist Stage*. Palgrave Macmillan, 2006.
Afzal-Khan, Fawzia. *Cultural Imperialism and the Indo-English Novel*. Pennsylvania State University Press, 1993.
Alkazi, Ebrahim. "Journal of South Asian Literature Interviews Ebrahim Alkazi." *Journal of South Asian Literature* 10, nos. 2–4 (1975): 289–325.
——. "The Training of the Actor." In *Indian Drama in Retrospect*, ed. Kastuar.
Allana, Amal, ed. *The Act of Becoming: Actors Talk*. National School of Drama and Niyogi, 2013.
——. *Ebrahim Alkazi: Holding Time Captive*. Vintage, 2024.
——. *The Theatre of E. Alkazi: A Modernist Approach to Indian Theatre*. Theatre and Television Associates, 2016.
Anand, Mulk Raj. *Conversations in Bloomsbury*. Arnold Heinemann, 1981.
——. "Indian Theatre in the Context of World Theater." In *Indian Drama in Retrospect*, ed. Kastuar.
Anantha Murthy, U. R., Ramachandra Śarma, and D. R. Nāgarāj, eds. *Vibhava: Modernism in Indian Writing*. Panther, 1992.
Appadurai, Arjun, Frank J. Korom, and Maragaret A. Mills, eds. *Gender, Genre, and Power in South Asian Expressive Traditions*. University of Pennsylvania Press, 1991.
Appiah, Kwame Anthony. *The Ethics of Identity*. Princeton University Press, 2005.
——. *In My Father's House: Africa in the Philosophy of Culture*. Oxford University Press, 1992.
——. "Rooted Cosmopolitanism." In Appiah, *The Ethics of Identity*.
"April 2010 Maoist Attack in Dantewada." Accessed August 15, 2023. https://en.wikipedia.org/wiki/April_2010_Maoist_attack_in_Dantewada.
Arac, Jonathan. "Anglo-Globalism?" *New Left Review* 16 (July–August 2002): 35–45.
Archer, William. "*A Doll's House* and the Ibsen Revolution." In Puchner, *Modern Drama*, vol. 1.

BIBLIOGRAPHY

Armstrong, Tim. *Modernism: A Cultural History*. Polity, 2005.
Ashvaghosha. *Handsome Nanda*. Trans. Linda Covill. New York University Press and JJC Foundation, 2007.
Ayub, Abu Sayid. *Adhunikata o rabindranath* (Modernism and Rabindranath [Tagore]). Trans. Amitava Ray. Sahitya Akademi, 1995.
Azad, Maulana Abul Kalam. "Opening Address," Sangeet Natak Akademi Inauguration. Accessed April 16, 2023. https://sangeetnatak.gov.in/sections/drama.
Bagchi, Amiya Kumar. "Reflections on the Nature of the Indian Bourgeoisie." *Social Scientist* 19, nos. 3–4 (March–April 1991): 3–18.
Bagwe, Anjali, ed. *Of Woman Caste: The Experience of Gender in Rural India*. Zed, 1995.
Baldick, Chris. *The Concise Oxford Dictionary of Literary Terms*. Oxford University Press, 2001.
Bandyopadhyay, Samik. Introduction to *Ghashiram Kotwal* by Vijay Tendulkar. Trans. Jayant Karve and Eleanor Zelliott. Seagull, 1986.
———. "The New Karnas of Manipur." *Seagull Theatre Quarterly*, nos. 14–15 (June–September 1997): 73–90.
Banerjee, Sumanta. "From Naxalbari to Chhattisgarh: Half-a-Century of Maoist Journey in India." *Southern Social Movements Newswire*, June 15, 2017. https://www.cetri.be/From-Naxalbari-to-Chhattisgarh?lang=fr.
Bapat, Gururao V., and Lata Singh, eds. *Performing Arts in India: Performances of/and Violence*. Indian Institute of Advanced Study, 2016.
Barba, Eugenio. "The Steps on the River Bank." In Lal and Dasgupta *Rasa*, vol. 2. ed.
Barlow, Judith E. "Into the Foxhole: Feminism, Realism, and Lillian Hellman." In *Realism and the American Dramatic Tradition*, ed. William W. Demastes. University of Alabama Press, 1996.
Begam, Richard, and Michael Valdez Moses, eds. *Modernism, Postcolonialism, and Globalism: Anglophone Literature, 1950 to the Present*. Oxford University Press, 2019.
Bell, Michael. "Myth and Religion in Modernist Literature." In *The Bloomsbury Companion to Modernist Literature*, ed. Ulrika Maude and Mark Nixon. Bloomsbury Academic, 2017.
———. "Myth and Literature in Modernity: A Question of Priority." *Publications of the English Goethe Society* 80, nos. 2–3 (2011): 204–15.
Bentley, Eric. "The Two Traditions of Modern Drama." In Puchner, *Modern Drama*, vol. 2.
Berman, Jessica. *Modernist Commitments: Ethics, Politics, and Transnational Modernism*. Columbia University Press, 2012.
———. "Neither Mirror nor Mimic: Transnational Reading and Indian Narratives in English." In *The Oxford Handbook of Global Modernisms*, ed. Wollaeger and Eatough.
Bhabha, Homi. "Spectral Sovereignty, Vernacular Cosmopolitans, and Cosmopolitan Memories." In *Cosmopolitanisms*, ed. Kwame Anthony Appiah et al. New York University Press, 2017.
———. "The Vernacular Cosmopolitan." In *Voices of the Crossing: The Impact of Britain on Writers from Asia, the Caribbean, and Africa*, ed. Ferdinand Dennis and Naseem Khan. Serpent's Tail, 2000.
Bhagat-Ganguly, Varsha, and Sujit Kumar, eds. *India's Scheduled Areas: Untangling Governance, Law and Politics*. Routledge, 2020.
Bhanj Deo, Pravir Chandra. *I Pravir, the Adivasi God*. ASIN: B00FG6GYWG.

BIBLIOGRAPHY

Bharati, Dharamvir. *Dharamvir bharati granthavali* (The works of Dharamvir Bharati). Ed. Chandrakant Bandavidekar. 9 vols. Vani Prakashan, 1998.
Bharucha, Rustom. *In the Name of the Secular: Contemporary Cultural Activism in India.* Oxford University Press, 1998.
———. *The Theatre of Kanhailal: Pebet and Memoirs of Africa.* Seagull, 1998.
———. "We Need a House of Our Own: The Impasse of Indian Theatre After Independence." In *2000: Reflections on the Arts in India*, ed. Pratapaditya Paul. Marg, 2000.
Bhatia, Nandi, ed. *Modern Indian Theater: A Reader.* Oxford University Press, 2009.
———. *Performing Women, Performing Womanhood: Theatre, Politics, and Dissent in North India.* Oxford University Press, 2010.
———. "'Provincializing English,' Globalizing Indian English Drama." *Postcolonial Text* 10, nos. 3–4 (2015): 1–15.
———. "Staging the 1857 Mutiny as 'The Great Rebellion': Colonial History and Post-Colonial Interventions in Utpal Dutt's *Mahavidroha*." *Theatre Journal* 51, no. 2 (1999): 167–84.
Bhattacharya, Sourit. *Postcolonial Modernity and the Indian Novel: On Catastrophic Realism.* Palgrave Macmillan, 2020.
Bhave, Pushpa. "Vijay Tendulkar: A Study." In *Contemporary Indian Theatre*, ed. Jacob.
Bhise, Manoj. "A Dialogue on *Ghashiram kotwal*." In *Vijay Tendulkar's Plays: An Anthology of Recent Criticism*, ed. V. M. Madge. Pencraft International, 2007.
Bhyrappa, S. L. "Mahabharata: My Attempt at a Recreation." In *The Mahabharata Revisited*, ed. R. N. Dandekar. Sahitya Akademi, 1990.
Bradbury, Malcolm, and James McFarlane, eds. *Modernism, 1890–1930.* Penguin, 1991. First published in 1976.
Bradshaw, David, and Kevin J. H. Dettmar, eds. *A Companion to Modernist Literature and Culture.* Blackwell, 2006.
Brooker, Peter, Andrzej Gasiorek, Deborah Longworth, and Andrew Thacker, eds. *The Oxford Handbook of Modernisms.* Oxford University Press, 2011.
Case, Sue-Ellen. *Feminism and Theatre.* Methuen, 1988.
Chakrabarty, Dipesh. *Habitations of Modernity.* University of Chicago Press, 2002.
———. *Provincializing Europe: Postcolonial Thought and Historical Difference.* Princeton University Press, 2000.
Chatak, Govind. *Adhunik natak ka masiha mohan rakesh* (Mohan Rakesh, the messiah of modern theater). Indraprastha Prakashan, 1975.
Chatterjee, Partha. "Talking About Our Modernity in Two Languages." In *A Possible India: Essays in Political Criticism.* Oxford University Press, 1997.
Chatterjee, Sudipto. *The Colonial Staged: Theatre in Colonial Calcutta.* Seagull, 2007.
Chattopadhyay, Kamaladevi. *Towards a National Theatre.* All India Women's Conference, 1945.
———. "National Theatre," *Natya* 1, no. 1 (1956): 7–10.
Chaudhuri, Amit, ed. *The Picador Book of Modern Indian Literature.* Picador, 2001.
Chaudhuri, Supriya. "Modernisms in India." In Brooker et al., *Oxford Handbook of Modernisms.*
Chaudhuri, Una. *Staging Place: The Geography of Modern Drama.* University of Michigan Press, 1995.

Ciuguraneau, Adina. "History and Myth in Pound's *Cantos*." *British and American Studies* 1 (1996): 99–108.
Contemporary Indian Theatre: Interviews with Playwrights and Directors, ed. Paul Jacob. Sangeet Natak Akademi, 1989.
Contemporary Playwriting and Play Production: Report of a Seminar, March 31–April 2, 1961. Bharatiya Natya Sangh, 1961.
Courbet, Gustave. *The Realist Manifesto*. Accessed March 10, 2023. https://www.scribd.com/document/370902364/Realist-Manifesto#.
Cuddy-Keane, Melba. "Modernism, Geopolitics, Globalization." *Modernism/Modernity* 10 (2003): 539–558.
Da Costa, Dia. *Politicizing Creative Economy: Activism and a Hunger Called Theatre*. University of Illinois Press, 2016.
Dalmia, Vasudha. "Neither Half nor Whole: Mohan Rakesh and the Modernist Quest." In *Poetics, Plays, and Performances: The Politics of Modern Indian Theatre*. Oxford University Press, 2006.
Das N. K., ed. *Exclusion, Discrimination, and Stratification: Tribes in Contemporary India*. Rawat, 2013.
Dass, Manishita. "Visions of Modernity in Colonial India: Cinema, Women, and the City." In *Oxford Handbook of Global Modernisms*, ed. Wollaeger and Eatough.
Dattani, Mahesh. "Contemporary Indian Theatre and its Relevance." In A. Dharwadker, *Poetics of Modernity*.
———. *Tara: A Play in Two Acts*. Ravi Dayal, 1990.
———. "Three Little Slices of Indian Urban Life." In *City Plays*. Seagull, 2004.
Decoste, Damon Marcel. "Modernism's Shell-Shocked History: Amnesia, Repetition, and the War in Graham Greene's *The Ministry of Fear*." *Twentieth Century Literature* 45, no. 4 (Winter 1999): 428–51.
Deshpande, G. P. "Fetish of Folk and Classic." *Sangeet Natak*, nos. 77–78 (July–December 1985): 47–50.
Deshpande, Sudhanva, ed. *Theatre of the Streets: The Jana Natya Manch Experience*. Jana Natya Manch, 2007.
Deshpande, Sulabha. "The Rest Is History." Accessed June 29, 2024. https://thebigindianpicture.com/2013/12/the-rest-is-history/.
Dev, Amiya. "A Note on Modern Bengali Writing." In Anantha Murthy et al., *Vibhava*.
Dharwadker, Aparna [Bhargava]. "Historical Fictions and Postcolonial Representation: Reading Girish Karnad's *Tughlaq*." *PMLA* 110, no.1 (1995): 43–58.
———. "The Ironic History of the Nation." In *Theatres of Independence: Drama, Theory, and Urban Performance in India Since 1947*. University of Iowa Press, 2005.
———. "Modernism, 'Tradition,' and History in the Postcolony: Vijay Tendulkar's *Ghashiram kotwal* (1972)." *Theatre Journal* 65, no. 4 (December 2013): 467–87.
———. "Mohan Rakesh, Modernism, and the Postcolonial Present." *South Central Review* 25, no. 1 (Spring 2008): 136–62.
———. "Myth, Ambivalence, and Evil." In *Theatres of Independence: Drama, Theory, and Urban Performance in India Since 1947*. University of Iowa Press, 2005.
———, ed. *A Poetics of Modernity: Indian Theatre Theory, 1850 to the Present*. Oxford University Press, 2019.
———. "The Really Poor Theatre: Postcolonial Economies of Performance." *Journal of Dramatic Theory and Criticism* 31, no. 2 (Spring 2017): 99–124.

———. "Representing India's Pasts: Time, Culture, and the Problems of Performance Historiography." In *Representing the Past: Essays in Performance Historiography*, ed. Thomas Postlewait and Charlotte Canning. University of Iowa Press, 2010.

———. *Theatres of Independence: Drama, Theory, and Urban Performance in India Since 1947*. University of Iowa Press, 2005.

Dharwadker, Vinay. "Modernism and Its Four Phases: Literature in South Asia." In *Modernist World*, ed. Ross and Lindgren.

———. "The Modernist Novel in India: Paradigms and Practices." In *A History of the Indian Novel in English*, ed. Ulka Anjaria. Cambridge University Press, 2015.

———. "Mumbai's Marathi Modernists: A Memoir from the Margins." *Journal of Postcolonial Writing* 53, nos. 1–2 (2017): 88–107.

———. "Nations, Modernisms, Anti-Nations: Five Theses on South Asian Arts and Cultures." Keynote address, conference on "Nationhood and Nation-Building in South Asia," Stanford University, April 29, 2010.

Dhingra, Baldoon. *A National Theatre for India*. Padma, 1944.

Diamond, Elin. "Modern Drama/Modernity's Drama." In *Modern Drama: Defining the Field*, ed. Knowles et al.

Doyle, Laura, and Laura Winkiel, eds. *Geomodernisms: Race, Modernism, Modernity*. Indiana University Press, 2005.

Dubey, Satyadev. Introduction to *Evam Indrajit* by Badal Sircar, v–ix. Oxford University Press, 1974.

Dubrow, Jennifer. *Cosmopolitan Dreams: The Making of Modern Urdu Literary Culture in Colonial South Asia*. Permanent Black, 2018.

Dutt, Michael Madhusudan. *Sermista: A Drama in Five Acts*. A. Pine Educational and Commercial, 1968. First published in 1859.

"Eighth Schedule to the Constitution of India." *The Constitution of India*, 30. Ministry of Law and Justice, 2007.

Eisen, Kurt. "Theatrical Ethnography and Modernist Primitivism in Eugene O'Neill and Zora Neale Hurston." *South Central Review*, 25, no. 1 (Spring 2008), 56–73.

Eliot, T. S. *The Poems of T. S. Eliot*, vol. 1, ed. Christopher Ricks and Jim McCue. Farrar, Strauss, and Giroux, 2015.

———. "Tradition and the Individual Talent." Accessed May 17, 2021. http://www.bartleby.com/200/sw4.html.

Elkunchwar, Mahesh. "An Interview by Ashish Rajadhyaksha." In *Contemporary Indian Theatre*, ed. Jacob.

———. *Atmakatha ani pratibimba*. (Autobiography and reflection). Mauj Prakashan, 1989.

———. *Autobiography*. Trans. Pratima Kulkarni. Seagull, 1989.

Elze, Jens. *Postcolonial Modernism and the Picaresque Novel: Literatures of Precarity*. Palgrave Macmillan, 2017.

Farfan, Penny. "Editorial Comment: 'Modernism.'" *Theatre Journal* 65, no. 4 (December 2013): i–iv.

———. *Performing Queer Modernism*. Oxford University Press, 2017.

Figueira, Dorothy Matilda. *Art and Resistance: Studies in Modern Indian Theatres*. Peter Lang, 2019.

Fiske, Shanyn. "From Ritual to the Archaic in Modernism: Fraser, Harrison, Freud, and the Persistence of Myth." In *A Handbook of Modernism Studies*, ed. Jean-Michel Rabaté. John Wiley, 2013.

Fordham, John. "The Revolution of the Scots Word: Modernism, Myth, and Nationhood in Gibbon and MacDiarmid." In *And in Our Time: Vision, Revision, and British Writing of the 1930s*, ed. Anthony Shuttleworth. Bucknell University Press, 2003.
Frassinelli, Pier Paolo, et al., eds. *Traversing Transnationalism: the Horizons of Literary and Cultural Studies*. Rodopi, 2011.
Freedman, Ariela. "On the Ganges Side of Modernism: Raghubir Singh, Amitav Ghosh, and the Postcolonial Modern." In *Geomodernisms*, ed. Doyle and Winkiel.
Friedman, Susan Stanford. "Paranoia, Pollution, and Sexuality: Affiliations Between E. M. Forster's *A Passage to India* and Arundhati Roy's *The God of Small Things*." In *Geomodernisms*, ed. Doyle and Winkiel.
——. "Periodizing Modernism: Postcolonial Modernities and the Space/Time Borders of Modernist Studies." *Modernism/Modernity* 13, no. 3 (2006): 425–43.
——. *Planetary Modernisms: Provocations on Modernity Across Time*. Columbia University Press, 2015.
Gangopadhyay, Rudrani. "Modernism in South Asia." In *Global Modernists on Modernism*, ed. Moody and Ross.
Ganguly, Sanjoy. *Jana Sanskriti: Forum Theatre and Democracy in India*. Routledge, 2010.
Gassner, John. "Forms of Modern Drama." In Puchner, *Modern Drama*, vol. 2,.
Gaston, Bruce. "Brecht's Pastiche History Play: Renaissance Drama and Modernist Theatre in *Leben Eduards des Zweiten von England*." *German Life and Letters* 56, no. 4 (October 2003): 345–62.
George, Rosemary Marangoly. *The Politics of Home: Postcolonial Relocations and Twentieth-Century Fiction*. Cambridge University Press, 1996.
Gerould, Daniel Charles, ed. *Theatre/Theory/Theatre: The Major Critical Texts from Aristotle and Zeami to Soyinka and Havel*. Applause, 2003.
Ghosh, Arjun. *A History of the Jana Natya Manch*. Sage, 2012.
Ghosh, Suniti Kumar. "Indian Bourgeoisie and Imperialism," *Economic and Political Weekly* 23, nos. 45/47 (November 1988): 2445–58.
Gikandi, Simon. "Preface: Modernism in the World." *Modernism/Modernity* 13, no. 3 (2006): 419–24.
——. *Writing in Limbo: Modernism and Caribbean Literature*. Cornell University Press, 1992.
Gokhale, Shanta. *Playwright at the Centre: Marathi Drama from 1843 to the Present*. Seagull, 2000.
——. "Tendulkar on His Own Terms." In *Vijay Tendulkar*. Katha, 2001.
——, ed. *The Theatre of Veenapani Chawla: Theory, Practice, Performance*. Oxford University Press, 2014.
Guha, Ranajit. *Dominance Without Hegemony: History and Power in Colonial India*. Harvard University Press, 1998.
Heffernan, Teresa. *Post-Apocalyptic Culture: Modernism, Postmodernism, and the Twentieth-Century Novel*. University of Toronto Press, 2008.
Hegglund, Jon. *World Views: Metageographies of Modernist Fiction*. Oxford University Press, 2012.
Hoffmann, Gerhard. "Myth, Ideology, Symbol and Faulkner's Modernism/ Postmodernism in *Go Down, Moses*." *American Studies* 42, no. 4 (1997): 661–78.
Hutcheon, Linda. *A Poetics of Postmodernism: History, Theory, Fiction*. Routledge, 1988.

Innes, Christopher. "Shifting the Frame: Modernism in the Theatre." In *Rethinking Modernism*, ed. Marianne Thormählen. Palgrave Macmillan, 2003.
——. "Modernism in Drama." In Levenson, *Cambridge Companion to Modernism*.
Innes, Christopher, and F. J. Marker, eds. *Modernism in European Drama: Ibsen, Strindberg, Pirandello, Beckett*. Essays from Modern Drama. University of Toronto Press, 1998.
Jain, Nemichandra, ed. *Mohan rakesh ke sampurna natak* (The complete plays of Mohan Rakesh). Rajpal, 1993.
——. "Some Notes on the Use of Tradition in Theatre," *Sangeet Natak*, nos. 77–78 (July–December 1985): 9–13.
Jameson, Fredric. *Postmodernism, or the Cultural Logic of Late Capitalism*. Duke University Press, 1991.
——. *A Singular Modernity: Essays on the Ontology of the Present*. Verso, 2002.
Jasanoff, Maya. "Narendra Modi Is Not Who America Thinks He Is." *New York Times* June 22, 2023. https://www.nytimes.com/2023/06/22/opinion/narendra-modi-india-democracy.html?searchResultPosition=1.
Jay, Paul L. "American Modernism and the Uses of History: The Case of William Carlos Williams." *New Orleans Review* 9, no. 3 (1982): 16–25.
Jiwani, Subuhi. "Vijay Tendulkar Is a Scathing Interpreter of Maladies." Daily News Analysis, *The Times of India*. October 7, 2005. https://www.dnaindia.com/analysis/report-vijay-tendulkar-is-a-scathing-interpreter-of-maladies-4810.
Joshi, Priya. *In Another Country: Colonialism, Culture, and the English Novel in India*. Columbia University Press, 2002.
Kambar, Chandrashekhar. "Folk Theater as I See It." *Sangeet Natak*, nos. 77–78 (July–December, 1985): 39–42.
——. "An Interview by Kirtinath Kurtkoti." In *Contemporary Indian Theatre*, ed. Jacob.
Kapur, Anuradha. Foreword to Anjum Katyal, *Habib Tanvir*, ix–xi.
Kapur, Geeta. *When Was Modernism? Essays on Contemporary Cultural Practice in India*. Tulika, 2000.
Karnad, Girish. *Collected Plays*. 3 vols. Oxford University Press, 2005–2017.
——. "An Interview by Kirtinath Kurtkoti." In *Contemporary Indian Theatre*, ed. Jacob.
——. "In Search of a New Theatre." In *Contemporary India: Essays on the Use of Tradition*, ed. Carla Borden. Oxford University Press, 1985.
——. "Performance, Meaning, and the Materials of Modern Indian Theatre." *New Theatre Quarterly* 44 (1995): 355–70.
——. "Theatre in India." *Daedalus* 118, no. 4 (1989): 331–52.
——. *Three Plays*. Trans. Girish Karnad. Oxford University Press, 1994.
——. *Yayati*. Trans. Girish Karnad. Oxford University Press, 2008.
Kastuar, Jayant. Introduction to *Indian Drama in Retrospect*. Hope India, 2007.
——, ed. *Indian Drama in Retrospect*. Hope India, 2007.
Katyal, Anjum. *Habib Tanvir: Towards an Inclusive Theatre*. Sage, 2012.
Kaul, Bansi. "Tradition All Around Us." *Sangeet Natak*, nos. 77–78 (July–December, 1985): 22–25.
Kaviraj, Sudipta. "The Two Histories of Literary Culture in Bengal." In Pollock, *Literary Cultures in History*.
Kelly, Katherine E. "Pandemic and Performance: Ibsen and the Outbreak of Modernism." *South Central Review* 25, no. 1 (Spring 2008): 12–35.

Kelly, Katherine E., and Penny Farfan, guest eds. "Staging Modernism: Introduction," *South Central Review* 25, no. 1 (Spring 2008): 1–11.

Khosla, Romi. "The New Metropolis: Nehru and the Aftermath." *Social Scientist* 43, nos. 3–4 (March–April 2015): 11–32.

Kirschen, Robert Michael. *James Joyce and Post-Imperial Bildung: Salman Rushdie, Tayeb Salih, and Tsitsi Dangarembga*. Digital Scholarship@UNLV 2013-05-01T07:00:00Z, 2013.

Knapp, James F. "Primitivism and Empire: John Synge and Paul Gauguin." *Comparative Literature* 41, no. 1 (Winter 1989): 53–68.

Knippling, Alpana Sharma. "Decolonizing the Modernist Mind." *South Asian Review* 33, no. 1 (2012): 13–29.

——, guest ed. *South Asian Review* 33, no. 1 (2012). Special issue on "South Asian Modernisms."

Knowles, Ric, Joanne Tompkins, and W. B. Worthen, eds. *Modern Drama: Defining the Field*. University of Toronto Press, 2003.

Kolocotroni, Vassiliki, Jane Goldman, and Olga Taxidou, eds. *Modernism: An Anthology of Sources and Documents*. University of Chicago Press, 1998.

Kolocotroni, Vassili, and Olga Taxidou, eds. *The Edinburgh Dictionary of Modernism*. Edinburgh University Press, 2018.

Kumar, Sukrita Paul. *Conversations on Modernism, With Reference to English, Hindi, and Urdu Fiction*. Indian Institute of Advanced Study, Shimla, in Association with Allied, 1990.

Lakshmi, C. S., ed. *Body Blows: Women, Violence, and Survival: Three Plays*. Seagull, 2000.

Lal, Ananda, and Chidananda Dasgupta, eds. *Rasa: The Indian Performing Arts in the Last 25 Years*. Anamika Kala Sangam, 1995.

Latham, Sean, and Gayle Rogers, eds. *The New Modernist Studies Reader: An Anthology of Essential Criticism*. Bloomsbury Academic, 2021.

The Laws of Manu. Trans. Wendy Doniger, with Brian K. Smith. Penguin Classics, 1992.

Lee, Steven S. "Revolution's Demands: Modernism, Socialist Realism, and the Manifesto." In Mao, *New Modernist Studies*.

Levenson, Michael, ed. *The Cambridge Companion to Modernism*, 2nd ed. Cambridge University Press, 2011.

Loncică, Diana-Eugenia. *Cultural Hybridization in the Contemporary Novel: Salman Rushdie, Michael Ondaatje, Kazuo Ishiguro*. Editura Uranus, 2009.

Lukács, György. "The Sociology of Modern Drama." In Puchner, *Modern Drama*, vol. 2.

Lyon, Janet. "Cosmopolitanism and Modernism." In *Oxford Handbook of Global Modernisms*, ed. Wollaeger and Eatough.

Lyotard, Jean-François. *The Postmodern Condition: A Report on Knowledge*. Trans. Geoff Bennington and Brian Massumi. University of Minnesota Press, 1984.

Macaulay, Thomas Babington. "Minute on Indian Education." In *Selected Writings*, ed. John Clive and Thomas Pinney. University of Chicago Press, 1972.

Machwe, Prabhakar. *Modernity and Contemporary Indian Literature*. Chetana, 1978.

Maeterlinck, Maurice. "The Modern Drama." In Puchner, *Modern Drama*, vol. 1.

The Mahabharata. Trans. and ed. J. A. B. van Buitenen, vol. 1. University of Chicago Press, 1973.

Malik, Neeraj, and Javed Malick, eds. *Habib Tanvir: Reflections and Reminiscences*. SAHMAT, 2010.

Mangai, A. *Acting Up: Gender and Theatre in India, 1979 Onwards*. LeftWord, 2015.

BIBLIOGRAPHY

Mao, Douglas, ed. *The New Modernist Studies Reader*. Cambridge University Press, 2021.
Mao, Douglas, and Rebecca L. Walkowitz, eds. *Bad Modernisms*. Duke University Press, 2006.
———. "The New Modernist Studies." *PMLA* 123, no. 3 (2008): 737–48.
Marinetti, F. T. "The Variety Theatre." In Puchner, *Modern Drama*, vol. 1.
Matthews, Steven, ed. *Modernism: A Sourcebook*. Palgrave Macmillan, 2008.
May, Brian. *Extravagant Postcolonialism: Modernism and Modernity in Anglophone Fiction, 1958–1988*. University of South Carolina Press, 2014.
Mee, Erin B. *Theatre of Roots: Redirecting the Modern Indian Stage*. Seagull, 2007.
Meister, Michael W. *Traditional and Vernacular Architecture: Proceedings of the Seminar*. Madras Craft Foundation, 2003.
Menon, Sadanand. "Reinventing the Political in Theatre." In *Habib Tanvir: Reflections and Reminiscences*, ed. Malik and Malick.
Mickalites, Carey. *Contemporary Fiction, Celebrity Culture, and the Market for Modernism: Fictions of Celebrity*. Bloomsbury Academic, 2022.
"Ministry of Tribal Affairs, Government of India." Accessed July 10, 2023. https://tribal.nic.in/.
Mishra, Urmila. *Adhunikata aur Mohan Rakesh* (Modernity and Mohan Rakesh). Vishwavidyalaya Prakashan, 1977.
Mitra, Samarpita. *Periodicals, Readers, and the Making of a Modern Literary Culture*. Brill, 2020.
Mitra, Shayoni. "Dispatches from the Margins: Theatre in India Since the 1990s." In *Mapping South Asia*, ed. Sengupta.
Mitra, Sombhu. "Amateur Theatre in India." In *Indian Drama in Retrospect*, ed. Kastuar.
Mitter, Partha. *The Triumph of Modernism: India's Artists and the Avant-Garde, 1922–1947*. Reaktion, 2007.
Moi, Toril. "Ibsen, Theatre, and the Ideology of Modernism." In Puchner, *Modern Drama*, vol. 2.
Moody, Alys, and Stephen J. Ross, eds. *Global Modernists on Modernism: An Anthology*. Bloomsbury Academic, 2020.
Moretti, Franco. *The Bourgeois: Between History and Literature*. Verso, 2013.
Morton, Stephen. *Salman Rushdie: Fictions of Postcolonial Modernity*. Palgrave Macmillan, 2008.
Mukherji, Tutun, ed. *Staging Resistance: Plays by Women in Translation*. Oxford University Press, 2005.
Muthuswami, Naa. "The Challenge of Tradition." *Sangeet Natak*, nos. 77–78 (July–December 1985): 78–84.
Natarajan, Nalini. *Woman and Indian Modernity: Readings of Colonial and Postcolonial Novels*. University Press of the South, 2002.
Nathan, Dev, and Virginius Xaxa, eds. *Social Exclusion and Adverse Inclusion: Development and Deprivation of Adivasis in India*. Oxford University Press, 2012.
Nerlekar, Anjali. *Bombay Modern: Arun Kolatkar and Bilingual Literary Culture*. Northwestern University Press, 2016.
O'Donnell, David. "Staging Modernity in the 'New Oceania': Modernism in Australian, New Zealand and Pacific Islands Theatre." In *Modernist World*, ed. Ross and Lindgren.
Panikkar, K. N. "An Interview by K. S. Narayana Pillai." In *Contemporary Indian Theatre*, ed. Jacob.

Parthasarathy, Indira. *Aurangzeb*. Trans. T. Sriraman. Seagull, 2004.
——. *Ramanujar: The Life and Ideas of Ramanuja*. Trans. T. Sriraman. Oxford University Press, 2008.
Pillai, G. Shankara. "Traditional Idiom and Modern Theatre." *Sangeet Natak*, nos. 77–78 (July–December, 1985): 43–46.
Pinkerton, Steve. *Blasphemous Modernism: The 20th-Century Word Made Flesh*. Oxford University Press, 2017.
Pollock, Sheldon. Introduction to *Literary Cultures in History: Reconstructions from South Asia*, ed. Sheldon Pollock. University of California Press, 2003.
Porselvi, P. Mary Vidya. *Nature, Culture, Gender: Rereading the Folktale*. Routledge, 2016.
Pradhan, Sudhi, ed. *Marxist Cultural Movement in India: Chronicles and Documents*. 3 vols. National Book Agency, 1979–1985.
Prasanna. "The True Significance of Habib Tanvir." In *Habib Tanvir: Reflections and Reminiscences*, ed. Malik and Malick.
Prateek. *Brecht in India: The Poetics and Politics of Transcultural Theatre*. Routledge, 2021.
Puchner, Martin, ed. *Modern Drama: Critical Concepts in Literary and Cultural Studies*. 4 vols. Routledge, 2008.
——. *Poetry of the Revolution: Marx, Manifestos, and the Avant-Gardes*. Princeton University Press, 2005.
——. *Stage Fright: Modernism, Anti-Theatricality, and Drama*. Johns Hopkins Press, 2002.
Rabaté, Jean-Michel. "Editor's Introduction: Cosmopolitan Modernism, Polylingual Strategies and Cultural Hybridity." *Journal of Modern Literature* 37, no.1 (2013): v–vi.
Raheja, Gloria Goodwin, ed. *Songs, Stories, Lives: Gendered Dialogues and Cultural Critique*. Kali for Women, 2003.
Raheja, Gloria Goodwin, and Ann Grodzins Gold. *Listen to the Heron's Words: Reimagining Gender and Kinship in North India*. University of California Press, 1994.
Raina, M. K. "Two Approaches to Tradition." *Sangeet Natak*, nos. 77–78 (July–December 1985): 29–32.
Rainey, Lawrence, ed. *Modernism: An Anthology*. Wiley-Blackwell, 2005.
Rakesh, Mohan. *Bakalam khud* (By his own pen). Rajpal, 1974.
——. "Looking Around as a Playwright." *Sangeet Natak*, no. 3 (October 1966): 16–21.
——. *Mohan rakesh ke sampurna natak* (The complete plays of Mohan Rakesh). Ed. Nemichandra Jain. Rajpal, 1993.
——. *Mohan rakesh rachanavali* (The works of Mohan Rakesh), 13 vols., ed. Jaidev Taneja. Rajkamal, 2011.
——. *Natya vimarsh* (Reflections on theater). Ed. Jaidev Taneja. National School of Drama, 2003.
——. *One Day in the Season of Rain*. Trans. Aparna Dharwadker and Vinay Dharwadker. Penguin, 2015.
——. *Sahitya aur sanskriti* (Literature and culture). Radhakrishna Prakashan, 1990.
——. "Theatre Without Walls." *Sangeet Natak*, no. 6 (October–December 1967): 66–69.
Ramachandran, C. N. "Folk Theatre and Social Structures: Tentative Comments." In *Drama as Form of Art and Theatre*, ed. C. D. Narasimhaiah and C. N. Srinath. Dhvanyaloka, 1993.
Ramanathan, Geetha. *Locating Gender in Modernism: The Outsider Female*. Routledge, 2012.

BIBLIOGRAPHY

Ranganath, H. K. *The Karnataka Theatre*, 2nd ed. Karnataka University, 1982.
Rangacharya, Adya. *The Indian Theatre*. National Book Trust, 1971.
Rao, V. Srinivasa, ed. *Disadvantaged Tribes of India: Regional Concerns*. Rawat, 2021.
Ross, Stephen, and Allana C. Lindgren, eds. *The Modernist World*. Routledge, 2015.
"Roundtable on the Contemporary Relevance of Traditional Theatre." *Sangeet Natak* 21 (July–September 1971): 5–74.
Roy, Amitav. "Folk Is What Sells Well." In *Rasa*, vol. 2, ed. Lal and Dasgupta.
Sangeet Natak Akademi Annual Report for 1986–87. Sangeet Natak Akademi, 1987.
Sangeet Natak Akademi Report, 1953–1958. Sangeet Natak Akademi, 1958.
Sathe, Makarand. "Editorial." In *The Vijay Tendulkar Omnibus*, ed. Makarand Sathe. Arvind Kumar, 2007.
———. *A Socio-Political History of Marathi Theatre: Thirty Nights*. 3 vols. Oxford University Press, 2015.
Sengupta, Ashis, ed. *Islam in Performance: Contemporary Plays from South Asia*. Bloomsbury Methuen, 2017.
———, ed. *Mapping South Asia Through Contemporary Theatre*. Palgrave Macmillan, 2014.
———. *Postdramatic Theatre and India: Theatre-Making Since the 1990s*. Methuen, 2022.
Shaw, Bernard. "The Technical Novelty in Ibsen's Plays." In *Dramatic Theory and Criticism: Greeks to Grotowski*, ed. Bernard F. Dukore. Holt, Rinehart, and Winston, 1974.
Sircar, Badal. *Evam Indrajit*. Trans. Girish Karnad. Oxford University Press, 1974.
———. *On Theatre: Selected Essays*. Seagull, 2009.
Sisodia, Yatindra Singh, and Tapas Kumar Dalapati, eds. *Development and Discontent in Tribal India*. Rawat, 2015.
Solomon, Rakesh H. *Globalization, Nationalism, and the Text of Kichaka vadha*. Anthem Press, 2014.
"Staging Transitions: Theater of the 90s in India." Alkazi Theater Archives: Notes from the Archive 2021–22. Alkazi Foundation for the Arts, 2022.
Subramanyam, Lakshmi, ed. *Modern Indian Drama: Issues and Interventions*. Srishti, 2008.
———, ed. *Muffled Voices: Women in Modern Indian Theatre*. Har-Anand, 2013. First published in 2002.
Sundar, Nandini. *Subalterns and Sovereigns: An Anthropological History of Bastar, 1854–1996*. Oxford University Press, 1997.
Szondi, Peter. "Theory of the Modern Drama, Parts I-II." In Puchner, *Modern Drama*, vol. 2.
Tanvir, Habib. "Brecht for One Producer." *Enact*, no. 15 (1968).
———. *Hirma ki amar kahani* (The immortal tale of Hirma). Pustakayan, 1990.
———. "The Indian Experiment." In *Theatre India*. Kerala Sangeet Natak Akademi, 1977.
———. "Journey Into Theatre." *Nukkad Janam Samvad* 7, nos. 23–26 (April 2004–March 2005): 101–2.
———. *The Living Tale of Hirma*. Trans. Anjum Katyal and Prabha Katyal. Seagull, 2005.
Taxidou, Olga. *Modernism and Performance: Jarry to Brecht*. Palgrave Macmillan, 2007.
Tendulkar, Vijay. *Ghashiram kotwal*, 5th ed. Popular Prakashan, 1995.
———. *Kanyadaan*. Trans. Gowri Ramnarayan. Oxford University Press, 1996.
———. "Lekhak ka vaktavya" (The author's statement). In *Vijay Tendulkar*. Katha, 2001.
———. "Majhe lekhan kashasatthi?" (What is my writing for?). In *Sahityatun satyakade* (Through literature toward the truth), ed. Pai and Tendulkar.

——. "*Majhe natyashikshan*" (My theater education). In *Natak ani mi* (The theater and I). Dimple, 1997.
——. *The Play Is the Thing*. Shri Ram Memorial Lecture no. 10. Shri Ram Centre for Art and Culture, 1997.
——. *Sahityatun satyakade: vijay tendulkar yanchya nivadaka sahityacha sangraha* (Through literature toward the truth: selected literary writings of Vijay Tendulkar), ed. Shirish Pai and Priya Tendulkar. Dimple, 1988.
——, "Samvad Tendulkaranshi: Shirish Pai, Priya Tendulkar" (A dialogue with Tendulkar: Shirish Pai, Priya Tendulkar). In Tendulkar, *Sahityatun satyakade*, ed. Pai and Tendulkar.
——. "A Testament." *Indian Literature*, no. 147 (January–February 1992): 55–61.
——. *Vijay Tendulkar*. Katha, 2001.
Tulsi, Trilokchand. *Bharatendu aur adhunikata: bharat mein adhunikata ka sutrapat* (Bharatendu and modernity: the inception of modernity in India). Vishveshvarananda Vaidik Shodh Sansthan, 1988.
Varerkar, Bhargavram Vitthal. *Majha nataki sansar* (My theater world), 2 vols. Swastik, 1941–1952.
"Vijay Tendulkar: The Man Who Wanted to Shoot Narendra Modi," *Daily News & Analysis*, May 19, 2008. https://www.dnaindia.com/india/report-vijay-tendulkar-the-man-who-wanted-to-shoot-narendra-modi-1165289.
Von Osten, Marion. Introduction to *Transcultural Modernisms*, ed. Moira Hill et al. Sternberg, 2013.
Walker, Julia A., and Glenn Odom. "Comparative Modernist Performance Studies: A Not So Modest Proposal." *Journal of Dramatic Theory and Criticism* 31, no. 1 (Fall 2016): 129–53.
Walkowitz, Rebecca L. *Cosmopolitan Style: Modernism Beyond the Nation*. Columbia University Press, 2006.
Wallerstein, Immanuel. *The Modern World System*. 4 vols. Academic Press, 1974–1989.
——. *World Systems Analysis: An Introduction*. Duke University Press, 2004.
Warden, Claire. "Modernism in European Drama/Theatre." In *Modernist World*, ed. Ross and Lindgren.
Williams, Raymond. "Excerpts from *Drama from Ibsen to Brecht*." In Puchner, *Modern Drama*, vol. 2.
Williams, Simon. "John Millington Synge: Transforming Myths of Ireland." In *Facets of European Modernism: Essays in Honour of James McFarlane*. University of East Anglia, 1985.
Winkiel, Laura, ed. *Transnational Exchange*. Special issue of *English Language Notes* 49, no. 1 (Spring–Summer, 2011).
Wollaeger, Mark. Introduction to *The Oxford Handbook of Global Modernisms*, ed. Wollaeger and Eatough.
Wollaeger, Mark, and Matt Eatough, eds. *The Oxford Handbook of Global Modernisms*. Oxford University Press, 2012.
Wood, Michael. "Modernism and Film." In *Cambridge Companion to Modernism*, ed. Levenson.
Zecchini, Laetitia. "What Filters Through the Curtain: Reconsidering Indian Modernisms, Travelling Literatures, and Little Magazines in a Cold War Context." *Interventions: International Journal of Postcolonial Studies* 22, no. 2 (2020): 172–94.
Zola, Emile. "Naturalism in the Theatre." In *Theatre/Theory/Theatre*, ed. Gerould.
——. "Naturalism on the Stage." In Puchner, *Modern Drama*, vol. 1.

INDEX

activism in Indian theater, 22, 26, 27, 28, 29, 67, 70, 71, 91, 214, 215, 267–68, 307n9

Adarkar, Priya, 58, 126, 127

Adhe adhure (Incomplete, unfinished) (Rakesh), 57, 86–87, 139, 144, 156–57, 180

adivasis (tribals) in India: geographical distribution, 305n58, 305n61; history in Bastar region, 244–45; problems posed by, 245, 305n59, 305n60; protections in Constitution, 246, 305n59; rebellions against British regime, 245; representation of, by Tanvir, 242–48, *250*, 252, 253, *253*, 254, *254*. *See also* Bhanj Deo; *Hirma ki amar kahani*

aesthetics: classical, 26, 169; of colonial theater, 75; of Indian modernisms, 5, 73, 74, 91, 115, 123, 232, 246; of modernism, 63; of modernist traditionalism, 224; premodern, 231; of realism, 162, 164, 200; of theatre of roots, 219; of traditional theater, 217, 221, 302n15

aesthetics and politics: of Indian modernism, 5, 7; of modernism's languages, 43–45; of modernist playwrights, 22, 28, 115; of modernist traditionalism, 220–26, 228, 232, 243, 246; of multilingualism, 62

Alekar, Satish, 98, 177, 270

Alkazi, Ebrahim, 96, 106, 181, 218, 264, 287n46, 288n47; audience development by, 104; as director of *Ashadh*, 107, 108, *108*; as founder of theater groups in Bombay, 100, 104; as NSD director, 99, 101, 104, 107

Alkazi Theatre Archives series, 266–67

Allana, Amal, 108, 264, 287n44, 299n70; *Act of Becoming, The,* 307n9; *Ebrahim Alkazi: Holding Time Captive,* 288n53; *Theatre of E. Alkazi, The,* 280n4, 288n53

Anand, Mulk Raj, 71; as Anglophone Indian modernist, 12, 99, 275n9, 280n5; *Untouchable* (novel), 175, 280n5, 297n35

Anantha Murthy, U. R. 18–19, 49, 280n4

Andha yug (Blind epoch) (Bharati), 28, 76, 262; based on *Mahabharata,* 76, 121, 125; Alkazi as director of, 104, 121; as condensed modernist epic, 262; as cosmo-modernist history of mankind, 289n3; Dubey makeshift stage for, 96; Karnad on, 95–96Anglophone writing, 14, 15, 33, 99, 259, 273n5;

Andha yug (Blind epoch) (Bharati) (*continued*)
  drama as category of, 25, 26, 32, 114–15, 275n8, 299n73; global audiences for, 64; prominence of, in contemporary literature, 12, 13, 17, 28, 32, 275n9, 280n5
Apparao, Gurajada, *Kanyasulkam*, 293n4
Anouilh, Jean, 95, 104, 132, 137, 262, 264
anticolonialism, 219, 221; bourgeois-nationalist forms of, 213; in theater, 118, 306n1
antitheatricalism: of colonial playwrights, 23; modernist forms of, 270; proto-modernist forms of, 69–70, 98, 181; Puchner on, 284n3; of realist drama, 165, 295n14
Arac, Jonathan, 274n7
Arbuzov, Aleksei, 81, 85–86
architecture: modernist, 13, 23, 33, 38, 41; transcultural modernism in, 41–42; vernacular forms of, 42. *See also* Correa; Le Corbusier
Ashadh ka ek din (One day in the season of rain) (Rakesh), 55, 68, 128, 292n25; 1958 SNA award for, 107; Alkazi as director of, 107, *108*; Carthage College and UW-Madison productions of, 59–60, *60*, *61*; critical significance of prefaces to, 92–93; performance history of, 67–68, 106–9, *108*; portrait of Kalidasa in, 86, 122–23, 138, 140, 141, 234, 262, 289n3; premier production directed by Jalan, 107; Rakesh interest in staging of, 93
Ashvaghosha (Buddhist monk), 125, 127, 128; Rakesh theatricalization of epic by, 142–49; *Saundarananda* (epic poem), 125, 127, 128, 149, 142–44, 152
Atmakatha (Autobiography) (Elkunchwar), 25, 192–201, *194*, 299n69; commentary on reality, fiction, and falsehood in, 193, 195, 199–201; as example of modernist realism, 192–94, 202; as family play, 163; literary culture of Marathi in, 197–99; mature gender relations in, 195, 196, 197; as metatheatrical play about writing, 163, 197

Atre, P. K., 171, 172, 293n4, 296n30; *Gharabaher*, 172
audience, 7, 60, 61, 64, 80, 94, 107, 120, 160, 175, 198, 224, 291n23; Alkazi approach to, 104; of colonial theater, 19, 65, 121, 131, 173, 291n10; Mitra on, 103; of noncommercial theater, 91, 102–9, 174, 207; Sircar approach to, 106; Subbanna approach to, at Ninasam, 105; of urban theater, 93, 94, 103, 159, 169, 173, 179, 191, 228
Aulak, Anita, 158
Awasthi, Suresh, 217, 218; as theorist of theatre of roots of, 218–19, 302n15
Awishkar (experimental Marathi theater group): Tendulkar association with, 88, 97
axis of language: creative grammar generated by, 32; defined by De Saussure, 31; defining modernism outside of, 33–43; critical acknowledgment of, 13–14, 273n5, 276n12, 277n14; power relations in, 9, 10; significance of, in modernist studies, 13–14, 23, 32–33, 260; volatility of, 9
Azad, Abul Kalam, 216

Bagchi, Amiya Kumar, 167, 295n24
Baki itihas (The rest of history). *See* Sircar
Barba, Eugenio, 81, 265
Barlow, Judith, 196
Beckett, Samuel, 21, 47, 81, 104, 190, 263, 264, 274n7, 293n30
Bengali language, 12, 13, 15, 16, 17, 18, 28, 29, 32, 33, 44, 46, 69, 72, 89, 102, 107, 137, 163, 173, 177, 215, 264, 182, 274n5; Dev on modernism in, 48–49; not as vernacular, 51–52; plays in, 29, 117, 118, 120, 121, 123, 125, 126, 129, 130, 137, 163, 173, 177, 215, 264, 269, 293n4, 294n6, 297n49
Bentley, Eric, 166
Bennewitz, Fritz, 228, 264
Bhagat, Datta, 26, 177
bhakti (worship or devotion), 15, 54
Bhanj Deo, Pravir Chandra: as model for Hirma in *Hirma ki amar kahani*, 244, 245, 246–47, 256, 304n56

INDEX

Bharat durdasha (India's plight). *See* Harishchandra

Bharati, Dharamvir, 76, 89; cosmopolitanism of, 262, 280n4; on crisis of modernity, 77–78; as iconic editor of Hindi weekly *Dharmayug*, 76; modernist definition of identity, 28; as postcolonial modernist, 73, 76–80; *Andha yug*, 28, 76, 95–96, 104, 121, 125, 262, 289n3; *Dharmavira bharati granthavali*, 77–80, 285n9; *Nadi pyasi thi*, 76

Bharat Rang Mahotsav (India theater festival), 101, 109

Bhatta, Krishna, 247

Bhatta, Narayana, 161

Big Fat City, The. See Dattani

Bjornson, Bjorn, 172

Bolt, Robert: *A Man for All Seasons*, 292n27

Bombay/Mumbai, xiii,19, 38, 40, 41, 81, 158, 230, 238, 255, 303n37; as setting in plays, 56, 179, *194*, 201, 202, 203, *204*, 205, 300n75; as theater location, 57, 65, 68, 72, 92, 100, 101, 102, 103, 104, 108, 117, 118, 127, *136*, 170, 181, 192, 231, 233, 264, 265, 287n44, 287n46

brahman, as caste category, 28, 29, 96, 129, 133, 135, 230; dominance of, in Hindu society, 230; dominance of, in Indian politics, 233, 236, 237–38, 241, 255, 303n37; satirized in *Ghashiram kotwal*, 231, 235–41, 236, 242, 286n24 *See also* caste system

Brecht, Bertolt, 21, 81, 105, 189, 231, 295n27; as influence on Indian playwrights, 189–90, 192, 239, 248–52, 263, 264

Brook, Peter, 265, 290n6

Budo saliker ghare ron (The old fool's fads). *See* M. Dutt

Calcutta/Kolkata, xiii, 19, 28, 38; as theater location, 57, 65, 68, 72, 98, 100, 101, 102, 103, 106, 107, 117, 130, *145*, *147*, 153–54, 170, 181, 264, 287n44, 287n46; as setting in plays, 182–83, 191–92, 297n49; as setting in films, 298n54

Camus, Albert, 81, 134, 190, 264

Carthage College: production of *One Day in the Season of Rain*, 59–60, *60*,

Case, Sue-Ellen, 196

caste system, Hindu, 14, 24, 28, 88, 167, 298n55; as subject in films, 87–88; as subject in plays, 29, 74, 122, 129, 226, 231, 234–41; *See also* brahman

center-periphery models, dismantling of, 23, 50–55, 261

Chakrabarty, Dipesh, 15

Chakravyuha (Battle Formation). *See* Thiyam

Chandavarkar, Bhaskar, 231

Chandigarh: designed by Le Corbusier at Nehru invitation, 38; as UNESCO World Heritage Site, 38, *39*

Chaplin, Charlie, 33–34, *34*, *35*

Charandas chor (Charandas the thief). *See* Tanvir

Chatterjee, Partha, 83

Chatterjee, Sudipto, 131

Chattopadhyay, Kamaladevi: ambivalence towards traditional theater, 216; bourgeois-nationalist vision of state-supported theaters, 99

Chattopadhyay, Mohit, 89

Chekhov, Anton, 15, 81, 165, 170, 173, 179, 231, 248, 263, 264, 295n16

Chopra, Pushpa, 158

Citizen Kane (film): influence on *Kagaz ke phool*, 34–35; Welles as director, *34*, *37*

Ciuguraneau, Adina, 124–25

closet plays, 21, 66, 68, 72, 73, 92, 170, 177, 291n10

colonialism: end of, in India, 5, 259; effects of, on Indian languages, 16, 281n18; Euro-Western cultural influences and, 7, 261; epistemic violence of, 10; legacy of, 182; limited growth of capitalism during, 167; modernizing effects of, 17, 18, 123, 162, 260, 283n39; economic "peripheralization" of India during, 54; reading habits and, 278n32; relation of, to modernism, 63, 74, 75; relation of, to precolonial culture, 17, 219; urban-rural divide in, 106

colonial theater: anticolonialism in, 118, 171, 295n26; closet plays in, 68, 73, 291n10; entertainment for profit model in, 102, 170, 181; extended ideological critiques of, 70–73, 174, 214; as incompatible with realism, 169–70; indigenized aesthetic of, 75, 170; legacy of classical Sanskrit theater in, 169; modernist rupture from, 72; modernity of, 65, 66, 261; myth and history leading narratives in, 115; Prasad on, 70; Rakesh distaste for, 84; as secular commercial institution, 68; variety of content in, 170
Communist Party of India (CPI), 71, 214
Communist Party-Marxist (CPM), 29, 180, 220, 256
Communist Party of India-Maoist, 256, 305n69
Communist Party of India-Marxist-Leninist (CP-ML), 305n69
Coppola, Carlo, 81
Correa, Charles: as architect of Kanchanjunga Apartment Building, 40, *40*, *41*
cosmo-modernism: activism as distinct from, 267–68; anatomy of, 23–30; as quality of authorial careers, 27, 64, 243, 247, 262–63, 265; of Bharati and Rakesh, 76–81, 262; chronology of, 266–67; as dimension of India/West relations, 162; definition of, 7, 261; effect of multilingualism and hermeneutic gap on, 207–8; as neologism, 7; playwright-director relationship and, 27; post-1990 landscape and, 268–69, 307n9; and theater in retrospect, 259–71; translation and, 263–64
cosmopolitanism, 19, 27, 28, 49, 64, 103, 243, 263, 269, 270; Anglocentric discussions of, 11, 12, 275; as quality in plays, 137, 175, 187, 188, 189, 203, 263, 271; IPTA rejection of, 71; as key term in modernism, 9; of modern Indian languages, 52, 261; relation to identity politics, 28–29; rooted forms of, 261; vernacular forms of, 51, 261
cosmopolitan modernism, 32, 52, 58, 73, 74–75, 81, 104, 124, 162, 271

Courbet, Gustave, "Realist Manifesto" (1855), 164
CPM. *See* Communist Party-Marxist
CP-ML. *See* Communist Party of India-Marxist-Leninist
cultural-nationalist platform: of Awasthi and Jain, for theatre of roots, 218–19, 302n15; Azad on, 216; K. Chattopadhyay on, 216; modernist opposition to, 49, 123, 132, 139, 228, 229, 232, 270; for MT, 220, 269–70; Seminar on Contemporary Playwriting and Play Production and, 217; SNA and, 215–16; SNA Roundtable and, 81, 217–18, 300n4

Dalmia, Vasudha, 49, 289n3
Dalvi, Abdussattar, 57
Dance Like a Man. See Dattani
Die Panne (A Dangerous Game). *See* Dürenmatt
Dattani, Mahesh, 89, 100, 101, 178–80, 265, 266, 297n49; English language and, 89, 202, 299n73; as founder-director of Playpen, 287n44; as proponent of urban social realism, 25, 74, 177, 178, 207; as postcolonial modernist playwright, 74; *Big Fat City, The*, 179; *Dance Like a Man*, 180; *Tara*, 25, 163, 201–7, 204, 300n75; "Three Little Slices of Urban Indian Life," 178; *Where There's a Will*, 297n49
Davis, Evan Grae, 300n76
Dharmavira bharati granthavali (Collected works of Dharamvir Bharati). *See* Bharati
Desani, G. V., 275n11
Deshpande, Arvind, 56, 88, 181
Deshpande, G. P., 26, 98, 177, 181, 218, 221–22, 224, 270; affiliation with Communist Party-Marxist, 29; *Ek vajoon gela ahe*, 29; *Uddhwasta dharmashala*, 29, 180
Deshpande, Sulabha, 88, 126, 181; as outstanding performer of realism, 56; on thirteen translations of *Shantata! court chalu ahe*, 283n37
Dev, Amiya, on Bengali modernism, 48–49

INDEX

Devi, Mahasweta, 26, 177, 181
Dharmayug (Hindi weekly). *See* Bharati
Dharwadker, Aparna [Bhargava]: 3–4; *Poetics of Modernity, A*, 5, 65, 280n40, 284n1, 284n2, 287n46, 299n70; *Theatres of Independence*, 197, 284n1, 289n3, 303n30, 306n3
Dharwadker, Vinay, 13, 59, 175, 297n35; on timelines for Indian modernism, 18; "Modernism and Its Four Phases," 49, 276n12
De Sica, Vittorio, 33–34
De Saussure, Ferdinand, 31
Dishantar (theater group). *See* Shivpuri, Om
Doyle, Laura, 273n5, 274n7, 275n11
drama: colonial, on contemporary topics, 161; Harishchandra on, 69; Ibsenian realism in, 175, 295n16, 296n34, 297n29; Lukács on modern bourgeois, 165; poetic, 69–70; Prasad on, 69; Rakesh reflections on, 80, 85; as medium for re-presenting past, 114; as palimpsestic form, 114, 115; radical contemporaneity of, 160; relationship with print medium, 66, 73, 97, 130, 270; shift from verse to conversational prose in, 166; Tagore on Sanskrit definition of, 70; as urban form, 118, 129, 137, 220
Dramatic Art and Design Academy, 287n44
Dubey, Satyadev, 101, 181, 182, 184, 264, 265, 283n36, 296n29; *Andha yug* directed by, 96; *Yayati* directed by, 126, *136*
Dubrow, Jennifer, 49
Dujardin, Filip, 40; "Untitled," *40*
Dürenmatt, Friedrich, *Die Panne*, 56, 263
Dutt, Guru: influenced by Welles, 34; *Kagaz ke phool* directed by, 34, 36, *36*, *37*
Dutt, Michael Madhusudan, 17, 66; *Mahabharata* used by, 161, 261; on Sanskrit aesthetics, 169; *Budo saliker ghare ron*, 293n4; *Ekei ki bale sabhyata?*, 293n4; *Meghnad badh*, 298n57; *Sharmishtha natak*, 125, 128–32, 261

East-West Seminar, 81
economics of theater production: colonial theater as commercial enterprise, 21, 65, 66, 68, 102, 169, 170, 207, 214, 260; decommercialization of postindependence theater, 22, 67, 70–73, 91, 98–106, 173, 288n48
education policy of India, three-language formula in, 281n14
Ekach pyala (Just one glass). *See* Gadkari
Ekei ki bale sabhyata? (You call this civilization?). *See* M. Dutt
Ek vajoon gela ahe (It's Past One O' Clock). *See* G. Deshpande
Eliot, T. S., 20, 63, 85, 89, 104, 124, 292n27; "Burnt Norton," 85; *The Criterion* (journal), 4, 281n5; "The Dry Salvages," 133; *Four Quartets*, 191, 262; "Gerontion," 262; "Journey of the Magi," 262, 281n5; *Murder in the Cathedral*, 292n27; "Sweeney Agonistes," 191; "Tradition and the Individual Talent," 26, 301n11; *The Waste Land*, 190, 262
Elkunchwar, Mahesh, 25, 89, 227, 263, 288n47, 297n49; on folk theater, 229; interview of, 179; Mehta director of plays by, 97; *Mi jinkalo! mi haralo!* impact on, 97; performance deferred, of plays by, 96–98; plays published in *Satyakatha* magazine, 97; as postcolonial modernist playwright, 74; as proponent of urban social realism, 25, 177, 178, 179; *Atmakatha*, 25, 163, 192–201, *194*; *Pratibimba*, 297n49; *Wada chirebandi* 197
English language: complex position of, in relation to Indian languages, 6, 11–12, 29, 32, 33, 43, 45, 49, 51, 75, 77, 80, 130, 175, 182, 254–55, 260, 283n9, 299n72; Dattani and, 89, 202–3, 299n73; as global medium, 11, 48, 64, 126, 137, 274n7; as language of modernism, 9, 273n5, 277n14; Macaulay on propagation of, 182; as national link language in India, 11, 213, 260; as official language in India, 43, 260; global readership of prose fiction in, 12; as target language of translation, 5,

English language (*continued*)
12–13, 29, 47, 55, 58, 59, 104, 108, 117, 125, 126, 130, 137, 161, 177, 246, 268, 284n1, 292n24, 294n6; vernacular model and, 50, 51. *See also* Anglocentrism; Anglophone writing

ethics of appropriation in traditionalism: Elkunchwar on, 179, 227, 229; Kaul on, 227; as modernist concern in use of traditional forms, 226–227, 229; Raina on, 227; as separation of form from content, 227–28; Tanvir on feudalism of folk culture, 228–29; tradition as spectacle for urban audiences, 179, 228. *See also* modernist traditionalism

Euro-American modernism, 48, 62, 68, 98, 124, 264–65, 266, 273n5, 284n3

Evam indrajit (And Indrajit) (Sircar), 58, 182–92, *185*, *187*; Calcutta as setting for, 183, 298n54; cosmopolitan reach of, 188, 189; Dubey on, 182; as example of modernist realism, 184, 191–92; included in *Three Modern Indian Plays*, 58; interchangeable characters in, 184, 186; metatheatrical elements in, 182–83, 186, 189; modernist influences on, 189–91, 262–63; as neocolonial wasteland, 182, 190; stylized structure of, 186–88; translation of, 294n6

Faulkner, Peter, 20
film. *See* Indian cinema
folk culture: as charismatic and liberatory, 197; as deeply political, 225; as artistic expression of "the people," 210; feudal roots of, 228–29; Kambar connection to, 211, 222; Panikkar connection to, 221, 222; precarity of, 227, 229

folk theater forms, 226, 227, 263; criticism of, 179, 217, 218, 221, cultural-nationalist support for, 179, 216–17, 249, 300n4; focus on gender in, 226; IPTA revival of, 71, 214, 215, 300n2; use of, in urban theater, 26, 29, 133, 134, 210, 222, 223, 243, 248, 304n49

Freedman, Ariela, 50, 275n8
Friedman, Susan Stanford, 14, 63, 75, 285n8

Gadkari, Ram Ganesh, 293n4; *Ekach pyala*, 170–71
Gandhi, Indira, 198, 233, 299n69
Gandhi, Mohandas K., 167, 171, 199, 213–14, 238, 263
Gandhi, Shanta, 218; *Jasma odan*, 26
Gangopadhyay, Rudrani, 13, 51, 276n12
Gargi, Balwant, 104, 226
Gassner, John, 295n14
gender, 17, 21, 24, 27, 28, 29, 142, 161, 162, 177, 224, 226, 267, 270, 271, 281n18; and authorship, 27, 199, 200, 201, 287n44; conflicts based on, in modernist plays, 26, 122, 129, 133, 142, 148, 149, 150, 156, 157, 166, 172, 195; inequities of, in India, 142, 168, 204, 205, 206, 220, 300n76
geomodernism, 5, 9, 52, 64, 259; singular Indian linguistic plurality in, 6
Gharabaher (Out of the house). *See* Atre
Ghashiram kotwal (Constable Ghashiram) (Tendulkar), 26, 212, 223, 229, 230–41, 236, 242, 298n64; attempted suppression of, 232–33; brilliantly collaborative production of, 231; court order relating to, 233; as controversial history play, 74, 233–34; 286n24; as exception in Tendulkar's oeuvre, 286n24; modernist subversion of religion in, 232, 239–41; Patel as director of, 231, 236, 242; PDA initial run of, 230–31; satiric representation of Pune brahmans in 234–40; theatre of roots movement and, 109, 231; use of folk theater forms in, 223, 304n49
Ghatak, Ritwik, 33, 36, 38
Ghorpade, Padmaja, 57
Ghosh, Amitav, 12, 50, 51, 275n11, 280n5
Ghosh, Girish Chandra, 66, 169, 120, 121
Gikandi, Simon, 52–53, 63, 281n18
global modernisms, 8, 10–14, 30, 32, 48, 62, 68, 87, 259, 260, 287n12; approached through world-systems theory, 53–54; geographical configurations of, 10–11; major languages added to, 9; positioning India in relation to, 12, 30, 48, 62, 68, 87, 259, 260
Gokhale, Gopal Krishna, 237

INDEX

Gokhale, Shanta, 172, 175, 177, 178
Gorky, Maxim, 81, 248, 263
group theater: defined by Sircar, 100–101, examples of, 287n44; as primary noncommercial model in postindependence theater, 99–100, 287n44
Gujaral, Satish, 40
Gujarati language, 17, 29, 32, 44, 46, 72, 102; plays in, 89, 173, 177, 180, 297n49

Haach mulacha baap (He is the groom's father). *See* Varerkar
Harishchandra, Bhartendu, 17–18, 23, 66, 69, 70, 72, 84, 170; antitheatricalism of, 98, 181; engagement with Sanskrit legacy, 66, 161, 169; *Andher nagari*, 293n7; *Bharat durdasha*, 293n7; *Natak*, 69
Hayavadana (Horse-head). *See* Karnad
Hellman, Lillian, 196
Hindi language, 12, 13, 16, 28, 29, 32, 33, 44, 45, 46, 47, 77, 92, 273n5; as film medium, 33, 76, 265, 283n36, 291n23; as link language in India, 43, 213; as major language of literature and theater, 29, 48, 49, 69,72, 80, 82, 92, 139, 170, 177; major modernist authors in, 17–18, 51, 76–77, 80, 89, 263–64, 297n35; new short story/novel and new poetry in, 82; not as vernacular, 51–52; as official language in India, 43; plays in, 26, 55, 59, 84, 102, 104, 107, 108, 121, 122, 125, 126, 154, 180, 212, 215, 243, 268, 269, 292n25, 293n4; Rakesh focus on theater in, 81, 92–93, 94, 262, 292n26
Hindu: fundamentalism, forms of, 115, 303n37; mythology, 116–118, 129, 241, 291; religious concepts and practices, 122, 184, 232, 235, 290n7; society, flaws in, 161, 167, 205, 238; nationalist thought, 237–38, 255, 306
Hinduism, 29, 116–17, 121, 141, 241, 291
Hirma ki amar kahani (The immortal tale of Hirma) (Tanvir), 212, 229–30, 243–44, 245, 246–57, 250, 253, 254; aesthetic and political strands in, 243–44; basis in history of Bastar region, 244–45; Bhanj Deo as model for, 244, 245, 246–47, 256; as Brechtian play, 248–49, 251–53; foreshadowing of Maoist insurgency in, 256; metatheatricality of, 247; modernist form and affect in, 248–55; as postcolonial text, 250; three-tier use of language in, 253–55
history. *See* myth and history
history play, 66, 114, 123, 262,292n26, 296n30; in colonial theater, 121; A. Dharwadker on, 289n3; as index of problems in Indian historiography, 118–20; as modernist form, 25, 123, 124, 133, 139, 140, 142, 234; theorized by Indian playwrights, 123, 124, 139–40, 233–35, 286n30
Husain, M. F.: "Horses" painting, 38, 39; quasi-cubist horses of, 38

Ibsen, Henrik, 15, 21, 70, 104, 114, 164–65, 170, 172, 173, 231, 295n16; Moi on, 166; as influence on realism in Indian drama, 175, 179, 264, 295n27, 296n29, 296n34
India: absence of national language in, 43; bourgeois-nationalism in, 22, 70, 71, 99, 199, 213; as challenge to word-systems theory, 54–55; and economic globalization, 24; end of colonialism in, 5; forms of capitalism in, 54–55, 167–68, 267, 306n5, 307n10; gender inequalities in, 168, 300n76; literary culture of, 6, 13, 49, 55, 59, 75, 76, 129, 195, 197–98, 283n39, 307n10; as location of geomodernism, 6, 52, 64, 259; nature of bourgeoisie in, 167, 168, 173, 174, 295n24, 296n34; nature of personal identity in, 28; neoliberalism in, 24, 267, 307n10; precolonial forms of modernity in, 15; shifting position in world economic system, 54; twenty-first-century conditions in, 255–57, 306n70; urban-rural divide in, 179, 210, 214
Indian cinema, 27, 33, 42, 55, 291n23; in English, 179, 245; film versions of *Shantata!*, 283n36; influence of Welles on G. Dutt, 34; influence of De Sica

Indian cinema (*continued*)
and Chaplin on Kapoor, 33–34, *34*, *35*; Marathi New Cinema movement in, 283n36; of Ray and Ghatak, in Bengali, 33, 298n54; in Telugu, 33; Tendulkar as screenwriter for, 76, 87–88; theater-film relation, 81, 85, 86, 92, 93, 96, 103, 106, 287n46, 290n6, 298n54

Indian Constitution: Eighth Schedule on Indian languages, 43; protection of adivasi and Scheduled Tribes in, 246, 305n59

Indian People's Theatre Association (IPTA): conflict with Nehru government, 71; critique of colonial theater by, 71, 214; left-populist approach of, 72, 77, 99, 212, 214–15, 219; major plays performed by, 215; as model for decommercialized performance, 99; as a national movement, 71, 72, 213; use of folk and traditional forms by, 71, 214, 215. *See also* Tanvir

indigenous performance forms, 10, 11, 19, 26, 66, 179, 209, 210–11, 214, 215, 219, 220, 264, 300n4; Bayalata (Karnataka), 210, 211, 223, 224; Dashavatar (Maharashtra), 210, 212, 238; Kirtan (Maharashtra), 238, 240; Nautanki (Uttar Pradesh), 210, 228; Tamasha (Maharashtra), 71, 210, 212, 215, 222–23; Kathakali (Kerala), 122, 210, 228; Kutiyattam (Kerala), 122, 211, 268; Yakshagana (Karnataka), 210, 211, 223, 228, 264

I Pravir, the Adivasi God (film), 245

IPTA. *See* Indian People's Theatre Association

"It's a Girl" (documentary film). *See* Davis

Jain, Kirti, 101, 299n70; as *Laharon ke rajhans* director, *150*, *151*

Jain, Nemichandra: theatre of roots and, 218–19, 301n9, 302n15

Jalan, Shyamanand, 57, 101, 181, 264, 287n44, 293n30, 296n29; as director of *Ashadh*, 107; as director of *Laharon ke rajhans*, 145, 147, *147*, 153; Rakesh collaboration with, 128, 149–50, 153–54

Jana Natya Manch (The people's stage) street theater group, 219–20, 267, 307n9

Jasma odan. *See* Gandhi, Shanta

Jokumaraswami. *See* Kambar

Joyce, James, 3, 4, 9, 20, 21, 280n5, 285n8; *Portrait of the Artist as a Young Man, A*, 280n5; *Ulysses*, 113

Kafka, Franz, 81, 190, 263

Kagaz ke phool (Paper flowers): *Citizen Kane* comparison to, 34–35; as cult classic, 36; of G. Dutt, 34, 36, *37*

Kalidasa, 105, 140; portrayal of, in *Ashadh ka ek din*, 59, 60, 86, 107, 108, 122, 138, 140, 234, 289n3; translated by Rakesh, 138–39

Kambar, Chandrashekhar, 98, 105, 218, 265, 266, 288; Bayalata folk form of, 223; contemporization of tradition by, 224, 225; on drama as essentially poetic form, 220–21; folk culture and, 222, 228–29, 263; theatre of roots movement and, 109, 231; *Jokumaraswami*, 26, 223, 224–25, 231; *Samba-shiva prahasana*, 26

Kannada language, 12, 28, 32, 44, 45, 46, 49; not as vernacular, 51–52; plays in, 26, 29, 57, 72, 89, 92, 95, 96, 102, 105, 108, 121, 122, 123, 126, 127, 129, 132, 137, 170, 177, 212, 226, 263, 264

Kanyasulkam (Girls for sale). *See* Apparao

Kapoor, Raj: interaction with Chaplin and De Sica, 33–34, *34*, *35*; in "Mera Naam Joker," 34

Karanth, B. V., 57, 219, 228, 264, 288n47, 296n29; supported as NSD Director, 101; translator of *Shantata!* into Kannada, 57

Karimkutty. *See* Panikkar

Karnad, Girish, 17, 25, 73, 74, 97, 101, 104, 160, 177, 265, 266, 288n47; career in film and television, 92, 96, 265; comparison with M. Dutt, 129, 131–32, 137; on decline in theater audiences, 103; on energy of folk theater, 226;

INDEX

on failure of realism in colonial theater, 296n34; interview in 1995, 160; Kannada language and, 89, 95, 126, 129; Kurtkoti challenge and, 96; *Mahabharata* and, 95, 159, 261; Parsi theater and, 96; as postcolonial modernist playwright, 73, 74, 96; on theater as parasitic genre, 290n6; traditional forms and narratives in theater of, 211; as translator of *Evam indrajit*, 294n6; as ultramodernist practitioner of MT, 222; use of Yakshagana, 211, 223; *Hayavadana*, 26, 135, 212, 223, 231; "Theatre in India," 95–96; *Tughlaq*, 28–29, 58, 96, 104, 234, 263; *Yayati*, 25, 95, 115, 125, 126, 127, 128–29, 131, 133–37, *136*, 159, 291n31
Kaul, Bansi, 227
Kaviraj, Sudipta, 18, 277n23
Kelly, Joshua Thomas, 59, *61*
Koi pan ek phoolnu naam bolo to (Tell me the name of a flower). See Rye
Koyma (The right to rule). See Panikkar
Kulinkulsarvasa (For the well-born, lineage is everything). See Tarkaratna
Kulkarni, Sudhir, 57
Kulvadhu (Dynastic bride). See Rangnekar
Kumar ni agashi (Kumar's terrace). See Rye
Kurtkoti, Kirtinath, 96, 291n21

Lagoo, Shriram, 181, *194*, 265; *Yayati* directed by, 126
Laharon ke rajhans (The royal swans on the waves) (Rakesh), 25, 86, 123, 139, *145*, 146, *147*, 148–56, *150*, *151*, 292n27; the Buddha as offstage presence in, 141, 144, 262; connection between Rakesh personal life and, 144, 157–58; Jain as director of, 128, *150*, *151*, 154; Jalan as director of, *145*, *147*, 153; lampstands and drifting swans symbolism in, 148–50; as palimpsestic play, 115, 125, 127, 148–59; as playwright's theater in practice, 1966, 153–54; Rakesh rewriting of, in 1966 and 1968, 128, 153, 155–59; *Saundarananda* as primary source of, 125, 127; O. Shivpuri as director of, 128; unresolvable gender conflicts in, 128,142, 149, 151, 153, 154, 156
languages of modernism: rapid proliferation of, in modernist studies, 8–9
Le Corbusier: influence on Correa and Gujaral, 40; Nehru invitation for design of Chandigarh, 38, *39*
left-populist platforms: dissociation of, from MT, 213, 220; of IPTA, 212, 214–15; Pradhan on, 214–15
Lindgren, Allana C., 15–16, 53, 63, 273n5, 275n11, 276n13, 293n5
lok kala/loknatya. See folk culture; folk theater forms
Lorca, Federico Garcia, 104, 221, 248, 263, 264
Lukács, György, 160, 165

Macaulay, Thomas Babington: "Minute on Education," 182
Mahabharata Sanskrit epic, 24, 28, 129; as epic of ambivalence, 25, 121; as major modern literary source, 76, 95, 117, 118, 121, 125, 130–31, 137, 159, 161, 211, 261, 262; Karnad perspectives on, 95, 159, 261, 290n6; Panikkar and Thiyam as directors of plays based on, 121, 211; Yayati section of, 128–29 See also *Andha yug*; *Sharmishtha*; *Yayati*
Mahindra Awards for Excellence in Theatre, 102
Majha nataki sansar (My theater world). See Varerkar
"*Majhe lekhan kashasathi?*" (What is my writing for?) See Tendulkar
"*Majhe natyashikshan*" (My theater education). See Tendulkar
Malayalam language, 13, 29, 32, 44, 45, 46, 49; plays in, 102, 122, 211, 212, 215
Manipuri language, 29, 44, 46; plays in, 109, 121, 122, 211, 212, 292n24
Mao, Douglas, 20, 48, 80, 275n11
Marathi language, 12, 13, 29, 32, 33, 44, 46, 49, 299n68; cinema in, 33; experimental theater groups in, 56, 88, 268; high-metropolitan bilingual literary culture of, 49; literary culture

Marathi language (*continued*)
of, 197–98; major authors in, 9, 51, 72, 87, 89, 92, 125, 175, 177, 180, 261, 293n4, 295n26, 297n49, 304n49; not as vernacular, 51–52; plays in, 25, 55, 57, 58, 66, 74, 97, 102, 117, 118, 123, 163, 170, 171, 172, 173, 180, 212, 223; as target language of translation, 91, 109, 126, 138, 264, 296n29. *See also Atmakatha*, *Ghashiram kotwal*

Marinetti, F. T., 293n5

Meherwal, Sheela, 158

Mehta, Vijaya, 218, 264, 265, 287n44; as director of Elkunchwar plays, 97, 101, 181, 265; as director of Tendulkar plays, 88, 101, 181; as founder of Rangayan theater group, 88

Meister, Michael, on vernacular architecture, 42

Mi jinkalo! mi haralo! (I won, I lost). See Tendulkar

Miller, Arthur, 15; *The Crucible*, 114, 292n27

Mistry, Rohinton, 12, 51, 280n5

Mitra, Sombhu, 99, 181, 233, 288n47, 296n29; on problems of noncommercial performance, 100; on theater audience, 103

modern Indian languages: classical origins of, 45, 46, 51, 52; center-periphery and vernacular models inappropriate for, 50–55, 197; demographics of, 46; dominance of, in literature and theater, 52, 66, 74, 275n11, 281n18; Eighth Schedule of Indian Constitution on, 43; geographical distribution of, 43–44, 44; historical development and continuity of, 5, 46, 47, 51, 54; marginality of, in modernist studies, 5–6, 8; problems of access in transnational frame, 6; rapid development of print culture in, 19; relationship to English, 11–13, 75; transnational presence of, 46 See also English language; multilingualism

modernism, Indian: as dominant aesthetic-political movement after 1950, 7, 162; autonomy of aesthetic in, 48, 73; defined outside language axis, 33–43; definitional problems in, 16–18; as distinct from colonial modernity, 18–19, 47–48; effective methodologies for recovery of, 61–63; excluded from Europhone global marketplace, 64; four phases of, 49, 276n12; intralingual and intraregional perspectives in, 62; intranational frame of, 5, 16, 55; as largest non-Europhone formation in global modernism, 5, 12, 13, 22; marginality of, in modernist studies, 8, 11, 13–14, 275n11, 276n12, 276n13, 277n14; and multilingual literacy, 11, 23, 53; timelines for, 18–19; tradition and, 26, 209–57; transnational frames for, 6, 38, 47–48, 262–63, 271; transnational modernist studies and, 8, 62–63 See also modernist Indian theater; multilingualism; translation

modernist classicism, 137, 265

modernist Indian theater: authorial self-fashioning in, 76–91; audience-centered initiatives in, 102–6; cosmopolitanism of, 137, 175, 187, 188, 189, 203, 263, 271; decommercialization of, 70–72, 91–92; deferral and actualization of performance in, 92–106; defining features of, 73–75; high period of, 55, 269; multilingualism of, 7; opposition to cultural-nationalist ideology in, 72, 217, 221, 228–29; post-1990 developments in, 267–69; principal forms of, 25, 115, 124–25, 137, 162, 174–75, 177, 210, 220–21, 265; proto-modernist prefiguring of, 69–70 ; rupture from colonial theater in, 72–73; timeline of, 19–20; perceived canonicity of, 270–71

modernist realism, 26, 29, 64, 207, 210, 266, 280n41, 297n35; actors with outstanding credentials in, 181; author-audience relationship and, 175; of Dattani, 180, 202, 297n49; of Elkunchwar, 178–80, 192–94, 297n49; leading directors of, 181; as deviation from realism, 162, 174–75, 180; Gokhale on, 175; in political plays, 26; qualities of, 26, 175–76, 180–81, 297n49; of Rakesh, 87; of Rye, 180, 297n49; of Tendulkar, 175–77, 212

INDEX

modernist traditionalism (MT), 266; aesthetics and politics of, 220–26; definition and qualities of, 210, 212–13, 219–20, 229–30; difference from left-populist and cultural-nationalist positions, 212, 228, 246; ethics of appropriation in, 226–30; major practitioners of, 210–12; of Panikkar as director of Sanskrit plays, 210–11; signature works of, 212; Tanvir as pioneer of, 210; Tendulkar use of, to represent Maratha history, 212, 232 *See also Ghashiram kotwal*; *Hirma ki amar kahani*

modernity: Bharati on crisis of, 77–78; Chakrabarty on, 15; P. Chatterjee on, 83; of colonial theater, 66; conflated with modernism in Indian languages, 8, 16–18; Friedman on modernism and, 14; India interest in precolonial forms of, 15; Kaviraj on, 277n23; Pollock on, 62; Rakesh on Indianness and, 83–84

Modi, Narendra, 255, 304n48, 306n5

Mohan rakesh rachanavali (MRR) (The works of Mohan Rakesh). *See* Rakesh

Moi, Toril, 166

Moody, Alys, 13–14, 273n5, 276n12, 277n14, 280n4

Moretti, Franco: Arac critique of distant reading of, 274n7; bourgeois defined by, 165

MRR. *See Mohan rakesh rachanavali*

MT. *See* modernist traditionalism

Mulgund, Krishnadev, 231

Multilingualism in India, 6–7, 16, 42, 163; codified in Indian Constitution, 43; demographics of, 46; effect of, on theatre, 46, 208, 287n46; geography of, 44; as fundamental feature of literary culture, 13, 48, 50; hermeneutic gap created by, 207–8; history, aesthetics, and politics of, 43–46, 61–62; intranational process of translation and, 55, 275n10; as simultaneous presence of works in many languages, 47; singularity of, 22, 45–47

multilingual literacy: as central to Indian literary culture, 5, 26, 27, 42, 47, 115, 260–61; effect of, on modernist expression, 23, 53; incompatible with single national language, 11

Murder in the Cathedral. See Eliot

musical drama. *See sangeet natak*

Muthuswami, Naa, 221

myth and history as narrative sources: in colonial theater, 115, 120–21, 161; heroic constructions of, 24, 120–21; Hoffman on Western approaches to, 289n5; modernist deconstructions of, 25, 74, 86, 121–24, 289n3; in modernist drama, 86, 114–15, 159, 211, 223; in modernist literature, 113–14; in palimpsestic modernism, 115, 124–28; in postindependence theater, 24, 87; as referents for the present, 133, 136, 171; talking cinema impact on, 291n23

Nadi pyasi thi (The river was thirsty). *See* Bharati

Narayan, R. K., 12, 275n9

Natak (Drama). *See* Harishchandra

Natak ani mi (The theater and I). *See* Tendulkar

Natakkar aur rangamanch (The playwright and the stage). *See* Rakesh

National Centre for the Performing Arts, in Bombay/Mumbai, 101

National Performing Arts Academy. *See* Sangeet Natak Akademi

National School of Drama (NSD), 56, 101, 249; Alkazi as director of, 99, 104, 107; production of *Ashadh ka ek din*, 107, *108*; production of *Laharon ke rajhans*, *150*, *151*; support of Alkazi and Karanth from 1962–1983, 101

Natya-vimarsha (Meditation on theater). *See* Rakesh

Naya Theatre: inclusion of folk and adivasi actors in, 243; indigenization of Western playwrights by, 247–48; productions of, 247–49; productions of *Good Person of Szechwan* (Brecht), 248; regional history and folklore portrayals in, 210; Tanvir formation of, 210, 243, 248

Nehru Centenary Theatre Festival, 102, 288n47

INDEX

Nehru Fellowship, 81
Nehru, Jawaharlal, 38, 71, 79; IPTA opposition to, 213–14, 215
neoliberalism, 24, 267, 282n34, 307n10
New Criticism, Anglophone modernists at center of, 9
Nilakanteshwara Natya Seva Sangh (Ninasam), 102, 105, 287n44, 288n55
Ninasam Tirugata Repertory Company, Subbanna establishment of, 105
NSD. *See* National School of Drama
NSD Repertory Company, Alkazi establishment of, 100, 104

O'Neill, Eugene, 15, 95, 132, 170, 262; *Mourning Becomes Electra*, 114
Orwell, George, 280n5
Osten, Marion von, 41–42
Ottayan (The lone tusker). *See* Panikkar

painting, 42; *Guernica* of Picasso, 38, *38*; "Horses" of Husain, 38, *39*
palimpsestic modernism, 25, 115, 124–28; Ciuguraneau on, 124–25
palimpsests of past. *See* myth and history; palimpsestic modernism
Panikkar, K. N., 212, 221, 224, 231, 266, 288; on drama as essentially poetic form, 220–21; folk culture of, 222, 223; as leading director of Sanskrit drama, 121, 210–11; multiple theater roles of, 100, 265; as theatre of roots contributor, 219; use of Kerala regional forms, 211; *Karimkutty* 223, 224; *Koyma*, 223; *Ottayan*, 224
paradigmatic axis, in language, 31
parampara (tradition), 17, 209–10
paramparagat (traditional), 209–10
paramparasheel (traditional), 209–10
Parsi theater, 170; antitheatrical attacks on, 69–70; Islamic narratives and Urdu language in, 291n10; Karnad interest in, 96; Rakesh distaste for, 84; supplanted by talking films, 70
Parthasarathy, Indira, 98, 124, 177; *Aurangzeb*, 123; *Ramanujar*, 123
Partition (1947), 15, 18, 38, 81–82, 125, 261
Patel, Jabbar, 231, 233, *236*, 242, 287n46, 296n29

PDA. *See* Progressive Dramatic Association
performance deferral, in postindependence modernism, 91–98; Elkunchwar and, 92, 96–98; Karnad and, 92, 95–96; Rakesh and, 92–95
photography, 42; of Dujardin, 40, *40*; of Singh, 50, 275n11
Phule, Jyotiba, *Tritiya ratna*, 170, 293n4
Picasso, Pablo: as friend of Anand, 280n5; *Guernica*, 38, *38*
Pinter, Harold, 81, 293n30
Pirandello, Luigi, 21, 189, 264
planetary modernism, 5, 9, 24, 47, 48, 87; Friedman definition of, 63, 285n8
Play Is the Thing, The. *See* Tendulkar
poetic drama, 69–70, 98, 262, 292n27
poetics of modernity, in urban theater, 65–66
Pollock, Sheldon, 47, 55, 62, 276n13, 281n18
postcolonial modernism, 5, 67, 261; Bharati and, 76–80; English and Hindi languages and, 213; Euro-Western cultural influences and, 7; Gikandi on, 63; of playwrights, 74; Rakesh and, 68, 74, 76, 80–87; Tendulkar and, 76, 87–91. *See also* cosmopolitanism; cosmopolitan modernism
Pradhan, Sudhi, 214–15
Prasad, Jaishankar, 66, 69, 70, 121, 292n26; antitheatricalism of, 69, 98, 181; as author of closet drama, 72, 291n10; as critic of Ibsenism, 70; history plays by, 121; on Parsi theater, 70, 84; Rakesh on, 84; and Sanskrit drama, 66, 69; "Rangmanch," 69
Pratibimba (Reflection). *See* Elkunchwar
Prithvi Theatre, in Bombay/Mumbai, 101, 102
Progressive Dramatic Association (PDA), 230–31
Progressive Writers Association, 214; founded in 1936, 77; Tanvir membership in, 242
Puchner, Martin, 278n34, 284n3

INDEX

Raat bitane tak (*RBT*) (Until the Night Ends). *See* Rakesh
Raghavan, V., 217
Raina, M. K., 218, 221, 227, 287n46
Rainey, Lawrence, 274n7
Raja, Arundhati, 126, 287n44, 292n24
Rakesh, Mohan, 15, 17, 25, 49, 80–87, 94, 137–42, 158, 177, 178, 217, 234, 285n9, 289n3; on Hindi language, 80; on Hindi stage and Indian theater, 81, 92–93; interview with Coppola, 81; modernist classicism of, 137–39; as modernist playwright, 68, 73, 74, 76, 80–87; on modernity and Indianness, 83–84; multiple works based on *Saundarananda* as source, 127–28; palimpsestic modernism of, 115, 148–59; on Parsi theater, 84; on playwright's theater, 153–54; preoccupation with remote Indian past, 137–42; on world theater, 81; *Adhe adhure*, 57, 86–87, 139, 144, 156–57, 180, 289n3; *Ashadh ka ek din*, 55, 59–60, *60*, *61*, 67–68, 86, 92, 93, 106–9, *108*, 122, 128, 138, 140, 141, 234, 262, 289n3; *Laharon ke rajhans*, 25, 86, 115, 123, 125, 127–28, 139, 141, *145*, *147*, 148–56, *150*, *151*, 159, 262, 292n27; "Looking Around as a Playwright", 84; *Mohan rakesh rachanavali* (Taneja), 138, 285n9; *Natakkar aur rangmanch*, 94, 153–54; *Natya-vimarsha*, 80–81; *Raat bitane tak*, 144, 146, 151–52; *Rangmanch aur shabda*, 85; "Samajik-asamajik," 82–83; "Theatre Without Walls," 93
Rangacharya, Adya, 226
Rangayan experimental Marathi theater group, 56, 88, 97, 101; Tendulkar association with, 56, 97–98. *See also* Elkunchwar; Mehta; Tendulkar
"Rangmanch" (The Theater). *See* Tagore; Prasad
Rangmanch aur shabda (Theater and the word). *See* Rakesh
Rangnekar, M. G., 171, 172, 173, 180, 293n4; *Kulvadhu*, 172
Rao, Raja, 12, 275n9

Ratan Sadasyata (Diamond Membership): conferred by Sangeet Natak Akademi, 102, 288n47
Ray, Satyajit, 33, 36, 233
RBT. *See Raat bitane tak*
realism: antitheatricality of, 295n14; avant-garde opposition to, 293n5; Bentley and R. Williams endorsement of, 166; bourgeois focus of, 165, 166, 295n16; Chekhov and, 165, 173, 295n16; classic Western qualities of, 162, 164–66; Courbet on, 164; feminist critique of, 196; Ibsen and, 175, 295n16, 296n29, 296n34; as incompatible with colonial Indian formations,166–68; Moi on, 166; Tagore on, 70, 169; Western origins of, 164; Zola on necessity of, 164, 165, 169; modern Indian theater and, 163–74
realism in Indian theater, 24, 25, 63, 67, 87, 124, 137, 163, 164, 166, 168, 173, 191, 207, 208, 215, 266, 271, 289; as mode for engaging with present, 162, 167, 174, 192, 207; compared to Western classic realism, 164, 169, 174, 192, 202; Elkunchwar positions on, 179–80; Ibsen-Shaw vogue in, 172; leading postindependence exponents of, 174, 177; not definable as bourgeois drama, 167; as opposite of traditionalism, 210, 213, 222, 234, 243, 293n3, 301n11; and political plays, 26; separation of form and content in, 164, 173; Tendulkar as exemplar of, 97, 175–77; two phases of, 170–73; urban plays and, 25–26 *See also* modernist realism
religious history as subject: in plays by Rakesh, 138, 141, 292n25, 292n27; in world literature and film, 292n27 *See also Laharon ke rajhans*
Renoir, Jean, 33
Ross, Stephen, 15–16, 53, 63, 273n5, 275n11, 276n13, 293n5
Ross, Stephen J., 13–14, 273n5, 274n7, 276n12, 277n14, 280n4
Roundtable on the Contemporary Relevance of Traditional Theatre (SNA), 81, 217–18, 300n4
Roy, Amitav, 227

Roy, Arundhati, 12, 51, 275n11, 284n9
Roy, Kumar, 126, 264
Rushdie, Salman, 12, 51, 275n8, 280n5, 292n27
Rye, Madhu, 89, 177, 180, 181, 297n49; *Koi pan ek phoolnu naam bolo to*, 180; *Kumar ni agashi* 297n49

"*Samajik-asamajik*" (Social-antisocial). *See* Rakesh
Samba-shiva prahasana (The farce of Samba and Shiva). *See* Kambar
sangeet natak (musical drama), 70, 170, 296n30, 304n49; dominance of, 172; *Ekach pyala* as, 171
Sangeet Natak Akademi (SNA), 57, 101; 1958 award for *Ashadh*, 107; 1970 award for *Shantata!*, 56; Awasthi as secretary of, 218; cultural-nationalist platform of, 215–16; Drama Seminar organized by, 71–72; Roundtable on the Contemporary Relevance of Traditional Theatre organized by, 81, 217–18, 300n4; Scheme of Assistance to Young Theatre Workers, 300n4
Sangeet Natak (journal, of SNA), 217; "Traditional Idiom in Contemporary Theatre" special issue, 218
Sanskrit: as classical language of India, 43, 51, 52, 54, 65, 205, 210, 283n3; M. Dutt, Harishchandra, and Tagore on aesthetics of, 169; Kalidasa as poet-playwright in, 59, 95, 122, 138, 289n3; 59; Tagore on aesthetics of, 169
Sanskrit drama, 65, 120, 131, 134, 138, 169, 171, 209, 220, 234; decline of, 117, 209; influence on *Chakravyuha*, 222, 225; legacy of, in modern theater, 19, 66, 69–70, 129, 1340, 131, 134, 138, 171, 252; Panikkar as leading director of, 121, 210–11, 212, 222; Tanvir adaptation of, 243; translations of, 66, 105, 130–31, 138, 139, 161, 290n6 *See also Mahabharata*
Sari ga sari (Rain, o, rain). *See* Tendulkar
Sartre, Jean-Paul, 81, 95, 104, 132, 134, 190, 262, 264
Satteche gulam (Slaves to entitlement). *See* Varerkar

Satyakatha magazine, Elkunchwar plays published in, 97
Saundarananda (Handsome Nanda). *See* Ashvaghosha
Scharnick, Neil, 59, 60
Seminar on Contemporary Playwriting and Play Production (1961), 217, 300n4
Sermista (translation of *Sharmishtha*), 125, 130, 131, 132
Shahane, Ashok, 51
Shajapur ki shantibai (adaptation of Brecht, *Good Person of Szechwan*). *See* Tanvir
Shantata! court chalu ahe (Silence! The court is in session) (Tendulkar), 55, 56–58, 263, 283n36, 283n37, 297n40; awards for, 56; English translation of, 58; film versions of, 283n36; similarities with Dürenmatt, *Die Panne*, 263; translation into multiple languages, 56–58, 283n37
Sharma, Akshay, 42
Sharma, Sudha. *See* Shivpuri, Sudha
Sharmishtha natak (M. Dutt), 125, 128–31, 261, 125, 261; Bengali and English versions of, 129; English translation of, 137; *Mahabharata* story line followed closely in, 130; moral and ethical issues dismissed in, 131; Sanskrit dramaturgical elements in, 234; Shakespearean structure of, 129–30; *Yayati* 1961 and, 131–32, 137, 261 *See also Sermista*
Shaw, George Bernard, 170, 173
Shivpuri, Om, 107, *108*, 181, *187*; as co-founder of Dishantar theater group, 56; as director of *Laharon ke rajhans*, 128; as director of *Shantata!* in Hindi, 56–57; on *Adhe adhure*, 180
Shivpuri, Sudha, 42, 56–57, 107–8, *108*, 181, *185*, 287n44
Shiv Sena (political party), 233, 236, 238, 241, 255, 303n37
Shri Ram Centre for Art and Culture, in New Delhi, 101
Singh, Raghubir, 50, 275n11
Sircar, Badal, 25, 28, 104, 106, 177, 181; accidental quality of authorship of,

INDEX

98; Bengali-speaking, of Calcutta, 28; on group theater, 100–101; as postcolonial modernist playwright, 73, 74; on urban-rural divide in culture and theater, 106; use of interactive actors and audience, 106; *Baki itihas*, 189, 297n49; *Evam indrajit*, 58, 182–92, 185, 187, 262–63, 294n6; *Third Theatre, The*, 106, 179, 192, 263; *Tringsha shatabdi*, 189
SNA. *See* Sangeet Natak Akademi
Souza, F. N., 38
Stein, Gertrude, 20, 21
Strindberg, August, 15, 21, 95, 104, 263, 264
Subaltern Studies, 119
Subbanna, K. V., 106; collaboration with Bennewitz, 264; experiment with theater audience, 105; as founder of Ninasam, 105, 287n44; Ninasam Tirugata repertory company and, 105; as translator of Brecht, 264; as translator of classic Sanskrit, modern Indian, and Western plays, 105; on theater and community, 105
syntagmatic axis, in language, 31
Szondi, Peter, 160

Tagore, Rabindranath, 17, 23, 49, 66, 275n11, 284n3; on realism, 70, 169; on Sanskrit aesthetics, 169; on Sanskrit definition of drama, 70; symbolist-poetic plays of, 170; "Rangmanch," 69
Taneja, Jaidev, 138, 158, 285n9
Tanvir, Habib, 26, 100, 249, 257, 265, 266, 288; adivasi politics and, 242–48; Brecht influence on, 248–52, 263, 264; as IPTA member, 210, 219, 242, 300n2; as leading practitioner of MT; modernist traits of, 243; as native of Chhattisgarh, 222; Naya Theatre formed by, 210, 243, 248; as proponent of folk culture, 178, 228–29; range and boldness of theater work of, 242; use of folk and adivasi actors by, 247, 248, 249; *Charandas chor*, 26, 212, 248, 305n63; *Hirma ki amar kahani*, 212, 229–30, 246–57, 250, 251, 253, 254; *Shajapur ki shantibai*, 248–49

Tara (Dattani), 25, 163, 201–7, 204, 300n75; Bombay as city in, 300n75; critique of gender inequity in, 205, 206, 207; English as controversial choice for, 203; as family drama, 163, 203–4; as modernist-realist play, 201–7; multilevel set in, 202; structure and characters of, 201–6; stylized space of home in, 300n75
Tarkaratna, Ramnarayan, *Kulinkulsarvasva*, 161
Tendulkar, Vijay, 25, 175, 212, 261, 288n47; absence of collected works of, 285n9; centrality of act of writing for, 88–89; controversial plays of, 176–77; Marathi as creative medium of, 76, 87; as modernist playwright, 73; modernist-realist plays of, 175; plays of, in English translation, 58; postcolonial modernism and, 76, 87–91; pursuit of impersonality and depersonalization by, 89–90; as screenwriter for cinema, 76, 87–88; Tamasha folk form of, 222–23; as theorist of realism, 176–77, 261, 297n39; as translator, 264; as ultramodernist practitioner of MT, 222. *Ghashiram kotwal*, 26, 109, 212, 223, 229–42, 236, 242, 286n24, 298n64; "Majhe lekhan kashasathi", 87, 88; "Majhe natyashikshana," 90; *Mi jinkalo! mi haralo!*, 97; *Natak ani mi* of, 87, 89; *Play Is the Thing, The*, 87, 88; *Sari ga sari*, 222; "A Testament," 87, 89–90
theater: Karnard on parasitical genre of, 290n6; marginality of, in modernist studies, 7, 8, 20–22; noncapitalized culture of, in India, 22; orientalist constructions of, 283n38; of protest and resistance since 1980s, 29; Rakesh on word-centeredness in, 85–86; translation and, 55–6
"Theatre Without Walls." *See* Rakesh
theatre of roots movement, 26, 231, 232, 293n5, 301n11; theorized by Awasthi and Jain, 218–19, 302n15; iconic works of, 109, 231; *Hirma ki amar kahani* and, 246
Third Theatre, The. *See* Sircar
theatrical illusion, G. Ghosh on, 169

Thiyam, Ratan, 100, 222, 266, 288n47; as director of *Yayati*, 292n4; multiple roles of, in theatre, 265; regional forms used by, 211; as theatre of roots playwright, 109, 219, 231; *Chakravyuha* 121, 224–225
three-language formula, in India education policy, 281n14
"Three Little Slices of Urban Indian Life." *See Dattani*
traditional Indian forms: as antithetical to Eliot definition of tradition, 26, 301n11; connection to folk culture, 210; connection to seasonal rituals, 210; major examples of, 209–10; modernism and, 26, 29, 220–55 *See also* indigenous performance forms
"Traditional Idiom in Contemporary Theater, The." *See Sangeet Natak*
traditionalist modernism. *See* modernist traditionalism
"Tradition and the Individual Talent." *See* Eliot
translation: cosmo-modernism and, 263–64; English as target language of, 12 ; and modernism, 48; and multilingualism, 45, 47; role in intranational circulation, 55–58, 275n10; role in transnational circulation, 58–61
Tritiya ratna (The third gem). *See* Phule
Tughlaq. *See* Karnad

Uddhwasta dharmashala (The ruined sanctuary). *See* G. Deshpande.
UNESCO World Heritage Site, Chandigarh as, 38, 39
Untouchable. *See* Anand
Urdu language: 13, 32, 43, 45, 46, 277, 280n4, 297n35; Dubrow on literary culture of, 49; plays in, 57, 177, 212, 215, 243, 263, 264, 291

Varerkar, Bhargavram Vitthal (Mama), 293n4; *Haach mulacha baap*, 170, 171; *Majha nataki sansar* 171; *Satteche gulam* 171
Varma, Sarojini, 57

Vartak, Shridhar V., 171, 180, 293n4; as co-founder of Natyamanwantar group, 171; *Andhalyanchi shala*, 172, 173; *Takshashila*, 172

Wada chirebandi (Old stone mansion). *See* Elkunchwar
Walkowitz, Rebecca, 80; on Anglophone modernism, 48, 275n8; on center-periphery model, 52–53; on modernism beyond nation, 75, 284n7
Wallerstein, Immanuel: 53–55, 282n34
Welles, Orson: *Citizen Kane* director, 34, 37; as influence on G. Dutt, 34
Where There's a Will. *See* Dattani
Williams, Raymond, 166
Williams, Tennessee, 15, 170, 263, 293n30
Williams, William Carlos, 3, *Paterson*, 113
Winkiel, Laura, 273n5, 274n7, 275n8, 275n11, 308n13
Wollaeger, Mark, 53, 62–63, 273n5

Yayati (Karnad), 25, 95, 261; Adarkar English translation of, 126, 127; ancient social hierarchies and tribal identities in, 135; based on *Mahabharata*, 125, 128–29; compared with M. Dutt, *Sharmishtha* (1858), 131, 137; Dubey as director of, 126, 136; Kannada and English versions of, 129; Kannada publication of, 126, 291n21; Karnad 2008 English translation of, 126–27, 137, 159, 291n31; Karnad ambivalence about, 126–27; Lagoo, K. Roy, and Raja as directors of, 126; translations into other languages, 126; as palimpsestic play, 25, 115, 125, 131–37, 159; Sanskrit dramaturgical elements in, 134; self-reflexive recursiveness in, 126–27; story background for, 132–35; Western influences on structure of, 95, 132, 135
Yayati section, of *Mahabharata* Sanskrit epic, 128–29
Yeats, William Butler, 3, 4, 9, 20, 21, 63, 113, 221, 278n34, 291n21

Zola, Émile, 21, 164–65, 169, 175

GPSR Authorized Representative: Easy Access System Europe, Mustamäe tee
50, 10621 Tallinn, Estonia, gpsr.requests@easproject.com